"I Love Learning; I Hate School"

An Anthropology of College

Susan D. Blum

Cornell University Press
Ithaca and London

This book was made possible, in part, by support from the Institute for Scholarship in the Liberal Arts, College of Arts and Letters, University of Notre Dame.

First published 2016 by Cornell University Press

Printed in the United States of America

Library of Congress Cataloging-in-Publication Data

Blum, Susan Debra, author.
  "I love learning; I hate school" : an anthropology of college /
Susan D. Blum.
      pages cm
  Includes bibliographical references and index.
  ISBN 978-1-5017-0021-7 (cloth : alk. paper)
  1. Motivation in education—United States.   2. College students—
United States—Attitudes.   3. Teacher-student relationships—
United States.   I. Title.
  LB1065.B56 2016
  370.15′4—dc23   2015030284

Cloth printing   10   9   8   7   6   5   4   3   2   1

For Kathi, Bobby, Linda, and Barbara

Long may we giggle play work learn worry eat rejoice
together, in good health

When a teacher's love of learning has been scorned she may find herself in despair. . . . Through exploring and understanding these teachers' despair, along with their love of learning in teaching and its loss, we may come to see more clearly the possibilities entailed in a larger love.

Daniel P. Liston, "Love and Despair in Teaching"

Proliferation of versions of a theory is a very usual symptom of crisis. . . . Scientific revolutions are . . . those non-cumulative developmental episodes in which an older paradigm is replaced in whole or in part by an incompatible new one.

Thomas S. Kuhn, *The Structure of Scientific Revolutions*

There are only two things wrong with the education system—
1. What we teach
2. How we teach it.

Roger Schank, on his website, RogerSchank.com

CONTENTS

"I Love Learning; I Hate School"

INTRODUCTION

What the Good Student Did Not Know

> For many students the experience of schooling is easily summed up: Nothing
> of real importance is a part of classroom life, nothing is connected to anything
> else, nothing is pursued to its furthest limits, nothing is ever undertaken with
> investment or courage, and nothing of lasting value is ever accomplished.
>
> WILLIAM AYERS, *On the Side of the Child*

The title of this book is a quotation from an interview with a high-achieving
college student. Actually, she mentioned several times how little she
liked school—how much she *hated* it. In this peer interview, my undergraduate research assistant (herself successful, enthusiastic, accepted at
an Ivy League college but attending Notre Dame because of the financial package) chimed in that she hated it too. But then the interviewee
went on to say, "I actually hate it, like, it makes me miserable . . . [but] I
want to be a teacher . . . because I feel like I can change the way school is
for people."

People like me love both learning *and* school. We become professors and
teachers. And so convinced are we of our passion that it is hard to understand how anyone *wouldn't* share it—or at least it was hard for me for fifty
years. I couldn't understand why so many students didn't care, much less
why they would *hate* this system I loved so much. But I've learned that
students have good reasons for hating it—learned with my head and with
my heart.

By the time the student actually uttered the sentence "I love learning; I hate school," not only was I not shocked; I was expecting it. Rarely, though, had I heard such a clear statement of the thesis of this book. Many of our students love learning and learn constantly and joyfully, because humans are born to learn. But the formal schooling that has been imposed on almost all young people until well into adulthood—now, that is a much tougher fit. Because people are adaptable, most can be shaped to endure, and some even end up, like the one quoted here, at first-rate universities. But that doesn't mean this is the way things should be.

"I Love Learning; I Hate School": An Anthropology of College tells the story of how I, a professor with twenty-five years of university teaching, an anthropologist studying this subject, a mother of two young adults, and a lifelong lover of schooling, lost faith in school but gained faith in my fellow humans.

Like many other college professors, I constantly asked myself and colleagues, "Why don't they care!?" But after a while I took the question as not just rhetorical but as a genuine one. This book is my answer.

Why Don't College Students Care about Learning?

Until I was fifty, I'd spent almost all my life living in, for, and through school. "Going to school" had been my primary activity, every day, for half a century. From nursery school through my Ph.D. and then as a professor at five universities, with side stints in Elderhostels, preschools, and everything in between, public, private, religious, I loved school. I was good at it, and it was good to me. I was a true believer.

I will tell you about critics' complaints such as that students "don't care" or don't learn, even at our best universities; I'll show why it is inevitable that schooling as we know it prevents learning. I see this as a crisis preceding a radical transformation. I end with suggestions about eliminating the automatic assumption that every young adult should go to college, and I discuss some of the good ideas floating around that can improve learning.

The bottom line is this: the more learning in school resembles the successful learning that is so abundant outside school, the greater the chance that some learning will take place. Learning occurs everywhere, all around us, often extremely effective and welcome. It can be observed in Bible study, book clubs, film groups, computer applications; in sewing, gardening, cooking; in dancing, playing sports, fixing cars, building things—in short most of what we do in most of our life.

The basic idea is that humans are born to learn, but not only cognitively. We are social, embodied, and emotional animals, with the capacity for learning any version of human culture. The more we take "learning" out of context and put it, cleanly and abstractly, into an institutional framework and ask students to perform in isolation, the less possible it is to learn. This now universal system of institutionalized schooling not only destroys joy and curiosity, and creates dropouts and failures, winners and losers. It also often fails to achieve even the goals we set, however assessed and however defined. This system that reduces humans to "thinkers" has existed for perhaps three centuries but has been widespread for only about a hundred years. Though people like me can operate at that abstract, cognitive, theoretical level, most people are doomed to fail if asked to work this way. As a result, we find cheating, alienation, resistance, corner-cutting, fixation on credentials. To combat all this, faculty and administrators increasingly focus on managerial approaches. Students learn plenty; they just don't learn the stuff presented by teachers in classrooms. Most classroom material is forgotten immediately; students even boast about it. This seems criminally wasteful.

I used to be frustrated by my students as individuals. I blamed them for their lack of devotion to the scholarly cause. Like other faculty, I grumbled and complained and, I'm sorry to say, disdained. And then I studied this problem anthropologically, but also as a human being. In the end, I discovered compassion for students struggling within a system they did not devise and that cannot possibly suit their human needs. And I changed my own heart, mind, and behavior as a result. I love the students; I deplore the system.

The factors influencing my reconsideration are both personal and professional, emotional and intellectual, accidental and deliberate. I spend most of this book describing the pieces that led to this turnaround which took me so much by surprise. My goal is to use one person's trajectory to provoke a larger rumination about these matters. By bringing to bear the wisdom of anthropology—the study of humankind—I suggest we establish radically alternative ways of raising our young. Youth need to learn;

workers need to know things; citizens need to be informed. But the system of schooling that keeps people virtual incompetents into their twenties, always trying to please teachers in order to be evaluated by uniform standards, stuffing unwanted information and skills into their distracted brains, delaying responsibility and promising an always deferred payoff—this familiar system of schooling is recent and peculiar. An anthropological look at learning reveals many of the flaws of this industrial educational model, which resembles the model of industrial agriculture similarly under reconsideration. (I explore the parallels in greater depth in the appendix.) And like the food system, education is ripe for a major overhaul, a revolution.

Dreams of a New Paradigm

I believe that before too long there will be widespread recognition of the ineffectiveness and inhumanity of universal compulsory schooling guided by an industrial model of predetermined, teacher-centered curriculum, measured by time-in-seat and assessed by high-stakes testing, with sorting (evident in grades and scores) as the principal goal. This dominant educational paradigm replicates race and class inequalities and distorts the natural human need to move around and have varied experiences. A new paradigm must come; the current one clearly works only for a few.

This dream of a new model has many facets. In such a vision, our young would be learning life skills and academic (cognitive) skills as motivated by need and desire, building on humans' natural—and I mean this in a truly evolutionary sense—curiosity and ability to discover patterns. This would happen through some formal, structured ways of learning but also through learning by observation, learning by doing, learning by apprenticeship in both the loose and the strict meanings. There would be many who find opportunities to earn a living by the time they are in their middle to late teens; we would accept the immense capacity of people at all ages. In fact, age would no longer be the defining category of personhood, the straitjacket that it has been across a century of industrial schooling.

By the time people reach late adolescence, many would find not just jobs but outlets for their enthusiasm and interests as well. (I understand that this requires an increase in the number of jobs.) Some would recognize a need for advanced training. This would take many forms. Some would seek short-term courses to learn specific skills; completion could be marked by demonstration of mastery (as in the "badges" and "competencies" movement). Some would want longer-term explorations of various forms of human knowledge; others would prefer to get just a taste of human wisdom, evident in classic works as well as contemporary forms. Some would aim for academic and professional paths involving something resembling our current college system, but it would no longer be the single preferred path for most young people. Some of these institutions might perhaps be residential, but all would involve components of integration into the broader world. Students at all levels would have multiple kinds of real-life responsibility and accountability. With no grades, no time-in-seat requirements, and no predetermined curriculum, each student's course of study and the time required to complete it would depend on individual goals.

Because experiences at lower levels would have been richer, such higher education as remains would not need the dreaded breadth requirements. Some students may *desire* breadth; others may desire—in consultation with guides—depth. Some would simply drift off (as they in fact do now, but it would be without stigma) and find their way into the community; others may produce culminating projects, portfolios, products that can be presented to potential employers, though that would not be the only goal.

It would be understood that entering students have diverse backgrounds, needs, and goals. Uniformity of "learning outcomes" would not be assumed; diversity would. This would require a lot of work on the part of the people serving as consultants and guides for the learners, but that is as it should be. Because students would have chosen freely to enter certain learning situations, teachers and learners would be aligned, not positioned on opposite sides of a battleground. There would be no need for subterfuge, cheating, going through the motions, because the motivational structure would be the reverse of what it is now. Just as you can't cheat in learning to walk, so you would not be able to cheat in learning what you yourself have chosen. There would still be challenges in learning to master the norms of academic citation, laboratory skills, scientific concepts, and so on, but these would be *educational* matters for a motivated few, not drudgery for the many.

Of course we all need to understand important scientific concepts such as evolution and climate science, statistical thinking, and the nature of cause and effect. But these can be learned in a variety of ways, and we know that they are *not* learned in the inch-thin and mile-wide mass-production system we have now.

In my much-reduced system of higher education, we would have no thousand-student lectures with almost everyone dreading the course and taking corner-cutting measures while they head off to do what really matters to them. Thus many of the mechanisms introduced to handle the volume of students would be unnecessary. And because age would have been downplayed as a determinant, students—or the minority of people who decide to become students—would not feel the need to demonstrate defiance of restrictions imposed on them in earlier years.

This vision depends on many societal changes that are unlikely to occur, but when I call it a "revolution," I really do mean that things would be profoundly transformed. This means addressing the social, political, and economic inequalities confronting society. Schools *mirror* and *replicate* social inequalities but do not create them and have been shown for a hundred years to be unable to reduce them. Thus the inequalities have to be addressed first. We would need to have jobs with dignity in abundance, and perhaps ways to welcome children into workplaces.

Above all, the image of docile students sitting passively for hours should be forever erased. As we now know, sitting for long periods of time leads to profound health problems. This is not the picture of a well-ordered classroom. It is the picture of pathology.

This is my revolutionary vision. But I've come to embrace it only through painful experiences and much deep learning of my own.

Hitting Bottom

Like all faculty, I've had many positive and many negative teaching experiences. But a certain moment really crystallized for me the troubles that had been brewing.

Notre Dame, a predominantly Catholic university where almost all students were involved in high school athletics, was rapidly establishing itself as a formidable academic institution with ever more impressive students. It had become one of the top twenty schools as ranked by *U.S. News & World Report*, and our students have superlative credentials. During my second year, four colleagues invited me to join in planning a core course, some version of which was required for all students in our college; our subject was childhood. We met weekly for an entire academic year, engrossed in discussions of ideas, curriculum, specific topics and readings, and assignments. One of the course goals was to produce cohesion by having the students remain together for two semesters, so they selected their class by time slot rather than by content.

Needless to say, many of my eighteen sophomores in that spring of 2002 were unhappy about being forced to take a class on childhood. They effectively sat with their arms folded the entire semester.

To add insult to injury—I'm not sure whose!—during the fall semester their teacher had been a benevolent older professor who had told them, "Write whatever you want about this topic," and who arrived in class asking, "What do you want to talk about?" (He never learned their names, but . . . whatever.) This vagueness was exactly opposite to the aims our group had designed. We'd built carefully from general themes to specific instantiation, then back to general topics, from ancient Rome to contemporary inner cities. We'd thought carefully about the skills we wanted to hone (autobiography, close reading, logical argument, visual analysis).

Our students were not especially interested. They were doers: athletes, Irish-, German-, English-, French-descended big-boned friendly Catholic achievers. I was a small, Jewish, liberal, unathletic dark-haired, intense woman, expecting impressive things from these students universally touted as "great."

The mismatch was inevitable.

That semester, one student wrote on the student evaluations, "I don't think Professor Blum likes college students."

That was true, then. (I can admit it now.) I was discouraged, wounded, disappointed. I grumbled to my colleagues that my students put almost no care into their work. They refused the intellectual bounty we offered them. I complained that they were smug about their accomplishments without making the effort to excel. They wanted praise and good grades simply for attending this school. Indeed, one student—the most memorable, of course—wrote in a reflection that because of his admission to this illustrious university his family had achieved greatness.

I tried to justify the subject, the class. I tried to get them to question their own lives, the university, education. They mostly refused to become interested. I dreaded going to class. (To be fair, *some* were hospitable to the topic of childhood and to me. In 2014 I got a letter out of the blue from a student I'd taught that year saying she still talks about one of my classes. She signed the letter "love.")

But it was then that I had the first inkling that I might make this topic—education and childhood—a subject of research.

After a decade of investigation and effort—my decade of obsession, my sentimental education—I have really come to enjoy college students. I understand their struggles and the ways they think about their own accomplishments. I feel vindicated; in fall 2009 one student, in writing about how enjoyable my class had been, added a comment: "I was worried about it because of the negative comments on [the unauthorized student course evaluation website]. I don't think they're true anymore." In spring 2010 I received a teaching award, nominated by students. In fall 2010 two separate students wrote to thank me for my kindness. By 2013 I was completely comfortable with students.

Something happened to me between 2002 and 2010, and since. This book tells the story of that journey, in part. But it also suggests a further journey, one to which I have not yet discovered the complete itinerary.

It is not that I have become an indulgent, coddling relativist who thinks anything students want is perfectly fine. Nor is it that the wimpy students all stay away from my classes in fear. I have grasped something new about teaching, about young adults, about myself, and about the world. I can't *cause* students' genuine learning, though I can try to create conditions to make it possible. We meet in our classrooms two or three times a week, all (ideally) having worked like dogs between our meetings. And something happens. It could be a miracle. A Jew teaching at a Catholic university might not have gone looking for miracles. But then again, it would not be a miracle if we expected it in the regular course of life, would it?

A Midway Point in the Journey

If my low point was in the 2002 course when I had to confront the question about whether I liked college students or not, and the high point (so far!) in the 2013 hugathon and chat fest you'll read about in the concluding chapter, a midpoint came in the 2005–2009 period, when I was completely absorbed in researching and writing *My Word! Plagiarism and College Culture*.

Like many faculty, I was shocked by figures that were emerging regarding the prevalence of student plagiarism and cheating. At the same time, I was finishing a project on deception (including cheating) and truth in China (*Lies That Bind: Chinese Truth, Other Truths*) and realized I knew little in an academic sense about U.S. cheating. I had additional theoretical questions about the relationship between speakers and their words, and notions of the individual, but one of the primary drivers was my discomfort with teaching and with the students.

I expected, when I wrote the first grant proposals in 2003, that I would find a lot of entitlement and laziness. I was disgusted by—or jealous of— the piled-on activities that contributed to my students' sense of accomplishment: the service projects and performances, the varsity and intramural athletics, the clubs and contests. Why oh why didn't they care as much about their academics?

I enlisted a series of undergraduate assistants to help me conduct and then make sense of research—both interviews and my daily experience teaching and thinking about teaching, what anthropologists call *participant observation*.

The undergraduate assistants were, every single one of them, wonderful companions along this path. They helped me see aspects of student life that had been invisible to me. I thought out loud about student interest, pressure, confusion. Once they could see that I genuinely wanted to know them, not to judge them, they relaxed. We had great conversations about what I was learning, and they continued to guide me as I began to understand the real experiences of the people I interacted with every day.

One of the conclusions I drew in *My Word!* was the eternal anthropological one: that students may have some degree of autonomy and responsibility, but like everyone else, they are immersed in a world not of their own making. And the specifics of this educational and social and economic world encourage them to cut corners, to act as "efficiently" as possible with regard to their time. Students are busy with nonacademic activities that interest them or that they believe will assist them in the process of attaining a comfortable life. All around them are competing narratives telling them to "be honest" and "do your own work" and at the same time "share!" and "make friends with your classmates/roommates/dorm mates" and "be clever; think of the bottom line." A lot of our schooling practices produce precisely the results we deplore. I came to understand some of the reasons why students might deliberately flout the overt rules about intellectual property stated in first-year composition courses and on every syllabus.

As a result of that study, I started to give talks at a variety of colleges and universities, usually in the context of "academic integrity" programs or writing-and-composition centers. I talked with faculty, students, and administrators about their struggles, and I began to see that something is profoundly wrong with the system, beyond what any one student or faculty member could possibly address. It is a systemic problem, built into the very nature of the educational system as we have it.

While there are fantastic success stories of engaged students digging in intellectually—please don't overlook this—many students often aim to skate through, untouched. They may long for something to matter to them, but they have learned that it is not likely to happen in their classes. They have often been taught that school is a game they must play. *Learn to perform, and all will be well.* School is a self-contained world, and the task of an achiever is to master its rules.

While I continued to teach, and to give talks about plagiarism, my inquiry went deeper. My discomfort lasted more than half a decade. I could not sleep. I could not settle down. I had to figure something out.

This book, then, has emerged from my deepest doubts. Only by sending my conclusions off into the world could I possibly put this topic out of my constant thoughts.

Unexpectedly, I learned to see students in an entirely new way. Instead of seeing them as trying to get away with doing as little as possible, I began to see them as agents attempting to navigate a flawed system. I stopped circulating the usual faculty complaints about how students were using words like *impact* as transitive verbs or how they didn't know who Marshall McLuhan was. I became an anthropologist of my own situation. And discarding a self-pitying perspective, I began to look at how all the pieces fit together.

And because I learn both by interacting, professionally and ethnographically, and by reading, I kept reading.

I delved into some of the literature on human nature and compared it to what I see in universities. I also began to read about learning in general, discovering earth-shattering (to me) news about what makes it possible. Research from the traditional field of educational psychology has been supplemented by newer work from cognitive science. I worried that Daniel Willingham's *Why Don't Students Like School?* would completely scoop my book. (It didn't.) And as I was putting the finishing touches on this book, I finally received, via interlibrary loan, John Taylor Gatto's *Underground History of American Education*. (It had had a detour into a colleague's mailbox; somehow this anti-efficiency feels correct for this book.) A four-hundred-page manifesto evoking the *Whole Earth Catalogue* from the 1960s, it sends energy blasting from every page. If I'd found it five years earlier, I might just have given up writing my own book.

Another resource was the anthropology of education and the anthropology of childhood, intersecting with linguistic and psychological anthropology. Education was a lifelong preoccupation of Margaret Mead; relevant research is found in the work of George and Louise Spindler, Shirley Brice Heath, Jean Lave, Frederick Erickson, Hervé Varenne, Harry Wolcott, Elinor Ochs, and Bambi Schieffelin, among many others.

I found kinship with the 1960s and 1970s educational revolutionaries following the progressive ideals of John Dewey. Some of these writers and their most well-known titles are Ivan Illich (*Deschooling Society*), William Ayers (*On the Side of the Child*), A. S. Neill (*Summerhill*), Eda Le Shan (*The Conspiracy against Childhood*), John Caldwell Holt (*How Children Fail; Instead of Education*), Paolo Freire (*Pedagogy of the Oppressed*), John Taylor Gatto (*Dumbing Us Down: The Hidden Curriculum of Compulsory Schooling*), Paul Goodman (*Compulsory Mis-education*), and Jules Henry (*Culture Against Man*). You can see the critique embedded in the titles.

Education has been a central part of a general social critique for hundreds of years, especially in the United States. All the authors mentioned locate a progressive critique of schooling within a more general social critique of inequality and since the 1980s of neoliberalism (a focus on competition, privatization, individualism, and the capitalist "market"). William Apple, Alfie Kohn, Kieren Egan, Linda Darling-Hammond, and Bradley Levinson, among many others, carry on this tradition. Many invoke John Dewey,

Lev Vygotsky, and sometimes Maria Montessori and the Waldorf-Steiner and Reggio Emilia schools. Many of these progressive theorists consciously or unconsciously echo a Rousseauian view of human nature, that (only) in the "state of nature" are humans psychologically, physically, and spiritually free, and only by living according to this nature can people flourish.

Oddly for me, many of the radical writers on schooling (and unschooling) talk about their own suffering at the hands of teachers, about being stifled, about the misery of classrooms. Though I have now grown to understand it, my own experience in school was never like that.

I loved most of my experience in school (except the social part around middle school). I liked worksheets, tests, homework. I loved writing and reading, math, French, German, Chinese, Japanese. I discovered linguistics and, eventually (not until graduate school), my beloved anthropology. I loved physics and chemistry, though I didn't really like lab work; that never made sense to me. Why spend so much time fumbling around measuring liquids when the pure abstract formula was available through calculation or introspection? I was a hands-off student, a Cartesian, preferring the beauty of ideas to the complexity of experience. And in a way, schooling was made by and for people like me. And I was made by school.

I played school. I thought about school. What I paid attention to in college was mostly my classes, though I had my first important romantic relationships there as well—a genuine distraction from the content of classes, to be sure. Graduate school fit me perfectly. I had lots of friends, all excited about school. There we were: a group of serious abstract thinkers relishing pure theory, eager to read and write. We loved our work and put off practical considerations like jobs, assuming things would work out somehow.

So my love of school took me to teaching.

I had always loved the Hermione Grangers in my classes: the young women with the organized planners who sat in front and took out their highlighted readings, the young men who asked hard questions about readings and their connections to life. I had some sympathy for the ones who tried but didn't quite get it. But I had no sympathy for the ones who were obviously skating, who did the minimum but were more engaged in life outside the classroom, who boasted to their friends about fooling their teachers and getting away with not reading. I couldn't understand students who didn't even buy books but relied on PowerPoint slides provided by their lecturers. I still don't quite understand—but in another way

I do—why it is so rare for students to be inspired to exceed minimum requirements. These are the ones who go to graduate school, the ones for whom school is not just a phase to be endured on the road to other things but is in itself satisfying, compelling, worthy of enjoyment and energy. But such students, the ones like me, are the exception.

And I have come to see that that's how it should be.

In general, people learn things when they care about them. People learn by doing. (In college—Carleton, in case you're wondering—my daughter Hannah discovered herself to be such a person, becoming bitter about having to sit in classrooms and learn any other way.) Lots of people are able to follow directions to do something concrete. But few are those who learn best by reading, or who relish the conceptual movement from the concrete to the abstract. Why should intelligence (whatever that is) be defined by the ability to abstract? Why should this be the sole measure of merit?

I have arrived circuitously but experientially (the way almost *everyone* learns, in fact), at Howard Gardner's notion of multiple intelligences, but I am interested in more than "intelligence." What is worth knowing? How can we get to know it? How do we decide what is good to learn?

It is good that some people know how to raise money for organizations by creating T-shirts. It is good that some people can charm others into working together. It is good that some people like to go off alone and create sculptures and others like to belt out songs in crowds. It is good that some people are finely attuned to others' emotions and that some are jovial clowns. It is good that some people are competent skilled laborers. Not just in work but in life, we need an assortment of people.

A final ingredient in this mix came from my children, and especially my younger daughter, Sassy. Like the younger daughter in Amy Chua's *Battle Hymn of the Tiger Mother*, the younger of two daughters in my family challenged our expectations.

My husband, Lionel, elder daughter, Hannah, and I are all oldest/older children and did well in school, pleasing our teachers and basking in the warmth of approval for our accomplishments. But high-spirited, fun-loving, passionate, and serious Sassy (whom we'd named Elena), then an aspiring writer and artist, found traditional school a straitjacket.

Like many creative and insightful children, our Elena chafed. From second grade, when her strict teacher repressed all her natural exuberance by keeping students chained to their desks, through high school, when she cried in the bathroom and kept her fingers, metaphorically, in her ears, Elena was defiant and resistant. She was not at all persuaded by her academic parents' love and respect for school. She had begun to defy her teachers in third grade. Her insight was, and has always been, pitiless. Insecure, incompetent, or inconsistent teachers were probed and dismissed. The fact that they were in a position to evaluate her was of no consequence.

In 2001 No Child Left Behind hit our daughters' poor urban school. Field trips were discontinued. Students were supposed to be at their "workstations" (did I make this up???) for ninety minutes of reading and ninety minutes of math. Hannah's fifth-grade teacher, who "looped" with this beloved class and had had creative ideas about combining social studies and English with reading groups that functioned like book clubs, disregarded the mandate to strip the curriculum of everything but a skeleton of meaningless, content-free, skill-infused "reading" and the math that none of the teachers really understood or liked.

At the end of sixth grade, representatives from the middle school came to do a presentation. We aren't entirely sure what they said. What Hannah reported was that they said that if kids got in trouble in middle school, it was not their parents but the kids themselves who would be held responsible. They would be led out of the school in handcuffs.

The following year we moved the girls to a Montessori school.

When Elena arrived, she instantly found a soul mate in the irrepressible and irreverent Helen Muffaletto, the assistant teacher, and a rock-solid calm anchor in Michael Poole, the head teacher. Helen understood Elena's need for snacks and movement, and invited Elena to accompany her on errands in the building. Elena formed a tight group of friends. Things were paradisiacal that first Montessori year. But by sixth grade she'd accumulated a pile of sixty uncompleted worksheets. (What business did a Montessori school have handing out worksheets?)

Elena struggled again in middle school, and by high school she was miserable, working at Starbucks during her senior year, graduating early, and spending a few months in Tanzania. She was curious, passionate, mesmerized by poetry and art, content to spend time learning—but only on her own. It became obvious that school *diserved* her. In the end she found Hampshire College, a Montessori-like "experimental" or alternative college, and as I write is completing her work there.

A Flawed Foundation

What I found through my reading and research and through looking at the world with different frames was a conceptual flaw at the center of conventional schooling. Whether looking anthropologically at hunter-gatherers, touring forms of non-school learning around the globe, or studying details of actual school, I saw that the way school is set up does not match the usual ways people learn. Our schooling takes people away from the flow of life, forcing them to please teachers, emphasizing cognitive and individual mastery of isolated pieces of knowledge or procedure, making every bit a morsel stuffed away for later. High-achieving students regard their primary goal as "getting good grades." Their meaningful pursuits largely occur outside classes. This is not effective. It has ill effects. It is wasteful on every level.

So it is no wonder that everyone complains. From faculty to the public, from students to parents, everyone laments one aspect or another of this expensive and virtually universal system. And now I see why. We can't fix it completely because its foundation is flawed. And we can't fix it piecemeal because it is a system. As with fundamental changes to conceptual systems in the history of science, the only solution is a radical transformation— ultimately, the reintegration of learning with life.

This book challenges my beautiful dreams of the Platonic ideal of higher education; it details my fall from the heights, my quest to understand what it is to learn and how humans of all sorts—hunter-gatherers, pastoralists, people in Asia and Latin America and France and Africa—are "raised up." I will tell you why most of our schooling goes against even the most flexible animal essence: human nature. I show how making school compulsory and disconnecting learning from use *prevent* learning. I make the case that learning with the body for real purposes, in company with others, is more effective than learning alone for someday. The fixation on pleasing teachers to get good grades and doing activities simply to gain credentials create falseness and mental illness.

Now, at least, I can genuinely answer the question "Why don't [most] students care about classes?" Students will find most of this obvious—a sign, to an anthropologist, that I'm getting it right. But it was not at all obvious to me before I did this work. Like many academics, I wasn't the average student: I loved the classes.

Much of what I used to accept as self-evident, many of the things I held dear my whole life, have been challenged by this quest. But I have emerged from it a more effective teacher, a more informed anthropologist, a more compassionate friend to people of all ages, and—strangely—a happier human.

This book mostly raises questions. I treat it like my classes: I don't have neatly packaged answers. There are no gimmicks. I don't prepare a set of PowerPoints that can replace the lecture. What will tell me I've been successful is if readers let me know they are thinking about education in a new way.

I could have waited until I figured it all out, but I don't think that day will come, and I didn't want to wait. I think I've learned something in this decade of obsession, and it could be useful to add to the conversation. I think of it as an offering, as at a temple. *This is what I have. Please accept it. Of course it is not enough, alone. But add it to the gifts of others, and maybe together we can build something sacred.*

The Book This Is and Isn't

Now for some disclaimers.

Disclaimer 1

This is a work of theory, a reflection, an essay, not a handbook. It is more diagnosis than prescription.

It is a coherent critique based on a particular view of humans as individuals and as members of social groups, as well as humans as a particular species of primates.

It has implications for practice, but it is not a manual.

It looks at the assumptions about human flourishing that are often unaddressed by more technical, practical, and measurable aspects of education.

It also does not address the monumental, wrenching inequalities of our society. These deserve, and have received, serious and nuanced treatment. If you know a disadvantaged young person, all other things being equal, that person's life chances are enhanced by going to college. My challenge is to the dominance of higher education as the prescribed path for *all* students, for the reasons that will unfold as you read.

I believe we took a wrong turn when institutional schooling became the overwhelming occupation of all modern children and youth well into biological adulthood. Like industrial agriculture and a petroleum-based infrastructure, industrial education has produced stellar accomplishments—especially the research and knowledge production of which we should be so proud—but it has also produced negative consequences and enormous waste.

Given the system we have, many relatively positive consequences can be seen. For those living *here*, *now*, this is the system within which success must be achieved.

But I am questioning the system. Mine is a dream, but new ideas have to come from dreams.

Disclaimer 2

This work focuses on highly successful students at elite institutions, especially at Notre Dame. That is not because I am unaware of struggling students, of students not privileged enough to find their way into those ranks, of institutions that are poorly resourced. In fact I have taught at a variety of schools, including Oklahoma State University and the University of Colorado Denver, which are not schools for the elite (though they too had brilliant and inspired students).

I focus on the elite because if even the successful aspects of the system have liabilities, we can see the flaws that much more clearly. Anthropologists have spoken of "studying up"—of focusing on the powerful—as one way to observe the workings of a cultural logic. It does not necessarily mean that attention should not be paid to those in other strata. But I can't do everything in one book.

Is Notre Dame "typical"? Of course not; every college and university has its particular aspects. Notre Dame is a highly selective private religious university located in the Midwest. Our students tend to be excellent at achievement but less focused on intellectual matters than students at some other schools. I use it because I know it intimately. But most of my argument is independent of the particulars of this institution.

Disclaimer 3

I assume good intentions on almost everyone's part. Teachers, administrators, researchers, students, parents—everyone wants the best and earnestly sets about to accomplish it.

Disclaimer 4

Some of the results of our system of higher education, especially the research it fosters, have been breathtakingly wonderful and have improved life for many, whether through a better understanding of the human condition or by generating practical solutions to concrete problems.

Colleges and universities of every sort are filled with amazing feats of learning and action, even among undergraduate students. The triumphant celebrations of research, awards, activism, creative output—all these are genuine, and should be applauded. But the students we don't hear about, the majority, are often just marking their days until they can, finally, get out of school.

Disclaimer 5

I am a passionate advocate of equality. But (more) schooling alone is not going to provide it, much as I wish it would.

Disclaimer 6

College works brilliantly for a minority of academically oriented people like myself. It can provide new directions, inspiration, ideas, skills, analytical tools, research paradigms. It can change lives, turn a muddling teenager into a passionate artist or scientist. But for too many, it is just a series of hoops to jump through on their way to the next thing. And this is a waste of time, energy, and money.

Disclaimer 7

This is an *anthropology*, not an *ethnography*. For me, *anthropology* is the study of humans, no matter how the information was gathered. *Ethnography*—long-term residence in a single place, especially using participant observation—is one method. I used that method, but only in part. Thus you do not find long discussions of how I spent time in particular schools, of who all the particular occupiers of positions of power were, of my interviewing techniques. I began with questions, a need to know something. And then I found ways to address those questions; my own disciplinary training provided some of those ways.

Disclaimer 8

Anthropology is known for its *cultural relativism*, or the idea that the first step in any analysis is to understand things on their own terms. My field is known for avoiding judgment. But there is also a long tradition of critiquing the anthropologist's own society. I thus am trying not just to understand but to assess what works and what doesn't.

Disclaimer 9

The book is about college, yes, but to a great extent understanding college depends on an understanding of schooling in general. College is, in important but often unremarked ways, not significantly different from "K–12." So you may find yourself reading in these pages about young children or high school and wondering if you got off the elevator on the wrong floor. In anthropology we believe everything is connected—so we can't really understand *college* without understanding *school*.

Disclaimer 10

This is not a book about the extraordinary costs of higher education, the staggering and sometimes incapacitating debt most students are incurring, or the lack of good jobs available to many college graduates. It is not about technological innovations, online learning, or credentials earned in high school. It is not about the two-tier employment system that has reduced tenured and tenure-track positions to about one-fourth of all faculty positions, filling the rest with poverty-level, no-benefits, contingent (adjunct) faculty. It is not about administrative glut, nor about college athletics.

All these are essential topics; many others have written about them brilliantly.

Disclaimer 11

I am not an expert on education. My perspective is that of a professor who happens to be an anthropologist. So I use the tools of my discipline, and allied others, to understand the predicament of a professor who plaintively wondered: Why don't they care? Why don't they like school?

There are lots of good reasons: What they learn. How they learn. Other preoccupations, including financial.

But these reasons have to be grasped in their entirety, not in isolation from the whole experience not simply of an individual *learner* but of a *person* in a social and cultural context.

Disclaimer 12

I have been teaching full-time since 1988. My regular teaching load has varied from two to three courses a semester, along with independent studies, senior and honors theses, and sometimes graduate courses or dissertation directing. When I was an adjunct, I sometimes taught four courses a semester. Small classes have generally not been below eight students. My largest classes were nearly a hundred. So in any given year I might teach between one hundred and two hundred students. Let's say it averages 120. In twenty-five years, then, I have taught three thousand students.

A few former students are my "friends" on Facebook. Some are actual friends. I have been to weddings and met some children. Once in a while a former student contacts me to say, "I saw this article and it reminded me of your class." Once I gave a lecture at a museum and one of my former students attended. Several years earlier she had sat in my class frowning the whole time, and I had assumed that she was one of the students who disliked me. At the museum lecture she told me how much my class had mattered to her. Because of it, she had majored in Asian studies and gotten a master's degree. That made me reconsider all my earlier thoughts. Out of my own insecurity I had assumed the worst, but maybe she just frowned out of concentration or habit. Maybe she needed new glasses.

It is impossible to know all the ramifications of our efforts.

Disclaimer 13

Here are all the ways you in particular, dear fellow faculty, may find my observations not relevant or my suggestions impossible to implement:

- You may have huge lecture classes.
- You may teach many courses.
- You may have imposed curricula.

- You may have strict outcomes assessment.
- You may have underprepared students.
- You may teach in a different cultural or national setting.
- You may teach online distance courses.

Teaching is really hard. Some problems and some situations may be improved only partially. Just as with students, there is no one-size-fits-all program that works.

Disclaimer 14

The book includes personal material because no observer can be disembodied, "objective," a viewer from nowhere.

And the story here is this: I, this particular person, did not understand. And then I did.

Disclaimer 15

Some of the complaints about education will seem to be more about society as a whole.

Exactly right.

Part I

TROUBLE IN PARADISE

Parents are slow in realizing how unimportant the learning side
of school is. Children, like adults, learn what they want to learn.

A. S. NEILL, *Summerhill*

At its best, U.S. higher education is extraordinary. It produces graduates
ready to do research, start NGOs, teach, work as engineers, write novels
and blogs, go to medical and law school, work as translators, and much
more. At the top of the higher education heap, students arrive already well
trained and eager to learn. Every faculty member can tell success stories—
of students whose lives were turned around and of students given opportunities they would never have had without college. College can provide a
ticket into the middle class and beyond and can introduce young people to
a broad world. At its best, U.S. higher education is the envy of the globe.

But like many things, it is not always at its best.

Educational ideals are beautiful: through teachers' expertise in a subject and in pedagogy, through eager—or at least diligent—engagement
in their classes, learners emerge educated, in whatever fashion that may
mean. But many faculty and much of the public, and certainly students
themselves, complain that these objectives are not being met. Furthermore, there is profound disagreement about what the system—expensive,
huge, complex—is for.

1

COMPLAINTS

Crisis or Moral Panic?

> Academics' complaints are not simply the inevitable self-serving grumbles of
> a public-sector group jostling for taxpayers' money. What education shares
> with health is that it does not and cannot register regular large efficiency
> gains, because it depends on human beings, not machines.
>
> ALISON WOLF, *Does Education Matter?*

Spend time with college faculty and you are likely to hear a lot of complaints. Some will be about employment conditions, as with any job. Salaries, raises, tenure expectations (for those lucky enough to be on the tenure track), workload, office space, parking, health insurance premiums, publishing, administrators . . . all the regular concerns of employees at virtually any large organization, though the changes in higher education have been extreme in the last thirty years or so. (Issues of economics and access in higher education are significant, but I will not address them centrally.)[1]

But the complaints that are relevant to my topic have to do with teaching.[2] Despite the fact that U.S. universities are among the best in the world in every ranking system and are widely admired and emulated, those inside it agree that all is not right in the world of higher education.

Students think they should get all A's.
They never do the reading.

They text all the time in class.
They don't care.
They can't write.
They can't read.
They can't think critically.
They only do what I tell them to and never go deeper.
They cheat/plagiarize.
They don't come to class.
They waste so much time on nonacademic things.
They binge drink.
They hook up [sexually].
They waste tuition money.

And those are just their teachers' complaints. Other, society-wide complaints concern students' not getting in, paying too much, staying too long without graduating, dropping out, owing too much, being unemployed in great numbers, and being unequally represented.

For my purposes, though, I want to focus on the complaints about students' behavior in school. You can find more comprehensive versions of these complaints in print.[3]

What's the Matter with Kids Today?

I have a whole shelf of books critical of college. The criticisms come from every possible direction, all with significant points to make; some are truly profound. They contradict one another, but it is still impossible to pretend that all is well. Faculty, administrators, and the public complain about grade inflation. Neighbors complain about student behavior. Employers complain about unprepared, undisciplined, and spoiled college graduates. College is too long, too short, too much fun, too distressing.

Richard Arum and Josipa Roksa's *Academically Adrift: Limited Learning on College Campuses* attracted public attention in 2011 with its claim that a significant percentage of students make absolutely no gains in terms of knowledge or skills during college. Students put in little effort, they charged. Students are not involved or engaged in the academic life, and learning outcomes are poor. And the situation is deteriorating: "While prior historical scholarship reminds us that U.S. undergraduates have long been devoted to pursuing social interests at college, there is emerging empirical evidence that suggests that college students' academic effort has dramatically declined in recent decades."[4] The average amount of time spent by full-time college students on academic activities, including attending classes, Arum and Roksa report, has shrunk to twenty-seven hours a week. (A survey I conducted in spring 2013 put it at twenty-one to twenty-five hours.)

Another complaint, bolstered by "hard facts," is that in tests administered to a more or less representative sample of students at more or less representative campuses, students do not improve on critical thinking. And critical thinking is what most faculty believe students should be learning in college.

That is so far from what students and their families believe they should be getting that it is worth a story of its own, though it will not receive one here. Do a survey: Ask the first five people you see what the goal of college is. Unless you ask college professors, I'd bet critical thinking is not on most people's lists.

(Are you back from asking? What did they say?)

Citing other research, Arum and Roksa put the problem clearly: "Many students come to college not only poorly prepared by prior schooling for highly demanding academic tasks that ideally lie in front of them, but—more troubling still—they enter college with attitudes, norms, values, and behaviors that are often at odds with academic commitment."[5] I used to be troubled by this, but no longer. It is a human norm to be at odds with academic commitment. Or, to reverse the formulation, academic commitment is such a peculiar form of what is humanly possible that it is only to be expected that most students do not possess it. What they learn is to mimic it during their time in school.

Movies such as *Animal House* and *Legally Blonde*, and fictional works like Tom Wolfe's *I Am Charlotte Simmons*, present in entertaining, exaggerated form the seamy side of college, with its apparently rampant drunkenness, corner-cutting, sexual debauchery, and slides into mental illness. Journalistic works on higher education, like Richard Hersh and John Merrow's *Declining by Degrees: Higher Education at Risk* and Barrett Seaman's *Binge: Campus Life in an Age of Disconnection and Excess*, point out how little actual academic learning is done even at the best colleges, while students devote themselves to pleasures and evasion. Those close to colleges, such as administrators, also weigh in. In 2006 Derek Bok, president of Harvard from 1971 to 1991 and again from 2006 to 2007, wrote *Our Underachieving Colleges: A Candid Look at How Much Students Learn and Why They Should Be Learning More*. Writers recall their student experience, as did Ross Douthat in *Privilege: Harvard and the Education of the Ruling Class*, and Walter Kirn in *Lost in the Meritocracy: The Undereducation of an Overachiever*. The shared message is that students aren't learning very much, academically speaking, but they should be.

Faculty write about higher education from oblique angles. Mark Edmundson, professor of English and prolific champion of the humanities, defends his profession, despite assaults from all sides, in *Why Teach? In Defense of a Real Education*. "Ultimately," he argues, "it is up to individuals— and individual students in particular—to make their own way against the current sludgy tide."[6] So the "sludgy tide" is to blame. In *In the Basement of the Ivory Tower*, "Professor X" provides the perspective of the increasingly numerous adjunct faculty teaching at "colleges of last resort," where students arrive with such poor training that more than half fail English 101. In *Shadow Scholar*, Dave Tomar writes about his ten years as a for-hire term paper writer; he even wrote dissertations for Ph.D. students too busy or panicked to do it themselves. He justifies his admittedly unethical behavior by his own miserable experience as one of hundreds warehoused in huge classes at Rutgers, where his only personal relationship with the school was with the parking office.

In 1996 Peter M. Sacks explained the new generation in *Generation X Goes to College: An Eye-Opening Account of Teaching in Postmodern America*. Andrew Delbanco writes about *College: What It Was, Is, and Should Be*. Derek Bok followed up *Our Underachieving Colleges* with the broad *Higher Education in America*. Applying business theories about "disruptive innovation" to higher education, Clayton Christensen and Henry Eyring propose *The Innovative University: Changing the DNA of Higher Education from the Inside Out*. Going further, Anya Kamenetz suggests *DIY U: Edupunks, Edupreneurs, and the Coming Transformation of Higher Education*. Kevin Carey argues, like me, that we have reached the end of the familiar form of higher education, in his book *The End of College: Creating the Future of Learning and the University of Everywhere*, but suggests a basically technological solution. Directly in contrast to those turning to technological innovations, William Deresiewicz in *Excellent Sheep: The Miseducation of the American Elite and the Way to a Meaningful Life* pleads for a return to the real value of liberal arts.

Anthropologists, sociologists, and other social scientists have written an array of books exposing the realities of higher education: Michael Moffatt demonstrated the strangeness of college in *Coming of Age in New Jersey*. Dorothy Holland and Margaret Eisenhart revealed female students' focus on relationships in *Educated in Romance*. Mary Grigsby showed how different types of students regard the academic enterprise in *College Life through the Eyes of Students*. Most colorfully, Rebekah Nathan in *My Freshman Year* writes about her own enrollment in college when she was already a professor in order to conduct clandestine research on the contemporary undergraduate experience. These works, and many more, explain what happens in college beyond the celebratory promotional advertising.

Similar complaints are voiced by teachers at lower levels of school, and hand-wringing about unprepared, undisciplined, unruly, defiant, lazy, erratic students proliferate. And don't forget their dreadful test scores.

Yet in some sense these same complaints have been circulating for millennia. A timeless lament variably attributed to Plato/Socrates, Aristotle, Cicero, Hesiod, "an old monk," and other Middle Eastern "ancients" (clearly apocryphal) criticizes the young:

> The children now love luxury; they have bad manners, contempt for authority; they show disrespect for elders and love chatter in place of exercise. Children are now tyrants, not the servants of their households. They no longer rise when elders enter the room. They contradict their parents, chatter before company, gobble up dainties at the table, cross their legs, and tyrannize their teachers.[7]

So the good old days included a time when students listened to their teachers, cared about their studies, did their reading, spent as much time as it took to do the work, walked five miles in the snow uphill in both directions ... Nostalgia for a fallen world of genuine learning in school brings with it much false memory. When we measure the present against an idealized past, it must fall short.

My Own Private Suffering in College Teaching

My own experience teaching in higher education had been typical. Here is how my complaint went:

> *I do a wonderful job preparing an organic feast, and the students spit in it.* Or *They pretend to eat, all the while filling up on cheeseburgers. Students are lazy, uninterested. They go through the motions. They pretend to be interested, just for the grade. They do only as much as they have to, and no more. They don't know how to write properly. They misuse so many words. They obviously haven't read past the first few pages. They haven't thought about my class since we last met. They are sloppy about their use of sources. And . . .* the most hurtful . . . *they don't care!*

It is not that my teaching always went badly. Sometimes students learned a lot. Some days were touched with magic: a discussion took off; a student admitted that she had been talking about the class with her parents; students wrote something absolutely inspired! I taught Chinese language and literature, and one of my students spent a year teaching English in China, where she met her husband. I taught classes about China, and some students went off to focus on Asian studies. I taught classes about anthropology, and some students earned Ph.D.s in anthropology, or went into teaching or health fields, or worked at NGOs. I listened to stories about emotional breakdowns and struggles with parents, about financial distress and romantic dissolution. Former students drop by to say hello. I advised a Ph.D. student from another country, disdained by other faculty; she named her daughter Susan.

There were always some gems, of course.

But then there was the bad stuff: cheating, plagiarism, complaining to the department chair about a grade (maybe a B), some nasty comments on evaluations. There were the days when we, teacher and students, sat staring at each other, waiting for something good to happen. The nights I couldn't sleep.

One of my strangest experiences came in a required anthropological theory course. One student had done a pretty good class presentation; he'd padded his work with a scarcely relevant video, but he understood the subject pretty well. I had given him nine points out of a potential ten. He gave himself eleven. The nine points were probably higher than I would have given a decade earlier. This student's writing tended to be B+ work. In a meeting he asked me how he could improve, and I gave him the usual line about "going above the minimal requirements." He complained to the department chair about my mistreatment of him.

That fall semester, on a bulletin board facing the elevator just outside our department, my photograph was removed twice. This had never happened before, and has never happened since. And in the course evaluations, still done on paper in those days, someone slipped in a typed sheet prepared in advance with complaint after complaint.

Months later, at the departmental end-of-the-year student honor dinner, the student stood behind me as I sat at my table and put his arm on my shoulder—threatening, dominating. (He was very tall and strong.) This moved far beyond the usual boundary between student and professor. "What are you doing next year?" he asked, in an anticipatory tone and with a smug smile. I would be teaching, of course. He seemed to expect me to say that I'd been fired because of his negative review. He'd certainly tried.

Entitlement and Privilege

Faculty and journalists write often about students' inflated sense of what they deserve—of their *entitlement*. Students act like customers, with faculty delivering a consumer good. Some may have had the experience in high school of being granted a higher grade if they even began to appeal. Faculty may be intimidated by students' implied threats and power: the power to evaluate *them*. Increasing numbers of publications address student or classroom "incivility"—anything from interrupting a fellow student to demanding concessions from cowed faculty.[8]

Some of this entitlement comes from socioeconomic privilege. In *Producing Success: The Culture of Personal Advancement in an American High School*, Peter Demerath reveals the complicity between suburban high school students from advantaged backgrounds and their parents, teachers, and school administrators. Observing the entire school system, analyzing marketing material, attending the graduation ceremony, classes, and faculty meetings, and conducting interviews, Demerath shows how everyone was determined to produce the success that would perpetuate the system.

Grades of 5.0 (out of a supposed 4.0) are given to students in the advanced classes. Ranking is eliminated, so colleges cannot compare the students. As students are awarded one honor after another, their profiles appear impressive, and their chances of getting into a selective college increase. Then the school can advertise the high success rate of its students.

Shamus Rahman Khan's *Privilege: The Making of an Adolescent Elite at St. Paul's School* similarly demonstrates how students are taught to put on an elite *habitus*, to demonstrate ease with their privilege through dining and dressing in certain ways, and in classes in which they learn to discuss course materials at an apparently high level, despite often not having actually done the reading. They are *assumed* to merit their rewards. And then, when they go on to Ivy League and other desirable colleges, they take with them the mantle of privilege.[9]

Without going too far into the topic of social and economic class in the supposedly equal United States, it is important to point out that ours is a winner-take-all system. From admission to work obligation to prior preparation to summer enrichment, students from affluent backgrounds continue to amass assets, "misrecognizing" their success, in Pierre Bourdieu's term, as stemming from their own merit.

Yet the system is entirely rigged.[10] Entitled, affluent students can gain access to internships more easily than other students. They have connections. Their parents can "make a phone call," or provide a car so the student can drive to the internship. They can afford to forgo earned summer income, and live away from home while not working, simply to gain experience and contacts. They have the cultural capital that lets them fit in with other successful people: they have shared experiences; they know how to "talk right," which topics to talk about in what way, even the proper pronunciation. Study abroad, volunteering at nonprofits, doing "service" while in college—all these are facilitated by lack of economic pressures. Some college admissions departments are now dismissing applicants' "summer service in Africa" as experiences that are simply purchased with their parents' funds.

Faculty and administrators continue to despair about high-achieving students who will not accept anything short of perfection, at least in terms of grades. Entitled students are accused (behind their backs) of "grade-grubbing." *She's a grade-grubber. I can't stand the end-of-semester grade-grubbing.* A decade or so ago at Notre Dame, at least in the College of Arts and Letters, students appeared to believe they deserved, as a default, a B+. Now it is an A-. In 2013 headlines once again reminded us that Harvard students get mostly A's.

Unsatisfied students may contest their grades, and although faculty dread these conversations, grading experts Walvoord and Anderson urge faculty to "Stay calm and focused, and concentrate on the learning."[11] This is hard to do, in the face of emotional or distraught students.

Students believe they deserve second chances; many were given them in high school. They believe they can and should get "extra credit" for attending lectures, reading something additional, doing more work. By their charm, by their insistence, by their standing out in a sea of people who appear not to care as much, they often succeed. While it may seem naïve to say so, *success*, not *learning*, is the obvious goal in college today. And success is measured automatically, by grades.

Grading Woes

The topic of grades, and grade inflation, is one of the major complaints about higher education, at least from the top of the education pyramid. University and college faculty often commiserate about grading, regarding it as the least enjoyable aspect of their work. They complain about its time-consuming nature, student resistance, the difficulty of remaining objective and consistent, their disdain for student competence, their wish to be more rigorous coupled with their fear of student retaliation. They seek assistance in learning how to be more precise, efficient, strict, objective, consistent.

Faculty have taken grades into their souls. When I first started teaching, I was proud of my "high standards," of being a tough grader. My husband, Lionel, teaching Chinese history and philosophy, was even tougher. Some semesters he gave no A's, and his students, he says, got "every possible grade." Holding the line on the evil of grade inflation pleases administrators everywhere.

I had a colleague who was quite unhappy at Notre Dame. Before I began to question my assumptions about all this, we commiserated about our students' weaknesses and our "soft" colleagues who failed to "maintain standards." His course enrollments were low. He left and went to another continent, where he is happier. We spoke about his new students, and he said with absolutely certainty: *I tell them that if they challenge a grade, they are questioning my integrity, and I will lower their grade.*

I, too, used to believe in the centrality of objective grading.

One commenter on a blog complains about students' inadequate understanding of grading and about their complaints:

> I serve as the grade appeal counselor for my science college and it always amazes me how little students understand the differential weighting of various components of course requirements. The most common complaint I hear from students is almost always like this: I made all As and Bs in my lab reports, and did very well on the quizzes and homework assignments and I don't see why I received a C grade in the course. They fail to examine the syllabus where the instructors would have *clearly stated* the weight for each component assignment for the course grade.
>
> Generally the in class exams tend to be weighted very highly (as much as 60–70 percent of course grade) while homework and quizzes may just be worth 10 percent of course grade. So you can make all As and Bs in homework assignments and still fail a class.
>
> It seems that every student wants to receive the A grade but their desire for the grade is often not matched by the hardwork [*sic*] and persistence necessary for the grade. The A grade means outstanding performance and should not be compromised at all by grade inflation.[12]

Here the complaint is that students lack understanding of the niceties of particular systems of grading. Faculty reinforce one another's confidence in their own criteria. It is in this context that the bugaboo of grade inflation enters the conversation. This form of moral panic has surfaced every few years since the 1980s, when grades, along with college enrollments, first began to rise.[13]

Amid the alarm about entitlement and grade inflation, faculty are often urged by administrators to give lower grades. One analyst distinguishes among *grade increase*, *grade inflation*, *grade compression*, and *grading disparity*, acknowledging the complexity of college grading and its multiple influences.[14] Another concludes a series of chapters on "grade inflation" by saying that "there is at present no received, orthodox view of what the purpose or function of grading is."[15] Some universities attempt to combat grade inflation with "grade deflation"—official policies mandating lower median grades. (More on this in chapter 5.) Faculty resist, and not only out of self-interest, though college professors throughout the United States worry that their own evaluations will suffer if they give the grades "students really deserve."[16] Others argue that if student "quality" as measured by incoming statistics (SAT, high school GPA, class rank, AP scores) continues to improve, outstanding students should be able to learn at high levels and their grades should acknowledge this.

At my own university, administrators argue that our very impressive students should work harder and produce superior results, and that routinely conferring the highest grades fails to motivate increased engagement and excellence. Annual salary reviews of faculty now include a printout of the grades each faculty member has bestowed, along with the median and mean. If these are too high, and if there is no "range" of grades, the department chair must (1) have a conversation with the professor; (2) if satisfied (for instance, the faculty member has permitted multiple revisions on assignments), then explain to the dean; and (3) if not satisfied, threaten the faculty member with salary consequences.

Administrative cajoling and anti–grade inflation discourse demonstrate belief in the validity and objectivity of grades. Faculty concern over grading similarly reflects the belief that grades are precise tools for learning. All agree that sorting should be an outcome.

But this is not how students see it. Faculty may aim to deliver nuanced messages through grading, but student efforts are directed toward the pursuit of high grades, good grades, A's.

For decades the focus on grades seemed to me, as a teacher, natural and right. Then it became irritating. And finally it signaled a grave mistake. In chapter 5, I explain more, but for now it is enough to understand that students see high grades as the basic goal—and many of our students have been taught to be goal oriented, above all else. They aim for the goal throughout the entire "game."

The Game of School: Playing the Teachers

An ambitious first-year student requested a meeting to discuss how I could help her "further her goals." I talked about this book, and like all students, she quickly grasped my distinction between learning and schooling.

Geometry was a good example: She didn't remember it at all (even as a college freshman). Why had she taken it? Because she needed it for Calc I and Calc II, which would help her get into Notre Dame, her ultimate and long-standing goal. She was clear-eyed about her utter lack of interest in the subject. There was no shame in admitting such a strategic approach to schooling. Only the most naïve would fail to be strategic.

Successful students have learned tricks. In *"Doing School,"* Denise Clark Pope reports on a clever, high-achieving student who raised her hand every ten minutes to "participate" in class discussion, even though she did homework for other classes while there. She knew what a successful student *looked like* (see chapter 4).

And if one of the goals of education is to learn something, but students are instead mastering techniques of *looking like* they are learning something, then we as teachers are both wasting our time and teaching something negative. The *game of school* involves mastering the rules and behaving in ways that maximize one's advantage, like collecting properties in Monopoly. School skills, developed to manipulate and control teachers,[17] have some transferable value outside the school setting, but they also have deleterious effects. One is the inauthenticity that comes from being for others.

While it is gracious and important to acknowledge other people's desires, it is also essential to ensure that something genuine and real occurs in the process of education. Learning to act simply in response to another's goals, while presenting them *as if* they were one's own, teaches that action is hollow. There is no solid core of motivation. It is all designed as a performance that will yield rewards.

This inauthenticity can be seen not only in the behavioral tactics of pleasing teachers but also in students' assignments. A large part of student effort is spent on sussing out what teachers want and then producing it. Saying something the students themselves believe in would require actually thinking about what they believe and risking teacher dissatisfaction. In *Professors' Guide to Getting Good Grades in College* and *The Secrets of College Success*, Lynn F. Jacobs and Jeremy S. Hyman advise students, for example, to choose a paper topic their professor seems to care about.

When my student interviewers talked with fellow students and asked about writing something they *did not believe* simply to get a good grade, most understood the question immediately and said either they'd done it themselves or knew that most of their fellow students did. A few expressed relief that they had never had to; somehow they'd been lucky.

This points to a great divide rather than harmony or shared intent between students and teachers, something well entrenched in most school situations, including higher education. Though we might expect teachers and students to be on "the same side," in fact evidence of many kinds—in both words and actions—shows a broad rift between them.

At gatherings, faculty complain about students' intellect, experience, discipline, writing, reading, speaking, focus . . . At a meeting I attended in October 2009, one humanities professor declared unequivocally that all his students wrote miserably. And yet each year the incoming students' scores are higher than the last: astronomical GPAs, AP exam scores of 5 (the top score), letters of praise. Students place out of freshman composition. And yet their teachers wring their hands at the students' lack of skill.

In the *Chronicle of Higher Education*, a three-part blog titled "5 Things Professors Don't Know" attracted hundreds of comments, mostly accusing "the other side" of childishness, of shirking, of whining. Faculty: *Students sit around playing games, have three grandmothers die during a semester, don't know the difference between "courses" and "classes," spend time making fun of their teachers.* Students: *Faculty think their course is the only one, don't have empathy, have thin skin, don't recognize genuine mental illness, and more.*

There is something very strange about the relationship—a Great Divide—between faculty and students. Are we as faculty more like parents, who know better than they do what's good for our "children," or are we help hired by our clients and employers? If we see ourselves as hired by customers, it is perplexing that students tend to want *less* of what we have to offer, in contrast, say, to hiring plumbers or doctors. The bitterness between faculty and students might seem shocking unless we regard education as a kind of medicine administered despite the patient's desires. The crux of the game is how to play the faculty, how to play the administration, how to get the most return with the least effort. Useful skills, surely, in the bigger game of life. But is this what we want to be teaching?

For a lot of students, school becomes the familiar game of getting as much as possible for as little as possible. What students *get* may vary. It might be a high grade, or a class passed and out of the way.

For teachers, the goal is often to get as much (learning? work?) out of the students as possible.

So there is a struggle.

And in the process of that struggle, in which the inequality of the relationship is always evident—analogous to an encounter with the police or other scary authorities—comes *resistance*.

The concept of resistance to domination was made widespread in anthropology and the social sciences through James Scott's *Weapons of the Weak: Everyday Forms of Peasant Resistance*. Building on insights of Antonio Gramsci and others about why unequal social arrangements persist without being overthrown, Scott showed that Malaysian peasants did in fact engage in acts of minor resistance, though they never challenged the social system as a whole.[18]

To help faculty understand their alien students—emphasizing a generational gulf—the Beloit College Mindset List, created in 1998, aims to explain each year's entering students, phrased in terms of what has always been their reality, with a focus on technology, popular culture, and terminology. For the class of 2017, entering in 2013, "Having a chat has seldom involved talking," and "Gaga has never been baby talk."[19] I find this list increasingly alienating, myself. It assumes little actual conversation between faculty and students and portrays the two parties as if living in two untouching worlds.

Contemporary students are described, sometimes favorably, as "digital natives," or less favorably as lazy, distracted, entitled, coddled by "helicopter parents."[20] Generational projects such as Neil Howe and William Strauss's *Millennials Rising: The Next Great Generation* and *Millennials Go to College*, suggest that they will accomplish great feats. A minor industry explaining the Millennials (group oriented, courteous, self-absorbed) has arisen; experts give workshops on the subject.[21]

Another faculty complaint concerns the dominance of course and teacher evaluations and the power these have come to exert in retention and promotion decisions, leading also to laments about "pandering to eighteen-year-olds." Those with good evaluations tend to find something of value in them, while those without tend to attack the method.

Faculty evaluations are supposed to measure teaching, but what they actually measure is student satisfaction—which often means walking a fine line between pushing and prodding students to work harder, and making things fun and easy. I do know many faculty who get excellent evaluations for pushing hard, but also many who are rewarded consistently for their congenial courses. Students *do* want to learn, it is clear, but they also want to manage the balance in their lives.[22]

Pearls before Swine: Evaluations and Pleasing the Customers

If you *really* want to get faculty talking, ask about course evaluations.

Since the 1960s, and especially since the mid-1990s, students evaluate every instructor in every course. It seems fair enough, in many ways, that students should have a voice in how they are taught. Terrible teachers should be called out. But course evaluations are used in ways that probably don't lead to the results intended.

Evaluations may be used (in the lingo) as *formative*, helping to shape future action and reveal areas of needed improvement, or as *summative*, summarizing the final product. Like student grades, or like reviews on Yelp (restaurants), Amazon (books or cameras or coffee makers), or Rotten Tomatoes (movies), faculty evaluations are on scales of A–F, or 1–5, or 1–10. Though there are multiple questions, they also tend—despite disclaimers from administrators—to be summed up in a unitary global measure, often a question like "How would you evaluate this class/instructor compared to others?" Such summary scores are considered when faculty are reviewed annually for their (often paltry) merit increases or contract renewal. At the time of tenure and promotion to full professor, committees everywhere pore over the figures. (At many universities, the desired result is that everyone be above average. And even though the middle option is phrased as "good," that is usually taken as a C, a grade that is supposed to be acceptable for students but not for faculty.) At many universities, especially public ones, these results are made available to help students select courses. Yet enjoying a class is not the same as learning a lot.

Evaluations tend to include questions about how organized the faculty member is, how available, how fair to people of diverse backgrounds, how enthusiastic, how helpful; about how useful the assignments and the readings were. Increasingly, questions inquire about students' own contributions: how often they came to class, how much time they spent on it, how much of the reading they did, their expected grade, why they took the class (requirement, elective), their class level, their major. There are plenty of numbers to crunch in multiple categories.

In the past these evaluations were done on paper. I still have mine from twenty-some years ago. Most institutions now do them electronically. When they were done in class, usually on the last day, just about every student who attended completed the evaluation. Attendance that day was a kind of proxy for students' interest in the class. At one university where I taught, my colleagues noted with a laugh that toward the end of the semester, only a third of their students attended. It is not only students who game the system. Some colleagues consciously massaged the evaluations by bringing donuts or pizza on evaluation day. I have heard of struggling faculty being coached: *Repeat often in the semester, "This is intellectually challenging." That way, when the students are asked how intellectually challenging the class is, they will answer that it is quite intellectually challenging.* Or I have heard that faculty should be hard graders early in the semester and easier later, so that when the evaluations appear, the students feel happy that they have improved so much. Or there is simply the perfect combination of joking, movies, food, little reading or writing, and easy grading that gets high marks.

Faculty who get "fair" or "good" evaluations are devastated. All faculty I know devote themselves to teaching. They really care. They lose sleep; they spend weekends grading and prepping instead of playing in the park with their children. They attend workshops about improving their teaching; they discuss it at department meetings and in hallways.

But when that payoff doesn't happen, when a professor has poured her soul into her teaching, when she has done absolutely everything she can think of and the students still claim they didn't learn anything, didn't like the class, didn't like the professor, would not recommend it, and then—the clincher—say that the only way to improve the class would be to fire the faculty member, you have never seen a more down-in-the-dumps adult. And so to bolster her, to remind her that she has done a wonderful job, colleagues comfort her: "Pearls before swine."

We offer pearls; they are swine.

Now, that is not a great way to conceptualize this relationship. Students may think we are their employees. Administrators may think we are *their* employees. But if teaching is somehow central to at least one of the missions of every college and university (research is another), then the faculty-as-teachers are the stars of the show. But miserable stars can't easily make themselves get up and go back out there. So we reassure them, we listen, we give suggestions. And we tell them, "You are just not appreciated."

I have had both kinds of evaluations. I have been "fired" and I have been beatified. My classes have taught students nothing and they have changed their lives—sometimes in the same course. I have been a terrible person and I have offered the best course in the university. I have sunk lower than the mud and I have floated in the clouds. These evaluations hurt or they feed the soul.

And even though I try to shield myself intellectually and emotionally, and wait for a moment when I will not fixate on them, I dread looking at them. Will this be the semester in which I thought everyone liked me and my jokes but secretly they were counting the minutes? Will this be the semester in which I thought students were lackluster but they loved everything about the class? Sometimes my expectations are right and sometimes I'm shocked by students' reaction.

It is in this context of students nonchalantly providing feedback about their classes—now often done late at night on their computers, bribed with some benefit, since the electronic evaluations have lower response rates and every college is trying to increase those rates—that faculty shape their classes.

Is this a good thing? Should there be better measures of "effective teaching"?[23] As Philip Stark, professor and chair of statistics at Berkeley, writes, "Students are arguably in the best position to judge certain aspects of teaching that *contribute* to effectiveness, such as clarity, pace, legibility, audibility."[24] Offices of institutional research and administrators, statisticians, and faculty have disputed for decades the meaning and value of these evaluations. Faculty contend that students favor easy graders, good-looking, young, sexy, hip, fun professors, and men. Student preference for male and white professors is well documented.[25]

Yet experts agree that it is almost impossible to measure genuine learning.

If learning means that things stick over time, shouldn't the evaluation be done a year, two years, five, ten after the class ends? Should it be about what students remember? Not just a pleasure/pain assessment at the moment. (*I'm mad at her because she only gave me a C on my last paper, so I'll get back at her on the evaluation.*)

Two "natural experiments," one at the Air Force Academy and one in Italy, have revealed that student satisfaction did not necessarily match learning. Students were randomly assigned to two sections of a required foundational course. Achievement in the second course could measure learning in the first course, and this could be compared with student evaluations of the first course. What they found confirmed the sense of faculty that "student evaluations of teaching effectiveness are *negatively associated* with direct measures of effectiveness: Evaluations do not seem to measure teaching effectiveness."[26] In other words, the students who had given the first course a higher evaluation had learned less.

Non-reading: The End of Civilization or a New Era?

In fall 2013 one of my undergraduate assistants reported a friend's boast that he had not read anything for school since fifth grade. A student at an excellent university, "clever," "smart," he successfully writes papers, takes exams, participates in class or online discussions. Why would he have to read?

Students sometimes don't buy the class books. Professors are shocked.

Several years ago a student told me that she regarded all assigned reading as "recommended," even when professors labeled it "required." Were professors so dumb that they didn't know that?

The idea of assigned reading, as the core activity of college students, is old. Students don't see it as central; faculty do.[27] Among many other educational crises, there is a perceived crisis that students are increasingly reading less and less.[28]

Student avoidance of reading is not an entirely new problem. One of my most indelible memories of graduate school in the 1980s was of a new classmate, straight out of a first-rate college, complaining in our anthropology theory class that we had to keep reading what other people thought. *When was it going to be time for us to convey* our *viewpoints? Why all that reading?*

Some college course evaluations ask students what percentage of the reading they did. Some report they did as much as 90 percent, some as little as 25 percent.

In a systematic study of college students' reading, Kylie Baier and four colleagues reported that students mostly (40 percent) read for exams.[29] Almost 19 percent don't read for class. In terms of time, 94 percent of students spend less than two hours on any given reading for class; 62 percent spend less than an hour. Thirty-two percent believe they could get an A without reading; 89 percent believe they could get at least a C.

When faculty enter new institutions, they often ask colleagues, *How much reading should I assign?* Some departments offer guidelines about the number of pages: *Assign twenty-five pages for each meeting of a first-year class but no more than one hundred pages a week for any course.* (This has always struck me as strange, given that a page of a novel and a page of a double-column textbook contain completely different amounts of text and take different kinds of attention and time.) In response to this faculty challenge, Steve Volk—named the Carnegie Professor of the Year in 2011, so he knows something about teaching—wrote on the website of Oberlin College's Center for Teaching Innovation and Excellence that there is no magic formula for numbers of pages. He suggests instead that faculty consider "What do you want the reading to do?"[30]

On a professional online discussion group, Languse, one faculty member asked in 2010 for help locating accessible readings that introduce the ideas of the sociologist Erving Goffman, because, he said, "I find that students no longer understand Goffman's prose." Responses ranged from helpful to hostile. *Do not water down the masters! It is our job to force students to read difficult material. I struggled through Goffman and came to love him, so our students should too.*

One commenter responded: *"No longer understand Goffman's prose? Whatever next? 'Modernised' [sic] Shakespeare? The beauty is worth the effort involved, and the effort involved increases the beauty."*

The original poster responded:

I share your love for Goffman's prose, but am not confident that that love is not a peculiar perversity. In any event, I know that I cannot expect my students to share it, because Goffman's prose requires that one spend time with it, and my students have no time. So many of today's students work, often full time, in addition to attending school.

Another chimed in:

Isn't what you're asking for . . . akin to having English Lit students read "modernised" or "simplified" versions of e.g. Shakespeare or Donne, on the grounds that the poor students don't have the time to read the more challenging original versions? Perhaps students are very pressed for time, but surely one of the basic principles we as university educators should steadfastly abide by is that seminal, classic texts must be read in their original versions. Summaries and secondary accounts of classic works are useful, but to my mind shouldn't replace the originals. And because almost everything in our field has been written in the last 60 years or so, the stylistic complexities are minute, compared to the aforementioned "classics" written hundreds of years ago. Maybe I'm being too idealistic, but some corners just shouldn't be cut, and this, to me at least, is one of them.

And yet another responded:

I am a non-native speaker of English. When I started my education in the US, my professors used Goffman's Interaction Ritual as textbook. I struggled for a short while, then I was quickly drawn to Goffman's detailed descriptions, and I even read all Goffman's books in the library on my own. The beauty in Goffman's writings is in the details. Now I am a college professor myself, and I take it as a part of my professional responsibilities to help my college students appreciate and love that beauty. I do not find that love either peculiar or perverse. To love academia and to love students do not necessarily contradict each other. Isn't it love to watch and ensure our college students grow intellectually?

The original writer weighed the comments.

I agree . . . that Goffman's examples are what make his writings so valuable.

Works that cover the concepts without illustrating them are awfully thin soup, and students will reject them as well for that reason.

But to those who say Goffman's prose, not his examples, are equivalent to Shakespeare's, and so must be thrust upon students for their own good, I wish to note that it is no diminishment of the value of literature to not teach it in every university course.

And to those who say it isn't really hard to read Goffman, I would note two things: first, you have very likely forgotten what it was like to read it for the first time; second, you are a Ph.D. and thus, one would hope, smarter than the average bear; third, as an interaction scholar you likely share my perverse pleasure in contortions of prose; and, fourth, as a social interaction scholar, your love of the phenomena would inspire you to grapple with nearly anything—including graduate school, Wittgenstein's crypticness, and, for God sake, Garfinkel's prose—to secure the hidden treasures lying beneath Goffman's prose style (particularly that in his Presentation of Everyday Life).

Reading original texts, and lots of them, seems worthy, of course—depending on the goals. When I teach a senior-level course, required of our majors, in anthropological theory, I do make them read the original. For a textbook I edited, I sorted through hundreds and hundreds of articles to find accessible, original works that students could read, enjoy, and learn from on a variety of levels—not summaries but actual original works.

Yet I am finding that it is increasingly difficult for students to sink their teeth into works that only a few years ago were not problematic. I don't think, as Nicholas Carr has it, that Google is making us stupid. But as we shape our brains through the activities we ask of them, we read differently. That has to do with technology, attention, pace of life, interests, motivations. And so we can lament, and blame, and grade down, and mutter to one another, insisting on "maintaining standards," or we can meet our students partway.

It is not only college teachers who worry about how much—or how little—people are reading. There is a widespread belief that Americans in general read less and less. This perception builds on public conversations about the lack of reading. In 2007 a National Endowment for the Arts study concluded that adults' reading habits were in severe decline. Only 57 percent of adults read a book voluntarily in 2002, down from 61 percent in 1992.[31] This was supposed to have all sorts of terrible consequences: educational, of course, but also economic, social, moral, you name it.

Reversing the glass-half-empty conclusion, a 2013 study showed that more than half of American adults read books for pleasure—just not what the NEA defines as "literature."[32] And the Pew Research Center's interpretation was that if reading for work and school is added to "voluntary reading," then almost all people read "books" at some point during the year: 79 percent of eighteen- to twenty-four-year-olds, and 90 percent of sixteen- to seventeen-year-olds.[33]

It is undeniable that people are reading (looking at) writing all the time. It may not be in physical books, however. In October 2013, *USA Today* argued that digital devices *increase* book reading (on the devices).[34]

Nicholas Carr wrote in 2008 about the decline in attention—and not only among students. I still received the *Atlantic* in hard copy in those days, so I remember vividly the cover of the magazine, asking in colorful letters, "Is Google Making Us Stoopid?" I still have it in my old-fashioned paper archives, even though, when I want to refer to it, I use the electronic version.

Mark Bauerlein's 2008 book *The Dumbest Generation: How the Digital Age Stupefies Young Americans and Jeopardizes Our Future (Or, Don't Trust Anyone under 30)* deplores the distraction and shallowness of the young, with the rewiring of the brain that accompanies frequent use of digital devices. Bauerlein is especially pessimistic about that generation because it is not engaging seriously with the ideas and knowledge required for genuine democracy.

Attention spans, focus, mindfulness—all these are shrinking. Technology plays a role, as many of us spend much of our lives looking at short items. The Onion, the humor website, puts most of its efforts into its headlines. Blogs should be at most one thousand words, but three hundred is better. Tweets are at most 140 characters long.

So if students are nibbling text constantly on their devices, and suddenly are asked to consume what sounds like an indigestible mountain of pages in some other form—and for what!?—they are likely to avoid it entirely.

A new model of teaching, "flipping the classroom," requires students to encounter material through reading or videos prior to class; in class they work on problems together.[35] (Some faculty have scoffed at the claim that this is novel. *Haven't they heard of seminars?*) This requires reading—but reading with a goal. Students often like to do that, as a kind of scavenger hunt for what is useful and important. Requiring students to read just for background ideas seems to be fading.

Actually, I have stopped worrying constantly about this. Students are reading. The public is reading. They may not sit for hours, still and attentive, focusing on one item. They may confuse their facts. They may miss a complex argument. Their reading may not be of physical books, nor of what is recognized as novels. A professor friend, an art historian, asked me, expecting shared disgust, if I regard graphic novels as literature. *We must maintain standards! We must protect the canon!*

Don't misunderstand. I worship reading. When I travel for three days, in addition to all my devices, I bring six books and five (print) magazines. Yet I cannot concentrate the way I used to. So as for those less devoted . . . Should we cut them off from the world, isolate them in soundproof rooms with no WiFi, and force them to read a book?

Writing has evolved, and will evolve. And with that, reading changes. From clay tablets designed to record debts to bronze proclamations of kings and emperors, from bamboo strips recording rituals to complex philosophical arguments on paper, from paintings for the royal afterlife to paperback novels, from stone tablets proclaiming a new moral code to infinitesimal elements on a shiny handheld device—from its origins, writing has transformed, and will continue to do so. It is not entirely that the medium is the message, but the medium affects the message. Since humans are the ones doing the writing, we get the writing that suits our purposes. Experimental research on brains shaped with and without computers indeed shows that our brains are molded by the tasks we ask of them, a characteristic known as *neural plasticity*. And whether the changes are good or bad, it is hard to imagine the world giving up on computers and returning to a time when weighty physical objects held a monopoly on knowledge, wisdom, and information.[36]

The Battle for Attention

Some of what I just argued came from a class I taught in which I did not know when I began what I thought about the subject. I always learn through teaching. In this case, it gave me an opportunity to learn something about that elusive quest for student engagement.

The class was on new media. Convinced of the value of looking at the topic anthropologically, I decided to open it up to all students, regardless of major, even though it was a 400-level course. Three of the students were seniors majoring in business who had waited until their very last semester to complete their social science requirements. They already had jobs lined up with important firms; they were checking the box.

Because it was a class on new media, I decided to allow technology in the classroom. We could always analyze its effects.

The class started out well enough. It was in my then favorite classroom—in a building since demolished and replaced. The windows were huge, and didn't entirely close. The desks moved. Some floor tiles (probably asbestos) were loose. Large black chalkboards could slide up to reveal additional writing space, and there was a projector and computer for contemporary needs. The paint was peeling. The room did not project the message that we were at the forefront of affluence and success; to me it said, "I have lived through decades of activity, with some scars, so use me as you will." These students, accustomed to sharp new facilities, commented regularly on how pathetic the classroom was.

After a few weeks, I noticed that the three seniors were becoming increasingly absorbed in their laptops. Finally one day, one of them jabbed her neighbor and pointed at something on the screen that made them both laugh. YouTube? Facebook? Something else? I could no longer pretend they were using their laptops for note taking and for the assigned reserve reading.

What to do? All along they had given me the clear message that they didn't much like the mandate for discussion; they didn't like the inconclusive readings; they knew what was real and they wanted answers. They didn't meet my eye in class and rebuffed my attempts at talking.

So as I lay awake, fretting, I decided I would forbid the use of technology from the next class period on.

I made the announcement, nervously, at the beginning of the hour. I explained that we had been talking about the effects of technology on social interaction, and that the pull of the Internet was too strong to resist. Since our task was to make the most of our precious face-to-face meetings, I would no longer allow the use of technology. The experiment had revealed results.

One of the students, accustomed to success, turned away from me (in our large circle of chair-desks) and pouted. She kept that up for about a week. But as the class discussions improved, eventually she relented slightly. (Students were aware of the requirement to participate in class; after all, it was part of their grade.)

But another student in the same class, also taking it to fulfill a requirement in his senior year, had the opposite reaction. A physics major, already accepted into a graduate engineering program, he was transfixed. He had never thought of analyzing the world this way. He was enchanted with Marxist analysis, and with the ethnographic work on cell phones and computers. In office hours he admitted that he was sorry he had waited so long to learn about a whole new approach to thinking about the world. We talked about his setting up social theory reading groups in graduate school, just for fun. And even though it has now been years since that class, occasionally I get an email from him when something reminds him of the subject.

Involvement and Engagement—or, Going through the Motions

I am not alone in my despair about students not caring, not putting effort into their classes. In the 1990s, education scholars began to investigate student involvement; in the early twenty-first century, the relevant term is *engagement*. This is studied through, among other things, annual surveys administered since 2000 to hundreds of thousands of students, the National Survey of Student Engagement, NSSE, pronounced "Nessie." According to the NSSE website:

> Student engagement represents two critical features of collegiate quality. The first is the amount of time and effort students put into their studies and other educationally purposeful activities. The second is how the institution deploys its resources and organizes the curriculum and other learning opportunities to get students to participate in activities that decades of research studies show are linked to student learning.[37]

Engagement is one of many desirable aspects of higher education participation, along with persistence (remaining in higher education until completion of degree), having good grades, and continuing to graduate school. Many researchers have attempted to specify not only correlations but causes among these and various educational experiences. The 1998 Boyer Commission Report on Reinventing Undergraduate Education identified serious misdirections and inadequacies in undergraduate education and proposed that "research-based learning" should be the standard at research universities, with all students involved in research and being guided by mentors.[38] Since the Boyer Commission's report, educators around the country have been trying to implement activities variously construed as "research," capstone projects, or senior theses.[39] The National Science Foundation funds Research Experiences for Undergraduates; many campuses provide funding for Undergraduate Research Opportunities. So now all over the United States, undergraduates conduct research, apply for research grants, organize conferences. Sometimes they do it because they really have a passion for the subject. Sometimes they do it because it has become just another expected item in their collection of accomplishments and they hope it enhances their record. New scholarship attempts to assess the value of such experiences.[40]

The important point, though, is that universities hope that through conducting mentored research, student engagement will increase—because so many students are known to be simply going through the motions.

I had a wonderful conversation with a young man early in his sophomore year. Raised in the southern United States by his adoptive family since the age of eighteen months, he wanted to go do research in his natal country on what the war there meant to people his age (and who looked just like him). He had spoken with political scientists and historians, but his passion lay in actually speaking with the people. I told him it was his destiny to become an anthropologist. He grinned.

"This is the only thing that has gotten me excited in school."

Ever?

This fellow was a student in our elite honors program. He had obviously done extremely well in high school, not just well enough to enter our highly selective university but to be among our most recognized students. He had been going through the motions all along. And he knew it.

In the online publication *Inside Higher Ed*, John Warner told of a deal he'd offered his students: A's for everyone, without coming to class or doing anything.[41] He wanted them to think about what it means to care only about the result of a class without any consideration of the content.

Sometimes students work hard, but if the work is perceived as meaningless, they resist by merely going through the motions. The *Atlantic* published an article by an earnest first-year student, Elif Koc, explaining how her "insane homework load" in high school taught her to game the system. She was heavily involved in activities (cross-country running, debate, mock trial, the newspaper, tutoring a student). "I worked hard," she said, "I loved school, and I was always stressed." Then in her junior year she realized that she did not have to do it all to pursue straight A's. She learned to become what teachers wanted—a "good student" rather than a "good learner." As she describes it, she and her classmates "were maximizing our academic success while minimizing our effort in certain subjects." For example, she did the easy math problems in her homework the night before and filled in the rest during class; smart students participated in class discussions of literature without having done the reading. "We understood our teachers' expectations and aimed to meet them, not to exceed them. There is a difference between being a good learner and a good student, and in high school, my peers and I learned how to be good students."[42]

And when the decorated journalist and writer Karl Taro Greenfeld tried to do his thirteen-year-old daughter's homework for a week—incomprehensible half the time—he too learned to cut corners. The goal became "How can I do as little as possible and still get an A?"[43]

In a system in which endurance is challenging, figuring out how to get by with as little as possible teaches students how to fake enthusiasm—while the professionals talk about "collaboration" and "engagement." This is not simply a waste; it also teaches inauthenticity, a focus on appearance rather than substance, and disdain for the institution within which students spend their entire youth.

I acknowledge that some students love every bit of the experience. There are engineers who love their engineering classes, poets who adore creative writing, history buffs who not only savor the facts and theories in their class books but also visit historic sites and watch the History Channel. Some students *like* the substance of school.

But get most students to talk about their work, their attitudes, and their goals, and you come away with the clear impression that most are only going through the motions.

A friend told me that her nephew hated all his classes for four years at Indiana University, usually considered a first-rate institution. He just had to survive those four years—those 1,200 days, those 360 hours of classes, and maybe 700 hours of work.

A waste.

In this sense it does not matter what we as teachers do in the classroom. We have lost before the students ever appear. They have been trained to perform their role. When we grade students on "participation," we are insisting that they act a certain way. The adept students have mastered that formula and can feed it back to us.

Poor, Unappreciated Liberal Arts

Across the United States, the liberal arts are neglected. They are shunned. They are avoided. They are fighting a desperate battle for survival.[44]

These "liberal arts" are the inheritors of one strand of educational history, the one that, according to the higher education creation myth, goes all the way back to the Greeks. It is here that we invoke Socrates, the unexamined life, Plato, and then the Romans with their *trivium* and *quadrivium*, the medieval universities and the Enlightenment, humanism, the Great Tradition, the idea of cultural literacy, standards, Oxford and Cambridge, and colonial America. Phi Beta Kappa, the national honors society, is devoted to the liberal arts. Almost all the "liberal arts colleges" adhere to a version of this story. St. John's College, in both its settings, teaches *only* through original sources, in seminars.

Liberal arts is essentially the core of higher education as it existed prior to land grant universities and massification. It could never be confused with vocational training.

Liberal arts is the bedrock of all educated life: English and writing and rhetoric, history, literature, philosophy, languages, "culture," even science and mathematics. It has expanded to embrace the social sciences: anthropology, sociology, psychology, political science, and economics. Liberal arts can include the study of film and television and theater, dance and music and the visual arts.

Liberal arts includes the subjects required of all students, no matter what their major.

Liberal arts is the major of the majority of community college students planning to transfer to four-year institutions. The liberal arts are the "gen(eral) ed(ucational requirement)s" that everyone has to get checked off. Community colleges are attractive because they allow students to get through their gen eds more cheaply. When you compare costs, cheaper is more attractive. Who can argue against that? Liberal arts courses may be fun or boring, hard or—best of all—easy, but students all have to take them.

A crisis has been brewing on almost every university campus: students are not selecting liberal arts for their majors. They are opting for, and are encouraged to major in, what they see as "practical" subjects: business, allied health fields. Interest in the STEM (science, technology, engineering, and math) fields is increasing, as it is in design, manufacturing, and much else. When students have a choice, they often flock to the vocational subjects that they believe will guarantee a job.

Liberal arts colleges—either the school-within-a-university called a *college* or the self-contained unit called a *college*—are fighting for their life. The elite liberal arts colleges, Williams, Amherst, Swarthmore, Middlebury, Carleton, Dartmouth, are doing fine, thank you, and applications are high as always. But the less selective ones are struggling to survive. There are enrollment crises and image crises. There are funding crises and staffing crises. There are crises of content. They can't get no respect.

Yet though students are running from our majors, we can't *force* students to choose liberal arts; we can only make them appealing.[45]

Business leaders, when surveyed, say that what they want is well-trained liberal arts graduates who can read, write, think, analyze. Students keep running.

Byron White, an ex-journalist, compared higher education with journalism. In the 1980s, surveys showed that readers viewed international news as the least compelling. Newspapers argued that they had to keep their bureaus open worldwide; they knew better than their readers. Their readers kept migrating. You know the end of that story. Its moral: "Adapt or die."

> So what if every reader survey ranked international news coverage near the bottom of what people wanted to read? Didn't they know our Africa correspondent had just won a Pulitzer Prize for international reporting? People needed international reporting even if they were too ignorant to recognize it, and we were determined to give it to them, no matter that the enormous expense of housing reporters all over the world was killing the bottom line.[46]

Educators keep talking about the importance of "critical thinking." That is not what students or the public regard as the goal of their education. Our students want cheap, easy liberal arts classes if they have to take them at all. They want something practical, something they can use immediately to make money.

We can keep preaching our gospel: The collective wisdom of humankind is assembled in the works of the past. The most profound knowledge and insight about the meaning of life are puzzled over in literary, cinematic, philosophical work. Questions of value and causality are thoroughly scrutinized in social science. Shakespeare knew everything about humans. But the students remain unmoved. I would not say that this reflects their lack of interest in learning; there are many ways to learn besides going to classes for which students pay tuition, following someone's instructions, and getting graded. People are learning all the time—just not necessarily in school. School for many is seen as a necessary evil for certain practical purposes.

To the extent that students separate school—a place in which to get their credentials—from the enjoyable or even meaningful part of learning, then liberal arts will seem not only undesirable but also unnecessary. And if they do need guidance with a subject that really appeals to them, there are always massive open online courses—MOOCs.

That Sinking Feeling

So, they don't read, they don't work, they don't care. Or so faculty complain, endlessly, about students today. Their complaints extend beyond these sins of omission to sins of commission. And the sense of moral panic rises.

Every professor who pays attention, for example, has had an encounter with cheating and plagiarism. If you ever need to find a subject to fill a lull in conversation—after student effort, grading, and course evaluations—ask a teacher at any level about her experiences with it.

My own personal experiences with cheating and plagiarism are not extensive. But they are memorable. There is a certain feeling you get in your gut when you are going along, reading papers, maybe planning to finish seven more and then pack up, get a cup of coffee, go home.

Maybe you're a little sleepy, or lulled into automaticity by the task. Maybe your back hurts, or your eyes. Maybe your pencil needs sharpening, or your email needs checking. Always there is a hope that it will be over sooner than expected. You try not to count every paper. Here's one, finished. And another. The "finished" pile is finally taller than the "unfinished."

And then . . . *zap!*

Having established the veracity of the historian's claims, we may now move on to question the applicability to the situation under consideration.

As I showed in Humpfelburger 1975, Tlingit tendencies toward cross-cousin marriage intersected with sibling taboo . . .

As Professor Lee said in our class . . .

Oh wow. Now you have to track it down. Are the sentences relevant? Lifted? Is the whole paragraph, the whole paper, borrowed from somewhere?

Every college and university has procedures for dealing with what are now referred to as "honor code violations" or "academic integrity problems," but before that bridge is crossed, professors spend time mulling over students' prose. Electronic services such as Turnitin.com may provide additional tools, but they cannot replace the judgment of an experienced teacher. They turn up both "false positives"—matches that do not stem from plagiarism—and "false negatives," or instances in which a student did in fact plagiarize but the electronic service does not possess the original against which to check the student's paper.

In the olden days I would trudge over to the library to try to hunt down plausible sources. Now, of course, students tend to rely on the Internet. And so can I.

I do pursue all such cases. Depending on the situation, I respond in varying ways. I have been increasingly torn by, on the one hand, a sense of compassion, combined with distrust over the entire educational enterprise, and on the other, my abiding belief in "standards" and academic practices for guiding the behavior of participants in the system.

When students are asked about academic misconduct—*Have you ever cheated on a test? Did you ever copy or permit someone to copy your homework? Did you in the last year include a sentence you did not attribute to its source? Did you ever permit someone to copy off you during a test? Did you ever fudge lab results?* (And don't get me started about how crazy some of the questions are. Allow someone to copy math homework? In what universe should this be considered cheating? If the homework is useless, who cares about it anyway?)—statistics show that anywhere from a third to 90 percent of college students engaged in this behavior at least once. So in every group of twenty-five students, anywhere between eight and twenty-two of them had done "bad things."

In thinking about my own students, I've had trouble connecting the statistics about cheating to the apparently polite and in some ways responsible young people in front of me. The two images couldn't be reconciled.

And yet they cheat, and faculty struggle to contain this misconduct. As one colleague lamented to me, "If I worked incredibly hard to make my degree meaningful, and someone else has earned the same degree by cheating, that makes my degree that much less meaningful." But—and here the question of disengagement arises again—if students aren't learning *meaningfully*, they may not see cheating and plagiarizing (however defined) as any sort of loss or violation. We can force compliance through brute power, but this is not what I aim for in my teaching.

The really central question for me is this: How can it be that the content of what we are teaching matters so little that students don't want to spend any time on it?

And that takes us to some of the things students do devote their time to.

Drinking and Hooking Up

I looked around my class at all the appealing students so concerned with their GPAs. I thought about the statistics I'd been so alarmed to learn: 30 to 80 percent (depending on the surveys) of them cheated and plagiarized, and 44 percent engaged in binge drinking (four drinks in a single setting for women, five for men). Some huge number of the drunken students engaged in demeaning sexual hookups.

But there they were in front of me at noon on Wednesday, looking like a million dollars, healthy, clean, polite. Which of them had been stumbling around sick and exposed on Saturday night? Was it possible that the eager young intellectual sitting with her notebooks so well organized had been debasing herself sexually just a few days ago?

Once, when I was director of the Center for Asian Studies, I received a CD of photos required of students who had won a summer scholarship for language study abroad. The photos were indeed of the student at her school, traveling to tourist sites, living with her host family. But by mistake—I assume—they also included images of drunkenness, of her lying by a puddle of vomit next to a toilet. This is what that statistical picture looked like on the ground. Misery, filth, humiliation: shameful images best kept from family and teachers.

A story in the *New York Times* in the summer of 2013 recounted the experiences of a young woman at the University of Pennsylvania and her demeaning casual sexual relations while drunk. She added that she did not want her need for sex to interfere with her résumé building.[47] Among the almost eight hundred responses, many challenged the generalizability of this report.

And sex (consensual but especially nonconsensual) and drinking go together. Almost every case of sexual misconduct between acquaintances occurs in the context of heavy alcohol use.[48] This is not to excuse the perpetrators; it is to acknowledge that drinking is implicated in a lot of undesirable behavior.[49]

Sex and drugs are sensationalized in media and movies, analyzed by academic and health experts. They are part of the fear and part of the thrill of going to college.

Certainly complaints about alcohol abuse may be deserved, whether because of alcohol poisoning, the development of alcoholism, or the loss of judgment that leads to risky and sometimes lethal behavior.[50] But they also follow a script: *Those unruly undergraduates* . . . Yet adults have complained about student alcohol consumption as long as we have had higher education—in ancient Rome, in Bologna, in Germany, in the Ivy League colleges during colonial times. (Perhaps the excessive drinking that alarms college administrators today would not be such a problem if our laws and mores allowed alcohol to be introduced gradually as part of ordinary consumption.)

One of the few biocultural anthropologists to study college drinking in a cultural context, Janet Chrzan, asks *why* students drink. Her research shows that in addition to the reasons adults drink—for fun, intoxication, relaxation—they also drink because they freely choose to, as well as to "facilitate sexual relations" or to explore the performance of gender identity.[51] Many of them are uncomfortable or genuinely ill at ease in social situations. Alcohol helps.

This connects with another troubling complaint about a problem that is real but is not recognized *enough*: the huge proportion of students suffering serious psychological distress.

The Campus Mental Health Crisis

A student with abdominal problems had been going on the usual wild goose chase from doctor to doctor. She had also been diagnosed as suffering from depression. One day she missed class, so I emailed to ask if she was okay. A junior, she said I was the first professor who had ever checked in on her. She admitted thinking she might be able to trust me, but it was very difficult to find someone to trust at Notre Dame. (I assume she meant among students, too.)

She was one of many students who suffer. Every semester I learn from several students that they are on medication or seeing therapists. They cry in my office, confess their tribulations.

Students are sadly lonely in the midst of what is supposed to be a four-year-long party. Their families go into debt, with all kinds of hopes for their beloved kids, and the kids can't be honest with their parents for fear they'll worry too much, make them come home, or decide it is not worth the pain. So they become more isolated. They "self-medicate" with alcohol, sex, and other drugs. In that sense, the "epidemic" of alcohol and meaningless sex is a symptom of the problem of unhappiness, which is rampant enough in this generation.[52] But add in the negative effects of schooling (the pressure for performance and achievement; a sense of alienation and fraudulence; loneliness and isolation; comparisons with others' apparent happiness) and it is no wonder these kids are seeking solace.

One year I had a student, Riley,[53] who told me that he had dropped out during his first semester of college, when for the first time he was unable to complete all his work. In high school he had, it seems, been quite a star. Now he seemed likely to drop out again. In his philosophy class, instead of writing a single-page response to a question, as required, he became obsessed. He could not sleep. He took to heart what was meant to be taken only to mind, and then only briefly. This is the attitude of a scholar, a poet, a madman. Which would he be?

Riley designed a brilliant independent major, but he came close to failing that, too. Or did we come close to failing him? One time he was supposed to respond to a blog post about the nature of a particular subject. He knew that he was supposed to reply breezily, off the cuff. But he felt compelled to bring in all the philosophical and disciplinary analysis of the topic and thus could neither begin nor complete the task.

Despite our claims to the contrary, schooling is built for reluctant learners. We don't know what to do with someone like Riley, who wanted time to think about things. Of course he "needed to learn" how to finish his work in a timely fashion. He needed to be able to dash off a two-page response, giving the professor "what she wants." Instead, he wanted to delve into topics. I feared all year that he would not emerge from his absorption. (Happily, he finished!)

I was really troubled by my complicity but was not sure how to respond. Should I have just accepted anything he gave me, anytime he could do it?

He suffered from (diagnosed) depression, anxiety, insomnia. That should be challenge enough. One professor told me she would call this student in the morning to make sure he got up. This struck me as both dangerous and humane.

Psychologists Richard Kadison and Theresa DiGeronimo, in *College of the Overwhelmed: The Campus Mental Health Crisis and What to Do about It,* discuss the substantial number of college students who are so depressed that they have trouble functioning. They report one 2003 study that saw a doubling of depression in thirteen years.[54] More than one-third of students in a survey were taking antidepressants at a particular time.[55] The Center for Collegiate Mental Health reports that as of the 2013–14 academic year, 48.1% of students had at some point in their lives attended counseling for mental health concerns, 32.6 percent had taken a medication for mental health concerns, and 30.9 percent of students seriously considered attempting suicide, though attempts had been made only by 8.9 percent.[56] Of the 25,475 clients reported on by mental health clinicians in 2014, they had seen 55.1 percent with anxiety and 45.26 percent with depression.[57]

And for those who want to claim that students have always been under pressure but now they name their discomfort *depression* or *anxiety*, note that the rates of mental illness and suicide have increased between ten- and twentyfold over the last fifty years. Some researchers blame not individuals and biology but the specific features of our society.[58]

Novels and accounts from the fifties, sixties, seventies, and eighties depict plenty of stress on campus, but it tends to be social or academic. Now it is more about personal issues like scheduling, sleeping, and so on.

Serious mental illness—bipolar disorder, personality disorder—have existed always and everywhere, but the forms and prevalence vary. And the uncertainty, the need to perform, the focus on achievement, the blaming of individuals for their fate—all these contribute to what may be a real increase in emotional distress.

Talking about This Generation

So now you have seen an assortment of complaints about college. Is this a genuine crisis? Or is it all a moral panic, a way to organize our discomfort at a rapidly transforming world? Does a golden age always lie in the past?

Are students the same as they ever were? Is the Internet changing them completely? Has our society lost its moral moorings?

I agree that there are tendencies toward unhappiness and acting recklessly, toward corner cutting and cheating, toward getting away with the minimum and just rushing to get things done in every time and place. But some of the details set today apart from the past.

Granted, generalizations are always dangerous. Students growing up in a two-professional household with a taste for classical music and organic food will not be the same as adolescents raising their younger siblings while Mom is in jail. If these last get a chance to go to college, they will have a different perspective on the whole experience. Nevertheless, here are some things that have changed over the *longue durée* of the twentieth century:

- The teenage years are named, set aside, and reserved for education, not for work.
- High school has become compulsory.
- High school and college have become differentiated.
- Colleges have a differentiated curriculum.
- Age-grading is ubiquitous and all-powerful.

There are some new aspects of education that have arisen in the last fifty years in the United States (and soon to follow elsewhere in the world, as other countries try to add the "American model"):

- High school diplomas are needed even for menial jobs, just because other people have them.
- More than half the population has attended some college, though completion rates remain relatively low.
- Community colleges have become in some sense the new high school.
- Highly selective colleges are more difficult to attend; children from privileged families spend their entire childhood in preparation for college admission.
- Education has come to be seen more as a private good than a public obligation; its focus on "sorting" has eclipsed its focus on citizenship.
- Reading and long-form writing are no longer the central component of education.

- As it is required that everyone stay in school, those without interest or ability must be accommodated (youth who would prefer to work, those too active to sit still, those with developmental delays) or medicated.

And even more changes have occurred in just the last several years:

- The Internet is ubiquitous.
- Economic insecurity has risen.
- Collaborative learning is common.
- Learning experts have challenged the idea of "sage on the stage" in favor of "guide on the side."
- Homeschooling and unschooling have increased.
- Alternative methods of education have proliferated: online universities, for-profit colleges, community colleges, charter schools, magnet schools, and private schools of a variety of types.

Through it all, some things endure:

- Social class remains predictive of educational success.
- The privileged continue to succeed beyond the non-privileged.
- Children prefer playing to sitting still.
- Children must be brought into the world of adults, slowly or abruptly.
- When stakes are high, there is motivation to risk unpermitted methods.

However we explain all these complaints, I certainly felt them deeply. By the time I received tenure in 2002, I was not sure I could go on. My disappointment was profound, constant, and personal. How could I possibly make myself plan courses enthusiastically, only to have students evaluate them on the basis of how little work they'd been able to get away with? Sure, there were good students, those who cared, worked hard, actually read everything. But I was focused on the numerous others. And it felt bad.

But then, as I studied the problem, expecting to see how lazy, wrongheaded, unintellectual, and entitled the students were, as I learned more and more about the students, the educational system, the history of education, and how people learn and grow up throughout the world, in short, as I used my anthropological skills to look at my own context, I found a different answer than I'd expected.

One of the remaining foundational puzzles has to do with confusion about what college is for, at all. Once we understand that, we can look more closely at college itself.

2

The Myriad and Muddied Goals of College

Education is not properly an industry, and its proper use is not to serve
industries, either by job-training or by industry-subsidized research. . . .
A proper education enables young people to put their lives in order, which
means knowing what things are more important than other things; it means
putting first things first.

WENDELL BERRY, *In the Presence of Fear*

*College is for growing up. . . . No, for getting a good job. . . . No, for having
fun. . . . No, for learning "transferable skills." . . . No, for learning content. . . .
No, for the credential. . . . No, wait, what was it for, again?*

When I was department chair, a colleague came to me with a problem.
A young woman in her first-year seminar wanted to revise a paper. Good
news, right? All students had been required to revise their papers, but this
particular student wanted to revise it a second time. Zeal for learning? An
exemplary student never satisfied with her efforts? Experienced faculty
and students in the know might guess the reason, which the student stated
explicitly: she wanted to do another revision because she was not satisfied
with her grade. She had calculated that even if she did very well on the
remaining assignments, she could not get an A in the course without an
A on this paper.

My colleague was disturbed. She wanted her students to learn to write,
to identify an argument, to improve—an idealistic perspective focused on
learning.

The student had entirely different goals. She wanted to achieve, to succeed, to get a good grade. Writing the paper was the way to get "the grade
she wanted." She never spoke of wanting to learn about writing. The
learning was a means to her ultimate goal: the grade. For my colleague,
the grade was a means by which to further *her* ultimate goal: learning.

It is obvious just from this little story that different participants in the
adventure of higher education have different goals—crudely put, *idealistic*
versus *pragmatic*—and we find many more, beyond grades and learning.
I've been collecting goals, like a fisher with a wide net, for almost a decade.
This chapter offers a sample of my multicolored specimens, far beyond the
two illustrated in the opening encounter, sorted into two main categories.

We have to decide what college is for before we can design the details,
such as who pays, who goes, what we teach, and how. As Stephen Covey
says, "Begin with the end in mind." But what, exactly, is the end?

The Idealistic Side of College: Learning

Colleagues speak movingly of knowledge, fascination, beauty, even
"love."[1] Faculty assign particular tasks, whether papers, projects, or tests,
in order to inculcate skills of composition, citation, argument, and structure, to teach professional preparation for academia, to introduce academic
fields of study, and more generally to promote critical thinking for life. In
this sense, "standards" are a means to a greater end, though sometimes
they appear instead to be the ends themselves.

Faculty might recognize here their own idealistic reasons for teaching
and the reasons we think students should be in college, especially liberal arts
colleges, in terms that are aesthetic, vocational in the religious sense, and
personal. These inspiring ideals are a far cry from a mechanized exchange of
credentials for a certain minimal amount of work, or a focus on the price per
credit hour of education as a purchasable good, or the pursuit of high grades.

The Liberal Arts: Learning for Learning's Sake

Learning for its own sake: How I have defended this idea over the years!
Many of my students completely accept this, or at least they can parrot
its tenets back to me when asked; it is one of the selling points of colleges

like Notre Dame. Businesses, when polled in surveys, agree that students with narrow vocational training are not optimal; they would rather seek graduates with general skills ("soft skills," like foreign languages, writing, speaking) that can be tailored to the specific needs of the task at hand.[2]

Phi Beta Kappa, the national honors society, vigorously supports the liberal arts. William Cronon's well-known essay "Only Connect" appeared in that society's superb journal, *American Scholar*, arguing that liberal education "aspires to nurture the growth of human talent in the service of human freedom.... [L]iberally educated people have been liberated by their education to explore and fulfill the promise of their own highest talents."[3] Admitting that it is easier to tinker with the components of a curriculum than to identify exactly how to educate for freedom, Cronon nonetheless gives it a go, attempting to identify the characteristics of liberally educated people:

1. They listen and they hear.
2. They read and they understand.
3. They can talk with anyone.
4. They can write clearly and persuasively and movingly.
5. They can solve a wide variety of puzzles and problems.
6. They respect rigor not so much for its own sake but as a way of seeking truth.
7. They practice humility, tolerance, and self-criticism.
8. They understand how to get things done in the world.
9. They nurture and empower the people around them.
10. They follow E. M. Forster's injunction from *Howards End*: "Only connect . . ."

My own checklist of goals for students at the completion of higher education might include the following "design features":

1. They possess sophistication in reading—and watching, viewing, listening to—a variety of materials.
2. They possess mastery of writing and creating a variety of types of texts and digital products.
3. They can make sense of and evaluate the enormous quantity of readily available information, whether mathematical/statistical, scientific, political, philosophical, commercial.

4. They are able to present material orally.
5. They understand the constructed and contested nature of theory.
6. They can place a current situation within broader contexts (historical, philosophical, cultural).
7. They can become their own teacher and judge.
8. They can take care of their own affairs—financial, logistical, health, sexual, social.
9. They can forge new relationships with a range of people.
10. They are able to stick to a task and meet obligations such as deadlines.

All this can be accomplished in any number of ways, which is why students' particular majors are not especially important. They can dig in and learn about interconnections between theory and application anywhere, but it probably helps to do it within a specific field, if only as a model of depth and intensity. Yet much of this list can be accomplished without formal schooling.

Idealism 101: Colleges That Change Lives

In the popular *Colleges That Change Lives*, former *New York Times* education reporter Loren Pope, writing until he was nearly one hundred years old, argued not for "value added" in economic terms, not for the transferable skills that would permit poets to work for General Mills, not for fun and football, but for *transformation*. This was a sixties value that, at least until the early twenty-first century, continued to resonate among a group of readers.

Each year the Higher Education Research Institute at UCLA reports on the National Survey of Freshmen, administered since 1965 to hundreds of thousands of incoming college students.[4] First-year students are asked, "What do you hope to get out of college?" Formerly one of the options—no longer included—was "learning about the meaning of life." Yet not all is crass. In 2014, in addition to wanting to "be able to get a better job" (86.1%) students had meaningful goals: "to gain a general education and appreciation of ideas" (70.6 percent); "to make me a more cultured person" (46.6 percent); "to learn more about things that interest me" (82.2 percent).[5] Students *do* want to learn. And some *are* eager to "be the change [they] want to see in the world"—a slogan commonly, though falsely, attributed to Gandhi.[6]

Saving the World

One night I attended a lecture by *New York Times* columnist Nicholas Kristof at Notre Dame's "sister" school, Saint Mary's College. More than a thousand people joined me—more people than attend SMC as students. Kristof gave some facts. He made fun of himself for getting Arabic wrong and inadvertently issuing a command to "f— yourself" (the meaning of a word sounding like "Nick"). He told heartwarming stories of girls rescued from poverty who eventually graduated from American colleges, and shocking stories of girls trafficked, two of whom he "bought" and then gave their freedom. He described fistulas and infanticide and, despite appearing at an avowedly Catholic campus, did not shy away from a question about abortion, which he answered by speaking of an "unmet need for family planning." He used his *Times* credentials and his experience around the world—Darfur, Pakistan, Bangladesh, China, Cambodia, various parts of Africa—to urge the students in the audience to travel to the developing world. *Don't go in a swarm of Americans to Paris; go to Ghana, and if you get malaria you get extra credit.*

It was a good speech. Not profound, but with some "action items." He had fantastic, huge color photos projected beside him (by *Times* photographers), and a PowerPoint theme from his book *Half the Sky*. Kristof reminded us that people born into middle-class families in the United States have won the lottery of life; it is necessary to use that advantage to alleviate the injustices and suffering of our fellows who have not.

If I'd been twenty and in the audience, I would have felt jolted into awareness and action, if I hadn't had that sense already. I would have wanted to take off for the hard places and *do something*! Just sitting and learning on campus could not possibly compete with a feeling of activity. Many of our students want to make the world better, and sitting in classrooms or libraries or dorm rooms highlighting passages in theoretical writings cannot compare.

While most students—in record numbers—are in college to get a job and make money, lots of them also feel impelled to improve the world.

These desires need not be entirely mutually exclusive. After a thirty-year-old makes her first million dollars, she can give fifty thousand to found a school in Afghanistan. After the first ten million, she can double or triple her contribution.

Academicizing

Challenging views such as Kristof's, provocateur Stanley Fish argues in *Save the World on Your Own Time* that college faculty should stick with what they know: teaching young people how to look at the world analytically. Anything, he claims, including the most contentious political and moral topic, can be "academicized," or subjected to academic analysis: examining its history, discerning the kinds of people supporting and attacking it, and dissecting the arguments and evidence that people use for their views. Professors' own opinions, political or other, do not belong in the classroom. Nor, he argues, should professors be in the business of counseling, role modeling, or any of the other tasks that would put them on a kind of pedestal. They are trained as academics and should function as academics. No more and no less.

This, of course, presupposes a certain view of the central function of universities as places for intellectual formation. But as all of us know, universities, colleges, and community colleges have many other roles as well. Fish does not ignore the other staff (student life, administrators) at universities but sees them as peripheral to the central mission of academics.

Ask a student about this and you are not likely to find much support for Fish's view. "Academicizing" the world is far from what most are seeking. *Professorial* is an insult for a politician, don't forget. And *academic* means useless.

Growing Up

At highly selective residential colleges nowadays, students are expected to do quite a bit of maturing; college is now the de rigueur *rite de passage* for the "emerging adults" who populate our classrooms. For many it is the first time they are responsible for caring for themselves.

This situation is hugely variable, to be sure. At nonresidential campuses or often at community colleges, students are older and have a great deal of life experience. Less affluent teenagers may have nothing like the luxury of an extended adolescence, as they carry the responsibility of caring for siblings or ill and overburdened parents. The sheltered and coddled upper-middle-class students described by prominent media outlets are distinctly in the minority.

Still, on traditional residential campuses, students' lives beyond the classroom are complex and intense, even if what outsiders see is indulged young people with trivial problems. Students are preoccupied with friends and roommates, with health, with their parents, and perhaps with serious romantic relationships. They often have money troubles and other practical problems. On one first-day-of-class questionnaire, along with ordinary questions like their major, I asked students what pressing issue was occupying them right at that moment. Most were really concerned about landing a job. One said he was trying to find a large box in which to ship something.

Like faculty, students are immersed in multiple aspects of their lives; getting them to focus on the academic side of college is often understandably challenging.

Student Life: A Parallel Universe

Faculty may not pay any attention to this, but an entire side of every college nowadays is devoted to "student life," "community engagement," and the "co-curriculum." As Richard Arum and Josipa Roksa pointed out in *Academically Adrift*, students at residential colleges generally spend more time and energy outside the classroom than on academics.

It may be that our distracted, stressed-out, and fascinating students are not compelled by classic works of literature and philosophy and the kind of academic thinking that faculty value. But they volunteer in homeless shelters and tutor at-risk kids. They perform in plays and concerts. They direct nonprofits. They take part in dormitory life or intramural athletics. They exercise and drink and play video games and spend time on Facebook or Snapchat. Some of their time is spent frivolously and some in extraordinarily impassioned pursuits. Much time is spent on the necessity of paid employment (more about this in chapter 6, "Campus Delights").

Moral Development

A dominant aspect of human development, according to the "student life" side of campus, is moral development. This includes learning more sophisticated ways of analyzing complex topics, taking multiple viewpoints, and developing internal values rather than acting out of fear or insecurity.[7] Some write of "character" and others of "ethics" and others yet of "leadership." People advocating the importance of moral development in college may invoke military academies, religious universities, or the service side of campus life. Some argue that moral development is one of the principal benefits of reading the classics.[8]

Citizenship and Social Value

Rarely mentioned now as a goal of college is advancing the collective good. The collective is brought up primarily when people argue that the United States is "behind" in international comparisons of the percentage of college completers or STEM majors, with the implication that this will have a negative effect on our GDP because of foreign competition. In contrast, when the Morrill Act was signed in 1862, the goal was to improve the substantive technical training of the American population.

But the collective is more than an economic unit in an international contest. In many countries, school is a tool for creating political cohesion. Véronique Benei's *Schooling Passions: Nation, History, and Language in Contemporary Western India* demonstrates the intersection of nationalism, education, and language in India. Similarly, one of the primary weapons in China's arsenal for inculcating a feeling of national identity is education.[9] (Students are cynical about it but do develop a sense of nationalism nonetheless.) As Benedict Anderson shows so well in *Imagined Communities*, teaching students to identify with the nation-state, even though they cannot actually meet or know most of their fellow citizens, is one of the primary burdens of contemporary education systems.[10]

Clearly, creating citizens is different from creating workers, and it is rarely heard as justification for higher education.

However expressed, this idealized set of goals is abstract, the noble gases of higher education. Many of our students want no part of our ivory tower, no matter how beautiful an orientation point it might provide. If you know students, you know what is missing, so far, from this account of the goals of college: credentials for getting a job.

The Pragmatic Side of College: Schooling

When surveyed, first-year students say what they want out of college is a job. They attend college with the understanding that employment will follow. Even in 1976, when the lowest-ever percentage of students offered that response, 67.8 percent said they were attending college in order to get a job. In 2012 the level reached an all-time high: 87.9 percent said this was what they were there for. And to get a job, most will need not just attendance but a degree, a credential.

Credentials and Economics

The idea of attaining a college degree, a credential, is a powerful motivator. One current national concern is with "completion," as in "the College Completion Agenda."[11] This is part of the international competition evident in the OECD (Organisation for Economic Co-operation and Development) and other rankings: the goal is to outnumber other countries' percentage of college graduates. You might ask if someone just short of a degree could still have *learned* as much as someone who graduates. But the point here is not learning. It is collecting enough "credits"—Carnegie units, in the interchangeable modular system once unique to the American factory model of education—to add up to the target (see chapter 4, "Wagging the Dog").

As a teacher, advisor, and former administrator, I can attest to the earnestness of faculty efforts to ensure that students "have enough credits" and "fulfill the requirements" so they can graduate. Students face serious financial consequences if they have to stay an extra semester or year, or if they can't go on to the next step.

There is a utopian fantasy that we can get the boxes right, and students will learn the right things in the right order, so that when it is all added up, they will—*presto!*—be educated, certified.[12] Yet a focus on credentials creates problems too.

For example, Marilee Jones, former dean of admissions at MIT, resigned in 2007 when it was discovered that she had lied on her résumé about having completed college.[13] Nobody claimed she was incapable of doing her job; she had done it brilliantly. But that called into question the idea that a degree is necessary, thus questioning the notion that the emperor has clothes on, and it was too uncomfortable to have her there. (She also had lied, an unacceptable misdeed; a student caught lying on an application would be punished, or at least denied admission.)

In 1903 William James, the prominent Harvard psychologist, wrote a satirical essay called "The Ph.D. Octopus," in which he mocked the institutional mandate that many who had already been successful and responsible professors of literature go complete a Ph.D., just so their institution could claim that all faculty had this credential.

Yet pursuit of credentials has only multiplied. Defenders of credentials claim that they matter because they are a proxy for or "signal" of something else, which is harder to discern.

Signaling and Sorting

When economists talk about a college degree possessing a "signaling" function,[14] especially in a competitive labor market, they mean that when comparing potential hires, employers are likely to find those with a degree more attractive because it indicates that they are the kind of people who persevere and complete tasks or long-term endeavors. It is not so much the *content* of the credential that matters as the fact of having one at all. It provides a way for employers to learn something about potential employees without having access to much direct information about them. So the signal is an indirect measure of their worth, value, knowledge, and potential. This is meaningful, of course, only if credentials are unevenly distributed.

Fifty years ago, when high school completion rates were low and college was the province only of the few, even a high school diploma could signal something important, and could lead to a decent job. Now, in the early twenty-first century, average U.S. rates of high school completion are in the neighborhood of 74 percent.[15] The percentage of adults twenty-five through sixty-four who have some higher education is only about 42 percent. Approximately two-thirds *begin* some form of higher education, but only around 38 percent complete it. Only about 20.1 percent of adults twenty-five and over had a bachelor's degree in 2013.[16] In this context, academic "attainment" sorts out competitors for jobs. (At the same time, some schools are giving "credit" for life experience—kind of a backward measure, if education is supposed to prepare us for life. If someone has already lived, what then is the need for education? Just signaling.)[17]

For individuals, increasing one's educational level is a preferred path to increasing one's cultural—and plain old economic—capital. But for a society, there is a question about how we can even out the levels of cultural capital. It seems like a race: I want to be faster even while everybody else is learning how to speed. We are all seeking to be above average.

We have contradictory and impossible goals: universal education along with sorting and conferring an advantage, a distinction, by amount of education. Historian of education David Labaree, in *Someone Has to Fail,* exposes the contradiction with utter clarity. In fact, sociologist Randall Collins claims that the simple problem of credential inflation is responsible for all that ails higher education, including grade inflation, disciplinary specialization, emphasis on academic publishing, and a two-tiered professoriate. This inflation is driven by "supply," by the easy access to higher education, not by "demand." "Most degrees," writes Collins, "have little substantive value in themselves; they are bureaucratic markers channeling access to the point at which they are cashed in, and guaranteeing nothing about their value at the point at which they are cashed." He points out a ludicrous possibility:

> In principle, educational expansion and credential inflation could go on endlessly, until janitors need PhDs, and household workers and babysitters will be required to hold advanced degrees in household appliances and childcare. Persons could be kept in school at increasing ages, up through the age 30s and 40s [sic], or in the distant future of the later 21st or 22nd century, even longer.[18]

Instead, each person tries to be the one with a higher credential than everyone else. For individuals it makes sense; for a society, it is impossible.

Transferable Skills

Liberal arts colleges try to compete with other forms of higher education by arguing that—practically speaking—they provide solid "transferable skills" that will serve employees well, perhaps beyond their first job. (In chapter 8, "Learning in the Wild, Learning in the Cage," you'll see that "transfer" doesn't actually happen.) Studying a field like, say, art history or anthropology could prepare students for jobs in marketing, public health, communications—because students will have "visual literacy" or "critical thinking" skills along with skills in reading and writing and presenting. This argument persuades many faculty but few students.

Getting through It

On *Inside Higher Ed*, a community college dean blogging as "Dean Dad" wrote a post called "Get Your Gen Eds Out of the Way." He lamented the fact that students—and, inadvertently, those who wish to help them—consider required classes useless, obligations to be dispatched as quickly as possible so they can get to "the good stuff."[19]

At Notre Dame we have something called The First Year of Studies, which is structured to force "exploration" in a range of basic subjects but ends up being treated like high school—compulsory, distasteful—as students and faculty complain bitterly and perennially about the worthlessness of the classes. This is one of several reasons students love advanced placement courses: with high scores on the AP test, they "don't have to" take any more history/English/math.[20]

There's another reason people give for the value of AP credits: they save money.

Return on Investment: Is College Worth the Money?

Finally we arrive at the focus of most of the public conversation about higher education in the early twenty-first century. Given the ever-increasing costs of college and the uncertain economy, it is reasonable to ask whether the entire enterprise makes economic sense. We do not live in a world built of ideas alone. It is essential for individuals to ask if college is worth the money, but given how much higher education is subsidized, the matter of social support is also appropriately queried.

The College Board—a frank advocate for higher education—has published four different reports (2004, 2007, 2010, 2013) called *Education Pays: The Benefits of Higher Education for Individuals and Society*, arguing that college graduates enjoy higher salaries and better health than those without a degree, while incurring less need for incarceration and other social costs. They are better mothers than those without college degrees at least as measured by the amount of time they spend with their children.[21] These are all quantifiable; the financial and economic advantage of higher education both to the individual and to society can be demonstrated. Yet some dispute the very nature of the question.[22] Some argue that it is not actually college that confers the advantage, that college students are already relatively advantaged; but this position is precarious.

The "college premium" is the amount of lifetime earnings, minus the costs (including wages forgone during the schooling period), for college graduates over those without a college degree. In 2010 a number of economists showed that the return on the investment in college was not paying off much at all, except at the very best universities:

> There are only 17 schools in the study whose graduates can expect to recoup the cost of their education and out-earn a high school graduate by [as much as] $1.2 million [over a lifetime], including four where they can do so to the tune of $1.6 million. At more than 500 other schools, the return on investment, or ROI, is less—sometimes far less. College, says Al Lee, director of quantitative analysis at PayScale, "is not the million-dollar slam dunk people talk about."[23]

In 2014 the Pew Center weighed in on this question, finding that the rising cost of *not* going to college makes getting a degree seem worthwhile. The Economic Policy Institute showed that the "pay gap" between college graduates and everyone else was the greatest it had ever been in 2013.[24] A *New York Times* article noted in 2014: "The pay gap between college graduates and everyone else reached a record high last year. . . . From almost any individual's perspective, college is a no-brainer. It's the most reliable ticket to the middle class and beyond."[25] (No one mentioned the content of that college education.)

Furthermore, the assumption that *where* students go to college matters has been challenged for more than a decade by economists. Studies in 2002 and 2011 concluded that students (at least white middle-class students) *accepted by* high-prestige colleges who nevertheless attended state universities had similar financial outcomes to those who actually attended high-prestige colleges.[26] Is all that childhood frenzy over what Gregg Easterbrook calls "Gotta-Get-Ins" wasted?[27] Financial guru Dave Ramsey scoffs at the idea that any particular expensive college is worth the money: "There's no undergraduate degree on the planet worth $250,000. The whole idea is absurd, and somebody needs to say that out loud."[28]

Richard Vedder lambastes universities for adding all kinds of expenses that contribute nothing at all to the educational mission; he, along with former Texas governor Rick Perry, financial columnist Michelle Singletary, and many other public figures, is trying to invent a $10,000 college degree. This would capitalize on the Web and other digital components. It would skip the climbing walls but would efficiently deliver the degree.

So one measure of the value of college is lifetime earnings. (This is reminiscent of studies that emerged in 2012 which showed that having a single "effective" teacher in lower levels of school result in higher earnings, such as the study conducted by Raj Chetty, John N. Friedman, and Jonah E. Rockoff.)[29] The buzzword is "value added," and the measure is economic.

With obvious credential inflation, even low-prestige jobs might as well require college degrees, even if the education is unnecessary to carry out the task. A 2013 article in the *New York Times,* "It Takes a B.A. to Find a Job as a File Clerk," explained that with so many applicants, employers had to decide on some winnowing mechanism. Among the more than a thousand comments posted online, several pointed out that a four-year college degree, as, for instance, required to work at the Metropolitan Museum of Art, mostly guaranteed the hiring of a middle-class employee.[30]

You Need It: Training

There is, of course, another aspect of education, but we often call this "training." Sometimes a person needs to learn something practical for a known purpose. Outside school, we do this all the time. You need to learn how to operate the new dishwasher, or you need to program the home theater that you spent thousands of dollars on. You take yoga classes, or Italian lessons, or cake decorating. Your boss sends you to learn the new software that will reimburse employees for their professional expenses. Factory workers may be sent to accumulate modules related to their precise needs. Sometimes we call these "workshops" and sometimes they are simply vocational education. This form of learning is regarded with distaste by those who prefer their educational goals more rarified. But there are many students who are in earnest about learning something with immediate application. Roger Schank suggests we completely transform universities into centers for professional training.[31] But conventional faculty would not be in a position to teach; we don't know how to do other jobs.

Both/And: Satisfying and Meaningful, Useful and Practical

In a 2012 article on *Inside Higher Ed* that made the rounds in liberal arts circles, Paul Jay and Gerald Graff charged that liberal arts faculty are afraid to convey how *useful* their training actually is; their pitch is defensive, as liberal arts faculty note the decline in numbers of liberal arts students and majors. They argued that the humanities need not be seen as antithetical to usefulness, that "credentializing" and "humanizing" views of higher education are not contradictory. That is to say, credentialism and vocationalism could be married to knowledge. We could have our cake and analyze it too. They term their suggestion "critical vocationalism," which resists both "an uncritical surrender to the market" and "a disdainful refusal to be sullied by it." And it yields the happy result that humanities graduates can "apply their training in meaningful and satisfying ways."[32]

At a meeting of administrators before the spring 2012 semester began at my university, our provost quoted from this article. I'd posted it on Facebook, and a young friend attending Harvard "liked" it. This resonates in selective schools. It is probably the path that we have to take in the real world in which we now teach, where the four (five, six) years of college are expensive and require justification—at least for now, before the inevitable wholesale reconsideration of higher education, before the revolution.

Order Out of Chaos?

If we were to lump together all these goals, we might end up with these categories as the focus of faculty aims, student attitudes, media coverage, and scholarship about higher education:

Idealistic

- Achievement
- Liberal arts education
- Saving the world
- Academicizing
- Growing up
- Student life (fun)
- Moral development
- Citizenship and social value

Pragmatic

- Getting a job
- Credentials
- Signaling and sorting
- Getting through it
- Return on investment
- Training

Or at a higher level of abstraction—that is to say, to "academicize" the list and explain who benefits—see Table 2.1.

TABLE 2.1   Goals of College

Type of goal	Commonly expressed form	Beneficiary/ies
Economic	Return on investment	Individual and nation
Vocational	Need it for a job	Individual, corporate
Political	Citizenship	Collective
Psychological	Rite of passage, development	Individual, collective
Cultural	Shared common knowledge, cultural capital	Individual, collective
Intellectual	Explore knowledge	Individual

So What Is College *Really* For?

To return to my colleague's dilemma at the beginning of this chapter, does it change anything to note that the student so fixated on her grade came from China? Education in China represents the extreme case of examination-focused competition, with education regarded largely as a credential and a commodity. She exhibited no shame in admitting openly her grade orientation as her goal, rather than cloaking it in the well-known obligatory language of "I want to improve." Is this honesty preferable to the deceptive and inauthentic lip service to learning as the goal of education that we often hear from students?

Rich Smorgasbord or Conceptual Mess?

When we look at the discourse about college, we find a host of functions for institutions of higher education: fostering adolescents' maturation through inculcating independence, practical knowledge, responsibility, and new relationships, including romantic relationships; aiding in moral and character development; providing intellectual enhancement in the form of both critical thinking and substantive knowledge of the world; preparing young people for the communal obligations of citizenship; providing job preparation through teaching of skills and knowledge, on the one hand, and providing credentials, on the other; and aiding in the pursuit of economic justice and equality of opportunity to the extent that discussions center on the costs and funding of college, access, and admissions. Different types of institutions—small liberal arts colleges, community colleges, religious colleges, large state universities, private universities, residential, commuting, online—appeal to students, parents, and supporters with diverse emphases.

In the national debate about higher education, we need to clarify what we think it is for. The central question is: *What do we need our colleges and universities to accomplish?* Only then can we figure out how to make this happen and where the support should originate. But we are far from agreed about the goals of college. We know that on average, college graduates earn more than high school graduates, who earn more than high school dropouts. But is it because college graduates are more advantaged to begin with? Is it because they have grown up in college? Does it have to do with our society's recognition of the credential of the bachelor's or associate's degree, or with something actually learned in school? We also know from the economists that the payoff to attending elite colleges is less than assumed, but students pursue such prestige nonetheless.

Until we can answer the question of what our focus should be, we will continue to spend huge amounts of money and have angry arguments that are akin to whistling in the wind. An expensive wind . . . And we will have millions of young people spending their childhoods in preparation for a stage that accomplishes someone's idea of necessity. Not only that: those of us "in the [educational] trenches" encounter demoralizing student resistance in James Scott's sense. We find foot-dragging, cheating and plagiarism, and all those corner-cutting methods for reaching the goal, along with mockery and other forms of counterhegemony.[33]

Challenges to the Status Quo's Version of Status

If we take as analogy Thomas Kuhn's notion of a *paradigm shift* preceded by increasing numbers of anomalies, then without doubt, higher education is in the midst of such a shift.

The dominance of credentialism has begun to be challenged, from a million angles. One of the more fun challenges is from the "tech" sector, holding that what you need to know can be learned by trying to do it. The notion of "hacking"—originally referring to trying to figure out how to make things happen on computers—is now expanding into domains beyond technology. Talk to a high school kid who has created a successful website or a musician who has learned how to artificially enhance voices (like the Gregory Brothers with their viral music videos). This is part of the Steve Jobs/Bill Gates mystique as well. These folks have learned on their own. Go to college for this? Whatever for?

In a nod to Scouts, some free online education sites are offering "badges"; they don't really "count" for anything, but they demonstrate a commitment and some kind of claim to mastery. Training results in certification, especially in "sectors" that recognize the need for constant learning. Badges motivate, they signal—and for now they do not cost anything. Clayton Christensen, Anya Kamenetz, and Cathy Davidson are among the best known of a crop of theorists about the new world of higher education. HĀSTAC is a site at Duke where ideas about technology and learning are bandied about productively, just as Khan Academy proposes to turn K–12 education upside down, to "flip" it in terms of what happens inside and outside the classroom.[34]

For-profit colleges now educate about 10 percent of all students, on average older, working, minority, female, parents. These colleges emphasize convenience: classes begin every five to nine weeks, and students can predict their entire four-year program. They have access to a team of counselors, academic advisors, and financial advisors, and though they may rarely interact with a faculty member, or with classmates, they can complete their credentials and get a job, or so the argument goes. (Most don't complete their diploma or get a job. Loan default rates are highest for these colleges; at this writing the federal government, led by Congress, is investigating.) All decisions are made as if in business. Faculty are commodities, classes are products, students are customers. Teachers are handed a preset curriculum because uniformity is one of the values. Students find the schools convenient; administrators like the potential for nimbleness.[35]

Comments on an article in the *Chronicle of Higher Education* point out that these schools are giving students what they *want*, not what they *need*; that they provide credentials rather than learning; that there is no research dimension to these schools, the curriculum is dumbed down, faculty are urged (forced) to pass almost everyone. This challenges the accepted model of higher education, the one that most writers, educated in more elite schools, experienced themselves. A June 2015 article titled "Face It: America's Experiment with For-Profit Colleges has Failed" recounts all the ways these institutions fall short, but its author acknowledges that they are still better than conventional colleges at meeting many of the needs of their students.[36]

For-profit colleges are one of many alternatives to the dominance of conventional four-year residential colleges attended full-time by young people aged eighteen to twenty-two. And more are to come.

According to Thomas Friedman, writing in 2014, Google doesn't hire people because of their credentials, their GPA, their schooling. What Google seeks above all is "learning ability"; least important is "expertise." And the proportion of Google's employees *without* a college education has been *increasing*.[37]

The education times they are a-changin', but there is no consensus yet about what, exactly, lies ahead.

So if we can't agree about what college is for, and if we see so much that is wrong with it, it is not surprising that, in the context of these muddied goals, college looks odd indeed.

Part II

SCHOOLING AND ITS ODDITIES

It's only recently in the long arc of human history—and only in some places—that teaching and learning has come to be conceived as something formal. . . . Most learning is in fact informal, experimental, slow, and idiosyncratic, like life in a family where kids imitate, mimic, imagine, play, and push in a largely safe [place—] and in the company of a largely appreciative audience—the apprenticeship of full and responsible personhood.

WILLIAM AYERS, *On the Side of the Child*

If everyone sees something wrong with schools in general and with college in particular, and yet we can't agree about what college is for, it might be helpful to go more deeply into the very strangeness of school. I can't possibly include *all* the oddities, only enough to make you wonder about the enterprise.

My intention in this section is, first, to make readers wonder about the very nature of college, the specific aspects that are so familiar that we rarely even notice them. Then I show how recently the entire system has spread throughout the world, just like highways and agricultural monocropping.

The broad overview is followed by reflections on two aspects of college that I have found especially perplexing and so investigated more thoroughly: students' focus on grades and students' preference for the extracurricular (co-curricular) part of their lives on residential campuses, at the expense of the academic side of things. I used to accept the value of grades, but I no longer do. I used to reject the dominance of the co-curriculum, but no longer do.

My aim is not necessarily to persuade you to join me in reversing long-held positions. But I hope you can better grasp students' perspectives, and this could help explain why so much of college is a costly and ineffective game that students dislike playing.

3

Seeing the Air

The Nature and Spread of Higher Education

> It is easy to fall into the habit of regarding the mechanics of school
> organization and administration as something comparatively external and
> indifferent to educational purposes and ideals . . . [but] it is precisely such
> things as these that really control the whole system, even on its distinctively
> educational side.
>
> John Dewey, *The Educational Situation*

Anthropologists often talk about how our field teaches students to see the air we breathe, to take note of things usually taken for granted. We sometimes express this as trying to "make the strange familiar, and the familiar strange." The idea of higher education—college—as a goal for all young adults is certainly familiar. In this chapter I aim to make it strange.

To do that, I will show where it arose, to defamiliarize ourselves with its forms and ubiquity.

To understand higher education, I ended up having to go back and understand something about the recent spread of compulsory, universal education in general. If schooling at all is so rare and strange, and if its history is really so shallow, and if it is unprecedented that it now lasts into people's twenties, how did this situation arise?

And what do we even mean when we speak of higher education? It appears *natural*, like a tree or a car. But it couldn't be further from that. Looking at it closely, we see that it is a conglomeration of oddities—recently created, at that.

The Nature of Higher Education: The Paradigm

Higher education, or *tertiary education*, or *post-secondary education*, or, for short, *college*, is an institutionalized level of "higher learning" that option-ally follows secondary schooling.[1] It is increasingly seen as culturally, if not legally, compulsory, at least for some socioeconomic groups. In the contemporary United States, higher education is quite varied, almost un-imaginably so, but I outline here only the quintessential form of four-year college or university:

- Students *apply* for *admission*, according to requirements set by each institution. Even if admission standards are lax to the point of being considered *open*, someone either is or is not officially a student at a particular college.
- The *curriculum* or course of study is *graded*, meaning that it has a progression from one level to the next. It is composed of *majors*, sometimes with *minors*, or *concentrations*, which are selected by the student. In addition to *requirements* in each major, most colleges have *distribution requirements* as well as *electives*.
- Courses have a beginning and an end. They are self-contained, named, and numbered units.
- Units in the curriculum are composed of time-evaluated compo-nents, usually based on the number of hours each course meets. Typically for a college using a fifteen-week semester system, a course meets three times a week for fifty minutes, and is worth three credits. This unit of accumulation is called a *Carnegie unit*. A certain number of Carnegie units are required for *completion* of the *degree*.
- Upon completion of the degree, a student is awarded a *credential* or *diploma*.
- Courses are taught by faculty. They may be one of a number of ranked "regular" faculty or adjuncts or graduate students. Each sta-tus is strictly defined and compensated accordingly.
- Faculty generally follow a *syllabus*, a pre-determined course of study that includes *readings*, *assignments*, *lectures*, and sometimes additional *activities*, which might include *laboratory work*.
- A common central occurrence in classes is the *lecture*, in which a number of students listen to and watch a faculty member explain

material set out in advance. A lecture can be digital, using video or PowerPoint.

- Some classes additionally or instead involve labs, discussions, or seminars.
- *Outcomes* are regularly *assessed*, in terms of both assignments (papers, essays, tests, lab reports, or less conventional assignments) and the course as a whole. These assessments are *uniform* for the class.
- Assessments result in *grades*. Grades *accumulate*; that is, earlier grades are averaged together with later ones.
- Many courses center on particular *readings*, which are selected by the faculty member.
- Interactions in class are directed by the faculty member, who can permit free discussions as well as control or revoke them.
- Students are expected to do some work between the regular meetings, either individually or with other students.
- The subjects studied are in some sense isolated from other subjects. They tend to be housed in *departments* or *divisions*, and sometimes in groupings called *colleges* or *schools* within universities.
- Many colleges have dedicated buildings or *campuses* that are set apart from the broader location. Some are quite beautiful and become tourist attractions.
- While students may have responsibilities beyond school, the goal is to master material in the curriculum rather than to work at other things.
- Many occupations require certain *degrees* or *credentials* as a matter of course.
- This educational system is costly. The costs are borne by students, their families, the nation, individual states, foundations, and donors, in varying proportions.
- The system is strictly stratified. Some forms of higher education and some institutions have greater prestige than others. Sometimes specific ("honors") courses or cohorts of students are also awarded greater status than others.
- Some colleges are residential.
- Some have athletic teams that draw hundreds of thousands of spectators, many not connected to the educational aspect of the college.

Each step of this interlocking system could be different. In fact in other times and places, learning occurs or did occur completely differently. It could be cost-free to the student; there could be no grades; there were formerly no majors; there could be an ongoing, unending "seminar"; students could hire and fire the faculty; there could be no buildings or campus at all; assessment could be done without concern about time spent; people of different ages could all be combined. And in most ways this system contrasts with how people learn "in the wild."

It is essential to point out again that this system could be different, because so much of it seems not to work very well. Yet the fact that components are intertwined means it is extremely difficult to change one piece at a time.

The Grammar of Schooling or The Hidden Curriculum

In terms of the "grammar of schooling" or of the "hidden curriculum,"[2] *college* differs little from other levels of *schooling*. David Tyack and Larry Cuban analyze some aspects of the enduring organizational framework of what people think of as "real schools" to explain why various types of attempted reforms are resisted: people often believe they are being cheated out of "real schools."[3]

Familiar as "real schools" are, for most of human history nobody went to school. People learned all manner of things as part of their innate, unbreakable nature. Sometimes, though not inevitably, there was something we would recognize as teaching. Once literacy took hold for a few elites—those who left traces of it in the form of books and essays, the ones that are assigned to current students—there was school, and even something that we might call "college" in some form.

But for most people, formal schooling was unknown. Still, like any Whiggish account (in which the past is assumed to run on a straight line to the present), history is written by writers, people who value literacy and schooling and who seek their own intellectual influences, continuities with "school" in the past. But does it startle you to learn that the entire graduating class of Harvard numbered nine in 1642 (the first commencement) and the total enrollment was only 366 as recently as 1856? That Ralph Waldo Emerson graduated thirtieth out of fifty-nine of his Harvard class of 1821?[4] That all students studied the classical curriculum in most colleges, with no science, until well into the nineteenth century? One of the chief pedagogical techniques was for students to recite by memory several pages of a textbook—a technique stemming from ancient Greek and Roman practices, and from the long past when book ownership was rare.

One of the few constants was composition, which was firmly associated with students' character. Half of Harvard's students failed the writing portion of the entrance examination in 1892; Stanford's success rate was even lower (only 40 out of 150 in 1894). To solve this problem, freshman English was born (the equivalent of today's "developmental" courses).[5]

Schooling in the past, even higher education, is much more unfamiliar than we might think.

The Spread of Schooling

Humans have existed for about 100,000 to 125,000 years in essentially the same form, with essentially the same physical, social, and cognitive abilities and needs, yet it is less than four hundred years since societies first *mandated* institutions set apart to teach all their children. Even with the existence of literacy—spanning at most four thousand years—only a few people actually went to school to learn to decipher the abstract symbols on clay, papyrus, bamboo, and ultimately paper.

The earliest sources suggest that some type of formal schooling existed, possibly as long ago as 2300–2100 BCE, in ancient Sumer, where scribes were berated for insufficient devotion to their studies. (Scribes were needed to keep track of market exchanges; their importance rose with the birth of credit.) There seems to have been a fixed curriculum, examinations, and some kind of certification.[6]

People often mastered the necessary range of skills and purposes of reading without the structure of school. Many families ensured that their children were able to read essential texts for whatever functions were widespread: religious, philosophical, historic, literary. Jews trained their sons to read Torah and to pray. Rome had academies, and China had *xueyuan*, attended by scribes and scholars and administrators. Each tradition had a set of commentaries, sometimes oral, that required transmission. It was this that took many years of devoted attention, and that left us records. We read back into them our own experience, but we should place all this in perspective. While the few were spending childhoods in school, the many were learning to work productively in whatever arrangement was customary in their own society: tagging along with their families, playing or working in groups of children, being lent to another family.

Neil Postman in *The Disappearance of Childhood* claims that the "Dark Ages" occurred because the majority of the population forgot how to read. One of the major consequences of the birth of the printing press in Europe was the Protestant Reformation and the responsibility it placed on individuals to read and accept the Bible on their own. In order for them to learn to read, some form of teaching had to occur.

In 1647 Massachusetts embarked on a radical transformation of human experience: a law was passed requiring that all children be educated. It was felt that those who wished to speak up against the colonizers needed to be able to read and write, and use numbers, on their own. Prussia in the early nineteenth century required schooling so that the young could learn obedience, along with reading the Bible. Under "the absolute state," this schooling included military service, physical education, and literacy instruction.[7] And in 1852 Massachusetts in turn followed Prussia by mandating that all children attend school, the "Common School" as advocated by reformer Horace Mann and others.

But school—in the iconic one-room schoolhouses of the U.S. past—was nothing like our contemporary notion.

The "(age-)graded school" was invented in the United States only in the 1830s. Prior to that, schooling had been "voluntary, episodic, and small-scale."[8] Just as in ancient Rome, in the one-room American schoolhouse, students were grouped by their level of knowledge, not by age; twenty-year-olds learning to read might be mixed with six-year-olds. There was a teacher, but much of the teaching occurred as students with greater proficiency helped those with less.

Discipline in the classroom may have been strict, but the lack of a physical outlet was not total; it lasted only during school hours. Students walked to and from school, using physical energy, and they had opportunities for unsupervised, sometimes rough play. Then they went home and did physical chores.

Schooling lasted only three to four years. Students left when their families needed them to work, or they got tired of it, or they had learned everything the teacher had to offer. Teachers often were just slightly more knowledgeable than their pupils.[9]

This was the form of schooling for most Americans until little more than the last hundred years.

In 1870 in the United States, almost 7 million students were enrolled in primary school, but only eighty thousand were in secondary schools; that year about nine thousand college degrees were granted. In 1990, there were 30 million students in public elementary schools and 11 million in secondary schools; more than 1.5 million degrees, bachelor's and higher, were awarded[10] (see Figure 3.1). Approximately 81 percent of public school students graduated from high school on time in the United States in 2012.[11]

Many of the features of "the grammar of schooling" arose bit by bit as schooling spread. From the one-room schoolhouse to the graded school, we have an industrial model with modular components and frequent assessment (grading), tracking, and sorting (vocational versus academic schooling). With the "Common School movement," starting with the Prussian efforts, we find the beginning of group instruction, for economies of scale, which in turn lends itself perfectly to comparison. It is impossible to measure "value added" if the "inputs" are not uniform, no matter how carefully the "outputs" are assessed. Thus it is more efficient—in this "Fordist" factory model of mass education—to divide students into groups as uniform as possible.[12] Even raising one's hand to ask a question started with the Prussians.

This familiar set of structures, this specific, often-taken-for-granted institution for learning is frequently "naturalized." That is, people rarely question its elements, purposes, or structures. (One study calls it the "black box" of the classroom.)

Schools differ—by setting, level, size, philosophy, and individuals. They differ by social class and nation. But many share the basic features of the "ideal type" of school:

- A building of its own
- Students divided by age
- A teacher in control
- A preset curriculum that fits with other levels
- Assessment of outcomes

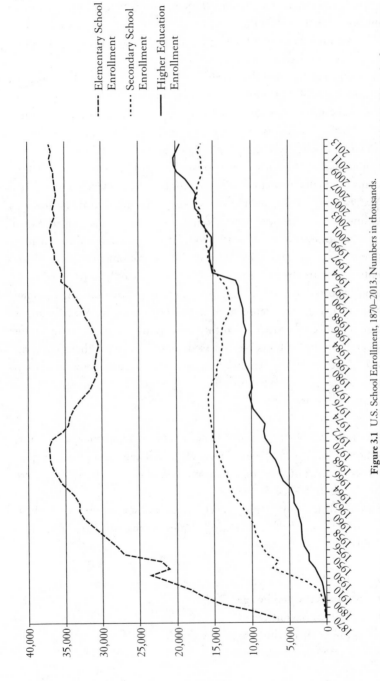

Figure 3.1 U.S. School Enrollment, 1870–2013. Numbers in thousands.

Sources: https://www.census.gov/hhes/school/data/cps/historical/TableA-1.xls and http://nces.ed.gov/programs/digest/d12/tables/dt12_003.asp?referrer=report.

- Stratification of students, some "higher" and some "lower"
- A setting apart from the flow of regular life
- An institution that includes not just the content but also social needs (Goffman's *total institution*)
- Emphasis on "school skills": literacy and numeracy
- Abstraction valued over concreteness
- Lack of work responsibility
- Artificial exercises (such as the teacher asks questions but already knows the answer)

Even after "real schools" arose, they were not necessarily part of every child's life. That has changed across the globe since the middle of the twentieth century.

Compulsory Education

Increasing educational access has been one of the principal projects around the world since the twentieth century, especially the second half of the century. In the aftermath of World War II, the Universal Declaration of Human Rights enshrined the right of every individual to an education. Article 26 states:

1. Everyone has the right to education. Education shall be free, at least in the elementary and fundamental stages. Elementary education shall be compulsory. Technical and professional education shall be made generally available and higher education shall be equally accessible to all on the basis of merit.
2. Education shall be directed to the full development of the human personality and to the strengthening of respect for human rights and fundamental freedoms. It shall promote understanding, tolerance and friendship among all nations, racial or religious groups, and shall further the activities of the United Nations for the maintenance of peace.
3. Parents have a prior right to choose the kind of education that shall be given to their children.[13]

From 1900 to 1950, for the first time in history many nations aimed to educate all children. East Asian countries have largely succeeded; now other developing countries are trying to catch up, and well-intentioned international entities are trying to make sure that happens.

The Spread of Higher Education

With the dawn of the twenty-first century, many nations have turned their attention to tertiary education.[14] Worldwide, between 1900 and 2000, the number of students in higher education grew *two hundredfold*, from 500,000 students (1 percent of the relevant population) to 100 million (20 percent).[15]

In 1972 Martin Trow devised a widely used typology to conceptualize these worldwide changes. Education systems might generally be divided into *elite*, with less than 15 percent participation; *mass*, with participation up to 50 percent; and *universal*, with participation exceeding that figure.[16] At the time, U.S. higher education had the world's highest level of participation, building on the gains of the GI Bill following World War II, and had recently become a mass system. Even secondary school participation was "elite" in the United States less than a century and a half ago; only 1.4 percent of the students in the Philadelphia school system were in high school in 1880.[17] Now, high school participation—though not completion—is nearly universal.

Graph after graph depicting the growth in higher education enrollments shows a slope heading straight up to the upper-right-hand corner. Whereas in the United States something like 2 percent of the population went to college in the late nineteenth century, about 60 percent at least begin now; in South Korea the figure is as high as 80 percent. (College completion is much more challenging, especially in the United States, because of financial pressures and extremely uneven preparation prior to college.)

As recently as the turn of the twentieth century, U.S. "colleges," many of them quite small, competed with "high schools" for students of the same ages. Compulsory schooling had just arisen, and truancy was a huge problem because teenagers so disliked going to school. They had to be forced by law to do so.

Advantaged families had been sending their children to "college," frequently as a kind of finishing school, for some time. Clergy were trained at colleges such as Harvard. But with the Morrill Land-Grant Act of 1862 and other factors, men and, to a far lesser extent, women who wished to learn more practical subjects began to attend college.

Many professions, such as law and medicine, still required no formal schooling. Remember Abraham Lincoln teaching himself law? It was possible to do that as recently as the 1890s; a few states even now permit someone to "read law" and take the bar exam without attending law school. As for medicine, before Abraham Flexner's report on medical education in 1910, a messy, unregulated assortment of paths toward the profession had proliferated. Only after it became regulated and standardized did it become reputable. As recently as the early twentieth century, many teachers in one-room schools themselves had emerged from that system; only later were "normal schools" for teacher training established.

The growth of professional societies began to make *credentials* gained through formal education a requirement. And that has led us far from the origins of higher education.

Medieval Universities and Academies

In *American Higher Education: A History*, Christopher Lucas begins by synthesizing everything we know about higher education, from Mesopotamia to China, from ancient Greece and Arabia to medieval and Renaissance Europe. Yes, there were universities of one form or another prior to the twentieth century. I have been fascinated to learn that many enduring centers of higher learning grew out of medieval cathedral schools in Bologna, Paris, and Oxford. They, like contemporary universities, had convoluted bureaucracies, competing multilingual communities, and status consciousness. But they differed in substantial ways from present-day universities.

Lest we get a mistaken impression about some golden age, it is worth noting that professors in Greece competed for students by advertising, often misleadingly, all kinds of perquisites.

There were institutions in ancient China that collected groups of highly educated men; later they became a version of some kind of academy. But they bear almost no resemblance to contemporary universities or colleges. Attended by a small minority of highly educated elite men preparing to be scholars or bureaucrats, some were private, usually surrounding a master;

some were supported by the government. And while they did include a curriculum and examinations (eventually), this model never, for two thousand years of China's imperial history, became widespread at all.

In the European Middle Ages, tertiary education was not just available but required for elite males planning to become professors or clergy. Medieval students sought practical training so they could quickly find work in these professions as well as in government, law, or medicine. The University of Bologna was established in the late eleventh century (1088 is the date usually provided). Before long there were about eleven thousand students, and in a striking contrast to today's universities, they were in control. Students arriving in Bologna spontaneously formed guilds to protect their interests; they derived enough power to force faculty to obey *them*, hiring, firing, and dictating behavior to their elders.

> It would hardly be an exaggeration to say that lecturing performance in thirteenth-century Bologna was continuously assessed by the students on both a qualitative and quantitative basis. A doctor who glossed over a difficulty or who failed to assign an equal emphasis to all parts of the syllabus would incur financial penalties. . . . Refusal to comply was pointless; no lecturer with fines outstanding was permitted to collect student fees for his teaching and thus his source of university income would be cut off. . . . Against the disadvantages of student controls, however, one has to balance the consideration that a successful lecturer in a populous university such as Bologna could expect to earn a good remuneration from student fees.[18]

It is tempting to attribute a kind of dignity and respectability to people in the past, but at medieval universities—not just in Bologna—the word that keeps appearing is *unruly*. According to Thomas Cahill in *Mysteries of the Middle Ages: And the Beginning of the Modern World*, around the same time in the Left Bank of Paris—the Latin Quarter—thousands of boisterous students speaking a wide variety of languages heard lectures in Latin while wreaking havoc outside the classroom. For centuries, students were deplored by the townspeople for their drunkenness and uncivil behavior. (Sound familiar?) Because most thirteenth-century universities, Jean Dunbabin writes, should be understood not as emerging within large cities, as NYU or Columbia did, but rather as themselves generating towns, as Amherst and Dartmouth have done, swelling student numbers alarmed the residents. "The town-gown conflicts of Orléans and Oxford were so bitter largely because the inhabitants of those towns were in serious danger of being swamped by the unruly aliens who flooded the place," writes Dunbabin. The students were called *invaders*: "Dwellers in most university towns in the thirteenth century were as helpless in [the] face of the invader as are middle-aged parents faced with a hyperactive toddler. Everything was moulded to the needs of the students."[19]

The *ideal* of a university, though, is beguiling. Jacques Le Goff, master historian of the Middle Ages, admired the magical moment when a number of factors converged to create the medieval universities that still exemplify the ideal of many professors—including me. An admiring analyst wrote of Le Goff's "vision of the medieval university at its fleeting moment of perfection, an open, dynamic powerhouse for its times, and . . . his choice of medieval theologians, combining learning, understanding and communicating, as model *engagés* intellectuals."[20] The important thing to note is the precariousness of this vision.

Still, most universities existed to disseminate *existing* knowledge. That changed only in the nineteenth century, with German universities' novel focus on contemplation and research. This ideal, as in Heidelberg, was promoted by thinkers such as Johann Gottfried Herder.

But even in the goldenest of golden ages, at the most revered of institutions, college students were rowdy, demanding, and ill-behaved. Far from spending all their time on their studies, they got drunk, visited prostitutes, and engaged in duels. An American academic, James Morgan Hart, who later went on to influence American graduate education and the research university along the lines of German universities (teaching at Johns Hopkins, the University of Cincinnati, and Cornell), wrote vividly and admiringly of his experience in German universities, beginning in 1861. Comparing German with American and English colleges, he points out that the freedom and independence of German students, no longer "school-boys," accounted for the simultaneous "extremes of lawlessness on the one hand, [and] models of industry on the other."[21]

So, though it is not quite accurate to suppose that there were no universities until a century ago, they were not quite the same as the ones of today. The last century in the United States has brought enormous numbers of young people to a specific form of institution, a model that is now being exported to the rest of the world. In Europe, where a variety of seminar-based, thesis-based, or research-based studies or degree programs, lasting various lengths of time, have existed for a long while, pressure to match and be interchangeable with higher education elsewhere has given rise to the "Bologna protocol" (or "Bologna process"). Emulating the grammar of U.S. higher education is the name of this game.

Expanding Higher Education in the United States

The U.S. Bureau (later Office, then Board, and now Department) of Education was established only in 1867. At that point, throughout the entire country, only 63,000 students—about 1 percent of the population of eighteen- to twenty-four-year-olds—were attending 563 institutions of higher education; this means each campus had an average of about 112 students.[22]

The most important moments in the growth of U.S. higher education were the establishment of "land grant" institutions through the Morrill Act of 1862 and the creation of "normal" (teacher training) schools, most of which have now become universities, and the GI Bill, which funded college for returning World War II servicemen and women. (In part this was to prevent massive unrest because of high rates of unemployment.) We might see the current emphasis on promoting universal higher education as another.

Of all people eighteen to twenty-four years old in the United States, 41 percent now attend college (2012),[23] with almost 18 million students enrolled in various types of tertiary education (2012).[24] Sixty-six percent of the 3.2 million students who completed high school in 2012 went directly to college, and of that percentage 40 percent went to two-year colleges and 60 percent to four-year colleges.[25] In 2012 public institutions awarded 63 percent of all bachelor's degrees and 74 percent of all associate's degrees; the corresponding figures for private nonprofit institutions are 29 percent and 5 percent. The private for-profit institutions awarded 7 percent of bachelor's degrees and 20 percent of associate's degrees.[26] Unlike the situation in many other countries, there is little centralized federal organization of higher education. Approximately 42 percent of adults twenty-five to sixty-four in the United States have bachelor's or associate's degrees (2011),[27] though two-thirds of the population has been involved in tertiary education in some form; "completion" rates of approximately 54 percent within six years are generally regarded as disappointing.[28]

Cost is certainly a factor. The economics of higher education are chaotic and troubling. Costs are largely borne by individuals, the institutions themselves, and the federal and state governments through grants and loans. In 2014 two-thirds of graduates of four-year colleges had student debt averaging $33,000, and the total amount borrowed has topped $1 *trillion*.[29] The number grows every year.

Many applaud the growth in college attendance, seeing in it democratization. If college is good for the advantaged, it should also be good for the disadvantaged.

I used to see it that way too.

But many critics, including sociologist Randall Collins, regard the growth of higher education as responsible for *credential inflation*, for the fact that a college degree no longer means as much as it formerly did, in an exchange system.

Evidence from a lot of places, including the much-touted almost-universal-higher-ed countries, South Korea and Japan, shows that the more people go to college, the more stratified higher education becomes. That is to say, sure, getting a degree is good. But not all degrees are equal. If everyone has a degree, it matters that your degree is from Seoul National University as opposed to a shady private school.

In Japan, less than half the relevant population was enrolled in senior high school in 1950; now the figure is 97.9 percent, though high school is not compulsory.[30] Fewer than one-fifth enroll in vocational programs. Of the 80 percent of that population that now attend some sort of tertiary institution, about 77 percent attend (less prestigious) private institutions.[31] Because of the expansion of institutions, overall admission is essentially nonselective, or open. Takehiko Kariya points out that "as higher education expands, the values of the degrees and credentials in the labour market tend to decrease."[32] In Japan, where there are more spaces for college students than there are students, given the contracting population and the proliferation of private colleges since government control over higher education relaxed in 1984, merely having a degree is insufficient to guarantee a desirable position. So stratification occurs somehow; in Japan's case, social inequality persists. Only a few may attend high-prestige institutions of higher education, not surprisingly predicted by having completed private elite secondary schools.[33] Formerly those without a college degree found employment in work such as sales; now those jobs are taken by people with less prestigious degrees. Kariya and others demonstrate conclusively "an inflation of credential in Japan that has developed together with university expansion and the arrival of a 'universal' stage."[34] Still, degrees from top-ranking universities have *increased* in relative value. He concludes that "social inequalities in higher education and employment persist and perhaps even become further entrenched even while university education becomes, and is celebrated as, 'universal.'"[35]

Selection and Stratification

Okay, in the introduction I said I was not writing about the sociology of education. But I have to say this.

With changing demographics and economics, since the late 1980s institutions of higher education have competed to attract the wealthiest and most high-achieving applicants, increasing their "selectivity" rate and permitting them to support less wealthy students through a complex formula of "sticker price," "net price," and "published price," along with financial aid, including both grants and loans.[36] Few colleges can afford to be "need-blind" in admissions and cover the full cost of attending; Notre Dame is one, but only for U.S. applicants. (Only six U.S. institutions include international students in full coverage.) The result has been the perception that for certain mostly affluent students, only the highest-ranked colleges are desirable. The rate of "selectivity" varies widely, from those 26 percent of four-year colleges that admit everyone ("open admissions") to the fifty-five or so that admit fewer than one-third of their applicants.[37] (Or the 200 to 250 "most competitive" in the Barron's guide.)[38] The college application process relies on scrutiny of high school grades, standardized test scores, faculty recommendations, student essays, and student experiences beyond the classroom such as athletics, music, or volunteering.[39] With some exceptions, the central measure is high school grades, and in particular the grade point average (GPA).

The students attending highly selective private universities represent the winners in this competition. And they largely understand how the system works. They may resist, but they demonstrate considerable expertise in all aspects of this strange, artificial amalgam. No one can be successful, can be a high achiever, without mastering the "grammar" of higher education.

Manual/Vocational versus Academic Schooling: Separate and Unequal?

Mirroring a general Euroamerican weighting of the mind over the body, spirit over matter, the abstract over the concrete, physical labor has been regarded as less worthy than mental labor. In turn, our academic schooling was designed to provide opportunities for students to overcome the need for "manual labor" (even though *someone* still has to perform such labor; training everyone to be "knowledge workers" in an "information economy" doesn't cause all jobs to be part of that economy). American (and many other) views of schooling reveal an enduring tension between academic education and vocational training, and between the realities of class stratification and the ideal of equal opportunity.

Since the nineteenth century, when academic schooling became more pervasive in U.S. society, disagreement has been the norm among experts and the general public alike about what school should consist of, and for whom. Academic education for the well-off, and for the less advantaged, "trades," "vocational education," "work preparation," and "training"?

The value of the *abstract* over the *concrete* has a specific history in connection with the triumph of *academic* over *vocational* education in the twentieth century.[40] This is visible as a focus on theory—quite rare worldwide[41]—or what Paolo Freire calls the "banking" method: putting knowledge away for use at some unspecified time in the future.[42] In most other settings, people learn by doing, learn as needed, or learn in practice.[43]

A tug-of-war between "tracking"—meeting students' needs and desires—and equality of opportunity should have exhausted even the most muscular competitors. Having a uniform curriculum (with all the localized variants made possible in our noncentralized system) has dominated, but that seems to be changing.

For a long time, the limited schooling for the poor was built on the assumption that they needed skills for jobs.[44] Inequality was accepted, as was what Pierre Bourdieu and Jean-Claude Passeron call "reproduction."[45] Schools, or tracks within schools, for the poor taught shop, home economics, metals—training for jobs. Schools and tracks for the advantaged prepared them for further schooling or for professions. But this division has been challenged, and now most schools maintain the ideal of equality, which means sameness.

So since the twentieth century a long path of well-intended policies has made academic schooling valued and vocational education a sorry second. And because of an ideology of equality, all children have been prepared—however inappropriately—for a life in college and the prestigious professions. It has been obvious that the "dropout factories" high schools have not been uniformly welcomed by those who are supposed to be the beneficiaries, but we hold to the ideal that all children should be prepared for college. This is the slogan at many charter schools.

In the twenty-first century, however, some people have been quietly raising the question again about the desirability of a uniform "common core" and the wishful-thinking dimension of a one-size-fits-all curriculum. New approaches to teaching students both academic subjects and practical subjects have emerged, sometimes in high schools that offer pre-career paths and sometimes in colleges. The kind of maturing that occurs in these two forms, I venture to suggest, differs too. Old-is-new-again experiments with work preparation are being attempted in high schools,[46] as well as in colleges, such as Berea College in Kentucky, which admits only low-income students (mostly from Appalachia), charges no tuition, and requires all students to work outside school at least ten hours a week. In the early twentieth-century high school, immigrant children were sent on work-study; in the 1960s colleges invented "co-op education," whereby students went and learned something practical. Now we have "internships," "service learning," and "community-based learning"—all attempts to de-academicize schooling.

In the twenty-first century, some are proposing models from other systems, such as in Germany and Finland, where vocational education, and in fact skilled labor, are valued, but where the split between schooling tracks occurs early. (One split is before fifth grade).[47] Students in the lower track go on to apprenticeships and vocational schools; only those in the upper tracks will go to college preparatory schools. In these countries and elsewhere, "polytechnical" schools, schools of higher learning that are nonacademic, are well funded, and (some) students find employment easily at the end. As in the within-school tracks in the United States, the tracking generally matches families' socioeconomic status. Furthermore, as Alison Wolf points out, no experiments with pushing vocational education have ever been successful on a large scale; when academic education coexists with vocational education, no parents or students prefer vocational education,[48] regarding it as an inferior option for less-advantaged populations: separate and unequal.

The tension between *training* and *education* is evident in the role of community colleges (formerly called *junior colleges*), now enrolling about 6 million students. In July 2009 President Obama announced a plan to provide $12 billion for retraining unemployed workers with decades of experience on automobile assembly lines. Two years of classes at community colleges might give them training for new industries—health care, computers, "green" jobs.

What nobody said was that they would receive an "education."

A further innovation in tertiary education comes with customizable courses for jobs, with modules at a particular cost and with no time limit on how long to spend learning the skills.[49] But the dilemma of equality of opportunity versus differentiation of curriculum remains.

Human Development: Sometimes Less Is More

When international development agencies, politicians, and aid workers attempt to measure "human development," obvious factors such as *income* and *health* (in terms of quantifiable life expectancy) are used for technical rankings such as the Human Development Index (HDI). But a third factor, or dimension, is *education*, which is usually ascertained simply by counting how many years of schooling citizens of various countries attain.[50]

Education levels can be seen as a measure of human development because of the rise of compulsory education across the world. But compulsory education does not come without costs. Japan has noted a phenomenon known as "school refusal," named in the 1960s, and sometimes considered a "culture-bound syndrome" in the sense that such a "disorder" does not exist universally. Approximately 127,000 students refused to attend school in 2006, out of a total of 10.8 million students. A large-scale epidemiological study of junior high and high school students in Japan reported in 2014 that 8.4 percent of boys and 7.4 percent of girls considered themselves unhappy at school, with higher numbers associated with older grade levels in high school.[51] Anthropologists see both school refusal and unhappiness as symptoms of a systemic problem, connected with the meaning of youth, notions of value, ideas of the self and family, and control over individuals.

Wherever compulsory schooling exists, we find resistance to it. That may take the form of failure and indifference, seen in skipping class, being late, illness, dropping out, "truancy." "Truant officers" locking kids up in school—that is quite an image, isn't it!

Nor does compulsory education encompass all the learning that people need in order to flourish in their societies. Standardized education may lead to forgetting of indigenous skills and knowledge, loss of minority languages, and disdain for social traditions. If more schooling leads to lack of learning, insecurity, bullying, debt, or alienation, then *more* brings the exact opposite of what is intended, and less would be preferred. In fact, compulsory education and the unexamined belief that more schooling is better than less may be leading nations and families in the wrong direction.

Such notions rest on an assumption that all significant learning occurs in schools, when in fact it occurs continuously and in all contexts. Academic learning is guided by a curriculum, often determined at the national or state level, and is formally assessed. This kind of learning takes on significance because of growing accountability efforts around the world, spurred by international comparisons of student achievement, measured largely by the TIMSS (Trends in International Mathematics and Science Study) and PISA (Programme for International Student Assessment) tests.[52]

Despite the recency of the system of schooling, it has come to appear *natural* because we refer to it daily, everywhere, without having to explain or justify it. None of my grandparents went to college. It was rare until very recently. Yet in two short generations it has completely taken over the expectations for our youth. This is not a natural occurrence; many agents have worked to ensure the increase in formal schooling.

It is only in this context—a mass spread of institutional education, uniform in its practices, competitive at its upper levels, definitive of daily occupation—that we can understand some of the oddities of schooling, including one of the greatest frustrations for faculty: the misplaced emphasis on grades over learning, and a focus on things that really matter only within the artificial context of school.

4

Wagging the Dog

Learning for Schooling

The pupil is . . . "schooled" to confuse teaching with learning, grade
advancement with education, a diploma with competence, and fluency with
the ability to say something new. . . . [S]chool is obligatory and becomes
schooling for schooling's sake. . . . Surrounded by all-powerful tools, man is
reduced to a tool of his tools.

Ivan Illich, *Deschooling Society*

One oddity of schooling at all levels—rarely regarded as odd because it is
so widespread—is that students spend substantial time and energy learning the tricks and arbitrary requirements of schooling. This includes attending because it is required ("seat time"), even if nothing substantive
occurs, and grasping the complexities and nuances of credits, requirements, and grades.

School Genres: Mastering the Fine Art of the Arbitrary

To be successful, students at every level must master the nuances of the
system in which they find themselves. One critical aspect involves forms—
genres—of performance and assessment that exist only within schools.
A college student, for example, might be compelled to gain proficiency
in certain genres that will be used in the accountancy examination or

in the MCAT, but once schooling is complete, will never be seen again. These school-specific forms include the ubiquitous syllabus; compare-and-contrast papers; five-paragraph essays; mandated avoidance of "I"; multiple-choice, matching, and true-false tests; "partial credit"; and term papers. All of these are bizarre, once you think about them. Multiple-choice exams, for instance, take time to construct (the choices have to sound plausible but most have to be wrong) but are a breeze to grade; this task can be automated so no human hands have to be involved. But out-side school, where do deliberately misleading options present themselves in time-limited form?

The website "HackCollege" explains how to approach multiple-choice tests. The assumption is that students have trouble actually learning, at least some of the time. (To the author's credit, he also offers tips on how to learn.) One strategy is this: "If two of the choices on the test are nearly identical in terms of spelling, one of them is probably the right answer. Professors like to throw two similar options at you in an attempt to trip you up. If you're guessing, this usually gives you a 50/50 shot." This is the free version of some of what is taught by expensive in-person test prepara-tion services, such as Kaplan, which affirms that "the most effective way to generate the highest score is with test preparation." This certainly is useful advice—but what in the world does it have to do with actually learning anything?[1] (I am not denying that it is handy to be able to do well on tests; I am showing how absurd that fact is.)

Testing rather impractical material is not unique to the contemporary United States. In China, the traditional civil service examination (*keju*) was the principal route to public service for about 1,300 years. One element of the examination developed out of composition skills, and for about a thousand years, a genre known as the *baguwen*, the "eight-legged essay," served as the focus of the examination, and therefore the focus of students' learning.[2] Contemporary sociologist of education Yong Zhao, writing of the examination, warns of the negative consequences when the tool of as-sessment becomes the principal determinant of the educational content: "Although the *keju* itself was not an education system but a political sys-tem, because of its high stakes it determined what education was about in China for centuries. Virtually all education activities were about preparing for the *keju*. What was tested was what was being learned and taught."[3] High-stakes testing, in which the learning is in service to assessment rather than the other way around, is evident everywhere. Students spend weeks preparing to master test formats; many such tests are poorly constructed and have little to do with the content of students' learning; they produce anxiety in teachers, students, and families; they narrow the notion of what counts as learning. As they increasingly dominate lower levels of education, they are also being introduced—without much success—in college.

But they are just one example of things that are valued only within the artificial universe of school. Deadlines are another.

A Real Deadline? Really?

Shaking voice. A message just before 8 a.m. on my office voicemail. "When I went to print out my project, it was blank!" It is the day before spring break, and the big semester project is due in my Linguistic Anthropology class. It is worth 50 points out of a total of 450. There are many different kinds of assignments, and this is the largest piece, aside from the final exam. My students have had two weeks to collect a conversation, record, transcribe, and analyze it. Most of them—or at least the ones I have heard from—recorded and began transcribing last weekend.

So Katie calls with nothing. She could show me her computer, prove that she created a document two (whole?) days ago and has modified it several times. I suggest she call the help desk at the Office of Information Technology. She calls back. They can't help her. I ask if she has backed it up somehow—a printout? A flash drive? Nothing at all. Just faith in a benevolent universe. And, failing that, in kind and compassionate teachers.

In some classes there are penalties for submitting work late; in others, no penalties; in some, penalties are only threatened; in others, they are enforced. I have some colleagues who post no deadlines for papers, allowing students if they choose to submit everything during the last week of class. The flexibility makes students happy, though sometimes they turn around and complain that the professor is "disorganized." It is not hard to understand students' confusion about what is real in college.

Real Learning and Fake-Real Learning

College faculty are increasingly trying to incorporate real-life activities in their classes, but often these are simply pretend-real. Students may be assigned to write blogs, but because of intellectual property and privacy concerns, they cannot be made public. Developing a genuine audience is a completely different activity, with completely different consequences, and thus completely different involvement, from writing for classmates and teachers. It is an improvement, in my view, from writing *only* for the teacher. But writing for "the world" is a real, and terrifying, and thus attention-grabbing activity.

A colleague discussed how he teaches writing to his students. "I tell them not just to write their papers for me, but to imagine writing them for their classmates too."

I asked the obvious question: "Do they actually read one another's papers?"

"No. We don't have time."

Such emphasis on crafting activities within the arbitrary boundaries of school are everywhere. Sometimes students are urged *not* to know something unless it can be known in the school way. I've had students ask if they are allowed to mention something they learned outside my class, even in a different course.

In *To Kill a Mockingbird* the precocious narrator, Scout, who could read the newspaper before she started school, is reprimanded by her inexperienced first-grade teacher: "Miss Caroline told me to tell my father not to teach me any more, it would interfere with my reading. . . . 'Now you tell your father not to teach you any more. It's best to begin reading with a fresh mind.'"[4] This ludicrous emphasis on school over learning epitomizes the dilemma inherent in a whole series of learning-for-schooling activities, from compare-and-contrast writing exercises to mastery of arcane grading scales to the pretense that teenagers can and must contribute original knowledge and interpretation in their class writings: *Your work must be original.* (To be fair, most professors recognize the limits to undergraduate originality.)

It is obvious, too, in foreign language courses. While it is certainly possible to learn languages in classes, most American students don't expect this to be the result; they are in the classes because they fulfill requirements.

Things can get pretty absurd.

A friend of my daughter Elena told me that despite the fact that his mom is from Honduras and they frequently travel there, he doesn't really know Spanish because in school they learned "theory of Spanish" rather than Spanish. For those of us with "good" theoretical minds, that is wonderful. We can contemplate to our heart's content. Rewarded at every turn, we can discuss verb forms or economic theory, ideas of symbolism or notions of history. But we may not necessarily be able to use any of it—and nobody cares. Compare that to the hands-on instruction in shop class that Mike Rose describes in *The Mind at Work*, where students building cabinets really need to know how to make things. They respect their teacher because he knows how to do it and they can test his answers against practice. In school, students respect their teachers because . . . well, because they have authority.

It's not just students like Scout who are punished for being real. In the 1980s, writer and English professor Cathy Davidson was teaching at Michigan State University. Her students from disadvantaged backgrounds were required to take fairly basic English composition courses. The standard expectation was that they would learn to write "term papers." But Davidson was appalled, as she tells it, by the enormous unemployment plaguing the area, and, with the agreement of her students, decided to spend the semester writing and revising and critiquing résumés and job application letters. She considered her class a triumph in that every single student was at least offered an interview, if not a job.

But she was reprimanded repeatedly for failing to uphold her mandate to teach the syllabus. So she left.[5]

Time in Seat: The Carnegie Unit Lives On

The "Carnegie unit" is an example of an arbitrary dimension of schooling that emerged at a particular identifiable moment and has come to govern all aspects of college: costs, completion, financial aid. And even while critics point out its drawbacks and limitations, it continues to be used—and even to spread.

In the early years of the twentieth century, the line between high schools and colleges was completely indistinct; as we saw in chapter 3, they even competed for the same students. The Carnegie Foundation for the Advancement of Teaching—initially established in 1905 for managing college professors' retirement benefits—tried to sort out high school from college. One way to do so was to establish entrance requirements for college, thus establishing a "college preparatory" curriculum for the "comprehensive high schools" that were now becoming available to a growing proportion of the population.

The entrance requirements included high school subjects, measured—so conveniently!—by time spent. It is a standardized way to assess attendance, but as Alvin Howard put it so clearly, "Critics pretty well agree that the trouble with the Carnegie Unit is that it interferes with good education."[6]

Snow Days Repaid

The winter of 2013–14 was known for a triple polar vortex. The weather brought snow, then deadly cold, then more snow and continued cold. The temperature exceeded freezing only once from December to February. To prevent kids from freezing at bus stops, the South Bend Community School Corporation called for eight snow or cold days. But the state requires 180 days of school, and with only two snow days built in, the additional six days had to be made up somehow.

Proposals for using spring break, cutting into summer vacation, or lengthening the school day were angrily debated. But few asked what would be learned; it was all about "butts in seats," about the counting of requisite hours. Students might be watching movies or having parties. As long as they were there, off the streets, in school, accreditation would follow.

How did we get to the point where time is all that matters?

The demise of the Carnegie unit was predicted, celebrated, advocated by a critic in the 1960s:

The Carnegie unit implies that all students can and should be exposed to the same material for the same length of time and that students can and should achieve at the same level in identical periods of time. . . . Few educators would actually profess to support the premises upon which the Carnegie unit is based.

This writer instead urges that "the instructional period . . . be based primarily on the tasks to be accomplished rather than on a predetermined master plan of uniform 45-, or 50-, or 60-minute periods."[7]

So half a century ago, the idea that school would be evaluated by the amount of time spent there—in terms of *credit hours* or *Carnegie units*—was challenged, yet it remains the only obvious way to measure progress.

What!?—you might say—how else could we know how much students have learned?

Well, there are answers to that question. There are many alternatives. One is *assessing competence*, perhaps with *badges* instead of *degrees* for *credits*. But these radical alternatives would have to confront "the machine."

Students are usually ineligible for financial aid, for example, if they fall below "full time," usually twelve credits a semester. A recent campaign in Indiana, 15toFinish, is aimed at teaching students and their parents that college students hoping to graduate in four years have to take fifteen credits every semester.[8] (For working adults, this is nearly impossible.) Yet prior to 1906, such a measure of college learning had not yet been invented, and at least three separate times—in the 1960s,[9] 1990s,[10] and today[11]—people have attempted to eradicate it.

Time as a measurement of education is part of the "grammar of schooling." Three decades after the 1960s revolutions, with little changed, David Tyack and William Tobin asked in 1994, "The 'Grammar' of Schooling: Why Has It Been So Hard to Change?" Yet, more than two decades on, we find it still kicking. Now even the *Carnegie Foundation itself* is considering whether the Carnegie unit—measuring student progress by time—is any longer appropriate.[12]

Ironically, in 1999 European universities, to make themselves more attractive to a new set of "customers," adopted the Carnegie unit in the Bologna protocol. No longer would different countries have different lengths of time for college, or different forms of evaluation (examinations and theses in Germany, seminars and examinations in France). All would sign up for the Carnegie unit model of modular courses—now called the European Credit Transfer and Accumulation System (ECTS), introduced in 1989[13]—each a semester long, with specified numbers of hours. Once a student completed a certain number, *Voilà!* Educated! (or at least certified).

Attendance in an Empty Room

We had a muddle: It was the last week of our challenging Elena's junior year of high school. On Monday and Tuesday she'd had her pre-calc final, and she'd turned in her art final project. So she planned to sleep in on Wednesday and Thursday. She was shocked that we, her devoted parents, would be unavailable to drive her to school late, so she called her friend Janella, whose mother agreed to take her. She set the alarm to get herself up at 9:00, instead of my waking her—trying to wake her, with gentleness, muttering, music, and when necessary repeated visits—at 6:45. Once at school, she planned to alert a friend to let her in, since the building was locked after the required 7:45 entrance time.

Lionel was opposed. Completely.

And I was ambivalent.

It was against the rules to skip class. It was forbidden to enter other than through the authorized front door. She was risking all kinds of penalties, I thought.

And yet . . . I was already immersed in thinking about this book. There were no plans to learn anything in either class, so the only reason for her to attend had to do with the rules set up by the school to teach discipline and obedience. Following rules is a good basic principle. Respecting authority is probably necessary. Attending school regularly is necessary for learning (sort of), or at least for ensuring continuity with classroom discussions and atmosphere.

But . . . to have a lively almost-seventeen-year-old who hated school sit in an empty classroom (seniors were officially exempt from attending) just to be marked "present" did seem to bow to the letter rather than the spirit of school attendance policies, to the structure rather than the substance of schooling.

We compromised: on Wednesday she went late, and on Thursday she sat alone in the empty room.

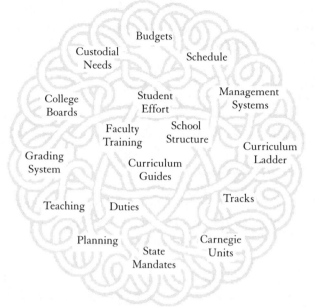

Figure 4.1 The interlocking systems of a Gordian knot: everything is connected.
Source: DiMartino and Clarke 2008:151. ©ASCD. Reprinted with permission.

This is only one example of a piece of the "grammar" of schooling. Each could and should be questioned, and each has been. But the hold remains. It took a short time for the landscape of the world to alter, but it is really hard to avoid the peculiar, arbitrary measures of educational success exemplified by the Carnegie unit. And the peculiarities—schedules, funding, advising, grading, planning—are intertwined. (See Figure 4.1.)

Submission to the Institutional Logic

Schools are institutions. A certain amount of expertise is required for success: understanding school genres; learning to produce acceptable attribution and citation to avoid the academic sin (crime) of plagiarism; knowing which teachers are softies and which are tough nuts; keeping track of those teachers who take attendance and those who don't, of the ones who want a bibliography and those who consider it unnecessary; knowing when collaboration is permitted and when it is strictly punishable by expulsion; being completely clear about what percentage of a grade is determined by participation and what by a journal, in case corners have to be cut. All this expertise is about the institution and its rather random rules. Those who master the rules win the game.

Academic learning starts at birth, for some. A classic article by Shirley Brice Heath shows that asking questions to which the questioner already knows the answer (*What does a dog say?*)—one of the most common school practices—is truly bizarre.[14] Such questions are "didactic," in that they exist only to test, not to become informed. Yet "school readiness" is so crucial to "school success," and so dependent on mastering school genres, that parents without a lot of schooling themselves are now being taught these genres. For example, the organization Parents as Teachers shows low-income parents how to function as in-home schoolteachers, just as advantaged parents do.[15]

Many students, especially those without the cultural capital that accompanies the middle-class birthright, flunk "schooling"; they fail to master the art of working the institution. They forget to turn in assignments. They don't get permission slips signed. In college they register too late, or forget to meet with advisors to check on their requirements. I know one young woman who finally finished her two-year degree but then missed the deadline to apply to a four-year college. Sure, these are skills that may transfer beyond school. But there are likely better uses of a person's entire childhood than learning to serve the institutional master.

Another aspect of schooling, one that dominates students' very sense of self, is that of grades. In the next chapter I explain why this is the case—and why it shouldn't be.

5

"What Do I Have to Do to Get an A?"

The Real Skinny on Grades

> The "C" students run the world.
>
> Harry S. Truman

Her self-control won, barely, but the sweet student who had recently lost her mother almost burst into tears because of the terrible new occurrence: she'd gotten a B+. Actually the paper received an A-, but because she had not followed the specified bibliographic format, her grade was reduced. *Which grade did I get?* The B+. *Is my writing so much worse now than at first, when I got an A? How can I bear this fate worse than death, something-other-than-an-A? What did I do wrong?*

This was a lovely student, one I'd spent several hours writing a graduate school recommendation for, extolling her moral sense, telling the admissions people that she was strong and willing to go against the crowd for her principles. And here she was, grade-grubbing. Not quite as bad as the threatening one who complained about me to my department chair and took down my photo, twice, from the departmental display. Not as bad as the one who actually did burst into tears. But still. She made it clear that this really mattered to her and she'd do just about anything to get a better grade. And let's face it. The grade is where it's at.

There isn't much I dislike more than this discussion about grades. Not discussion, really, but obsession. My task-completing students produce fine if rarely excellent work. But they arrive at college having been told that only misdeeds can remove them from their pedestals, and mere mediocre writing is hardly justification for their dethronement.

Faculty Faith in Grades

"Grades are the measure of college success. Like the salary at a job, the batting average in baseball, or the price of a stock, your grade-point average is an objective indication of how you're doing."[1] Like education bloggers Lynn Jacobs and Jeremy Hyman, I too used to believe that grades were genuine, objective measures of student accomplishment and worth. Like IQ and SAT scores, these precise numerical packages seemed to have the power to reveal inherent and enduring merit.

As a faculty member I spend a lot of time grading, and talking and thinking about grading. During the period in which I wrote *My Word!* I came up with the idea that grades had three functions: *sorting*, *motivating*, and *communicating*. Since I didn't really care to sort, and since I'd already learned about the deleterious results of extrinsic motivation (see chapter 9), I wanted to emphasize only the communication function. But I've gone further since then. I'd like to abolish grades entirely. They dominate discourse on education. But they don't work. In fact they backfire and produce ill effects.

Sorting

One common view is that faculty have to *sort* "excellent" from "good" to "mediocre" to "failed" assignments and then, cumulatively, students. Some faculty use a preestablished "curve" with a specified grade distribution. One colleague reported (surprise!) negative reactions when he announced at the beginning of the semester that he would award A's to only 35 percent of the class. Princeton implemented "grade deflation" in 2004, mandating an average maximum of A's in each level of courses. In 2014 it reversed that policy, while Yale was considering it.[2] Elsewhere faculty are simply encouraged to be strict. Many believe that the more low grades they award, the more they demonstrate that they uphold "standards."

I used to be horrified at a colleague, a charismatic teacher, beloved on campus, who awarded about 95 percent A's and A-'s. Many hundreds of students are desperate to take his classes every year. Kind, gentle, and entertaining, he has a way of making it sound as if he is talking to each student individually, even in a class of three hundred. I have heard some students brag about how easy the classes are, but I have also seen hundreds of students become anthropology majors because of the inspiration that this teacher provides. He gives online quizzes that students can retake until they reach the grade they want. They submit huge portfolios at the end of the semester, in boxes that line the department hallway, and he reads them all himself. Students get few comments, and certainly a percentage of them cheat. The high grades reflect my colleague's sense of *rewarding* the students for their attention and for being young and curious. *They do not sort.* They do not mean the same thing at all as a strict colleague's grades. But I no longer believe this matters and I no longer disapprove.

Motivating

I have tried to use grades to *motivate*. I want my students to come to class prepared so we can have meaningful discussions, not so I can introduce material that they should have encountered first on their own. I want them to read difficult material that they might not have chosen themselves. I want their work submitted on time so that they can get used to meeting deadlines (part of their real-world skills preparation), and so I can grade it all at once. Promptness also ensures that they will have completed the assignment in time to learn from it, which can occur only in a well-thought-out sequence of activities. I understand that students have many demands on their attention. But I want my class to count for *something*; otherwise there is no point in my being there.

I used to use grades both to reward and, sometimes out of desperation, threaten.

Clever students trained in this system—clever as foxes—admit that they get away with whatever they can and do whatever they have to. They do not do the reading just because I assign it, they tell me, but only if their grade depends on it. So in some classes I used to implement small quizzes. Since the quizzes *count*, students would do at least some of the reading, or so I believed. They would be informed and we could have meaningful conversations. This, I thought, would lead to the higher-level learning that I value. I'd prefer that they read just because they find it interesting or worthwhile, but there are so many more urgent things calling to them that unless there is a "price tag" on the work, it will be viewed as valueless.

But as you'll see in chapter 9, *extrinsic* rewards and threats rarely lead to *intrinsic* motivation.

I have now stopped giving the quizzes; a thoughtful student challenged me about them. After all, I'd become increasingly frank about my distrust of grades. I now try to make the motivation more genuine by creating situations in which students have to *use* the content of the reading somehow. That's harder.

Communicating

I have attempted to use grades to *communicate* standards of excellence. Students who go through the motions and do everything expected may get a B, I have proclaimed, but cannot get an A. And though I have come to have grave doubts about the objectivity of grades, many faculty retain their faith.

A professor in the humanities explains why, despite all their problems, she believes in grades:

> Although some professors abuse the privilege of grading, the system of grades per se remains the best way to assess the quality of student performance. Students complain about grades, but they at least understand them. Grades form an integral part of the unwritten contract between students and professors whereby professors agree to teach–and evaluate or judge students–and students agree to follow the professor through a course of study. In humanities courses, letter grades (as opposed to numerical grades) offer a form of *shorthand communication* for the many words that would be necessary for professors to explain to students how good their work is. In other words, letter grades offer students an assessment that goes beyond quantification of student performance and instead assesses the quality of their work.[3]

Humane and enlightened counsel from within the academy aims to "make our grading fair, time efficient, and conducive to student learning." Barbara Walvoord and Virginia Johnson Anderson see grading serving five roles: *evaluation, communication, motivation, organization,* and *faculty and student reflection.*[4] Workshops, books, and websites offer assistance in, among other things, better communicating one's grading standards, as this suggestion by learning specialists reveals:

> A-level work is, on the whole, not only clear, precise, and well-reasoned, but insightful as well. Basic terms and distinctions are learned at a level which implies insight into basic concepts and principles.... The grade of B implies sound thinking and performance within the domain of a subject and course, along with the development of a range of knowledge acquired through the exercise of thinking skills and abilities.[5]

Despite ever-longer syllabi and instructions on assignments, faculty are often accused of inadequate communication, both by students and by education consultants. *She didn't really tell me what I did wrong.* Or *Professor Jones needs to communicate more clearly his standards for grading.* Increasingly employing professional management terminology, pedagogy experts plead with faculty for better use of the communicative function of grades, which they argue can be used to improve student learning outcomes by breaking tasks down into their smaller components, as in factory work. For them, grades are the natural form of assessment, "formative" (helping learning) as well as "summative" (giving a single final evaluation). Faculty have even been encouraged to use "rubrics," as do teachers at earlier levels of schooling.

> A rubric is a scoring tool that explicitly represents the performance expectations for an assignment or piece of work. A rubric divides the assigned work into component parts and provides clear descriptions of the characteristics of the work associated with each component, at varying levels of mastery. Rubrics can be used for a wide array of assignments: papers, projects, oral presentations, artistic performances, group projects, etc. Rubrics can be used as scoring or grading guides, to provide formative feedback to support and guide ongoing learning efforts, or both.[6]

In my experience, students have come to see rubrics as indicating the formula for success, not as information to help them improve: education by numbers. But I sometimes use them.

A diffident but seething student in my linguistic anthropology class, Rory, asked to see me after I returned the major class project, one that involved recording, transcribing, and analyzing natural conversation. The project was worth 50 points; he'd gotten 36, similar to his grade on the previous assignment. I knew he cared about his grades and that he disliked the way I taught the class. We were in a room with flexible seating. I preferred the dinner club style of clustering around four large tables; he preferred rows facing forward. We tended to leave the room as we found it; he and I rejoiced—visibly, loudly—at opposite configurations.

Rory came in to ask what he "could do better." I began by showing him how much interesting material he had missed. (His analysis was just over three pages; some students had written twelve. I had specified the point values of the components of the project when I gave the assignment; he had dismissed in a few sentences some that were one-tenth the value of the project.)

He started to catch on. So I asked the question that I always ask: "When you looked your project over, did the grades and comments make sense?"

What he said stunned me, though I should have expected it.

"I never read over what I've written. I hate to see it."

Never mind that I had told students I'd be happy to meet with them about their papers, but only *after* they'd reread the assignment, my comments, and their paper. My short-term instruction from my one-semester class could not undo the trouble here, a problem as big as a boulder, put there by his entire lifetime of schooling—the schooling that had led him to a high-prestige college.

All he looked at, I thought, all he cared about, was the bottom line. (Later he protested this characterization.)

I lectured him about the importance, indeed centrality, of editing, of revising. I brought in my own experience as author of several books, my tendency to rewrite and rewrite, sometimes up to twenty or thirty times for a chapter.

"How can you improve if you don't look critically at what you've written?" I had begun to see that self-assessment is one of the keys to learning. "And," another thought dawned on me, "what do you think all those comments we write are for? If you never look at them and think about them, why do we bother?"

These rhetorical questions were likely lost. Rory knew what he needed: a higher grade. It seemed to be all about the number, the letter, the magic sign of his worth. He did something; the universe responded. If everything went according to plan, the number was a high one. He played the lottery to win, and apparently often did.

Later he and I had a heart-to-heart conversation when I posted this account, careful not to identify him, on my blog. He was appalled; he *did* love learning. He just had been trained to behave in a certain way with regard to his grades.

It isn't entirely Rory's fault. Our society sets students up for this attitude by focusing only on the bottom line of their accomplishment. Scholars have written of *achievement discourse*, of *learning for grades*, of *extrinsic motivation*. High-achieving students "do school" and play their teachers and learn, above all, how to succeed without learning anything else. Such students have risen to the top in a system that rewards a certain calculated and steady focus on the measures of accomplishment.[7] For them, grades emerge as a topic everywhere. Grades are dropped offhandedly into conversations about college in general, as their importance is assumed. A staff member at my university told me that her son's doctors calibrate his ADHD medication by his grades: when his grades improve, they know they have the dosage right. Clearly this attention to grades is established early.

All Conversational Roads Lead to Grades

In what follows, I draw on my decade of interviews with nearly three hundred Notre Dame undergraduates, using peer interviewers, about a broad range of questions regarding their college experience.[8] Having mastered the educational system in junior high and high school, these students bring this expertise to college, where they expect its application to yield the same success.[9] Since the interviewers were also students, respondents assumed mutual understanding as they circulated their strategic expertise in analyzing their own, their professors', and their fellow students' behavior.

Although the interviews generally weren't meant to focus on grades, students *volunteered* to talk about them, especially "good grades," "4.0," "A's," about which they demonstrate considerable expertise. Students recognize and sometimes deplore the centrality of grades and their dominance over their school life. Some assume "getting good grades" is the overall goal of college. Some have come to ignore grades, learning despite them. Some see grades as actually *preventing* learning. And most identify the fixation on "getting good grades" as the reason for "doing whatever it takes," including cheating.

So this exercise in listening in to students' accounts of their lives—accounts not directed initially at the subject of grades, but ending there— shows how a long apprenticeship in going to school teaches a particular kind of expertise. Some may resist, but most who remain in such a selective and desirable environment nonetheless accommodate.

When Grades Are the Goal

Grades are often seen as the very point of college. For example, to a question about specific things to accomplish in college, one student volunteered,[10] "I really want to, like, get good grades and meet different types of people and, . . . I don't know, develop a passion for something, . . . realize something I would love to do." Similarly, when a premed junior from Indiana observed that during the first year, many students "go out" (that is, drink excessively) four times a week, but over the years they "calm down," he assumed the overall goal of good grades: "They've begun to realize that this is college, they're going to school to get good grades, to get a job or go to wherever they're gonna go, so, yeah, they've definitely all grown up with all their immaturities freshman year. . . . They've definitely calmed down, . . . become much more mature."

Several students reported their "job" or responsibility in high school and college as getting good grades. As a double Spanish and economics major put it:

> I give myself my responsibilities. Kind of, like, doing my schoolwork, getting good grades, . . . keeping in touch with friends. . . . [In college] people are really focused on classes. And, like, . . . from Monday to Thursday, Sunday to Thursday, people are really focused on . . . their best friends and their classes. And then on weekends people are more focused on social life, like, hooking up and everything, and not as much on classes at all.

Asked, "What are they trying to get out of it, do you think?" the student answered: "People are generally just trying to get good grades. So if that means doing a lot of homework and studying a lot, that's what they'll do. But if they can get away with good grades without it, then they won't." The focus on grades—good grades—needs no justification.

Sharing Strategies

One aspect of student expertise, circulated widely, is how easy a class is. *Easiness* is one of the four desirable traits (along with *overall quality, helpfulness,* and *clarity*) evaluated on the online anonymous faculty-rating site RateMyProfessors.com.

One day on campus at registration time I heard a student shout encouragement to his friend across the sidewalk: "Take that class, man, for sure! Professor X is awesome! I didn't even go to class and I got an A!"

Another planning to become a psychiatrist consulted friends when choosing classes. One in particular seemed an ideal complement to her organic chemistry, biology, and statistics courses: "I ended up taking [the class] because a friend of mine had taken it and the same professor was gonna be teaching it, they were gonna be using the same textbooks and she said overall it was a really easy class."

Grades as Necessary for the Next Step

In addition to trying to balance their workload, some students focus on the practical—and realistic—use of grades for admission to the next level of schooling. In a system in which ranking is assumed to be a natural product of schooling, grades are in fact needed to "sort" students. A first-year business major from a Micronesian island explained that her plan to attend law school required a focus on "doing well":

> The very competitive law schools, which I do want to go to, they look at your grades and . . . you have to have a certain GPA or you have to graduate with certain honors. And I do feel like, since my plan is to go into law school, I have to do well here in my undergraduate studies. So, I definitely felt that kind of pressure. If I don't get a certain [grade] that I want in a class, that just makes me even more focused to . . . to put in more time and effort into studying that material, so I can bring up that grade. . . . So I definitely feel that I have to do well, in undergrad, in order to get into law school. . . . [This university] is ranked very high in the nation and . . . if you score well or you graduate with good grades and stuff, then you'll pretty much be accepted anywhere you want to go. Just 'cause, I think that where my education is now will definitely help me in the future.

This pragmatic motive—not unrealistic, of course—can govern the undergraduate experience of many achievement-oriented students.[11] But grades also represent the ultimate goal in perplexing ways, leading to cynical calculation or desperate measures, but not to the learning that is purportedly represented by high grades.

It is true that students demonstrate significant expertise in the game of school, but many nonetheless recognize the negative effects of this game. For an opening exercise in one of my classes, The Anthropology of Childhood and Education, I asked students to write about their educational philosophy. One student charged that testing causes students to focus on the wrong thing:

> I think spending too much time teaching students how to take a test can make them view an education as a means to an end (a grade, an achievement score, etc.) and it keeps them from appreciating education as an end in itself—as a valuable process by which we can better ourselves and learn all sorts of information for the pure joy of our interests. At Notre Dame I have had to catch myself on a few occasions and contemplate where my behaviors were coming from. For example, I have sometimes looked for ways to cut corners on reading assignments or evaluated the exact amount of effort I could get away with spending on studying for a test. These strategies, of meticulously strategizing the allocation of my time and effort, served me great from kindergarten through high school when it seemed so much of my education was a multiple choice race against the clock. But now they have become bad habits that can at times keep me from really grasping the material offered to me in class and from truly taking advantage of the tremendous opportunities to learn I am presented with every day here at notre dame.

In a system in which students regard their main task as getting good grades, they, more than their teachers, recognize that grades *suppress* learning. This all makes sense, given the "minimax" principle of motivation: when extrinsic motives for performance dominate, all people prefer tasks that are less challenging, complex, or risky.[12]

Grades in Contrast to Learning

Not all students are "grade-grubbers." Some are genuinely motivated to learn, conscious of the contrast between learning and doing something

Figure 5.1 Refrigerator Reward Center. Photo by Meredith S. Chesson.

purely for the grade, even to the point that they blame grades for *preventing* learning.

A prelaw student from a mid-Atlantic state with many majors and minors (political science, philosophy, Middle Eastern studies, and African American studies) answered the question "How would you measure whether or not you're doing well in school?" this way: "I like measure based on grades, which is I know not [laughter] the way you're supposed to look at it." She blames the "pressure" of grades for her lack of "outside reading"—or what faculty would call "reading"—doing only "what it takes to get an A and I don't go above and beyond that." Asked why she thinks that is, she answered:

> Probably because of the emphasis that . . . the academic system itself puts on grades. . . . Like it doesn't even ever seem like learning is what the outcome should be. It's more like the grades [are what] the outcome could be. And then just like, obviously, like getting into law school, so that's . . . huge.

"Where do students learn to focus on grades?," the interviewer asked.

> I went to a private elementary school so . . . you had to get A's . . . to get into
> the best high school and then in high school, get A's, get into the best col-
> lege, getting A's, get into law school. But it wasn't ever like the point was to
> learn. . . . A lot of the classes I'm more interested in, so like I go to class and I
> like am interested in the material and I retain more of the information, but
> I like don't do the outside reading unless I think I have to. So I feel like if
> there wasn't as much pressure to get an A, I would be more inclined to, you
> know, read more and learn more.

Though she says she likes to learn and read in the summer, and might
even take a class, she enjoys it only because of the lack of grading. Professors may regard this as rationalizing her choice not to do any of the course
reading, but she regards the system as itself preventing learning:

> Pretty much everybody who's here did really well in high school and like
> they're just used to doing well and being the best and getting good grades
> and perfectionist syndrome and [laughter] like you know it's just like pres-
> sure to keep doing well or get into med school or get into grad school or get
> into law school, so . . . If I was a professor I would be upset by that, like . . .
> [I'd want students to] care about something more than their grade. But on
> the other hand, like the way the classes are set up, it's why we care about
> the grade. You know, like I think it's the professors themselves that add to
> [this]. We can't all get A's and we all know that but like if the point is to
> learn and we all learn, then why can't we all get A's? . . . [laughter]. They
> make grades the goal in class. They make getting an A hard to do. . . . Pro-
> fessors kinda add to the emphasis on grades over learning.

Another student, an accounting major, contrasted her satisfying learning experience studying in London with the frustrating grade focus back
home.

> I wanted to learn the material so I would know it. . . . I didn't have to . . .
> but I'd go to the library every day and just like look into some of the sub-
> ject matter. Like art history, we were talking about an artist, I would just
> go and research him and just learn some things about him. . . . Like I felt
> like there was more emphasis on learning instead of like assignments and
> the grade.

She appreciated the encouragement to learn and deplored her need to complete "all of these stupid, meaningless assignments that I'm not really getting anything out of. . . . I'm doing stupid like journals and things like that, you know?" She had ceased completing assignments she regarded as meaningless, instead reading the *Wall Street Journal*, to which she had just subscribed.

> I'd definitely say that I'm just focused again on grades. [In London] because I wasn't so worried about like the end grade because there wasn't many assignments, I actually was able to like become knowledgeable on the subject. . . . [College is] your opportunity to find something you really enjoy and just learn all you can about it. . . . I'm here to expand my learning, not just to get, you know, a 4.0 and you know, like go to a great job or whatever.

In rejecting "just getting a 4.0" she also acknowledges the ordinariness of such a goal. But grades cannot be ignored; she still worries about them, and this, she says, destroys her ability to learn. While resisting, she complies.

Are Grades the Self or Self-Alienating?

Not only do grades often prevent learning, but they have other ill effects as well. The quest for grades can lead to the sense that students are in school to pursue high grades no matter what the cost. One method is to discern the teacher's desires. In R. D. Laing's sense, this may produce a profoundly divided self in which the student's behavior has nothing to do with her or his own intention.

Psychologists Ohmer Milton, Howard R. Pollio, and James A. Eison note: "It is our impression from working with students that grades become equated with the self for far too many. It is as though an A means 'I am a good or a smart person' and an F means 'I am a failure as a person.'"[13] The reified sign becomes internalized, replacing other motives.

A high-achieving first-year student taking Chinese, math, science, music—a total of nineteen credit hours—didn't mind yielding to the professor's demands:

> The professor ask/tells us to, you know, write a paper and format it in a certain way, you know? Some people might like complain about it, 'Oh you

know he's just going against everything I've ever learned,' like, you know, it's really is like Professor X's choice. You know, you might as well follow along since he's the one who's giving you the grade.

The quest for high grades can also lead to anxiety, depression, and challenges to students' sense of self-worth. An architecture student who said she thought being successful was important to everyone clarified:

> It's important for me just to—just to find like my potential. . . . I always kinda struggle with like wanting to be better at things, like especially with like sports and stuff, so I think that kinda carries over with academics too because . . . some grades just aren't good enough and you really wanna just keep going.

With such perfectionism, the quest for good grades can be literally life-threatening. I had a successful student who developed obsessive-compulsive disorder—the perfect student gone too far. During her junior year she began fixating on memorizing the details of theoretical readings instead of grasping their overall point. She started running fifty miles a day. Her handwriting became tiny and perfect. After she left school for a year of treatment, she returned, healthy and relaxed, even about her grades.

Several other students got me preaching the gospel of imperfection. One was thin, well groomed, conscientious, ambitious. She wore tasteful jewelry and traveled widely. She seemed to be put together. But in a Chinese language class she was about to get an A-. This would ruin her perfect GPA. If this occurred in one three-credit course during college, her GPA would fall from 4.000 to 3.99. Twice, and she would plummet to 3.98.

Despite the infinitesimal difference, it caused her such anxiety and fear that she trembled and cried. It was as if opening up the possibility of imperfection would crack the hull of a seaworthy vessel and the next thing you knew, the boat would be taking on so much water that it would capsize. The only hope was to keep patching the cracks.

Two family friends were similarly perfectionistic. The high school valedictorian carrot was one incentive: only a student with a perfect 4.0 could be valedictorian. But these two students were nervous wrecks much of the time. They worried and worried, worked and worked.

When I hugged them as they set off for college, I urged them, "Try to get a B." I thought it would be good for them.

One spent most of her first year at a very prestigious college studying, reading, trying to master every bit of every subject, just as she had in high school. But something changed in her second year. When I saw her that summer, she reported triumphantly that she had earned a C+ in a science class. This was part of a critique of her fellow premed students, but I took the fact that she now grasped the foolishness of spending every waking moment fixated on a number as a sign of health.

Grades Cause Cheating

Students often explain that cheating results from a focus on grades. One female premed and psychology major stated:

> I'm just like trying to do the best I can. Like get the best grades I can. I can't really worry about like what everybody else is doing but where a lot of people who are just like completely taken over by it. . . . If they didn't care what their grade was gonna be, they wouldn't bother cheating.

This student laments the unfairness—even when there are no quotas—when those who use improper tactics meet with success. She is glad that unearned good grades may be caught by software; the "playing field" in the game of school should be "even."

> [Turnitin.com] helps to force people to make sure that their work is their own. . . . It doesn't make it an even playing field if people aren't submitting their own work. . . . They will get good grades on things that they don't do themselves. And then there you are, you're doing the work yourself and if you get a worse grade than they do, they don't deserve that and . . . you feel that . . . something should be done.

A female Asian American premed student suggested that shortcuts (such as cheating) should be resorted to only if an A is not guaranteed:

> Well, if I have a paper, I don't usually take shortcuts because I feel . . . like the answers are right there and the potential to get an A on that is like so close to like your reach that there shouldn't be any reason why you don't get an A on it and there shouldn't be any shortcuts taken with that.

Yet another student reasoned, "I think people would cheat because they either don't wanna do the work or they don't feel confident enough that they'd get an A on their own," adding, "I guess a lot of people have problems with people who cheat because they think it's not fair that somebody is getting an A without doing the work and like they got an A and did the work."

Recognizing the pressure of competing goals, another student gave an explanation, "If [cheaters] think that college is just a way to get good grades and get a job, then they probably don't feel any shame [in plagiarizing], . . . but if they saw college as a learning experience geared to increase your knowledge on a subject, then they probably would feel shame." Students recognize the lack of focus on learning in much of their school experience. (How learning in school is related to doing a job is usually overlooked—because so much of the emphasis is on completing the requirements and credentials.)

My Grade and I

A high school student once contacted me for some help on a project. I tried to clarify the background of her topic, sociolinguistics, and made some suggestions. In response she wrote, "My grade and I thank you." Jocular, perhaps—but this Frankenstein creation, The Grade, has indeed come to possess independent life.

Facts (and Fantasies) about Grading

We may believe that there are "standards" in grading student work, just like with eggs, cattle, tomatoes, Red Delicious apples, but despite beliefs about the objectivity of grades, there is not and has never been anything objective about them. They are always comparative. They are always arbitrary.

I can determine a scale and then use it, but my decision to count a certain question as "worth 5 percent" or "worth 10 percent" of a test, or an essay as "worth 10 percent of the course grade" or "worth 25 percent of the course grade," comes entirely from my own capricious determination. I can decide to count attendance, participation, punctuality of submission— or not. I can assign a five-hundred-word blog post or a twenty-five-page term paper. "Objective" tests are built on a series of arbitrarily selected questions.

All the research on faculty grading shows lack of consistency. At best we get within a full letter grade or so of our norm over time, and inter-faculty standards remain shaky.

Though I used to believe that smaller gradations of grade categories would help refine this process, experts on grading actually advise instead using broader categories. The best suggestion I have read is to offer "Satisfactory" and "Unsatisfactory" with a rare option of "Meritorious." (This is the path used by elite law schools that deemphasize grades.)

But how, my colleagues will ask, *can we tell the difference between what is really great and what isn't? How can we decide who will go to medical school?*

Sorting Humans and Eggs and Steel

When grades are used to *sort* or *rank*, it is assumed that humans line up in a neat row in order of quality: worst to best. Standardized tests operate on that assumption. It is convenient, of course. Machines and computers can take the numbers and run.

But once people leave college, the absolute ranking is no longer even relevant. Even for doctors.

My father and brother are pediatricians. They hire associates pretty regularly. I asked my brother what they are looking for and he said, "Personality. That's it." Board scores, transcripts, all the rest: none of it has anything to do with how well they will perform in a primary care setting. Maybe specialists need to know more organic chemistry and pharmacology; researchers certainly do. I understand that a certain baseline competence is measured by boards. But the absolute ranking of students has little to do with how well they will function once they have finished being students.

Grades simplify the admission process. But as soon as students are out of school, or even enrolled in the revered professional schools, such numerical measures no longer have much meaning, except at the very extremes.

Stanford Law School dropped letter grades in 2008, joining Yale Law School and the School of Law at the University of California at Berkeley, arguing that doing so would reduce unnecessary pressure and improve learning. Grading at Stanford Medical School is pass-fail only; Yale Medical School doesn't rank students until the third year. True, given students' obvious stature simply for having attended these schools, their employment prospects are not diminished.[14] But the fact that these elite professional schools recognize the negative effects on learning that grades create should make everyone ask questions about this pervasive aspect of schools.

A Short History of Grading

Even though grading systems, whether a hundred-point scale or letter grades or any other scheme, seem like part of the natural world, they are relatively recent. They are modeled on industrial quality-control measures, just like the ones used to sort factory-made products, and use the very same terminology. The "factory model" is derived from ideas of "management" stemming from Prussian military theory. ("The school, like the factory, is a thoroughly regimented world.")[15] Arising simultaneously in factories and schools in the nineteenth and early twentieth centuries to create uniformity and efficiency,[16] this model required metrics of quality assessment. In order to ensure uniform "inputs" (raw materials), students were narrowly age-graded.[17] "Outputs" were also assessed and all wrapped up into a single letter or number that was supposed to reveal quality—just like with factory products ("Grade A meat").

And while it makes sense to evaluate interchangeable uniform products such as ball bearings with a single scale, it makes much less sense to do so with humans. Not only does it miss a lot of useful information, even about valuable job skills such as work ethic or perseverance. It also creates ill effects: the system gets internalized, at least for the ones with a chance to excel in it, while the dropouts, the disenfranchised, the angry ones who resist, all eventually come to understand that they can't be "reduced to a number."

Debates about the nature of education intersect with debates about grades. In the early twentieth century, John Dewey's "progressive" whole child education competed with the "scientific measurement" approach of E. L. Thorndike (to oversimplify a long, complex tale). Thorndike's won,[18] resulting in the ubiquitous focus of schooling on measurement against a norm.[19]

Sorting was not entirely unknown prior to the existence of factory schools. Whenever entry is limited, some sorting system appears. For about 1,300 years, China's examination system identified the most qualified to serve as government bureaucrats.[20] Medieval and early modern European universities had examinations, but they were oral and public, involving disputations among the community of scholars, until the shift to written examinations at Oxford and Cambridge in the eighteenth and nineteenth centuries. Some written examinations may have been included as early as the sixteenth century, especially in mathematics but also in the humanities, but the dominant form of examination was oral. This changed when the increasing number of candidates made oral examinations impractical. Christopher Stray notes that with the move to self-contained written examinations, "socio-moral criteria were giving way to cognitive evaluation."[21]

Oral disputations continued well into the nineteenth century. There were always substantial preparatory negotiations over the content and participants—with the aim of avoiding trivial or risky topics. In U.S. higher education, the dissertation defense retains this flavor.[22]

France continues to rely on examinations, the *concours*, for admission to the prestigious *grandes écoles* that dominate French higher education.[23] European universities, such as the great German institutions that gave the world the notion of a research university, never used grades at all. Students passed or failed, and could try again as many times as their economic resources allowed. With the twenty-first-century spread of the Bologna protocol, using the U.S. system of credits, credentials, and modularity, grades are being introduced—though with difficulty and resistance. An international trial of the U.S.-style GPA will compare it with conventional grading systems for five years. Early reports are that employers like it.[24]

Grades in higher education have a specific genesis. They began in the late eighteenth century at elite institutions such as Cambridge and Yale, where they were both supplementary[25] and disdained,[26] a method of sorting the top students. Students at Cambridge had been ranked since the sixteenth century, with competition among students prominent. Oxford downplayed the ranking of candidates; the Greek letters alpha, beta, and gamma indicated classes of candidates, but it was possible for all to be first class.

The origin of "grades" is often attributed to William Farish, chair of mechanical engineering at Cambridge; the common history says he began to use "marks" in 1792 to evaluate individual questions, but there is little evidence for this claim.[27] Oral examinations were marked with letters and pluses and minuses—reflecting the importance of mathematics at Cambridge.

In the United States, differentiating students into four classes occurred at Yale in the late eighteenth century. At Harvard in 1830 a scale of 20 was used in rhetoric examinations. The University of Michigan went from a numerical system to pass/no-pass in 1851, modifying it slightly but in 1860 returning to a scale of 100. Every school experimented with different ways to communicate student quality, using numbers, abbreviations for passing, absences and behavior, and more. But the familiar letter grades were first used by Mount Holyoke only in 1897.[28] Since then, grading has become ever more complex, elaborated, and indeed consequential.[29]

The elaboration of grading intersects with standardized testing, which developed in the early twentieth century[30] to identify "raw intelligence" and increase access to higher education for the less advantaged; it is interwoven with eugenics and other classification schemas having to do with "intelligence" and comparison.[31] In the second half of the century, standardized tests proliferated. Critical analysts challenge the high-stakes testing that has become the focus of national education policy, schools for disadvantaged youth, the test-prep industry, and college admissions—in short, most of the lives of the young until they are well into their twenties.[32]

To the dismay of faculty, grades also motivate "the game of school," which involves clever guessing about pleasing teachers rather than meaningful expression or exploration of students' own perspectives.[33] Many students become adept at "playing" and managing their professors in order to secure high grades.[34] As Wendy Nelson Espeland and Michael Sauder note, reliance on numbers frequently confuses measuring with influencing ("teaching to the test").[35] College students often pursue the high grade rather than the learning that the grade is supposed to reflect.[36]

But it gets stranger yet. In the 1990s in Denver, I encountered the new phenomenon of students earning above-perfect grades in advanced placement or honors classes. To encourage them to take academic risks—so goes the official story—they were able to earn 5.0 out of a possible 4.0. I considered it only a local oddity until I came to Notre Dame, where the vast majority of my students have attended schools that award such super-high grades.

In the affluent suburban high schools that feed selective colleges, Peter Demerath analyzed "hypercredentialing," that is, "the process of artificially high credentials intended to strengthen students' positions on education and job markets,"[37] as well as the conferring of "weighted grades" for honors and advanced placement courses; hence the possible grade of 5.0 on a 4.0 scale. In this system many students graduate from high school with GPAs above a "perfect" 4.0. One such school had forty-seven valedictorians—every student who earned a 4.0 or above. Colleges in turn publicize the extraordinarily high GPAs of their incoming students.

Grades do many things, but one of them is to communicate a sense of worth. And students who are in a position to earn 5.0 points on a 4.0 scale are being told that they are worth more than others who can earn only a maximum of 4.0. Their parents are in on this, and the colleges like it too.

There is nevertheless something both logically and socially problematic about this practice. The fact that it is mostly affluent white students who enjoy such a cushion (AP and honors classes are abundant at schools with mostly middle- and upper-middle-class students, and rare at schools serving disadvantaged students) is not beside the point, though it is often clothed in the language of meritocracy—or what Stephen J. McNamee and Robert K. Miller call "the meritocracy myth."[38] (The term *meritocracy* was initially meant as satire.)[39]

Grades, as measures, indicators, assessments—what Sally Engle Merry calls "simplified numerical representations of complex phenomena"— form part of the fabric of modernity.[40] Such measures have become obvious and powerful, illustrating the usually unnoticed contingent nature of such a system.

The Fallacy of Misplaced Concreteness

Progressive writer and scholar Eric Zencey argued in 2009 that we should get rid of the gross domestic product as a measure of economic well-being. It is simply convenient but oversimplifies complex reality through a reified measure. Grades are similar.

We assess students because we can. How smart is Jennifer? Pretty smart; she is a 3.5 student. How about Joey? Not so smart; he's only a 2.8 student. And what about Connie? Well, she's an underachiever. She got a 2100 on her SAT but is only a 3.2 student.

Testing and measuring blossomed in the early twentieth century. One test was of IQ, which measures "g," or general intelligence. Originally a ratio ("intelligence quotient"), representing mental age over actual chronological age, it assumed a regular progression of "human development" that grew out of certain specific views of humans as biologically programmed just as plants are. Individuals and societies could similarly be measured against a standard, which was a white European male of upper-middle-class status and excellent education. "Primitives," lower-class people, and "ethnics" fell below the standard, which was of course unquestioned. Women and girls, too, often fell behind.[41]

Another was the SAT, which grew out of "college boards" administered since 1900 by the College Entrance Examination Board. From an attempt to measure achievement in high school, the SAT originally claimed to measure "aptitude" (Scholastic Aptitude Test), one measure of which involved testing for exotic vocabulary,[42] relying on the argument that familiarity with uncommon words must stem from diverse and engaged reading, which does not necessarily entirely depend on financial advantage—for even the poor are theoretically able to use libraries,[43] though the practical obstacles to their doing so can be quite significant. Eventually the College Board acknowledged that "aptitude" could be influenced by test preparation, and the word was quietly retired. Now families may spend thousands of dollars on SAT preparation courses to enhance their children's likelihood of admission into highly selective schools. (Those attending community colleges or local state schools, the majority in the United States, need not worry so much.)

Arguments about the usefulness of the SAT—does it in fact predict college success?—are leading increasing numbers of colleges to reject its use for admissions. Some argue that high school grades correlate better with college grades than does the SAT, more accurately predicting school success. It is important to note, however, that school success and grades *do not* predict life success or happiness. C students do better at business. They are happier people.[44]

Audit Culture

As assessments—grades, tests, faculty evaluations, departmental outcomes assessment, student satisfaction, school evaluations—have proliferated at all levels of institutional schooling, critical analysts query the external discipline that becomes internalized by those preparing for their places at the top of the system.[45] Analyses of "audit culture" with its fixation on measurement, evaluation, and competition demonstrate its spread with twenty-first century neoliberalism (faith in free markets, privatization, and competition, with denigration of social explanations and shared responsibility).[46] First the people who are being assessed have to play the game. "Neo-liberal governance relies on individual agency, and . . . individuals, as active subjects, are co-opted into regimes of power."[47] The assessments and "indicators" (numerical and statistical measures) then have effects on personal views of the self. "In some of the most successful examples, such as grades in school, the indicator comes to shape subjectivity, defining for the individual his or her degree of merit," in Sally Engle Merry's terms.[48] We become the sum of our evaluative measures.

Critiquing the "Magic of Numbers"

The real problem with grades is that they are like Dr. Frankenstein's creatures: conceived for a certain purpose but coming to take on a life of their own. In that way they resemble money and other signs and indicators (think of GDP). When you hear "B+" or "$12" or "annual income of $42,000," it seems as if something precise and concrete is being referred to. But is the B+ the result of excellent work turned in late, or was the work just pretty good? Was the $12 a six-year-old's monthly salary for walking a dog or the cost of an airport sandwich? Is the annual income of $42,000 a maximum in a low-income country or a median figure for someone in a developed country?

Grades—like money and other indicators—*flatten* experience by making it all *commensurate*. That has bureaucratic appeal.

But surely everyone would agree that schools do not exist purely for their own institutional convenience. Like other signs such as money, grades are multivalent symbols that simultaneously have and do not have instrumental functions.[49] As both social and subjective, they perform psychological and institutional work that may be undesirable,[50] but they are reified and fetishized through circulation.

Like money, grades spill over far beyond the purposes for which they were invented. Grades, unlike money, are "inalienable"[51]—that is, they cannot be conferred on others or exchanged, but stick to their owners' selves alone. Like money, a grade as a type of "indicator" may transition from the utilitarian to the objective and absolute valuation of human beings,[52] providing the *appearance* of comparability, or commensurability.

> A comparison [of indicators] with money is instructive because it is the quintessential unit that flattens difference into commensurate values. . . . Indicators rely on a similar alchemy: they create a commensurability that is widely used to compare, to rank, and to make decisions even though the users recognize that these simplified numerical forms are superficial, often misleading, and very possibly wrong.[53]

And in that sense, as naturalized forms of discipline and subjectivity, grades intersect with other cultural developments. Grades emerged along with the rise of statistics, measures, and the focus on numbers.

> Numbers are the epitome of the modern fact because they seem to be simple descriptors of phenomena and to resist the biases of conjecture and theory because they are subject to the invariable rules of mathematics. Numbers have become the bedrock of systematic knowledge because they seem to be free of interpretation and to be neutral and descriptive. They are presented as objective, with an interpretive narrative attached to them by which they are given meaning.[54]

One further effect is the way such measures are internalized so individuals discipline themselves.[55] Schooling is one powerful aspect of such governance, transformed into self-governance.

Once the categories are in place, people's behavior increasingly conforms to them. This is not the obvious power of coercion but the more elusive, passive power of discipline, increasingly self-inflicted. The validity of censuses, test scores, or public opinion polls requires complicity from their subjects. Individuals are made governable . . . and numbers become self-vindicating . . . when measures guide the activities being measured or shape the images of those whose characteristics they measure.[56]

This and similar critiques emphasize that "the magic of numbers" provides "an appearance of certainty and objectivity."[57] In this way grades may be further abstracted, as is evident in discussions of the four-digit GPA. A GPA of 3.0 could indicate all B's or half A's and half C's—surely reflecting two different student experiences. But we can compare 3.712 and 3.722 and believe there are meaningful distinctions.

And like other forms of measurement, indicators "cause people to think and act differently."[58] Grades initially were intended to measure phenomena. Yet "an indicator may even create the phenomenon it is measuring instead of the other way around. For example, IQ is whatever it is that the IQ test measures. Here, the process of measurement produces the phenomenon it claims to measure."[59]

Against Grades: Moving to Self-Assessment

Grades teach students that others are the only judge. Students finish the assignment, forget about it, and hope for the best. They learn to please: "What does *this* professor want?" They learn that someone, somewhere, will tell them if they are any good.

I have begun to give my students, in smaller classes, rubrics without grades. I tell them that if this causes too much anxiety, I'll be happy to tell them what grade the rubric would translate to. (Nobody has requested this, so far.) In addition, I make them evaluate themselves, try to develop a sense of their own standards. What do *they* think is high quality? This forces them, instead of shutting their eyes and jumping, to open their eyes and think about genuine standards—the sought-after *metacognition*. After all, if they are going to go out in the world and become active agents, they have to know when they have achieved something worthwhile and when they are doing a superficial job. The focus on grades teaches them that the universe is irrational and sometimes the superficial job wins the prize.

I believe this is absolutely the wrong lesson. But they have been learning it their entire schooling lives.

In my 2009 Anthropology of Childhood and Education class I decided to go for broke with an unconventional approach. I had taught the class before. I was in the fortunate position of having been promoted to full professor. What did I have to lose?

I wanted my students to learn to be learners, to learn how to teach themselves. That includes learning to evaluate themselves, not to submit a half-baked assignment and pray for grace.[60] They had to internalize their own standards and live up to them, not try to get away with doing as little as possible.

I began the class with no grading policy and no assignments. (Well, I had one up my sleeve, with the usual details about the relative weight of each assignment, due dates, and so forth.) These were good, able, responsible students, many of them planning to become teachers. We had already spoken for several class periods about their identity between adulthood and childhood, about them as students and teachers. So I took the question to them: How should their grades be determined?

You need to understand that Notre Dame is no Hampshire or Antioch College. There has never been an antiestablishment movement here. Our students love the system within which they have been rewarded. So the experiment was new for them. It could have allowed them to throw off the yoke of oppression under which they had suffered for twenty years. It could have given them the tempting freedom to say, "We all get A's."

Gimme Good Grades!

At a talk I gave at the Culver Military Academy in Indiana, I asked students what grades were for. They knew grades determined who got into college. I showed an image of a range of grades and asked—tongue in cheek, of course—which one they liked. They were a little nervous, as if they might somehow get stuck with an undesirable grade if they even whispered the wrong answer. What kind of trick question was I asking? Multiple-choice questions that appear easy must have some twist. Why would "A+" *not* be the obvious answer?

My students at Notre Dame had nothing to say. They thought it was a trick, a prelude to giving them all "bad" grades. I gently introduced the critique of grades, and once they trusted me, they admitted their own misgivings. When I taught the class the next time, I had students grade themselves on every assignment. Uncomfortable at first—Is it a better strategy to give themselves undeserved high grades and hope I'll let them stand, or to give themselves modest low grades and hope I'll raise them?—they began to embrace this exercise and take it seriously. Almost all showed impressive self-awareness about the strengths and weaknesses of their work. At the end of the course, students reflected that they could never fully return to the old model of writing for their teachers.

On a self-evaluation, one of my students wrote the following, explaining why her paper might not have lived up to her own goals and standards: "I just wanted to get this paper done. . . . I tend to finish writing it then never want to look at it again (the pain is too much to bear . . . haha)."

Compare the student's view (*I never want to look at my work again*) with an athlete's: to improve one's stroke or form or time, one has to look frankly at the entire effort, all of it. But the goal is different. At a faculty gathering at a very highly regarded liberal arts college, one faculty member spoke of the "black box" of grading: students thrust their work out into the world, and for some reason a particular evaluation comes back. I wanted them to open their eyes and look.

So from any number of perspectives, the dominance and value of grades should be challenged.

Some critics emphasize the stratification that accompanies the ranking.[61] Failure, built into assessment, is correlated with social position. High grades are especially bestowed on students possessing social and economic advantages,[62] with teachers' often strategic, if unconscious, compliance.

Others, as you'll see in chapter 9, focus on the loss of personal motivation that accompanies extrinsic motivators like grades.[63]

Still others point out differences between learning in schools and nonschool settings,[64] where assessment never occurs in such an arbitrary, decontextualized, uniform fashion. The high-stakes testing that now dominates K–12 education is particularly inimical to learning.[65]

The critical analysis of education, huge and multidimensional, largely challenges the dominance of grades. Yet those responsible for conferring them reveal few such qualms.

So why can't we just get rid of them?

It must be acknowledged that grades are in some contexts consequential in a real-world setting. For those pursuing higher levels of education, grades are used to determine admission. Some employers also rely on grades (GPA, transcript) in hiring, at least to distinguish among potential candidates who don't yet have work experience. Higher grades get students reduced car insurance rates. And even though grades have little correlation with success, happiness, or other lifelong aims,[66] they remain a convenient tool for sorting people.

Students confess to me, to my colleagues, to my student interviewers, and in much published scholarship that they are after the grade, pure and simple. One of my colleagues was exasperated at his student's unselfconscious question: "What do I have to do to get an A?" In Peter Demerath's book *Producing Success,* Alexandra Robbins's *The Overachievers*, Denise Clark Pope's *"Doing School": How We Are Creating a Generation of Stressed Out, Materialistic, and Miseducated Students*, and David Labaree's *How to Succeed in School without Really Learning*, we see how this works in high school, and of course students' "expertise" in schooling is brought with them to college—especially to high-prestige colleges.

But I don't want my classroom to exist for the convenience of professional schools.

Still, it is the *belief*—sometimes quite rational—in the consequentiality of grades that seems persuasive, not the *fact* or degree of consequentiality.

In contrast to the anxious fixation on individual achievement and competition that forms the bedrock of high-achieving students' academic life, in the next chapter you will hear about the other half—the delightful half, the part where students find meaning, fun, and friends.

6

CAMPUS DELIGHTS

Nonacademic Engagement and Responsibility

A preponderant body of research documents that the social and emotional
gains that students make during college are considerably greater than the
intellectual gains over the same span of time.

SUSAN A. AMBROSE ET AL., *How Learning Works*

As a professor I used to be a little bit jealous. I used to regard the non-
curricular side of college as in competition with what I saw as the central
focus of college—the academic side. Then, as part of the turnaround I've
experienced over the last decade or so, I began genuinely to wonder why
students were so committed to all those activities. Why were they spending so much more time on them than on their classwork? Why did they
seem to care so much about everything but classes, which they treated as
necessary evils?

I also began to notice how competent many students were. On U.S.
residential campuses, students direct plays; function as quasi-professional
athletes fought over by recruiters; produce dance parties; tutor disadvantaged children; build houses for previously homeless people; organize food
drives; play in bands. Students who are mediocre at classwork sometimes
thrive once college is over.[1]

I came to wonder about the contrast with classrooms, where students
are frequently treated like irresponsible children and overseeing adults are

largely regarded as adversaries rather than as partners.[2] Students often sit passively, awaiting instruction on how to act. Or they resist.

Studies going back to the 1980s—well before smart phones and the Internet—show that in classes, about a third of students, at any moment, are thinking about something other than the course.[3] As human beings, students naturally focus their time and energy not just on classes. They also hold down jobs, have relationships, care for dependents, volunteer, enjoy entertainment and exercise, cope with illness and disabilities. For some students, a substantial amount of time is spent on extracurricular activities. Once I awoke to the reality that students were putting in dozens of hours weekly on all kinds of interests outside classes, I wanted to understand this better. So, using surveys, interviews, and observation, I conducted a small research project to discover what students spent their time on, and why. I came to admire the work students do outside class and to understand why they value it so much more than the academic side. I also came to see why many experts believe that students "develop" socially and emotionally more than intellectually.[4]

In contrast to the painful "get-it-over-with" attitude that students often have toward the academic side of college, where grades are the goal, non-academic activities are often their own reward.

Just as I reversed my views about grades, no longer believing that they were useful or important, I reversed my views about the nonacademic side of college, no longer seeing these pursuits as frivolous distractions from a more important task.

Extracurriculars and the Co-curriculum

As higher education was transformed in the late twentieth century in the United States from an elite to a mass system,[5] and with the proliferation of professional non-faculty staff, a new discourse of the importance of the "co-curriculum" was born.[6] Some students had always been involved in activities apart from the academic side, but this trend increased dramatically, owing to two mutually reinforcing factors: (1) habits developed in high school among students aiming to enter selective colleges by building up their extracurricular record,[7] and (2) the increasing numbers of professionals devoted to these campus activities.[8]

The disciplinary institution of school is intimately entangled with the decades-long process of achieving adulthood. Students are novices, and their activities—like their consumption—are to be directed by experts, "real adults," conducted in institutions separated from the outside world by physical, social, and legal barriers. In the total institutions that represent the version of higher education that I have been studying for over a decade, we find contradictory discourses about the relative value of academic and nonacademic activities.

Administrators support nonacademic activities, to some extent. In certain cases, seen as supplementary to the important academic concerns of the university, they are also useful in marketing. They provide that central element of "fun" as a self-evident good, as Michael Moffatt, among others, has discussed, while also conferring social and cultural capital that can be exchanged for employment.

Extracurricular participation in the United States has been studied deeply at the high school level, especially its correlations with academic success, engagement, and healthy behaviors.[9] It has been studied less in college, though some studies reveal the powerful correlation between extracurricular participation and socioeconomic status and race/ethnicity.[10] Social capital, already present, increases through participation in extracurricular life, enhancing positive attitudes and dispositions toward academic and social engagement.[11]

Yet the academic and nonacademic sides of higher education rarely speak. Most faculty largely ignore the existence of the nonacademic life, being aware, perhaps, of the most successful athletic teams and the marching band, or attending student multicultural events. On residential campuses most faculty have never entered student dormitories or fraternity and sorority houses. Most have rarely attended student performances. Many do not read student publications. A colleague proclaimed proudly to me that she had never read the student newspaper. Most never take into account students' need for employment.

While the student affairs folks see themselves as contributing in a coherent way to the "development" of post-adolescent students, faculty may regard this "development" as detracting from the real work of school: learning school subjects.

I used to see it that way too. I saw my job as central to the purpose of a university, and assumed that students *should* expend most of their energy on their classes. A common conversation among faculty details the number of hours students should spend in class and devote to class work outside the meeting time (reading, writing, studying); the total is supposed to be equivalent to a full-time job, approximately forty hours a week, as academics are seen as students' principal focus. When figures come in revealing a total of perhaps twenty-five hours—including attending classes—horror and lamentation follow.[12] I once shocked a colleague when I lectured about student time use; he was still operating as if his students were like himself: devoted entirely, full-time, to their studies.

But as you know, I have come to see things differently.

Students involved in the most absorbing extracurricular activities, such as varsity athletics and band, spend more time on that activity than a full-time job would require. They willingly put in countless hours rehearsing dramatic performances, organizing charitable operations, leading religious retreats, traveling out of state every weekend for athletic events.

It became clear that the pull of a real-life and real-time group activity, a performance or competition, could vastly outweigh the tepid words on a page or screen that dominate school learning. It began to dawn on me that some students in residential colleges were entirely engaged in their lives—but in their *campus* lives, not so much their *academic* lives. As young adults, many were competent and reliable, with responsibilities for budgets and management that far exceeded those of their teachers. I wanted to understand this better.

In Search of Engagement

As you saw in chapter 1, college students are the focus of many complaints: they are academically adrift;[13] earn excessively high grades for inadequate work;[14] engage in binge drinking[15] and meaningless sexual encounters;[16] waste time and money;[17] focus on sports instead of academics;[18] cheat;[19] and are generally uninterested in their studies.[20] Critiques of faculty,[21] the curriculum,[22] and corporatization[23] are plentiful. One moral panic after another has looked to education for solutions to social problems, beginning with the compulsory education designed to combat "juvenile delinquency" and its obvious side effect, "truancy." One of the latest fears is that our students are not "engaged." They lack academic seriousness. They waste their time on unimportant and self-indulgent activities. This critique reflects a general American distinction between "work" and "play." According to this dominant trope on campus,[24] the learning that happens in class is "work," authorized as valuable. "Play" is dangerous, chaotic, unruly, or at least frivolous.

Articles and books have been written in the attempt to define *engagement*. My own version has included both "caring" and time spent. I too was horrified over the years (though less now) at the self-reported amount of time students spent studying.[25] Self-righteously, I recall that I spent almost all my time in school studying. (This is probably untrue, but it is my memory.)

Alexander Astin in the 1990s tried to get at *student involvement*, including topics such as *flow*. George Kuh extended this to *engagement*, with quantitative measures that can be compared across time and institutions and individuals, with the goal of increasing academic and institutional involvement or engagement in order to improve graduation rates.

By nature, humans are learners and doers. We are born needing and able to learn in a variety of ways,[26] and continue from birth to death to absorb new skills, information, concepts, and practices. People often do so avidly (consider the popularity of TED talks, Great Courses lectures, *NOVA*, or Wikipedia), spending resources to attend classes, picking up new interests and hobbies. We learn to work at new jobs,[27] master popular songs, write novels and poetry and fan fiction. The joy and engagement found in these pursuits contrasts instructively with the resistance and frustration often observed in the kind of learning forced upon students in schools.[28] In *Why Don't Students Like School?* Daniel Willingham shows how the cognitive practices common in academia do not match our innate patterns of thought, while Howard Gardner explains why human thought sticks to its own patterns of the "unschooled mind" no matter how much schools attempt to change it.[29]

But humans are not all "mind." We know that sociality is central to human nature.

The extension of childhood throughout the world beginning in the twentieth century, with most activities replaced by compulsory schooling, has meant that children and youth spend much of their daytime hours doing activities for the sake of school itself. Child labor is abhorred. Children and youth are, ideally, to be protected from the need to make a living,[30] though clearly this is possible only for students of a certain economic class—the class largely represented in my research. But even such students often chafe at their lack of consequentiality.

In many societies at very young ages people are given real, substantial responsibility for contributing to the well-being and needs of their families and communities.[31] Work is seen as necessary, not an evil to avoid. Even in industrial society, many youth enjoy work and in fact prefer it to school.[32] When we observe how people learn, and the forms of engagement that accompany "real-life" learning, we find substantial contrasts in every dimension with what is seen in schooling.[33] Every institution of education possesses cognitive goals. But in their role as total institutions, not only boarding schools but also ordinary high schools and most colleges, especially for the advantaged, offer a varying assortment of extracurricular, or co-curricular, activities. High schools emphasize athletics, some argue, because without *something* compelling them, many students would simply leave.[34]

Analyzing the Academic/Nonacademic Dichotomy

While dichotomies can exaggerate, in Table 6.1 I schematize folk understanding of the distinction between "academic" and "nonacademic"—drawn

TABLE 6.1   Academic and Nonacademic Activities

Curricular, Academic	Extracurricular, Co-curricular, Nonacademic
Teacher-centered	Student-driven
Cognitive	Embodied, multimodal
Assessed	Consequential
Predetermined	(Spontaneous?)
Serious	Fun?
Individual	Social?
Extrinsic rewards*	Intrinsic rewards
Official	Unofficial
Central	"Extra"
Scheduled, disciplined	Free time
Knowing that	Knowing that, knowing how
Uniform	Uneven (social capital, individual choice, talent, etc.)

* Many co-curricular activities have both intrinsic and extrinsic rewards. Think of Division I football.

by college faculty as much as anyone. "Nonacademic" may include a range of activities, from leisure to extracurricular to employment, though employment has many complicated connections to academic values.

We could look at nonacademic activities in terms of (1) engagement, measured in time, energy, effort, self-bestowal, sincerity; (2) motivation; (3) affective response; (4) learning; and (5) value or meaning. Here I consider the first three topics only, aiming to grasp differences that might be recruited into educating young adults—or any humans.

Hypotheses

As I zoomed out, as it were, to look at the broader goals of early adulthood and reached a deeper understanding of motivation and mastery, my attitude changed about the enormous amounts of time and energy students spent on nonacademic pursuits. Even though some of the motives for nonacademic activities were extrinsic—such as the strategic focus on résumé building—I wondered if learning about these activities could give insight into things that truly absorb students' attention. I hypothesized that many students value and are engaged more in their nonacademic activities than in their academic activities because the activities (1) are embodied (modality); (2) are social; (3) involve "play" (i.e., they are fun); (4) are freely chosen; (5) include direct real-life consequences, effects, and rewards; (6) require responsibility; and (7) treat students more like adults. Though these questions ran parallel to the investigation of "student engagement" in the academic side of college,[35] I was not concerned about the effects of extracurricular engagement on academic achievement; rather I wanted to enter an entirely different universe where learning, growth, and change occur—driven by students' own passions.

Methods

For this small study I asked two undergraduate researchers to conduct thirty-six peer interviews in spring 2013. With their help I also administered an anonymous survey taken by nearly two hundred current or recent college students (within three years of graduation). We posted it on Facebook and emailed it to family, friends, and acquaintances, who circulated it to their contacts and networks. As a convenience sample it is not representative, but it does include students from diverse backgrounds and with varying experiences. The students skew white, midwestern, and Catholic. Most (91.2 percent) attended universities—48.5 percent private, 25.7 percent each public and religious. Many of their universities were either highly selective (58.1 percent), accepting fewer than one-fourth of applicants, or selective (20.6 percent), accepting about one-fourth. The respondents were 69.1 percent female—greater than the average female population in higher education of 57 percent. They represented all years of school; one student had left without graduating. Their majors were in every field, but most were strong students: 53.7 percent had grade point averages (GPAs) of 3.6 to 4.0, and 38.2 percent of 3.1 to 3.5. Only 7.4 percent had GPAs below 3.0; one student had a GPA below 2.0. They reported themselves as upper class (10.9 percent), upper-middle class (48.2 percent), middle class (29.2 percent), working class (6.6 percent), and struggling (5.1 percent).

Surveys can provide overviews of topics; interviews deepen understanding. Notre Dame students are not representative even of private, highly selective residential colleges; they may exhibit a greater degree of sociality than students at many other schools. They are often achievement- and performance-oriented.[36] The selectivity involved is social, cultural, and economic. As Shamus Rahman Khan points out,[37] building on Pierre Bourdieu,[38] the sense of privilege is circular: those from such backgrounds wear their knowledge easily, in turn being invited into the next bastions of privilege—while claiming a meritocratic organizing principle open to all. The groups represented then believe that they *as individuals* have earned their place through hard work and native ability rather than recognizing either luck or the scaffolding afforded by their family background. And while these students cannot possibly represent all college students, there is a certain pure logic revealed by "studying up."[39] If students at even the most desirable institutions, with the (perhaps) best facilities and greatest concentration of knowledge, prefer nonacademic to academic pursuits, this has implications for the entire system.

I should reiterate that I am not assessing the efficacy of these activities for learning skills or information nor their contribution to academic engagement; I am concerned with attitudes toward them and subjective reports. Education by definition requires the student to bring subjectivity along; without it, nothing could be accomplished to change the person.

Findings

The surveys and peer interviews yielded information about the amount of time and energy students invest in nonacademic activities as well as their perception of the value of that devotion. They discussed their reasons for engaging in their activities and made predictions about their future memories of current activities. Intriguing contrasts emerged between nonacademic and academic pursuits.

Time and Engagement   On the 185 survey responses to the question about how they apportioned their time, 2.7 percent of respondents said they had no outside activities, half spent 75 percent of their time on academics, 36 percent spent equal amounts of time on academics and outside activities, and 12 percent spent three-quarters of their time on outside activities. Academic activities—including attending class—occupied a mean of twenty-one to twenty-five hours, with classes accounting for about half that time. But 9 percent spent more than forty-one hours a week on school, and 12 percent spent thirty-six to forty hours. This certainly does not suggest an overall picture of students "blowing off" the school side of school; some students *are* academically oriented.

When asked about nonacademic organized activities, such as clubs, dorm activities, athletics, and service, the most common response (29.5 percent) was that students spent zero to ten hours a week on them. But the time spent varied greatly: 22.1 percent, eleven to fifteen hours; 15.3 percent, sixteen to twenty hours; 12.1 percent, twenty-one to twenty-five hours; 10 percent, twenty-six to thirty hours; 4.7 percent, thirty-one to thirty-five hours; 1.6 percent, thirty-six to forty hours; and 4.7 percent, more than forty-one hours. Most commonly students participated regularly in two (34.4 percent) or three (28.0 percent) activities, but some went beyond this, reporting four activities (13.2 percent), five activities (7.4 percent), six activities (2.1 percent), and seven or more activities (2.1 percent).

Students also reported on their motivations for participating; they could choose more than one, as seen in Table 6.2.

These students reported an enormous variety of *primary* activities, as listed in Table 6.3, and they liked many overlapping aspects. (This is spelled out in Table 6.4.) They nonetheless disliked some aspects, but far

TABLE 6.2   Reported Motivation for Extracurricular Activities

Fun	86.6 %
Friends	82.9
Importance of activity/believe in its mission and value	65.2
Community	61.0
Résumé building	57.8
Physical outlet	47.6
Skill building	39.0
Like the sense of responsibility	29.4
Other	1.6

TABLE 6.3   Primary Nonacademic Activity

Music, theater, dance, literature, arts	18.9 %
Club athletics	18.2
Marching band	14.9
Academic or intellectual	12.8
Dorm activities	12.2
Service or philanthropy	12.2
Religious	6.1
Student government	6.1
Political	4.7
Professional or business	4.1
Ethnic or national organization	3.4
Sorority or fraternity	3.4
Varsity athletics	3.4
Film, radio, television, or other media	2.7
Gender or sexuality organization	2.7
Newspaper, yearbook, other publication	2.7
Health	2.0
Military	1.4

Other: Zumba, Take Back the Night March, outdoors, exercising independently, student manager of varsity football team, golf

fewer than they liked. Five of the 125 who answered the question took the trouble to note that they disliked nothing at all.

Enthusiasm abounded. In answering a question about whether they expected to remember this activity in ten or twenty years, almost all thought they would: 86 percent said absolutely, 12.0 percent said probably, and

TABLE 6.4   Positive Aspects of Principal Nonacademic Activity

It's fun	86.6 %
It's meaningful	65.8
I like seeing people I like	62.4
The results are rewarding	60.4
It's a break from studying	60.4
It's a good workout	34.9
There are nice perks	34.9
I like keeping in shape	31.5
I like helping people	24.8
I like winning	16.1
I like getting attention	13.4
It will help with networking for jobs	12.1
Other	4.0

only 2.0 percent said probably not. What stood out for them was people (87.2 percent), interest (62.4 percent), a sense of accomplishment (55.7 percent), and prestige (23.5 percent).

Many (56.7 percent) felt that their own contribution was moderate, though some (29.3 percent) considered it substantial, and a minority (12.7 percent) characterized their contribution as negligible. Most believed that they had learned "skills" through their principal activity: either many skills (52.8 percent), some (31.5 percent), or maybe a few (11.1 percent); only 6.5 percent thought they had learned no skills as a result of the activity.

Sociality   Given our human need for interaction, many students at all levels are drawn to the social dimensions of extracurricular activities. (This varies by individual but also by campus. Notre Dame is an intensely social place.) A notable example comes from Allie, who is especially active as president of her "hall" (dorm). She says:

> I place a lot of importance on my schoolwork, like, I'm pretty dedicated to that, but I wouldn't say that's the most important thing. It's more like social interactions, like being with my friends, and then like especially with girls in the hall. . . . There are so many wonderful people at this school and I want to get to know as many of them as I can.

One student, Brad, was president of his dorm and of a club sport, possibly planning to go to medical school. He was pleased at the time management skills he had learned and emphasized that what he'd learned in college had much more to do with "dealing with people" as a "leader" than with classes or academic subjects.

Extrinsic and Intrinsic Motivation: Résumés, "Real" Outcomes, and Genuine Responsibility   In addition to the social aspects, another prominent source of satisfaction had to do with the real-life consequences of the activities.

Most of schooling, at every level, is essentially an investment in the future. Few of its products are real. Students are motivated to undertake activities because they will get something else that they want: credit, a grade, a requirement checked off, a credential, eventually a job, and somewhere down the road, satisfaction. The "banking model" explains this process in part; this is extrinsic motivation par excellence.[40] Furthermore, the valuing of school over work means that students are rarely given genuine responsibility. That will follow the completion of school. Their responsibility is only for classes.

The only extrinsic motivation listed in Table 6.2 is résumé building. About 58 percent of respondents acknowledged this as an important dimension of their activity, but other motivations dominated.

Ivy, a business major, was explicit. In addition to the time-consuming but nearly required business club, which at its peak absorbs full days of her time, she worked in the ad department of the student newspaper, originally because she hoped to meet new people, make a little money, and build her résumé. Because the ad department is open only during business hours, whereas most of the intense editorial work—the bonding time— happens late at night, she was a bit disappointed. Asked if she would stay with it, she answered:

> Yeah, I think so. Like, I like the work, and it's good for . . . like when I'm interviewing for jobs, because you're doing something like outside of school. . . . They want really hard workers, so like, if you can get like an ideal candidate, 4.0, working to pay off loans and stuff, then that's like what they like. . . . The skills I've learned there, and like having to contact new people, and like do customer service stuff in, like, investment banking . . .

it's good for me to talk about in interviews. . . . That's one plus, one résumé builder [laughs].

Apart from the extrinsic rewards, most of the nonacademic activities in which students are most engaged, however, could be considered "real." That is, they have effects on the world, now. Students themselves have responsibility, and results are immediately evident. Even though Ivy did the newspaper job for the sake of her résumé, if people made mistakes—for example, if the paper had to run an ad twice because it was done wrong the first time—it cost real money.

Table 6.5 shows responses to a question about who was in charge of the activity. While only some students claimed to have had the greatest responsibility, most were satisfied with the quality of the relations, as seen in Table 6.6.

Like Brad, Arnie considers "time management" the most important thing in college. He spends fifteen to twenty hours a week on his involvement in dormitory government (president of dorm), intramural sports, Student Union Board (SUB), tutoring student-athletes, and (volunteer)

TABLE 6.5 Principal Person in Charge of Extracurricular Activity

Other students	50.3 %
Faculty member	19.5
You	8.1
Coach	6.0
Staff member	6.0
Community member	4.0
Other adult(s)	2.7
Other: Other students for 3 years, me for 1; faculty directors, student drum major, and section leaders; a variety of adult and student staff	2.7
Religious individual	0.7

TABLE 6.6 Relationship between Respondent and People in Charge of Extracurricular Activity

Equal	53.4 %
Unequal and nurturing	38.4
Unequal	6.2
Unequal and combative	2.1

science research, with his position as dorm president dominating. He likes SUB because

> our students actually run everything, it's not something like where we just tell administration, like, "Hey, can you get this to happen?" I mean, yeah, we have some guy who, like, submits a contract to like an artist or whatever, but like ninety percent of the work is all students, like ideas from students, or, you know, like work from students, like all the art SUB puts out is from kids in SUB, all the like, working . . . at movies and events is just students volunteering their time to, like, try to make like campus more fun for other kids, which I think is just like a good mission, . . . a good goal to have. It's a good purpose.

Because the activities are generated by students for students, he is compelled to do the work well.

Sometimes the relative contrast between classes and outside activities is ironic, as when a student who had successfully founded a nonprofit foundation with chapters in many states and on many campuses was warned by a professor to focus on school so she could get a job after graduation—perhaps doing the kind of thing she was already doing. Molly explains why the organization absorbs more of her time than schoolwork. The outcomes are real, not hypothetical:

> Just 'cause it's . . . like realistic results, actually helping people, right now, where it's like schoolwork, I'm just like "sure like I need to do this." This sounds bad, but like I just don't see why I should do my accounting homework before I make this call to [take care of a person through my club], like it just doesn't work out that way in my mind unfortunately, so that's why the time is so different. . . . My parents, definitely they've questioned [spending my time like that] 'cause obviously I need to graduate from here to have legitimacy in my life. . . . I was talking to [one of the administrators in the business school] about [my nonprofit] stuff. He was just like, "Hey, well, don't spend all your time on this, like you don't want to fail out of business school."

Students actually operating organizations are likely to find frustrating the unreal and hypothetical introduction to such activities, as found in classes. Not only do people "learn by doing," but also learning without doing can be an obstacle.

Flow   Psychologist Mihaly Csikszentmihalyi's notion of "flow" refers to the experience of being so absorbed in an activity that you do not worry about the time. You are involved for intrinsic reasons, and satisfaction is the result—even when the work is hard. Flow contrasts with pleasure, but it can contribute to happiness.[41] It also contributes to learning. Flow generally results more from chosen activities, though it can also come from required ones when certain things align. Ryan is a typically busy student, spending fifteen to twenty hours a week on his position on a club athletic team, but atypical in his admitted acceptance of and respect for authority and the hierarchy of bosses and coaches, in (Catholic) church and in his activities. He also admits that he is an introvert. He recalls an unusual moment of "flow" that occurred while he was working with one other person: "Freshman year with this engineering project, me and this guy had great synergy, like we literally just got together, like one night we got together and we wrote this really cool thing, like we were just sittin'—five hours went by like that. It was a really neat project." Students with what Mary Grigsby terms an "academic" orientation,[42] like many faculty, may find flow in academic pursuits, but many students report feeling it in their other activities.

In my survey I asked about "flow." Students reported that in engaging in their activity they "lost track of time" (49.7 percent) or sometimes did (48.3 percent). Only 2.0 percent watch the clock the whole time, and nobody reported resenting every minute. Given that they basically participate freely in these activities, it should not be surprising that they enjoy them.

Chrissy, who has a central role in a sport she played in high school but vowed to avoid in college, sometimes resents practice but loves the races. "There's times where it's like pulling rocks and you're like, 'Can this race be over!' but . . . I've never felt that during . . . an actual race. Like, I felt that during . . . practice, like 'Can this be over?' like, but I've never [felt it racing]." Given the zest many students reveal about the nonacademic side of their lives, it is worth noting that they are aware of the contrast with the academic side.

Comparisons with School   Some students explicitly compared their nonacademic life with their academics. Arnie, for instance, hopes to go to medical school, or at least get "a really good job right out of college." He builds his résumé and attends to his GPA, but not purely.

If I want to do . . . either of those things, I have to have a pretty solid résumé and a good GPA. And also, I enjoy a lot of the stuff I do. Like, kids often-times say they like hate school, and I actually like learning, some of the stuff I learn [laughs], like, not necessarily chemistry, but like, I like my account-ing class, even though I don't like my actual philosophy class, I like a lot of the stuff we read, and I like doing stuff for hall government, I like going to, like, interhall sports or like intramurals too, that's the big thing, is like, en-joyment. So . . . if you enjoy what you're doing too, it definitely helps with like the purpose part. It takes some stress off of you too, I think. . . . I don't think college should just be about the education. I mean, you're learning about life, not just a topic. So like, I think it's important that you get in-volved in, like, as much as you can 'cause you'll meet more people. . . . Learn-ing about people is more important than learning about a thing, I think, and that's one of the reasons, one of the main reasons I do it. And I just think it's important to have a bunch of different people who I can call a friend.

Enjoyment helps make the activity sustainable, and the social part of it contributes to learning.

Many students are thoughtful about their own learning and even con-sider how it is assessed. Lee began devoting himself, three times a week at least, during his senior year to the martial art of Taekwondo.

It's just fun to see kind of your own progress because it's physical, you know, it's like tangible progress . . . because each time you test and get a new belt and it's like "Yes! I earned it, I hope!" [laughs]. . . . There's like a test every so often and like you have to go to it and you have to know forms up to a cer-tain level and like you have to be able to do things like reasonably well. . . . It's pretty much all the same kicks and punches but it's like how well you execute them . . . and like our master will say like, "There's no such thing as a perfect kick, like you will never kick perfectly." . . . I feel like, like in school . . . like you get a one hundred if you . . . know everything, whereas this is kind of like you kick kind of above this line and you get the belt, so it's like as long as you're making progress . . . It's a really nice backdrop to learning because it doesn't pressure you to be perfect and you, you can make mistakes and it's okay and like . . . you'll try again and it's not like a big deal.

Lee understands the artificiality of school assessment, in which perfection is possible, but he appreciates the reward for progress in his martial art, and that mistakes are not punished.

Chrissy is the most explicit in weighing classes against everything else: "Sometimes like when I am in class obviously I just don't want to be in class so I'll think like, 'Oh, let me think about what it would be like on the quad this afternoon, hanging out there,' or like in the winter, 'Oh, let's go sledding tonight or have a snowball fight.'" Asked what she thinks she will remember about college, she does not falter:

> My friends. I know for sure there are certain people I will definitely be in contact with, like guaranteed, not a question . . . so I think just those experiences we shared together, and I think the knowledge I've gained from the conversations that we've had. . . . I feel like that's what I'll remember most, like, the friendships.

"Do you think you'll remember any classes?" she was asked.

> Honestly, like, not first semester, actually I really love my philo class, that was great. . . . I don't think I'll remember exactly what I learned but I'll remember that it was great. . . . This semester—I'm trying to think. I'm not really in anything super-memorable but I am doing all my prereqs, so it's not very . . . it's just stuff I had to do, I guess.

Finally she lets loose with her feelings:

> Actually, this is probably awful and you don't want to hear this but I actually hate school. . . . Okay, actually hate it like it makes me miserable. . . . I love learning! I love learning, I hate school. . . . So—but this sounds really awful because I want to be a teacher. Is that, is that the worst? [The interviewer comments, "*Oh my gosh,* that is the most ironic thing I've ever heard."] Because I feel like I can change the way school is for people. . . . Like I hate being told what to learn. I like being led in the direction to learn, you know, so I feel like there's too many teachers that lecture and teach you what to learn. They force-feed you your information: lecture, quiz, test, done. I feel like you need to develop the understanding of your material or like your knowledge yourself. You need to . . . come to it in your own way and I feel like as a teacher I could help people do that.

If only.

Affective Responses and Efficacious Learning   Many of the students interviewed offered, unsolicited, that they liked learning and found school an
obstacle. Contemporary cognitive science research supports what teachers
know: that emotion influences even the purely cognitive kind of learning
prescribed in conventional schools.[43]

In comparing their "best moments," 45.1 percent found them more in
their nonacademic activity, and 29.6 percent found them in both their activity and academic pursuits; 25.4 percent did find them in academic activities. Students commented variously that they were in school to focus on
academics, or that they found activities more meaningful, or they enjoyed
the challenges of classes, or they liked the real-world nature of activities.

There were some negative aspects to their activity, especially the time
required and friction among participants (see Table 6.7). But when asked
about their "worst moments" in college, 71.8 percent responded that they
occurred in class or in academic pursuits. Some, 13.4 percent, found them
in both, and 14.8 percent found them in the activity.

TABLE 6.7   Negative Aspects of Principal Nonacademic Activity

Time commitment	48.0 %
Friction among participants	38.4
Cost	16.8
Difficulty	16.8
Doesn't really accomplish anything	12.0
Not successful	3.2
Boring	1.6
Other	8.8

Fun, Play, Happiness, and Learning

In a guest lecture in a first-year anthropology class, I conducted a
brief exercise asking why the students were in college. After jobs,
money, and careers, a number of them listed "fun" as a compelling
motivation. Instead of dismissing this as frivolous and a distraction

from the central purpose of turning out workers, I have begun to attend to it as one of the principal aspects of our humanity. Students like play—as do all people, as Google knows, with its attempt to introduce fun into the daily activities on its corporate campus.[44] Play not only fosters productivity and creativity but also makes life more meaningful.[45] And it helps learning. Gregory Bateson decades ago asked what the function of play is.[46] Answers remain unclear, just as the purpose of sleep is unclear. All we know is that without sleep, and without play, the human spirit withers. And at the very least, we know a withered spirit cannot learn.

Discussion and Implications

What I found from my 2013 study of nonacademic engagement bears out many of my initial hypotheses. When reflecting on their activities, students overwhelmingly report that what matters, what is memorable, and what they enjoy are the people with whom they engage. They sometimes note that the outcomes are significant, such as when they help someone, or that they like the physical activity, such as with intramural athletics. Overwhelmingly they report more negative aspects to classes and more positive experiences with their activities. Many students explicitly, spontaneously contrast academic and nonacademic learning. And while I did not measure the "efficacy" or "outcomes" of their experiences, we know that many college students are willing to throw themselves into time-consuming and demanding activities, and in the process may learn a wide range of things. In the increasingly important "co-curriculum," not only do students master complex "leadership" and "team-building" skills for their résumés, but also they enjoy them. The structures of authority and responsibility, the absorption, the feeling of satisfaction, the voluntary enlisting combine to make these aspects of the college experience valuable.

The implications for academic learning are clear: the features that promote engagement, motivation, and positive affective response—which in turn promote learning—are present in large amounts in nonacademic, voluntary activities and largely absent, or perceived by students as being absent, in academic activities. The enforced compulsory and disciplined nature of much academic activity is at odds with student—I daresay human—inclinations. Understanding students' response to the work/play and compulsory/voluntary dichotomies (among others) helps explain the apparent lack of engagement with the academic side of college.

This sampling of voices shows why so many nonacademic activities are enticing and absorbing. Students are not isolated, disembodied minds; they have significant needs as embodied social beings. Humans seek, and find, meaning somehow. It is up to faculty to see that they find it in their classes, too.

But do we need college, tuition, and credits for all this?

The next section of the book examines the mismatch between *schooling* and *learning*.

Part III

How and Why Humans Learn

Explaining the Mismatch

> The drive to learn in humans is something so strong, so defining of human
> nature according to anthropologists, that it should still amaze us as truly
> remarkable that we have been able to design a social institution that can
> teach children to fail at learning.
>
> Ruth Paradise, "What's Different about Learning in Schools
> as Compared to Family and Community Settings?"

As I have shown so far, many people see a lot wrong with college and find it frustrating.

Beyond that, there are so many goals that it is hard to imagine how any single institution or set of practices could possibly satisfy all of them. Some are contradictory.

I have also shown some of the odd features of formal schooling in general and of college specifically. I went into depth about two phenomena that exemplify this strangeness: students' fixation on that contradiction-filled and diverting entity, *grades*, which looms so large, and their strong preferences in traditional colleges for the nonacademic side of their lives.

This section of the book reveals the broader context for the mismatch between *learning*, which students may love, and *schooling*, which many students hate. The reasons lie in several aspects of human nature, including the need for a long period of learning and dependence, our innate curiosity, the depth of emotional complexity, our nature as social beings, the fact that we are not just minds but bodies, the many ways humans learn, and how we decide what we want or need to do. Only when everything aligns can we find the well-being that is surely everyone's goal and that leads to successful outcomes of the process.

The rarity of this alignment explains why so many humans are so miserable in school and learn so little. The combination of misery and lack of learning means that the goals of schooling, of college, can never quite be met.

For this reason, unless college changes fundamentally, we are doomed to keep hearing all the complaints set out at the beginning of this book.

7

Beyond Cognition and Abstraction

Notes on Human Nature and Development

> Humans are born with a lot of development to do outside the womb.
>
> John Bock, "An Evolutionary Perspective
> on Learning in Social, Cultural, and
> Ecological Context"

Students, we've seen, may simultaneously love learning and hate school. In large numbers they may try to skate through classes, focused only on grades, and spend their considerable energies outside them. This makes quite a lot of sense, at least if we look at the broadest context of who humans *are* and what we are like as a species. If the school side of college mostly focuses on individual cognition and abstraction, a competitive game to endure, this is completely at odds with all that we know about us: we are born needing to learn, and we do it in ways that benefit from our intertwined emotional and physical being. In the words of an essay titled "We Feel, Therefore We Learn":

> Our brains still bear evidence of their original purpose: to manage our bodies and minds in the service of living, and living happily, in the world with other people. . . . [L]earning, in the complex sense in which it happens in schools or the real world, is not a rational or disembodied process; neither is it a lonely one.[1]

Humans Are Immature Capable Curious Emotional Social Animals

If my field has staked its principal claim on detailing human variation, then how can anyone suggest that there is such a thing as *human nature*? Scholars argue about whether it is more important to identify commonalities or differences. Anthropologist Stephen Levinson argues that the really interesting thing about humans is our variation, in contrast to linguist Noam Chomsky, who believes that it is the sameness that matters.

Anthropology and Psychology: It's Complicated

You may wonder why an anthropologist, not a psychologist, is writing about growing up. After all, doesn't the field of psychology pretty much own the topic of *human development*?

You may think so, but in fact anthropologists have been investigating this subject for a century at least. The fields twist and twine, sometimes more kindred and sometimes less. *Cultural psychology* and *psychological anthropology* have formed at the intersection, with a lot of the same foundations but slightly different aims. I have read a huge amount of psychological research, and I admire and rely on it.

What's important, though, is that we often use different *methods*.

Psychologists devise clever experiments to hold everything constant except one variable, in order to illuminate causes and reasons.

Anthropologists tend to observe people in the course of their everyday lives. It's a lot messier. We tend to avoid claiming that we *prove* anything. In answer to questions about "Why do the X do Y?" our default answer is "It's complicated" and the questioner moves on. But we believe that the artificiality of laboratory settings often changes the entire set of behaviors.

We also have a different *scope*. Psychologists tend to be talking about contemporary people in industrialized, developed countries. So common is that focus, though usually not noticed, that the authors of one paper termed the subjects of psychological experiments

WEIRD: Western, Educated, Industrialized, Rich, and Democratic.[2] This is one of the most important behavioral science papers written in a decade. The lead author, Joseph Henrich, you won't be surprised to learn, is an anthropologist who has done fieldwork.

Anthropologists tend to collect a lot of examples from, as we like to say, "across time and space." That way, we can get a sense of whether what we're seeing is unique to a single group (and that's important, too) or if it is the general way things work.

We also consider our biological place within the animal kingdom and what we know of our evolutionary endowment.

So anyone generalizing about *human development* needs a big-picture idea of what it is to be human. And that's the scope of anthropology.

It seems that everyone everywhere, not only philosophers and theologians (though not recently cultural anthropologists), has written on this question.[3] As with any topic, the answer depends on your goals and framework. From the perspective of comparing humans to, say, earthworms, it is enough to point out our general anatomy, social organization, cognitive capacity, and so forth. But if we are trying to figure out which language uses clicks and which one uses fortis consonants, we will need to be precise and detailed. The level of detail depends on the question.

Work on human universals has tended to be somewhat vague. *Humans have language, live in societies, and have marriage and verbs. On average, males are larger than females within any given "population." People tend to like their own kind of people more than others.*[4] In venturing some ideas about human nature, gingerly stepping around this minefield, I hope to find a safe inch or two where I can stand. I'm being really cautious: these are only notes.

I'm talking about just the aspects of humanity, maybe not often mentioned, that are relevant to schooling in general and to college in particular. These are things that we really need to keep in mind as we attempt to make education worthwhile, things that have often been factored out. Their absence can help explain students' dislike of and failure to engage in school.

I. Immature but Capable

One of the first things to note is how immature humans are at birth, biologically speaking. The very evolution of the phase of childhood—costly and dangerous—is a burning research question.[5] The risk of having defenseless immature beings needing care from and protection by others, diverting attention and energy from those others' caring for themselves, seems to be balanced by benefits that include greater complexity, leading to increased survival.

Immature and Needing to Growing Up

Primatologists and others interested in evolution and animal behavior have written extensively about learning, and even about whether "teaching" in some form exists in other animals, perhaps as an evolutionary, adaptive advantage. That depends on how "teaching" is defined, and whether it must be intentional.[6]

In the evolutionary context, I have learned, all species balance two mandates: the need to reproduce and the need to grow. Biologists distinguish organisms that are born or hatched nearly ready to move on their own—the *precocial* species. Others, like humans and many other mammals and birds, are born quite immature, and require a long period of growth prior to reproduction. These are the *altricial* organisms. Humans are born helpless, defenseless. Unlike other mammals, we do not possess the ability to survive on our own at birth.[7] Horses can stand the day they are born; humans cannot survive on our own until we are approximately five or six years old. But along with this helplessness comes the fact that children are born to learn. Since we have few inborn instincts, we have both the opportunity and the need for social learning—which is enormous.[8]

Another trade-off involving human immaturity leads to humans' being born with a huge amount of brain growth still to be done—more, relative to our body mass, than in any other primate species. That is partly because the size of the human brain—bigger is better—has to be balanced against the advantages of *bipedalism* (walking on two feet), which leads to a certain kind of pelvis. In childbirth, the smaller the baby's skull the better. But after childbirth, the bigger the brain relative to body mass (*encephalization*) (compared to other species') the better. So there is some advantage to, as the biological anthropologists put it, a lot of brain development continuing to occur outside the womb.[9]

Born to Learn   Anthropologists studying learning in the context of our human nature point out that one of the factors distinguishing humans and other animals is our reliance on socially transmitted knowledge. Because there is so much to learn, we are different even from most other primates; humans keep learning well after we are capable of production and reproduction.[10] Education, or what has classically been called "socialization,"[11] is central to the development of every human into a full-fledged member of her society, necessary for psychological, social, and economic well-being. Thus our social groups have an obligation to determine methods of inculcating the skills and knowledge children need to function as members of their own particular society, not only our species in general.

But after that, divergence is wild. The period of learning has no fixed end point.

Another trade-off, generally speaking, is that the simpler the society, the earlier each member can fully participate in productive work. Delaying entrance into this world permits the amassing of a wide set of skills. John Bock explains:

> Where resources are easy to extract, either because they are highly abundant or because a relatively low level of skill is necessary, children become competent at earlier ages and there is a shorter period of provisioning. Conversely, when resources are difficult to extract because of scarcity or a hazardous environment, or because high levels of skill are necessary, the period of learning is much longer, requiring consequently a longer period of provisioning. In industrial societies, it seems that this period of dependence can be quite long because the duration of skill acquisition is so extended. . . . In fact, borrowing against future returns is the most common form of financing a college education in the United States.[12]

In societies in which simple skills are generally known, children can work with their families from their very earliest years. In societies like ours, it may take two decades, at least for the most advantaged—perhaps an unnecessarily lengthy delay in terms of actual usefulness.

Every society builds on and transforms a universal biological baseline that takes into account birth, the first set of teeth, walking, elimination control, talking, the second set of teeth, puberty (secondary sex characteristics, menarche), fertility, childbirth, loss of fertility (for women, and sometimes for men), senescence (sometimes), and death. Yet beliefs and practices vary about each of these milestones, which may or may not be recognized, along with diverse beliefs and rituals regarding pregnancy and birth, family arrangements, expectations about infants' and toddlers' abilities, responsibility for minding the young, and children's activities. Societies vary in the phases they mark, or even in whether the phases are abruptly or gradually noted. Childhood can begin prior to birth, as in contemporary American "pro-life" discourses about abortion killing "children." It can be regarded as beginning only months or even years following birth, as personhood is delayed (relative to a North American standard) in some places.[13] Some amount of dependence is the norm, but beyond that, variation is also the rule.

But in the human sweep, the North American version of childhood, extending so far into the twenties and filled with schooling, is relatively peculiar. David Lancy terms it a "neontocracy," in which children are the most valued people.

The few commonalities involve an "age of reason" in middle childhood (about age seven), when children worldwide are expected to take a certain amount of responsibility and exhibit a certain amount of mastery. This coincides in the contemporary world with the beginning of school, and is recognized in religion with, for example, first communion. And some moment of puberty is often acknowledged, though the precise details differ. All societies recognize the need to shape and control sexuality and marriage. Among the more commonly noticed markers are those indicating the onset of female sexual maturity, such as menarche (the beginning of menstruation), and male sexual maturation; sometimes, but not always, they are observed with rites of passage.

Rites of Passage   In 1909 Belgian anthropologist Arnold van Gennep's work *The Rites of Passage* analyzed the principal ritual occasions on which people's identities underwent transformations (birth, puberty, marriage, and death). Van Gennep's work was especially influential in calling attention to the second set of rites, initiation rites, though he was careful to point out that puberty is not marked everywhere, and it tends to be marked differently for boys and girls.

These ceremonies may emphasize variably rites of separation, transition, or incorporation.[14] The ritual process takes time, because it has to convince everyone that some profound transformation has occurred such that the original person (a child, a single person, a newly dead relative) has been replaced by a new one, often with a different name or title (an adult, a married person, an ancestor). Work, then, is done on both the individual and collective fronts.

Rites of passage are often undertaken by cohorts, or "age-grades," groups that share an ordeal and create bonds of solidarity that may endure throughout a lifetime.[15] Sometimes the ordeals are traumatic, sometimes celebratory.

In some sense, in "modern" countries with schooling, I see the entirety of childhood as a rite of passage, a long ordeal that doesn't end until release from college and entrance into adulthood. Many have also written about formal rites of passage, which are few in contemporary U.S. society. (Getting a driver's license is pretty thin as rituals go, especially compared to the colorful months-long rituals of African tribes or Oceania.) Some write of high school or college, or alternatively graduation from high school or college, as a rite of passage.[16] Some have proposed that the problem with adolescence in the United States is the lack of meaningful rituals marking the entry into adulthood.[17]

Even within the history of American childhood, told by Joseph Kett in *Rites of Passage*, Jon Grinspan, and others, we find instability of expectation, term, age, responsibility, independence, ability, expected virtues and vices, and more, until the twentieth century, when compulsory and universal schooling was seen as the solution to many problems, among them unemployment, and resulted in assumptions of uniformity.

Historical accounts of people variously referred to as "child," "youth," or "young man" are completely disorienting to me as a middle-class twenty-first-century reader. Before the age of twenty, John Levy, a young man born in 1797 in the West Indies, made his way to Boston, having been a carpenter's apprentice and a sailor, having been robbed by pirates, forced into the British navy, from which he deserted, and having had his own crockery business on the Isle of Man. Another, William Otter, was born in Yorkshire in 1789. His father beat him and he left home on a ship bound for Greenland. Otter was shipwrecked and forced into the British navy; he also deserted. He went home only to find that his parents had left for America, so he stowed away on a ship to the Americas, where he became an apprentice—all before he was sixteen.[18]

Expectations for children and youth varied. Grinspan reports that in the nineteenth century, British travelers to the United States were shocked to find children drinking and smoking cigars at age ten, and that parents encouraged their children's "wildness."[19]

Ideas about who could do what, and when, were not absolute. Age was far from determinative, and notions of "human development" were not at all uniform.[20] Schools, colleges, and academies were often unregulated collections of people of a variety of ages who attended for unpredictable periods of time. For instance, at Exeter Academy—like many others, with sporadic and seasonal attendance—in 1812 students ranged from age ten to twenty-eight.[21] School attendance was not expected, so there was no notion of "truancy," for "the idea of truancy presupposes an anterior concept of normal attendance, and the latter could not exist as long as students drifted in and out of [district schools] at random, at virtually any hour of the morning or afternoon." In 1828 one district school included boys aged six to twenty and girls aged four to eighteen.[22]

By the late twentieth century, though, American childhood and adolescence had settled on a specific model, one with distinct and "scientific" phases, the most contentious of which was *adolescence*. Each phase is in turn associated with a type of formal education.

Coming of Age: Adolescence   For the last hundred years or so it has been customary to recognize a phase between childhood and adulthood: that of *adolescence*. Some use the term *youth*, though for others this actually points to a period following adolescence, while still others substitute the new term *emerging adults*.

Panic! Teenagers Are Coming!   Though we in the twenty-first century have completely become used to the idea of "teenagers" as a natural category, and "adolescence" as a problematic phase of life, it has not always been so.

Around the world and across time, the people we think of as teenagers have married, borne children, led armies (Joan of Arc, Alexander the

Great), and fought in wars. They have supported families and worked in factories. They make carpets and sell trinkets. They write memoirs and poetry, and create new musical forms (from Mozart to the Beatles).

In the late nineteenth and early twentieth centuries in the United States, adolescence itself became something of a "moral panic,"[23] the fear that there was something new and alarming that required treatment by the good folks of the law-abiding middle class. David Tyack calls 1890–1920 "the age of adolescence."[24] Restrictions on child labor coincided with the birth of compulsory education. It was only in about 1870 that compulsory education laws became widespread, and one of the main goals was to eliminate juvenile delinquency.

Many scholars trace the focus on adolescence to 1904, with the publication of psychologist Stanley Hall's two-volume book *Adolescence*, in which he set out some of the particular characteristics of this age and tried to explain the juvenile delinquency that seemed rampant then. Some say he "invented" adolescence. Others say he simply gave voice to a growing tendency to identify a particular phase in the life cycle. Some dismiss his contributions. In *Adolescence: An Anthropological Inquiry*, anthropologist Alice Schlegel and psychologist Herbert Barry dispute the origin myth of this period, noting widespread recognition of social adolescence, with the beginning determined, in part, biologically but the end determined socially. They detail the biological and evolutionary characteristics of adolescents: developing brains, shifting patterns of hormone secretion, emergence of secondary sex characteristics. Whether or not a given society *recognizes* this cohort as an age apart, they show why it is "natural" to do so and how this is unique among primate species, though with some nonhuman homologues, as in gorillas; it's part of being an ape.

In 1925 anthropologist Margaret Mead went to study Samoan youth to show that the supposedly universal "storm and stress" (*Sturm und Drang*) of adolescence had everything to do with particular features of U.S. society (nurture) and were neither inborn nor universal (nature).[25]

In *Teenage: The Creation of Youth Culture,* journalist Jon Savage attributes the category to its value as a cohort of *consumers* of particular products marketed to them. The World War II period gave us bobby-soxers and Frank Sinatra. The baby boomers brought rock and roll. Generation X found itself consuming MTV, and Generation Y/the Millennials have been at the forefront of Facebook, instant messaging, the iPhone, and many other devices designed for and sometimes by them.

As Nancy Lesko points out in "Denaturalizing Adolescence: The Politics of Contemporary Representations," the very notion of adolescence depends on (1) a focus on age as definitive of personhood; (2) a contrast between "regular people"—the unmarked, understood "adult," who is usually a white male—and those who are problematic; (3) the notion that the determinants of behavior and being are biological, such as hormones; and (4) a sense of a problem that must be solved, as in "What can we do with these alien creatures!?"

There is no shortage of material on adolescents, each absolute in its declarations of what this phase of life is.[26] Soldiers. Apprentices. Delinquents. Problems. Angels. Sex-obsessed. In need of control. Able to learn, not able to learn. A group apart. A group just like others.

A number of interrelated factors have created the contemporary concept of adolescence: compulsory schooling and mandated years of school, laws regarding child labor and work, and ideas of competence and responsibility. When "school is children's work" and "play is how people learn," school and learning are valued above work and play. The role of school is especially relevant in the attempt to locate the end of childhood. If the beginning of adolescence is seen as containing a biological dimension, the end has none. Whatever the label—older adolescents, youth, emerging adults—it is often believed that college is intimately connected to the creation of this period.

Becoming an Adult   "Even if it is not really a 'crisis,'" says psychologist Jeffrey Jensen Arnett, "emerging adulthood is experienced as a time of new and not always welcome responsibilities, a time of not just exhilarating independence and exploration but stress and anxiety as well."[27] Arnett has analyzed the phenomenon of, in the industrialized countries of the twenty-first century, adolescence extending well into young people's twenties, as middle-class offspring return home from college and continue their financial dependence on their parents, who are delighted to hang out and listen to boss tunes with their now appreciative children. (What Arnett calls "emerging adulthood," others call "extended adolescence"; David Brooks tried out "the Odyssey years," but it doesn't seem to have caught on.)[28] The period from about eighteen to twenty-five or so has become an in-between but very long phase of exploration of self. The sense of identity formation and exploration that Erik Erikson regarded as central to adolescence now, according to Arnett, lies rather in the older period, when "kids" are independent of parents and have few responsibilities. He argues that this period is not simply a consequence of sociological changes such as increased college attendance, later age of marriage and childbirth, and the like but rather has psychological meanings and causes.[29] The period includes faith that work will be fulfilling and meaningful but also poses dangers and frustrations (depression, suicide, aimlessness, lack of confidence, a sense of waiting for real life to start). Arnett describes emerging adults' sense of instability and their felt need to develop a "Plan" even though it changes frequently.[30] The period is also "self-focused."[31]

Arnett notes three criteria that young respondents use to evaluate their own entrance into adulthood: "(1) Accept responsibility for yourself. (2) Make independent decisions. (3) Become financially independent."[32] (Anthropologists would want to issue a reminder right about here that none of this is universal or unchanging.)

The worldwide responsibilities expected of and capabilities attributed to adolescents, youth, and emerging adults vary considerably—and these reflect only official policy, not the variations among individual viewpoints or actual behavior:

- Age of majority ("adult"): fourteen in Albania, eighteen in most countries, twenty-one in some countries.
- Age of voting: sixteen in Austria, eighteen in most countries, twenty-one in many countries, twenty-five in a few.
- Drinking age: from none specified to sixteen in some, eighteen in most, and twenty-one in a few; some distinguish beer and wine from spirits, and some forbid alcohol entirely.
- Age of candidacy for political office, usually specified for president: eighteen in some places, thirty in others, thirty-five in the United States, forty in some, and fifty in Italy, whose president is by design an elder politician.
- Draft age: seventeen or eighteen.
- Age of criminal responsibility: mostly eighteen. (The United States is the only country to imprison, without possibility of parole, children under eighteen, and some as young as thirteen.)[33]

- Legal dependence: sometimes up to sixteen or eighteen; sometimes through college; sometimes until marriage, especially for women.
- Health insurance: In the United States, beginning in 2010 youth were able to stay on their parents' health insurance up to their twenty-sixth birthday.

Youth struggle practically, economically, culturally, and psychologically to sort out their proper roles vis-à-vis their families of origin, with tension between dependence, interdependence, and independence. In many societies, such as the East Asian societies that I have spent my life studying, *independence* of adult children is a nightmarish worst-case outcome. The goal of families is to foster their children's continued involvement in their parents' lives, with children ultimately accepting financial and practical responsibility for their parents' well-being. In others, including to a great extent the United States, independence is the aim.

The lines between dependence, semi-dependence, and independence shift constantly, like a deep string on a bass vibrating visibly over a large range. There is no "natural" specific moment at which youth become— *Presto!*—capable.

Capable

In 1979 Urie Bronfenbrenner wrote:

> In the United States it is now possible for a person eighteen years of age to graduate from high school without ever having had to do a piece of work on which somebody else truly depended. If the young person goes on to college, the experience is postponed for another four years. If he goes on to graduate school, some might say the experience is postponed forever.[34]

While humans may be quite capable of carrying out actual tasks at an early age, in a complex society like that of middle-class North America, children from families that can afford it often have little genuine responsibility. They may be told that "school is your job," or they may have tasks such as babysitting or lawn-mowing, but mostly they spend their waking hours, the bulk of their days, in school and engaged in school-related activities.

Societies differ in expectations of children's responsibility. Elinor Ochs and Carolina Izquierdo argue that "task participation" has a number of consequences, including fostering awareness of others' needs.[35] ("Responsibility" can also include autonomy.) To investigate and clarify the practical and moral aspects of responsibility, they compared domestic responsibility in several different societies. I'll convey only two of their stories, striking in their contrast.

A middle-class mother in Los Angeles is preparing breakfast for her children, aged eleven, twelve, and fifteen. She is also making their lunches and has gone repeatedly to wake them up. She asks her twelve-year-old son to take out the trash. He refuses. After he goes upstairs the mother yells and asks what he's doing. He is playing. And then she says *she'll* take out the trash, though in fact she merely puts the bags near the door. Eventually he does take it out—but only after pointed battles.

In contrast, a six-year-old Matsigenka girl in the Peruvian Amazon accompanies an anthropologist and other local people on a five-day trip away from the village. She takes care of herself, carrying everything she needs for the whole time. Without being asked, she helps collect roofing materials to take back to the village and participates in the fishing that is one of the goals of the trip. She cleans up and cooks for the whole group.

As this story illustrates, in some societies, as David Lancy, Barbara Rogoff, and many others have pointed out, children's responsibility is real from the earliest years, though they also often play at increased responsibility.[36] Three-year-olds use machetes, four-year-olds tend fires, six-year-olds watch babies, seven-year-olds herd sheep, and eight-year-olds cook dinner for the family. Suzanne Gaskins observes that among Yucatec Mayans there is no pleading or bargaining with children to do tasks; adult work—family work—is seen as nonnegotiable and the children must help when they can. There is no "allowance" for chores, no sense of children doing the parents a favor. There is work, and hands are needed to do it. (This is true as well in the United States in less-advantaged families.) And yet in the United States, even twenty-year-olds are not expected to do much that is genuine work.

Responsibility Deferred   Even older adolescents in the contemporary United States, at least in school, are given limited responsibility. Their "job" is to master a curriculum designed to serve as the intellectual foundation for life. As you saw in chapter 3, hands-on work is judged inferior—for children as well as workers. The supremacy of mental and abstract work over the physical and concrete is evident in every aspect of coming of age.

The United States imposes strict limitations on teenage employment (except for agricultural work), on the theory that for the young, school is more important than work, and that too much work would interfere with school. Sometimes this makes no sense: when my daughter Hannah wanted to work at a *summer camp* when she was fifteen, we had to get permission from the school district.

Those with economic hardship—a significant portion of the population, to be sure—may work in the informal economy, and may be doing some of the same household tasks I just mentioned. But the ideal for those who can afford it is to be free of such labor.

By the time students are in college, they have heard the outside message—without by any means accepting it—that classes and studying are more important than actual work, though many students, such as the working adults I taught at the University of Colorado Denver, an urban university, are forced by circumstances to see it the other way around. Work for them is real, consequential, absorbing, while classes appear (to many) an irrelevant interruption. Those preparing for concrete work, in contrast to the ones who are free to study abstraction (and complain about it), are often pitied,[37] though the tide may be turning on that—or the pendulum swinging back.[38] A new experiment involves a six-year high school in place of the conventional four, funded by corporations, at the end of which students find a job and are awarded an associate's degree.[39] (I think that six years is *far* too long, especially since I've seen what happens in high schools, and there is no need for most of the time spent there. But we would not be able to employ all those teenagers, so we have to keep them in school.)

For teenagers without the need or expectation that college is appropriate for them, having access to a job is appealing.

One non–Notre Dame student who chose to work instead of going to college explained to my interviewer Addie that she had begun working at a local Jimmy John's sandwich shop between her sophomore and junior years of high school. By the time she was seventeen she was managing the restaurant; by eighteen she was assistant general manager.

That's probably a big part of why I decided I didn't want to go to college. 'Cause I decided that I really wanted to do that, I really enjoyed it, I liked it a lot more than school. I didn't like school at all and I really liked this, I could do this and be happy, and be successful. And I was going to do it forever. And then I finally snapped out of it last minute and realized that it wasn't what I wanted to do, and I wouldn't have a backup plan and I needed to get a degree. And so I quit there.

She enrolled at a local university, but not for long. "I like to do things and teach things on my own terms, and at my own pace, and kinda just like fill myself in and self-teach. I don't really like someone sitting there instructing me and telling me like how they see it and how they want me to learn it, and how they think it's done." So college seemed a way out of a dead-end job, but the autonomy and responsibility she had enjoyed at work were then taken away once she went back to school.

There is little agreement across cultures in terms of responsibility and expectations for the young. The variation in ages and restrictions is a reminder that human development is not entirely age-specific. For human beings, whose development from birth to adulthood is influenced not only by biology but also by culture, this path can take almost an infinity of forms. Though the general goal for society is identical—to create responsible, reproducing people with the values of their culture—variation exists even within a particular society and often for individuals.

College as Rite of Passage toward Adulthood   One thing that many have noticed in the contemporary Western (WEIRD!) world is that "childhood" has become extended, elongated, and that college plays a role in this. Yet while college may be the primary location for "growing up" for U.S. middle- and upper-middle-class adolescents, there are many other locations for doing so.

- Working-class adolescents often grow up on their own, in high school or after dropping out of high school. They support themselves financially, sometimes have children, and are not at all coddled the way traditional college students are.
- Military service in some contexts provides the kind of training and responsibility that force maturity. In Israel, for example, military

service is obligatory for all but the most observant Orthodox Jews, and Israeli Arabs. The two- or three-year service requirement follows high school, and university follows military service for the minority who decide to pursue academic higher education. The same is true for men in South Korea.

My own view is that the middle-class extension of deferred responsibility into the twenties is deleterious. Yet I am delighted, and not only as a parent, with undergraduates' attachment to their parents. The continuity in such relationships provides security, and suddenly discarding that primary relationship seems radical and unnecessary. (Though as Margaret Mead argued, fixation on the nuclear family also forces relationships to be too intense and irreplaceable.) The normative middle-class severing of familial bonds when children leave the nest—as spelled out brilliantly by Terry Castle in her controversial piece, "Don't Pick Up: Why Kids Need to Separate from Their Parents"[40]—is almost nonexistent in the ethnographic record. Hyper-individualism is not entirely liberating from the shackles of tradition; it can result in precarious solitude, or knee-jerk opposition to anything inherited. Young adults can accept the dominance of familial bonds and yet develop a genuine sense that not everything is pretend, and practice for later.

We need to figure out ways to foster simultaneously interdependence and self-reliance (knowing how to do laundry, to wake up in the morning). Options include gap years or mandatory service. Like military service, these would help sort out the "growing up" mandate from the "learning" mandate.

Adulthood must arrive. Not through trauma and expulsion from Eden, but through a constant and gradual increase in responsibility. Taking care of others—as teenage mothers or army conscripts or responsible siblings do—reduces the self-absorption that can end in narcissism. Making school the sole focus of two decades of life is unnecessary and harmful to students both as people and as learners. A much broader understanding of the mandates of growing up would help all around. Just as toddlers can tend livestock and wield knives, so can adolescents lead armies. Or they can sit and wait, their energies channeled toward taking SATs and pleasing their teachers. But should they?

II. Notes on Characteristics of the Human Animal

In our (too?) long period of dependence and learning, humans have other characteristics that in some sense must be expressed, though they are often suppressed in conventional schooling. Studies of human nature have revealed several features with significant implications for the mismatch between the learning that occurs in life and the learning that is supposed to occur in school. In this section I touch on a few of the relevant features of human nature that scientists are currently investigating. These are fragments, intended simply to whet your appetite. Each paragraph could easily be its own book.

Curious

Jaak Panksepp and Lucy Biven observe: "The ancient affective foundations of mind are essential for many higher mental activities. In short, to understand the whole mind, we must respect the ancestral forms of mind that first emerged in brain evolution."[41] In their magisterial work *The Archaeology of Mind,* they aim to show the enduring evolutionary basis of affect that permeates all of humankind. They identify seven dominant "systems," of which the most powerful is what they refer to as SEEKING-EXPECTANCY. One aspect of this system is the quest for exploration, yielding pleasure in the brain—similar to what other researchers have called the "brain reward," separate from other rewards such as food, water, sex, sleep (or grades). SEEKING is found in humans, other primates, other mammals, and birds. Exploration for its own sake is observed everywhere; curiosity may have killed the cat, but it also drove it.

Curiosity has been honored and deplored in Western thought: it drives the quest for truth and science; it is too passionate; it is restless; it is unquenchable. Thinkers from Aristotle to Hume to contemporary psychologists and cognitive scientists, educators, and artists have weighed in, arguing variably that curiosity is a vice, a virtue, or a necessity.

Societies have to confront it, one way or another, because it appears to be a human constant. And educators are usually urged to foster curiosity, which is the precursor to seeking knowledge or understanding.

But the key here is that the seeker must be the one to do the wondering; having it satisfied prior to the longing is sure to backfire—like stuffing someone with food who is not hungry.

Emotional

Though all teachers, parents, and students know that emotion is part of our experience every minute of every day, most of school is designed to be purely intellectual. Yet this is fighting an aspect of our nature that cannot really be suppressed. Panksepp calls himself an *affective neuroscientist*; Mary Helen Immordino-Yang and Antonio Damasio similarly use neuroscience to show that affect (emotion) is central to learning: "When we educators fail to appreciate the importance of students' emotions, we fail to appreciate a critical force in students' learning. One could argue, in fact, that we fail to appreciate the very reason that students learn at all."[42] They show that it is not just that we add emotion to our cognitive learning. "It is, rather, that the original purpose for which our brains evolved was to manage our physiology, to optimize our survival, and to allow us to flourish."[43]

So while it is often expected that students, in earlier levels or in college, should somehow entirely manage and repress their emotions while learning cognitively, increasingly research shows the impossibility of dissociating these two facets of humankind. Furthermore, morality depends on social and emotional factors—which, as Immordino-Yang and Damasio argue, form the foundation for the decisions that should be the outcome of education. "At its best, ethical decision making weaves together emotion, high reasoning, creativity, and social functioning, all in a cultural context."[44] (See Figure 7.1.) And without emotional direction we can't use, or "recruit," rational thought and logical reasoning.

Yet the explicit goal of much of formal education is the exclusion of everything except "reason." So when our students seek laughter, intensity, or some other aspect of emotional life in their school lives, they are simply trying to find a reason for its importance.

Evidence from brain-damaged individuals suggests that interference with emotion leads to impairment in reason. We *must* and *do* have powerful emotions at all times, whether they are called to consciousness, suppressed, or welcomed.[45] Panksepp and Biven similarly argue that "the neocortex—the source of our human intellect—is the servant of our emotional systems."[46]

Teachers should regard emotions as resources. But they are often ignored.

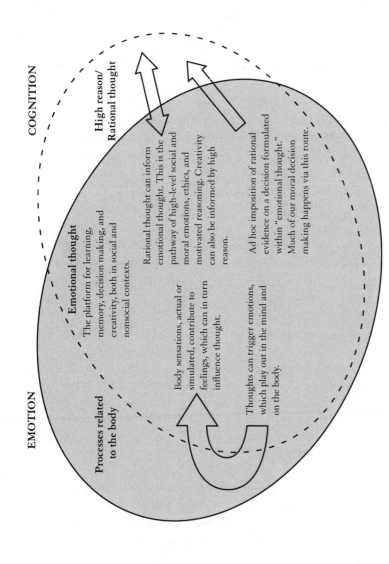

COGNITION

High reason/
Rational thought

Emotional thought

The platform for learning,
memory, decision making, and
creativity, both in social and
nonsocial contexts.

Rational thought can inform
emotional thought. This is the
pathway of high-level social and
moral emotions, ethics, and
motivated reasoning. Creativity
can also be informed by high
reason.

**Processes related
to the body**

Body sensations, actual or
simulated, contribute to
feelings, which can in turn
influence thought.

Ad hoc imposition of rational
evidence on a decision formulated
within "emotional thought."
Much of our moral decision
making happens via this route.

Thoughts can trigger emotions,
which play out in the mind and
on the body.

EMOTION

Figure 7.1 Overlap between emotion and cognition.

Source: Mary Helen Immordino-Yang and Antonio Damasio, We feel, Therefore We Learn:
The Relevance of Affective and Social Neuroscience to Education, *Mind, Brain, and
Education* 1(1): 3–10, 2007. P. 8. Used by permission of John Wiley & Sons.

Social

The nature of the human brain and the human body, the whole problem presented by evolution, shows that on our own we are unable to survive. We require long and substantial input from our social group long past early childhood. Our "adaptive niche," as the evolutionary scientists have it, is that we are *social*,[47] or as one group of researchers assert, "Humans are not just social but 'ultra-social.'"[48] (The technical problem is the *evolution* of sociality, because it challenges some Darwinian notions about our wish to protect our own genes.) We don't have claws or fur or fangs or shells. What we have is *interaction*. Language and other forms of semiosis (meaning-making) are part of that, probably the most important part, and we evolved to speak with our vocal tracts even though we risk choking because of the specific construction of the throat. Our brains are metabolically expensive, requiring a fourth of all our caloric intake (which, before cheap agriculture, was challenging to attain), but they too are worth it because we can learn specific and technical information that is socially transmitted.

What this also means, though, is that we are remarkably attuned to others, and we are primed to interact with them.[49] N. J. Enfield and Stephen Levinson call attention especially to our *intersubjectivity* and the power of *joint action*:

> Supported by uniquely human abilities, and responsive to context-specific motivations and accumulated cultural conventions, human social interaction exhibits striking properties not found elsewhere in the animal world. It involves frequent, intense, and highly structured interaction, using complex communication systems, on which the rest of culture depends for its realization. . . . What makes human interaction qualitatively distinct in the animal kingdom is that it is built on intersubjectivity, enabling a brand of joint action that is truly open-ended in goals and structure.[50]

Almost all forms of human learning rely on transmission from and with others, in meaningful ways, whether we learn by watching,[51] playing,[52] following the "chore curriculum,"[53] or serving as apprentices. Hunter-gatherers often learn in a socially shaped fashion.[54] (More on this in the next chapter.)

In contrast, in much academic life the emphasis is on the individual as central, with the individual responsible for attending class, reading, conducting experiments, doing "homework," writing, being examined. Sharing knowledge is *cheating*; using someone else's words is *plagiarism*. Yet everything about the nature of humans builds from our natural interdependence.

Animals (Embodied)

Humans may have disabilities and increasingly incorporate nonbiological components as we become hybrid *cyborgs*, but by nature we inhabit, have, or *are* bodies. We have physical needs. We are animals.

And a principal insight of evolutionary scientists is that one of the aspects of our physicality is *bipedalism*, our ability to walk on two legs.

For almost all of the time since humans diverged from the (other) apes, about 6 million years, we have been characterized by our astounding ability to *walk*. This has all kinds of consequences, including the freeing of our hands; the ability to meet, speak, and have sex face-to-face; possibly the development of the white part of our eyes (sclera) so we can observe others' gazes from a distance; problems with childbirth; and more. As anthropologists study contemporary hunter-gatherers, people whose lives most resemble the state in which humans existed for most of our history (but they are *not*, decisively not, "living fossils"), they observe people such as the Hadza foragers of northern Tanzania, who regularly walk distances from three and a half (women) to seven (men) miles daily.[55] Kim Hill, who studies both the Ache of Paraguay and the Hiwi of southwestern Venezuela, reports that the Hiwi might walk eighty to one hundred kilometers—fifty or sixty miles—just to visit another village for an hour![56]

I raise this not to say that we must live a Paleolithic life. Humans vary. There is no single agreed-upon way to be human. But it is obvious that the body must be understood and factored into our plans for our young. If we don't do it, they will!

The physical dimension of learning is often seen not as a resource but as a problem. Our embodiment is frequently denied in our everyday lives. For many in industrialized societies, we have to pay to get more exercise, while we try to see how little exercise we can get away with.[57] Yet we are made to move. We are made to live in our body/minds. We can't compartmentalize all this and expect well-being. A pill can't replace our need for loping among the trees. We have to smell things and touch things, and not just screens and keyboards or even just pages. We have to live through our bodies and textures, not just our minds. We are not the "ghosts in the machine" that Descartes tried to show us, when the independent mind was such a new discovery. All research on humans reminds us that even our minds have something to do with our brains, in turn with cells, chemicals, hormones, connections, oxygen, environmental influences, and more.

Even our genetics is influenced by our experience and context. "Nature or nurture" is not the correct way of framing the interaction. Our brains are shaped by our behavior, which is in turn shaped by our brains, in turn shaped by our environment. And everywhere we turn is body.

Learning through the Body   A lot of noise has been made about losing the knowledge of handwriting. Many lament this disappearance for aesthetic reasons, and because lack of understanding of handwriting cuts future generations off from the past. (Handwriting and printing forms do change through time. It is difficult for contemporary Americans to read the original of the Declaration of Independence, for instance.) But what is really at stake, I think, is the lack of involvement of the body.

As one who once wrote everything by hand, then typed, and then entered everything into the computer, and now composes on the computer, I know that there is a difference not only in speed but also in style that accompanies these forms of writing. The prose style of Friedrich Nietzsche famously changed when physical decline forced him to write on a typewriter beginning in 1882.[58]

When musicians or dancers or actors prepare, their aim is "getting it in the body." This is true for writing as well. One study shows that students who take notes by hand learn and remember far more than those who use laptops for the same material.[59]

The Body in School   The role of the body in learning, whether teacher-centered learning or student-centered learning, is not prominent enough—especially in college. We know definitively that people learn not through passive reception but through activity. Even in a discussion, the multisensory experience reinforces the messages. There was a fashion in second-language acquisition for a time called "Total Physical Response," which aimed to build on the physical and social and connect it with the cognitive.[60] Students were taught to associate actions with speech and deepen their understanding. Another approach in second-language teaching is to use *realia*—real objects—to make connections between what is said and what is done, recruiting the body and its powerful connections. Students often like their (well-taught) foreign language classes a lot; at their best they are filled with interaction and maybe even real physical action. Computer language classes can at best invoke a memory of the physical experience.

Bodies as Problem, Bodies as Resource   The embodied nature of humans as learners is especially noteworthy in small children. Since humans evolved to move, it takes a huge amount of effort to repress that urge. The youngest children have this channeled into games, running around, sitting in circles. In preschool they learn to control their need for excretion. In elementary school they learn to line up, to raise their hand. It is a gradual disciplining of the body, with fewer and fewer outlets as they get older.

Those who cannot successfully internalize this bodily discipline, who cannot "sit still" and focus, are provided pharmaceutical assistance. The use of medication for attention deficit (hyperactivity) disorder (AD[H]D), and the eightfold increase in diagnosis between 1980 and 2007,[61] are notorious. More than one out of every ten children in the United States has received such a diagnosis.

If we think, though, about the nature of humans, and our human evolution, it is obvious that we can restrain that nature only so much. Humans need to experience the world through *haptic* and tactile interaction. The kinesthetic dimension of learning is enormous.

Abstraction Means Absence of the Body   Just as in early levels of schooling, in higher education the body is often regarded as an impediment. The body must be fed and watered, sitting somewhere. But sitting is problematic. And now with much of our lives spent on screens, the places for physical action in daily life are fewer.

Imagine a contemporary student. Class may or may not be physical. A lot of classes post "the PowerPoints" (ugh, I regret that formulation, smuggling in assumptions about almost every class having them and their containing the packaged information that will be required for tests). In those cases, many savvy students choose to skip class. Why bother watching an inept performer read from slides? Students can stay in their pajamas and read them all in a rush the night before "the test."

When we compare this kind of imperfect performance with the top faculty chosen to present MOOCs—massive open online courses—it is no surprise that the MOOCs have some appeal.

Even a regular class could be appealing, or could be repellent. An auditorium with five hundred seats, in which the premium last-row seats are stereotypically occupied by large athletes, may offer some little professor far away at the front, probably nervous, lecturing at the class, "the PowerPoints" appearing on a screen, maybe sharp and clear but maybe fuzzy and indistinct. But there are things that could draw students: A charismatic teacher. Interesting material. Friends. Threats of points docked for lack of attendance.

An administrator reported with concern that when he stood in the back of an auditorium auditing a class, everyone's computer was filled with Facebook, YouTube, and other fun and games.

And even if an eighteen-person seminar seems a different kettle of fish (though many students at large public universities never have such a class), this does not guarantee engagement. My niece at the prestigious University of Michigan reported that even in small seminars, students are texting the whole time, despite the fact everyone can see them do it.

(In my small classes, thank goodness, students have mostly not texted. I am grateful for their politeness, though in 2015 they began to, so ubiquitous and pervasive is the sense that communication should happen everywhere and always.)

How can we wrest attention back?

With the body.

Get people standing up. Get them to shake one another's hands. Have them move furniture. Have them jump up and down to illustrate . . . anything! Surely there is a movement or a posture or a shape or something that applies in every field.

Learning in the wild—real-life learning—is always multimodal. It involves doing things with ears, eyes, and hands, and with other people. The tests are not always comparable and statistically significant, but they are real.

So if we know so much about how humans are, and how humans mature, and if we compare this with what school is like, it should not surprise us that the match is not, as it were, made in heaven.

The quintessential college situation has students without genuine responsibility, being force-fed; not allowed to let their curiosity guide them, presented with reason and logic and facts over emotion or passion, being assessed individually, and lacking any physical or practical activities. There are exceptions to each of these, but not necessarily all at once. We can aim to overcome these deficiencies by insisting on responsibility: requiring "service-learning"; allowing students to make choices or design independent projects, including theses. We can try to get students to feel passion: moral outrage, desire, admiration (for beauty, say). We can foster social interaction of any sort, or physical engagement, such as in lab courses, vocational training, taking notes, making something. But the less any of these appears in a given course, the less likely students—typical students—will find it engaging.

So a study of the nature of humans, compared to the nature of schools, begins to solve the mystery of why students don't care and why they prefer to get their learning outside school.

And not only do we know all this, but also we know a lot about how humans learn—not just in familiar classroom ways but everywhere.

8

Learning in the Wild, Learning in the Cage

We learn from the company we keep, throughout our lives, without effort, without awareness, and with no forgetting. . . . We are learning all the time—about the world and about ourselves. We learn without knowing that we are learning and we learn without effort every moment of the day.

Frank Smith, *The Book of Learning and Forgetting*

In the last chapter we saw that humans are born to learn. And whatever people may argue about the goals of college, everyone would claim that at least one of them is learning. And one of the principal complaints has to do with how *little* students learn in college "these days."

But what do we know about learning? And how does learning in school match up with learning outside school?

The knowledge required to survive as a human, naked (no fur or feathers), vulnerable, has to be learned after birth, through transmission by meaningful others and by participating in a social group. Our brains thus all contain the *capacity* for complex learning, but unlike many other species, we have few inborn, instinctive bodies of knowledge.

Furthermore, human contexts differ like mad. Anthropologists have spent the past century and a half cataloguing some of this variation. What is important to remember is that there is never a single "natural" way to be human. We learn to be members of our own groups, more or less, but it is not quite as tidy a process as that suggests.

Looking at how people learn "in the wild" (that is, outside our familiar institutions), we find learning by doing, learning through play, observation, imitation, trial and error, guided participation, and apprenticeships, in which young people or novices are assigned to an expert to learn a craft or trade.[1] What we find little of, in general, is the peculiar institution of schooling or anything resembling it.

A. S. Neill, founder of the revolutionary school Summerhill, charges that "only pedants"—those annoying people fixated on precision, rules, and academics—"claim that learning from books is education."[2] I was such a pedant, I fear, but no longer.

Until I began this project and the struggles leading up to it, I had never questioned the need for school. I had assumed that learning brought joy, and that if only students would open themselves up to school learning, they would find joy too. I had never paid much attention to the rest of the learning that occurs all around us, effortlessly or effort-fully, yet without the schooling apparatus. I was too busy concentrating on the deliberate, packaged learning that is the focus of schooling.

But, it turns out, humans learn in extremely varied ways, and I don't mean to invoke here the "auditory" versus "visual" typology that has become popular (and, finally, discredited).[3] I mean that people learn to cook, and speak languages, and ride bicycles, and pray, and recount Middle Earth arcana. People learn all about the Civil War, and they learn about their children's rare medical conditions; they learn to drive, or play guitar, or install bolts on lamps, or play *World of Warcraft* or beer pong. They learn to ski down tall mountains and to write computer programs. They do it on their own, or using YouTube videos, or from after-school lessons, or by hanging out with relatives or age-mates. They do it because it's fun, or because they have to; they learn because it satisfies their curiosity or because it helps them "get the girl." They do it because they are addicted to thrills or because they can't afford to hire somebody to teach them. They learn because it will allow them to eat. They do it without tests (often) and without someone forcing them.

Every activity we engage in—social, personal, aesthetic, pragmatic—requires learning, defined by educational psychologists as "any relatively permanent change in thought or behavior that occurs as a result of experience."[4] Yet an ethnographic look at learning in the world rarely reveals anything resembling the way classrooms function. Most people learn most of what they know without direct instruction. Teachers—and sometimes teaching—are often optional. Babies learn to walk and talk. We are born to learn—but how?

You might think professors would know something about learning. But the kind of training we get is to be scholars. Any knowledge about how people learn generally comes from apprenticeship, from our own experiences as learners, then as teachers, and sometimes as parents. Nothing systematic or academic comes our way about how people learn unless we take teaching workshops—which are usually voluntary. But I have plunged into the topic of learning, and what I found amazed me.

I. Learning in School: Abstract, Solitary, Cognitive—and for Later

"Why *don't* [students] learn what we teach them?" John Holt asks in *How Children Fail.* "The answer I have come to boils down to this: *Because* we teach them—that is, try to control the contents of their minds."[5] School learning is supposed to be abstract, independent, cognitive, predetermined, squirreled away for future use and transfer. As Daniel T. Willingham puts it in *Why Don't Students Like School*, "Abstraction is the goal of schooling."[6] And Susan Ambrose and her coauthors in *How Learning Works* state that "far transfer is, arguably, the central goal of education: we want our students to be able to apply what they learn beyond the classroom."[7]

The basic idea for required courses, at all levels of education, is this: Curriculum experts, the public, and teachers or professors get together and figure out what information and skills children or students are likely to need at some point in the future. Faculty attempt to stuff it all into their heads while they are young and expect that even though they learn it in classrooms, later they will be able to use it in "real life." (Paolo Freire famously termed this the "banking" model.) We learn algebra in high school so we can buy carpet when we are forty, one argument goes. Liberal arts colleges celebrate and advertise the "transferrable skills" such as analysis and writing that can be used in a variety of jobs.

Almost everyone assumes that schools are the best places to learn. I assumed that our students would somehow store the material they learned and find it later—even though all evidence suggests they forget most of it very quickly. It shocked me, therefore, to see what research shows.

Jean Lave, the prominent anthropologist of learning, set out to study the assumed prevalence of "transfer." Her conclusion was that it essentially never happened. Lave compared what students are supposed to be learning in school with people's actual *use* of it (math, in this case) in everyday life, not in the laboratory. Using practice theory to consider cognition as "stretched across mind, body, activity and setting,"[8] *Cognition in Practice* shows that people use a wide range of resources in accomplishing actual tasks, such as shopping for the best prices at supermarkets or figuring out how many cartons to put on a truck to send out to clients. Some tasks are incredibly involved; dairy-loading personnel, for example, had to fulfill orders accurately, when some cases contained sixteen cartons but others held thirty-two or forty-eight, and some were only partially filled. Their skill at work does not correlate with their grades in school math or with their years of schooling. And as soon as their actual knowledge is translated into school-like tests, adults often fail. Lave concludes that "everyday activity . . . is a more powerful source of socialization than intentional pedagogy."[9]

Similarly, Howard Gardner recounts a famous experiment. Students at Harvard who took a course in physics and astronomy were tested before and after the course. Almost none of them before and almost none of them after could explain the workings of the solar system. Twenty-three out of twenty-five of these students, despite excellent grades and the ability to restate the words required on tests, could not explain the reason for the earth's seasons.[10]

The uselessness of school learning is brought out in *How to Survive in Your Native Land,* James Herndon's poignant book which had me laughing and crying at the familiar absurdity and wastefulness of school. He tells of a class for the lowest of the low students: "the dumb class." Herndon—critical of the whole system in the late 1960s in the San Francisco Bay Area—used a range of creative alternative methods to try to help his eighth-graders, who couldn't add or subtract. One day he came across one of his students, the dumbest kid in the dumb class, at a bowling alley. The kid had a paying job there, keeping score for two teams, each with four people, eight scores at once, the fast-paced strikes and spares being added precisely and steadily. The kid couldn't do math worksheets, but he could do math in real life. And then it turned out a lot of the kids had paper routes, or went shopping, and kept good track of money. So Herndon tried to create math problems about bowling scores, paper routes, buying shoes. As always, they couldn't get any of it straight. The problem, Herndon concludes, is that the kids had been assigned to the dumb class by the schools, and that the real dumb class is the teachers who make ordinary life more complicated than necessary.

> What we [teachers] are supposed to do is something which, like adding, everyone knows how to do. It isn't mysterious, nor dependent on a vast and intricate knowledge of pedagogy or technology or psychological tests or rats. Is there any man or woman on earth who knows how to read who doesn't feel quite capable of teaching his own child or children to read? Doesn't every father feel confident that his boy will come into the bathroom every morning to stand around and watch while the father shaves and play number games with the father and learn about numbers and shaving at the same time? Every person not in the dumb class feels that these things are simple. Want to know about Egypt? Mother or father or older brother or uncle or someone and the kid go down to the public library and get out a book on Egypt and the kid reads it and perhaps the uncle reads it too, and while they are shaving they may talk about Egypt. But the dumb class of teachers and public educators feel that these things are very difficult, and they must keep hiring experts and devising strategies in order that they can rush these experts and strategies with their papers asking Is this right? and What's my grade?[11]

So maybe one part of the answer to why students love learning but hate school, why they appear helpless within our walls, as if every move must be approved by grade-bestowing judges, is to be found in the mistaken ideas about learning that teachers bring to school—that things are hard to learn. To improve, we need to pay much more attention to the many ways that people learn, successfully, outside school.

II. Learning outside School: Doing, Observing, Trying, Playing, Working . . . with Others

To understand the full range of human education, it is not sufficient to look at one other society, not even a hunter-gatherer society, because what is immediately apparent is that humans learn by using a range of methods.

Early anthropologists such as Margaret Mead and Meyer Fortes focused on *socialization* as a way of understanding how individuals become psychologically shaped in specific ways, emphasizing variation. Anthropologists of education such as George and Louise Spindler mined the ethnographic record, uncovering gems like the rites of passage among the Arunta (indigenous people of Australia) or Hutterites, to note that education in most human societies produces only successes—no dropouts and no failures.[12]

Some societies establish settings devoted to learning. In others, children are just expected to learn on their own. Some societies recognize that humans must be helped in their learning, though the nature of that help varies considerably.

Our most specific human capacity, that for (spoken) language, is and must be learned, though we learn it without direct instruction. (Babies have to be exposed to some *meaningful* and *consequential* use of language in social encounters; just hearing or watching television does not teach language.) For example, not until a Kaluli (Papua New Guinea) infant or toddler produces the words meaning 'mother' or 'breast' is that child addressed directly.[13] Any child born anywhere of parents from any background will learn the language to which she or he is exposed. Take a child born in China and raise her in Texas and she will speak like a Texan. The same is true the other way around. There is no *inborn* language—only the *capacity* for language. Experts argue about whether some of the specific deepest structures of language are somehow pre-loaded into the architecture of the human brain. But all agree that children learn very fast and that the way language is learned is still somewhat mysterious—but we know that it is not, mostly, *taught*. By the age of three or four, children master all the essential elements of their language—sound system, grammatical system, thousands of words, intonation, joking. And they can sort out multiple languages without difficulty, though this does sometimes slow down production for a brief period.[14]

The attention paid to language in schools involves the acquisition of a very specific version of language, the version that has the greatest prestige and is appropriate for a range of settings that differs from the home: public, institutional, and eventually professional. Schools correct aspects of speech that are especially stigmatized (*ain't*, double negatives), and teach unfamiliar vocabulary. Writing—a recent invention in the broad scope of things—is usually learned and refined in school, but the basics of spoken language are learned, without anyone knowing much about the process, at home and in the community, and have been for all the 100,000 or so years that we have been modern humans.

Families and communities teach—or are the context for learning—basic orientations to the universe. Such orientations, powerful and enduring, are physical and aesthetic, emotional and relational. Outside institutions can rarely compete with them.

The Brain Learns: Neuroplasticity

Over the last two decades or so a revolution in thinking about the brain has occurred. With the model of "hardwiring" and the brain viewed as a machine, experts formerly believed that only in childhood did anything like neurological growth occur. Evidence included the effects of strokes and brain damage, when injury to a particular location in the brain prevents restoration of specific functions. But using new techniques and asking new questions, cognitive scientists have shown how *plastic* the human brain is. It is now clear that the brain retains its plasticity, its ability to change according to the demands made of it, throughout life.[15] Even adult brains undergo *neurogenesis* when learning occurs; as long as people are learning, their brains continue to change.

The recent focus on *metacognition* aims to make the learning process conscious, though awareness is usually a stage only at the beginning of learning. Doing things over and over until they become automatic alters the way the brain manages them. Once something is deeply learned, it moves from a "conscious" to an "unconscious" part of the brain. (This is an extreme simplification.) Try explaining to your fifteen-year-old what you are doing when you drive.

So when Yo-Yo Ma plays Bach, he is not thinking about it the same way a beginning cello student is, reading each note (*A sharp, up-bow, third finger*), and when I write a paper, I am not thinking about the structure the same way a beginning writer is (*introduction, claim, support, linking sentence*). You probably don't think about the "values" of the letters (*t+h = a sound like the word* the; *the* gh *in* caught *is silent*) when you read, but a new reader of English has to.[16]

Any form of learning involves a physical, neurological, psychological *change*. This is the definition of learning.

Learning "rewires" the brain: things learned in tandem create pathways in the brain that easily work together. In *The Brain That Changes Itself*, psychiatrist Norman Doidge cites an aphorism from Carla Shatz: "Neurons that fire together wire together." And unused pathways get "pruned" to increase efficiency of connection. The synapses (places where neurons meet) become more efficient the more they are used. Many aspects of brain function rely on adjacent structures, and can reinforce (or replace, if necessary) one another. For example, vision and affect may intersect, so when people learn in a multimodal fashion, the learning is multiply reinforced. Synesthesia—when two or more of the five senses are experienced together automatically, as when someone hearing a number spoken "sees" it as a color—is an extreme example.

All of this can help us understand the successes and failures of schooling because it makes clear how many things happen all at once when people learn: emotional, biological, cognitive, sensory, interactional. Despite the goal of much of modernist education to strip everything of its complicating factors in order to be able to assess it, to sort out "inputs" and "outputs," to specify tidy "outcomes," everything we know about learning in the wild shows how powerful the combination of factors can be.

Other recent findings from neuroscience are also relevant to an anthropological understanding of learning. On a basic level, we are made to imitate.

Learning through Imitation

Humans are acutely observant of one another (we learn to notice other drivers' glances from across intersections so we can predict whether we will be cut off by a sudden left turn) and possess an innate tendency for mimicry. Joint attention arises within the first year of life; babies follow the eye gaze of those around them.[17] Infants attend to faces and imitate the expressions they see. The discovery of "mirror neurons"[18] has given a cellular foundation for what we have always known: we want to please others and tend to act like them; behavioral styles tend to converge. It is not only teenagers who aim to "ape" their social models.

Much that the young learn is unconscious imitation; explicit description and didactic narration are not needed. Humans are so attuned to one another that our "reading" of others is effortless, instantaneous, and sometimes not even available to consciousness. One neuroscientist, Marco Iacoboni, compares the innate sort of learning with the kind that is more valued: "Mirroring behaviors . . . seem implicit, automatic, and pre-reflective. Meanwhile, society is obviously built on explicit, deliberate, reflective discourse. Implicit and explicit mental processes rarely interact; indeed, they can even dissociate."[19]

Learning through Careful Observation

Suzanne Gaskins and Barbara Rogoff, among others, have been studying human development among Maya communities in the Yucatán peninsula and Guatemala for decades. Straddling the line between anthropology and psychology, they conduct fieldwork in non-laboratory settings. The Maya among whom they have worked for so long are "indigenous" (though like all people categorized this way, they have interacted with and been influenced by the dominant national society and themselves have a specific history). Both scholars challenge much of conventional educational and psychological dogma about human development.

Among the Maya, a good portion of their learning occurs without teaching, without trial and error, and without play. Young people simply watch, with what Gaskins terms "open attention."[20] That is to say, they do not appear to be fixated or focused on the activity in question, but they are aware of their entire surroundings. Native Americans such as the Apache studied by Keith Basso similarly do this, not only in childhood but well into adulthood: their eyes continually scan the horizon and the environment.[21] Richard Nisbett has also claimed that "Asians," to use an extremely broad category, pay more attention to the "ground" and "North Americans" to the "figure."[22] Gaskins and Ruth Paradise emphasize that in addition to the common understanding that children need to be integrated into activities with people who are important to them and that they have intrinsic reasons to take the initiative to learn actively, children also attend in a wide-angled and abiding way to their environments. Learning, they point out, may be an "incidental byproduct of social life."[23] In such settings children and youth are legitimately present, or engaged in "legitimate peripheral participation."[24] They have a right to be there; every day is "take your child to work day."[25]

The Maya whom Gaskins studies may watch people weave or cook or make tortillas, and then suddenly one day they can do it. The learning is *observational* but it is also *active*, if not physical. But wide-angled attention would be considered wandering in, say, a Euro-American classroom. Maya children are expected to retain their awareness of their surroundings, as they may have responsibilities—for instance, watching younger siblings—even while they are practicing a new skill or playing with a cultural script.

In contrast, North Americans often expect to be *taught* if they are to learn anything. David Lancy reports an observation he made at a Utah ski resort. Just ahead of him in line for the ski lift was a group of teenage boys, passing the time and chatting comfortably. Finally it was their turn. Despite having had the opportunity to observe dozens of other snowboarders mount the lift, they stood there completely uncertain about how to get on. Nobody had taught them, so they hadn't learned.[26]

"Learning" for those raised in school is often assumed to occur principally that way. But the report from elsewhere shows something different.

Learning by Doing, Trying, Guided Participation . . . without Teaching

Lancy has been showing for years that learning does not require teaching. "Teaching is very rare in the ethnographic record," he reports.[27] He shows how, throughout the world, people have learned without teachers. Children in villages learn from "near-peers" how to be safe in their environments, how to use machetes, and how to care for younger relatives. Adults are scarcely present—a bit like the childhood world of *Tom Sawyer.*

It is not only in the technologically "underdeveloped" world that non-instructed learning occurs. Sugata Mitra has become well known for his hole-in-the-wall experiments.[28] In a poor Indian village he installed a computer in a wall. Within a few months illiterate, non-English-speaking children had figured out how it worked. He termed this *minimally invasive education*, emphasizing that when children are curious, they work together (distributing tasks and relying on distributed knowledge) to accomplish goals, retaining what they have learned because it has included social interaction (and, I would point out, some physical manipulation). They are motivated, and given the freedom (since nobody has assigned it), to use trial and error.

With hunters and gatherers—the basic but not uniform state of humans for 99 percent of our history—children are entirely incorporated into the lives of their society. The youngest are strapped on someone's back for most of the day and observe all the events surrounding them, or they are placed in a sling and kept safely out of the way. Older children spend their time largely in mixed-age groups. There are some specialized tasks, such as butchering or cooking, and these are similarly learned through watching and being given small—and real—tasks with consequences.[29]

There are disciplinary differences in explaining learning. "Social anthropologists suggest that teaching is absent or rare in small-scale cultures, whereas developmental psychologists tend to assume that it is part of human nature."[30] Following their detailed qualitative and quantitative investigations of Aka and Bofi foragers in Central Africa, compared with farmers, Barry Hewlett and his colleagues accept that *pedagogy* is a human universal, but that it occurs much less than other forms of social learning, such as observation and imitation.[31]

Parents do engage in teaching, such as by making small (not pretend) implements for children to use; half the episodes Hewlett and his associates observed included knives or machetes. A twelve-year-old girl and an adult woman sat right next to Bonnie L. Hewlett for three weeks, patiently teaching her to make an Aka basket. They "scaffolded" her new knowledge in a pedagogically skillful way, guiding her hand and teaching her to weave, though the instruction was not verbal.[32]

So while pedagogy of some sort exists, observation and imitation are even more widespread. A good deal of the teaching is done by other children and by non-parent adults. The pedagogy observed on videotapes and by the technique of "focal following" was not principally verbal or explicit, perhaps because of respect for the autonomy of all—even young children. Most learning is at the learner's own request, and "since learning is self-motivated and directed and takes place in intimate and trusting contexts, hunter-gatherer children are generally very confident and self-assured learners."[33] How many of our students would be considered "very confident and self-assured learners"? So much of our schooling system seems designed to destroy confidence: *Am I doing this right? Is this the right answer? What's my grade?*

Barbara Rogoff reports an eleven-month-old in the Ituri Forest of Zaire entrusted with a machete and toddlers among the Fore in New Guinea using fire and knives. In some cases, but not all, adults surrounding them keep an eye on things, and surely there are mishaps. Rogoff and Patricia Greenfield report on "guided participation": experts break down weaving

(Mayan and Mexican) or tailoring (Liberian) tasks and jointly lead novices to mastery in something resembling a curriculum but with genuine outcomes. In the Orinoco delta in Venezuela, Guareños teach their children to work in a sequential and additive fashion, but through "learning by doing."[34] The basic assumption is that children are human beings with capabilities and that they are useful.

Barry Hewlett and colleagues distinguish *modes of cultural transmission* (that is, from which direction the knowledge is shared: vertical, horizontal, oblique, conformist, prestige-bias) and *processes of social learning* (teaching, emulation, imitation, collaborative learning).[35] They conclude that young children learn especially from elders and middle children from peers and near-peers, and that while some forms of deliberate "teaching" exist, these are far overshadowed by imitation and observation. Like Yucatec Mayan children, hunter-gatherers observe the world around them, and when they are ready, they have mastered skills and knowledge—all without attempting it, playing, or being coached, taught, or graded.

Learning in Shared Practice: Distributed Cognition

In the context of contemporary formal education, learning is usually assumed to be individual and cognitive. But Edwin Hutchins demonstrates convincingly that in life and in complex work, learning is also shared and social. Hutchins studied navigation on a U.S. naval ship and among Micronesian navigators in order to demonstrate that learning was not entirely or even principally explained or understood as occurring within an individual's head. Though he was trained as a cognitive anthropologist, once he began to observe learning "in the wild" rather than in the artificial conditions of the laboratory, he argued that it was necessary to include the entire context, including the other people, in which learning and action take place.

Hutchins further defines learning as "adaptive reorganization in a complex system."[36] This is important because it points out the multiple resources brought into all real-world tasks. His notion of "the relevant complex system"—the unit of analysis—is not simply an individual mind but "a web of coordination among media and processes inside and outside the individual task performers."[37] Unlike students taking examinations in empty rooms with no resources, in real life, people need to know how to use resources, including other people.

Just as debates about calculators were prominent in the 1960s and 1970s, when the calculation of math facts was regarded as a central part of the skills being tested, so the question of what needs to be included in the study of learning is a genuine, theoretical biological and social-scientific question. While cognitive science can help us understand how the mind works, it has limitations. Cognitive science has largely had "methodological individualism" at its core, measuring and accounting for only an individual, not social groups; only thinking, not feeling or acting; only the present, not the past; only decontextualized performance, and not the entire colorful cultural context. When we think of human minds as analogous with computers, we miss some of the other dimensions. Hutchins aims to "re-embody cognition," among other things, emphasizing the body.[38]

Learning in Doing

As an example of learning, we could look at driving. Driving is taught both theoretically and as an apprenticeship, with both cognitive and physical dimensions. Students are taught in class for a semester, or a condensed two-week all-day session in the summer or during a vacation. They learn about signs and signals, rules, strategies. Some learn online. According to my daughter Hannah, they also learn new vocabulary, including the marvelous word *velocitation*, which describes the sensation of becoming accustomed to speed after a while (for instance, on the highway). The theoretical part of the test is written. At my daughters' expensive driving school ($425 for the course, *after* the prepayment discount), they also had to submit a scrapbook of articles about accidents.

But then they get in a car.

Both my daughters had great difficulty coordinating the accelerator and the brake, the steering and the turning. (We had not taught them before their class.) They really did not know what to do at an intersection. My brother-in-law asked Sassy, "Didn't you take drivers' ed?" when she had no idea who had the right of way after a stop.

The total disconnection between the abstract rules that she had never wondered about and the need to have that information once she was driving make it clear that for Sassy, and for many people in the world, there is little to no transfer from abstract learning to actual practice, just as Lave has shown.

So what are we teaching in college?

Most of our students are going to have jobs like managing insurance offices or representing companies to buyers, filling cavities or advising wealthy people about their investments. Some will be nurses and some will paint houses. Most of these jobs will be learned by doing. They will also learn how to pay taxes and to research issues they will vote on, and they'll learn ballroom dancing or how to play new video games. They will teach Bible study or raise money for community gardens. They will also wonder about the meaning of life and death, good and evil, chance and destiny. How much of this is informed by anything learned in school is debatable.

Professional/Vocational Education and Apprenticeship

Even the most prestigious professions are learned principally through apprenticeship, albeit one preceded by a period of classroom and "theoretical," foundational instruction.

Medical school evolved into academic training following the 1910 Flexner Report. Previously medical education had been a diverse set of apprenticeship, shoddy lecturing with and without dissection, and more. Abraham Flexner used the "hyper-rational" model of German education to reform it completely; some argue that the "scientific" aspects have improperly superseded the "caring" dimension, and that a rebalancing is long overdue.[39]

In some countries, medical education is still a four-year program, completed after high school. During those years students learn how to practice medicine. They spend less time than their American counterparts taking classes in foreign languages they will never use, or studying art history, or even learning about elaborate rituals in remote parts of the world (a favorite of anthropology). They learn the biology and chemistry that they need. They have rounds. And then they are practicing.

American students study biology, inorganic and organic chemistry, physics, calculus—all so they can do well on the MCAT exam so they can enter medical school after four years of majoring in something else (perhaps something obscure like peace studies or anthropology) which would make them stand out in the application process, but which they might enjoy. They spend two years in classrooms memorizing terms and learning about theories of medicine. And then once they pass their boards, they are finally moved to rotations, where they actually see what doctors do in practicing. For most of them, this is what they have wanted. All the preceding six years, or even ten years, if we include high school, are preliminary.

What keeps people going that long? Is it love of healing? Sheer endurance? Desire for wealth? Deferring until someday?

Somebody told me the story of a family friend, Trey, whose ambitions were stymied by the schooling that stood between him and his dreams. An enthusiastic young man, he had initially planned to go to a big state university and bide his time until he could go to medical school. His professional parents had always had very practical aims for his education and insisted on knowing what kind of job he was training for. Trey had done well in high school. At college he made good friends. He played sports. He was active in religious life there. He stayed up late, learned to make mixed drinks, got a job as a bartender, and loved everything about his school—except the academic part. He was ready to go be a doctor, but he struggled in his required classes.

He lasted about two years at college, and then his parents "brought him home." He got a job at a blood bank and loved it. It was obvious that he would be extremely competent at the activities required in a real job. He liked the setting, the people, the responsibility. He organized blood drives and spoke passionately about them. He went to the local branch of the state university and even liked a few of the classes. He did well, applied to, entered, and completed nursing school. Now employed as a nurse, he seems finally fulfilled.

For some people, like Trey, traditional college is too irrelevant and too disconnected from their real enthusiasms. It is as if someone were a marvelous musician but first had to study, for four years, how to make breakfast cereal. Some few skills "transfer," and learning anything well teaches the perseverance and fortitude to do something else well. But other than that, the connection seems unclear.

So why are we making so many of our young people submit to this discipline? Is it just to show who is boss? If they can follow the rules, sit still, and succeed, then we'll allow them to do something meaningful?

Learning through Work, or The Reluctant Learner

In 2009 two books appeared in defense of manual labor, appealing to a sense of the "real" or "authentic": Matthew Crawford's *Shop Class as Soulcraft* and Alain De Botton's *Pleasures and Sorrows of Work*. Both celebrate the idea of genuine work, with real-world, observable, physical consequences, in contrast to abstract, lifeless, fake work, exemplified by academic theorizing or financial sleight-of-hand games such as "credit default swaps." While practitioners of the latter manipulate formulas invented by (mostly) men in suits, people engaged in the former sweat over engines and fix cars or get dirt under their fingernails and grow the crops that sustain us all.

This seems to me to be connected to the choices that even privileged adolescents are increasingly considering: whether to follow prescriptions for a good—leisurely, well-paid—life or to pursue some sense of meaning without schooling. One trend is that of educated younger adults becoming organic farmers.[40] Agriculture students are motivated to learn certain things about botany, zoology, and so on, but to learn them in a different way from those preparing for, say, admission tests to professional schools. An option for our society would be for youth to begin with work, perhaps at a lower wage—a *learner's wage*—and to pursue additional education if desired.

Instead, we force the young to learn, and they resist. Compare resistant students with novice Mayan weavers as studied by Rogoff. All are expected to learn successfully because it is part of being a person in society. Evading learning would be evasion of social identity.

Learning through (the Right Degree of) Challenge

Don't get me wrong. I am not saying that all learning should be painless and effortless. In fact, a slight amount of discomfort leads to greater learning. From a lot of different angles researchers have demonstrated that to achieve "flow" or absorption in learning, people need to concentrate on meeting an interesting challenge. David Shernoff calls the sensation a mix of "concentration, enjoyment, and interest"; it comes from the combination of high challenge and high skill. College students studied were more engaged and attentive during cooperative learning tasks than in large-group instruction. Harvey Whitehouse has been showing for a long time that ritual contributes to vivid memories and that high-arousal but rarely occurring practices (such as rites of passage) can enhance memory.[41]

People pay attention when they are scared. Richard W. Brown, Henry L. Roediger III, and Mark A. McDaniel write that some difficulties, which they regard as "desirable," increase learning and remembering. So it is not the case that all learning should be painless and effortless. For decades it has been demonstrated that on their own, people will choose a medium level of challenge, the sweet spot between "too hard" and "too easy." They don't want simply to be told the answer, for example, to a puzzle; they like working it out, but feeling that it is possible to do so.

Learning through Play: Taking Play Seriously

Do human beings die if they don't play?

Some scholars think so, and have evidence for the lack of play going beyond making a person dull. (*All work and no play makes Jack a dull boy.*) Evolutionary scholars argue that there are biological, physiological, and social needs for play, in humans and other mammals as well.[42] Without play, we don't thrive. We don't learn. And in some cases we don't even live.

All mammals play. Dolphins, according to Gregory Bateson, clearly demonstrate the ability to differentiate between genuine and pretend fighting that defines intelligence. We simultaneously say "this matters" and "this is not true." And this works between mammals of different orders: Dogs can play with gibbons and humans with dolphins—and maybe beyond mammals even to birds (at least corvids).[43]

Have you ever played peek-a-boo with a one-year-old child? The child knows it is a game, and delightedly squeals each time the expected face appears from its momentary hiding place. How exactly we communicate the frame *play* (the *metamessage*) is an enduring question.

The academic and intellectual study of play—an oxymoron?—is vast. In 1938 Johan Huizinga wrote *Homo Ludens: A Study of the Play-Element in Culture* about the need for play. In 2013 Peter Gray published *Free to Learn*, with the same message, and some updated social science research along with personal experience to support his claims.

Howard Chudacoff defines *play* as "amusing activities that have behavioral, social, intellectual, and physical rewards."[44] That makes it sound so . . . serious. In "Deep Play" Clifford Geertz argued that the Balinese cockfight reflected the social categories and meanings of that society. And Diane Ackerman's luminous book also called *Deep Play* (both she and

Geertz acknowledge Jeremy Bentham, who distrusted play) introduces a kind of transcendence (transcenDANCE), when life becomes fully meaningful, akin to Csikszentmihalyi's "flow." It is this that makes us fully aware of the joy possible to us, and allows us to lose ourselves at the same time. Perhaps watching others play (as in spectator sports) counts, but I don't think so.

And though everyone *really* agrees that children have to play, we should pause before we exaggerate our sentimental idealizing of merry "cherubs." Despite the ubiquity of the phrase "play is children's work" or "play is the work of the child," is it true?

Fred Rogers, "Mr. Rogers," among many others, made this claim.

Anthropologist Garry Chick says no, in "Work, Play, and Learning," arguing that the separation between "work" and "play" is much less clear in many societies than was assumed by researchers.[45] Anthropologists observing children often have to categorize the principal activity in which the child is currently engaged. Many of children's productive activities may count as "work" but also incorporate aspects of enjoyment and liberty that we might consider "play." So play may be serious and work may be pleasant and play often interweaves with productive activity. When Chick conducted fieldwork in the late 1970s in the highlands of central Mexico, where maize agriculture is the main preoccupation and occupation of the thousand or so residents, he observed the combination:

> Boys chased each other, played simple games, clearly enjoyed throwing sticks or stones at marauding birds, and occasionally at each other, while they guarded fields. Washing clothes was generally a pleasant activity for village women and their daughters as it was time outside the home away from its routine and an opportunity to socialize with others engaged in the same chore.[46]

So distinguishing work and play, or work, play, and learning, is often impossible. Ethnographic and development studies of the need for play are inconclusive, according to Chick,[47] though it is *assumed* to be beneficial.

Play is often divided into types: fantasy play, creative play, role play, and games with rules. David Lancy has written about "rough-and-tumble" play, the big-muscle rolling around and fake fighting, wrestling, chase, tag that are nearly ubiquitous. (He also writes about children learning through "the chore curriculum"—work if there ever was any.)

But play and work are both hard to define and then hard to differentiate. (In the words of one expert, Tom Sawyer, "Work consists of whatever a body is *obliged* to do . . . and play consists of whatever a body is not obliged to do.")[48]Adults and children may differ about which activity is being done. If the activity is evaluated for its consequences, then it's work. Some have distinguished "child work" (for use value) and "child labor" (for exchange value).

We might also point out that adults "play" in the sense that all societies have enjoyable activities without practical consequences. From decades of research on hunters and gatherers, we know that they spend only about five hours a day on subsistence activities (collecting food, cooking, building shelters); the rest of their time is spent in gossip, storytelling, sexual activity, and other enjoyable practices.

All societies have verbal art, too—song, ritual, chant, poetry, stories—and all have dance.[49] All have some kind of music, and all have ceremonies. These activities have social consequences and economic requirements, but their goal is partially entertainment.[50] We can invent useful purposes for such activities: they cement social ties; they reinforce grammatical patterns; they circulate resources. But they are also deeply pleasurable. Pleasure is an intrinsic part of human life. And children find pleasure in work and play.

College Play   At many colleges students love to utter the phrase "Work Hard Play Hard" or "Work Hard Party Hard." "Play" has come to mean "party" (in fact, one of my research assistants automatically substituted "party" in the question we asked of all students), which means drinking. This is clearly not developmentally or joyfully needed—nor does it "teach" anything constructive. I used to believe the primary reason college drinking has become the intense preoccupation it has since the 1980s is mainly connected to the rise in the drinking age from eighteen or nineteen to twenty-one, but perhaps it also has to do with the fact that so much of the rest of students' lives is focused on achievement. They need a release from this fixation on measurable outcomes.[51]

In American culture, with a puritanical emphasis on drawing a line between "work" and "play," drinking is reserved for the category of "play."[52]

Can there be play in accompaniment to learning in college classes? Or do classes have to be purely about duty, obligation, discipline? A video of a master teacher shows Harriet Ball singing multiplication facts rhythmically and physically with her elementary school students.[53] I couldn't turn it off!

Fun and Games in Class   In my fall 2010 class Doing Things with Words, I commented on the pen games that one student, Nathan, had learned the previous year in my Anthropology of Childhood and Education. Another student, Athena, informed us about the YouTube videos of pen games, teaching a huge variety of games that we can practice during class.

But the sheer expenditure of energy and attention on something so silly reminds me of the joy in challenge. As Diane Ackerman points out, even crows play. They amuse themselves by watching things fall, or catch pieces of straw in midair. It could be regarded as "training" for something serious, but it doesn't seem to her to be that at all. She compares it with extreme sports, like climbing huge mountains. People love to do things that are hard, that absorb their attention, and that they can survive and succeed at. She is especially interested in the way real danger or fear focuses the attention, so that one is almost not even thinking. That chattering, monkey mind is banished and a single point of light draws every iota of physical, psychic, emotional concern. It is, in its way, relaxing.

Like Riding a Bicycle: If Learned, It Cannot Be Forgotten

Learning is memory, essentially.

A psycholinguist with the all-American name—though he was born in England and lives in Canada—Frank Smith wrote in *The Book of Learning and Forgetting* that when we learn things, really learn them, they can never be forgotten. If students forget everything, they have not learned it—and forgetting is a common school experience. Students boast about their memories being erased immediately after the test. Cognitive scientists now demonstrate aspects of memory that are counterintuitive, such as that simple repetition is less effective at cementing memory than other forms of "retrieval" such as reflection or even testing (which could be self-testing).[54]

The "riding a bicycle" example is exemplary for a reason.

There may be steps along the way. There may be some teaching for a while. There may be some period in which the pieces—steering, pedaling, braking—have to be mastered separately. But once a kid knows how to fly effortlessly down the block, the task is learned. And it is remembered all her life. (There could be strokes or rustiness, and muscles could atrophy. But barring all that, this skill is not forgettable.)

Students will use their bike riding for whatever purposes they need. They will go off in dozens of directions, some to churches and some to prisons, some to malls and some to forests. Some few will create new forms of bike-craft, and some will crash. Some will invent generators and some will tow neighbors' dogs. Some will be able to ride to a job and support their families.

As a teacher, I want all my subjects to be like bicycle riding.

I want students to want to learn. I want them to find elation in mastery. I want them to go off on their own, forgetting that they ever had to learn.

I want the process to be just challenging enough to engage their attention. I want the teaching to be incidental. I want the learning to become part of their nature.

Compare this to regular classroom learning, at any level. Students arrive with no reason to learn. No elation. Instant forgetting. Focus on the teacher. A plan mapped out in advance. Automatic expectation that many will fail. Anxiety about evaluation.

Lots of subjects are like bicycle riding: Reading. Foreign languages. Musical performance. Philosophical analysis. Historical, sociological, anthropological reasoning. Scientific analysis. If students really learn, they can never forget. And they are changed in the process.

And if we think about testing and grading: In bike riding the test is the ride. The grade . . . is the ride. What should the grade distribution be? How many A's should we expect? Who has a natural aptitude for riding? Do we exclude those not born to ride?

The more we can help our students become free to go off, holding them upright just long enough for them to get their balance, the better we can attain our goals, which should be their goals too.

As each new semester begins, I hope to remind myself that a child who learns to ride a bicycle is free to roam. What kinds of freedoms am I helping my students develop? I have to accept that I can't predict their paths; I celebrate their many roads.

I hope at least a few will send postcards.

Learning in College

We know that disagreements abound about what is supposed to happen in college, from whether the emphasis should be on "content" or on "learning to learn" or on "transferrable skills" or on "cultural literacy" or "facts" or "procedural knowledge," to how these various things should be taught (lectures, seminars, online, labs, service learning) and how they should be assessed (tests, portfolios, projects, conferences, oral exams, "clickers," one-minute jottings). New ideas are suggested by the teaching and learning centers that abound on every campus—often with deep understanding of how people learn, but faculty and administrators, and students and the public, cling to their notion of what "real schools" look like.

The tension between what is known about learning and what is done in college (see Table 8.1) is evidence that we aren't necessarily succeeding in our aims.[55]

The more courses diverge from the super-conventional stereotype and resemble learning "in the wild," the more likely it is that actual learning—with remembering—will occur.

Jean Lave puts it this way, contrasting *practice theory* with *functionalist* accounts of learning:

> Functionalists argue that verbally transmitted, explicit, general knowledge is the main prerequisite that makes cognitive skills available for transfer across situations. Social practice proponents argue that knowledge-in-practice, constituted in the settings of practice, is the locus of the most

TABLE 8.1   Learning in School and Learning in the Wild

Super-Conventional Class	Learning "in the Wild"
Lecture	Action
Extrinsic motivation	Intrinsic motivation
Individual	Social
Abstract	Concrete
Cognitive	Physical/cognitive
Multiple-choice tests	Actual use
Factual knowledge	Procedural knowledge
Cramming	Natural repetition
Outcomes: grade, credit	Something real

powerful knowledgeability of people in the lived-in world. Practice theory, in short, suggests a different approach to cognition and to schooling than that embodied in functional-schooling theories, educational ideologies, and cognitive theory.[56]

Or, we might say, most schooling does not teach the way most people learn.

Zesty Learning Outside School

As we continually have seen, students, like all people, often love learning. After college, people sign up for clubs, for travel tours with guides, for MOOCs. They take art classes and watch YouTube videos teaching them how to do things, or about new ways to understand the universe. "Big History" is one favorite topic. TED talks and the TEDx talks that have become an authorized franchise show how eager people are for learning.

Advertised in the *New York Times Book Review* and the *Atlantic*, the "Great Courses" lectures available on CD and DVD provide, at some expense, a series of courses on a huge range of topics, from traditionally academic (calculus, philosophy) to practical and inspirational (mindfulness, gardening, exercise). The number of courses seems to be proliferating; in 2011 Great Courses had $110 million in annual sales.[57] Various forms of adult education abound: continuing education, elder hostels (renamed Road Scholar, formerly one of its dimensions, in 2010),[58] "free universities." The Chautauqua Institution was established in 1874 for the American goal of "self-improvement through lifelong learning." Evidence is everywhere of opportunities for learning, for enjoyment, without credit or grade. Some researchers call this *informal education*.[59] So there are people among us who want to learn, just 'cause, and many who are satisfying that desire.

Opening Up Learning

Recall the tests used to support the claims in *Academically Adrift* that we saw in the "Complaints" chapter: Do students know certain kinds of information? Can they be shown to engage in "critical thinking"? At a talk I gave, one faculty member lamented that students now do not know how a bill becomes a law. (I'm rusty on the details. But I know how to find out!)

And in 2006 media charged that two-thirds of Americans couldn't locate Iraq on a map.[60]

In 2011 two technophile researchers interested in challenging conventional views of school, Douglas Thomas and John Seely Brown, repeated the Iraq test. But they permitted the use of computers. Unlike the 63 percent who failed to locate it when given a conventional test, every one of the eighteen- to twenty-four-year-olds could do so. The young folks also understood that there were multiple capabilities involved in using electronic maps; they wanted to know *what else* besides this trivial task of location they were supposed to do with their information.[61] Because parroting context-free information is not that interesting.

This is completely connected to the topic of motivation.

9

Motivation Comes in at Least Two Flavors, Intrinsic and Extrinsic

The Master said: "Knowing something is not as good as loving it; loving
something is not as good as delighting in it."

The Analects

When I started graduate school in anthropology in 1986, having completed a master's degree in Chinese literature, I was already in my late
twenties. I had been out of school for four years prior to entering graduate school at all, and once entered, I had also spent a year in Taiwan,
working on advanced Chinese. I had finished a master's thesis on metaphor in the Daoist philosophical text *Zhuangzi* (Chuang Tzu), filled with
literary and cultural theory; that led me to change to anthropology. Our
fairly traditional program insisted on a year of reading a lot of old texts in
our theory class—between five hundred and a thousand pages a week, by
my count, of very dense theory. We read Herbert Spencer, Lewis Henry
Morgan, Karl Marx, Franz Boas, Émile Durkheim, Bronislaw Ma-
linowski, Claude Lévi-Strauss, and the like. Old dead white men (Lévi-
Strauss was still alive), to be sure (later many women), but filled with
passion and color and brand-new insights at the time. Some of the old issues—as I tell my students now—have simply been repackaged and have
stayed around unsolved. We read them not only to do honor to our ancestors but also to learn how ideas get proposed, attacked, defended. Along
the way we learned about the Iroquois and the Dobu and the Trobriand
Islanders, the Orinoco Valley and the aboriginal peoples of Australia, the

Inuit and the Hopi, the Ndembe and Azande. We learned about totemism, about fetishes, about moieties and potlatches and means of production, about witchcraft and symbols. It was a wonderful education about the sociology of knowledge along with a lot of specific details regarding the world's many peoples, described and analyzed by Europeans and Americans who willingly went to live among the "primitive" (a term we repudiated) for years at a time, learning languages and reverently collecting information and artifacts to show to their fellow educated citizens back home. They relied on their privileges, and some served imperialist purposes; a good number tried to demonstrate how rational were people often regarded as simple. We students organized discussion and reading groups on our own. Friends, ideas, books, anthropology, food and drink: a heavenly combination—for people like me and others who became academics.

You can probably tell from the enthusiasm of my description that I loved this experience. We anthropology graduate students might have seemed pretentious, regarding ourselves as intellectuals, but we were motivated by a love for the field. Few conversations revolved around jobs; we assumed that all would work out in due time. We were in no hurry to finish our studies, though financially it was often challenging; hardly anyone had a complete fellowship, and most of us had to teach and take out loans to make things work out. But those of us in graduate school in the late 1980s, in our late twenties and early thirties, were baby boomers and dismissive of material concerns as primary motivation. Once we began having children, looking for jobs, we became more "practical," but those early years of our graduate education were luxurious. We learned for learning's sake, devouring ideas and readings. We were motivated by the academic process.

But imagine our surprise, then, when we first faced classrooms full of students who had completely different concerns. For many of us there was a long period of shock, disillusionment, and even pain, leading to the complaints you read about earlier.

I struggled for decades, trying to understand how to "motivate" students. All I ever really wanted was that they should *want* to learn. Yet it was clear that they want all kinds of other things. How could I *force* them to want what I want?

But then I learned something profound, indeed life-changing, from the psychologists, and especially educational psychologists.

Who Teaches the Teachers about Teaching and Learning?

I heard about the subfield of psychology known as "educational psychology" only after having taught for more than twenty years. Many cognitive and behavioral psychologists specialize in how people and other animals learn through focus on individual cognition and on rewards and motivation. Educational psychologists apply these and other theories to school. Neurobiological and cognitive science research are just beginning to be incorporated into these discussions. (An exception is Willingham.)[1]

Educational psychology has been the primary research component of schools of education—"the one area within education schools that has been able to establish itself as a credible producer of academic knowledge and thus establish its faculty as legitimate members of the university professoriate," according to David Labaree.[2]

While the majority of research on learning has for decades demonstrated the greater effectiveness of "guide on the side" models, observation and even policy usually reveal a preference for "sage on the stage" models (as in "real schools"). Teachers rarely replace their many years of experience about how schooling works with the knowledge gained through a few years' worth of education classes. What is actually seen in classrooms—teacher-centered "stand and deliver" lecturing—is quite different from the student-centered learning that the research considers "best practices." Most teachers usually teach as they were taught, even when such methods are known to be ineffective. And so it is that the "grammar of schooling" persists.[3]

This information is old hat for people trained in education, but because we professors never study this field, we learn the hard way—through trial and error, in our long and high-stakes apprenticeship.

What I am about to tell you here changed my life. It started with a writer named Alfie Kohn.

Motivation

In my reading about school, learning, and grades, the topic of *motivation* kept appearing.

Psychologists distinguish two types of motivation: *intrinsic* and *extrinsic*. The line between them is not always clear, and definitions are challenging, but the basic idea is this: *Intrinsic motivation* means doing things for their own sake, or because the outcomes of the activities matter. The reason for doing something comes from *inside* the self or the activity. *Extrinsic motivation* comes from things that are *outside* the doer or the activity itself: pleasing someone, getting approval, trying to use the activity as a bargaining chip for something else.

Differentiating the two is not simple, as we all internalize external values and motives in the process of growing up.[4] So we may be motivated by something outside ourselves that also matters to us inside ourselves. And many activities combine both types of motivations; we may love our work but still need the money we earn. But the basic principle is that when people are involved in activities that matter to them intrinsically, they are more likely to enjoy and delve into them and less likely to be distracted.

Obviously, everyone must at times force themselves to stay focused even when tasks are boring, unimportant, or difficult. We cannot simply act on instinct; as our social rules remind us, we are part of culture, not nature. All societies require some degree of self-control. And children have to learn some tough lessons. *We can't always get what we want. We have to wait our turn. We should not grab.* But along with the necessary repressions that, as Freud pointed out, permit us to live in society, we learn and practice things guaranteed to divert us from fulfillment. Certainly schools must inculcate at least some degree of capacity to sit still, concentrate, and follow directions even when they make no sense.[5] But school can't *only* be about developing the ability to master the undesired.[6]

In *Punished by Rewards: The Trouble with Gold Stars, Incentive Plans, A's, Praise, and Other Bribes* Alfie Kohn argues that extrinsic rewards *cannot* improve education. He reports on decades of research consistently showing that merely changing the way activities are rewarded changes people's motivation for performing them—and *increasing* extrinsic motivation *decreases* intrinsic motivation.[7] Take a task people enjoy and give them rewards, and they stop liking those activities. Take workers in fairly mundane jobs, give them some autonomy and scope, and they flourish. When hobbies become professions, people love them less.

Behaviorist psychology, which ruled the day, claimed that rewarding desirable behavior increases it, and punishing undesirable behavior decreases it; in other words, they claimed that external rewards would enhance or create intrinsic motivation. But in the 1970s several psychologists challenged this simplistic model of human motivation.

Edward Deci conducted a study with a result so amazing that nobody believed it. College students were divided into two groups. All were given a challenging puzzle to work on, but half earned money for solving it. Researchers left the room and observed the students. The ones who had been paid showed *less* interest in the puzzle than the other group.[8] This finding has been replicated again and again and again.[9]

In another study Mark Lepper and his colleagues gave children drawing materials. They randomly divided the students into two groups. One was allowed to draw as before, and the other was given prizes for their drawings. A week or two later, the children were observed. Those who had been randomly assigned to the "rewarded" group seemed *less* interested in using the materials, but those who had earlier just been allowed to draw still enjoyed it.[10]

Extrinsic rewards often lead also to decreases in *quality*. Seeking to maximize rewards, people often apply minimal effort; one group of researchers calls this the "minimax principle."[11]

The message is obvious but shocking: *Rewarding backfires.*

When people are told that they need a reward aside from whatever satisfaction or use they derive from the activity itself, it signals that they should not like it because they have to have some other sign of their accomplishment. Nobody has to be rewarded for eating chocolate. It is its own reward.

Extrinsic rewards could be as simple as praise, or as lavish as payment for grades (a double removal from the intrinsic activity). Grades and scores are the obvious extrinsic rewards in school, but credentials, degrees, credits, requirements, and all the rest are also extrinsic rewards. Lower-achieving students are often bombarded with threats and higher-achieving students with promises of *rewards* (but also threats of decreased rewards—always a danger because there is always another threat around the corner).

This counterintuitive conclusion, repeatedly tested,

confirms that virtually every type of expected tangible reward made contingent on task performance does, in fact, undermine intrinsic motivation. Furthermore, not only tangible rewards, but also threats . . . , deadlines . . . , directives . . . , and competition pressure . . . diminish intrinsic motivation because . . . people experience them as controllers of their behavior. On the other hand, choice and the opportunity for self-direction . . . appear to enhance intrinsic motivation, as they afford a greater sense of autonomy.[12]

So where does that leave our students?

Credentials versus Learning

College is filled with both rewards and threats. As predicted, students often limit the energy devoted to academic work in order to maximize rewards and minimize threats.

Colleges construct curricula and requirements to force students to develop curiosity, expose themselves to new things, become "well rounded" and knowledgeable about a range of activities. But even such well-meaning structures backfire. Kalamazoo College requires first-year students to attend five events, choosing among topics ranging from college success to multiculturalism to health and safety to community involvement.[13] But I'm told that many students discover in April that they have not filled up their checklist and must rush around and randomly complete the requirement. Academic distribution requirements are intended to serve the same purpose, but students regard them as onerous obligations as they race to "get the gen eds out of the way."

In Hawai'i I watched kids learning to surf. They had boogie boards or little kickboards, and older kids would show them a few tricks, or the younger ones would just watch and figure it out. They could do this for hours, trying over and over and over, varying their approach, and really *learning*. Give them a teacher, a grade, a curriculum, credit, a certificate, and this pleasurable activity would become drudgery, just like math class or biology. Things that are inherently interesting can be made less so by the structure and expectation of schooling.

Learning for *Use* and Learning for *Exchange*

David Labaree's book *How to Succeed in School without Really Learning* reminded me of the Marxist distinction between "use value" and "exchange value." *Use value* derives from the nature of the thing itself. Shoes have *use value,* for example, because they protect our feet. But shoes can also have *exchange value* if they are important only for how much we can exchange them for (other goods or money). Owners of shoe stores may have decided on this kind of store because they love shoes or because they have done research on how much profit they can make, with each pair of shoes an inventory unit. Pork bellies are important to suit-wearing guys with Blackberries and iPhones not because they're farm boys who love pigs but because they can exchange them for other commodities and money.

Education works the same way.

You can take a class because it gives you something you can exchange ("one credit of social science" can be swapped for "one credit of multiculturalism") in an economy of requirements, or you can write a paper because it gives you some units ("each response paper counts for 15 points"). Or you can take a class because you will learn something you need to know ("In my phlebotomy class we learned how to start IVs") or something interesting ("In my Ecosystems and Economics class we learned about the interrelatedness of the two domains, and my life was changed forever").

You can see where this is going.

When we talk about whether higher education is worthwhile in terms of its contribution to finding a job or increasing earnings, we are weighing it purely in terms of its exchange value. When we talk about its opening up the world, or providing a window onto the "meaning of life," or preparing students for work, we talk about it in terms of use value.

It can't be the fault of each of our young "customers" that they have absorbed the exchange-value lingo about education when it is all around them.

But the question is: Is there any way to change this?

In practice, aspects of intrinsic motivation in school classrooms might include intrinsic interest, usefulness or applicability, responsibility to others, self-esteem or self-worth, and building blocks for further learning.

If a class, or even an assignment, offers none of these things, students are less likely to spend time and effort on it, unless the threats and rewards are substantial enough. If a homework assignment in math yields nothing but points, students feel no compunction about copying from others. They learn nothing either way. But if something valuable is derived from it, then they may calculate that it's worthwhile.

Performance Goals versus Learning Goals

In *How Learning Works*, Susan A. Ambrose and colleagues contrast *learning goals* with *performance goals* in an effort to explain that there is often a disconnect between professors' and students' motives: "A . . . form of mismatch often occurs when we want our students to pursue learning for its own sake but they are motivated primarily by *performance goals*. . . . Performance goals involve protecting a desired self-image and projecting a positive reputation and public persona."[14]

Students also have "learning goals" and "work-avoidant goals," which means they want "to finish work as quickly as possible with as little effort as possible." But the authors are hopeful that students' goals and those of their teachers can align in some ways. They conclude that "if an activity satisfies more than one goal, the motivation to pursue that activity is likely to be higher than if it satisfies only one goal. Relevant to this point is the fact that *affective goals* and *social goals* can play an important role in the classroom."[15] That's because humans are immature capable curious emotional social animals.

So Now I Know . . . Why We Can't *Make* Them Care

Throughout this book I have talked of many aspects of both the "learning" side of things and the "schooling" side. In important ways, they contrast. To put it all together—for those of us who find it helpful—I have mapped a number of contrasts that show connections among various factors. (See Table 9.1.)

All I ever wanted was for my students to *care* about the subject. And now I understand why this outcome was unlikely. The deck was stacked with *extrinsic* motives. And though I believed that through exposure to enough of them they would discover some *intrinsic* interest, the research

TABLE 9.1   Comparing Learning and Schooling

Category	Learning	Schooling
Value	Use value	Exchange value
Motivation	Intrinsic	Extrinsic
Dominant styles	Student-centered	Teacher-centered
Role of teachers	"Guide on the side"	"Sage on the stage"
	Partners and advocates	Disciplinarians and adversaries
Goals	Personal development	Employment
	Collective social good	Individual private economic good
	Citizenship	"Return on investment"
	Interest, use, skills, knowledge	Credentials, grades
Emphasis	Valuing the steps	Bottom line
	Process	Product, commodity
Social relations	Cooperation, equality	Competition, stratification
Affective result	Happiness, satisfaction	Misery or relief, fragile pride
Model	Apprenticeship	Factory
Relationship with outside	Integrated	Separated
Key symbol	Doing, enjoying	Grade, diploma
Writing for . . .	Discovery, communication, completion, self	Requirement, grade, minimum, others
Self	Authentic	Performance

shows that things are more likely to go the other way: the more *extrinsic* motivation is involved, the more everyone focuses on points, grades, credits, credentials, and jobs, the more it will destroy *intrinsic* motivation.

Granted, some students always have cared, and some continue to. But I now see how the system is made to deflect that outcome. With such contradictory aims built in, it is inevitable that students focus on the easy-to-see extrinsic motives, which kill intrinsic ones. And we teachers all end up frustrated, unable to attain the most important goal of all: our students' well-being.

10

On Happiness, Flourishing, Well-Being, and Meaning

> When I was five years old, my mother always told me that happiness was the key to life. When I went to school, they asked me what I wanted to be when I grew up. I wrote down "happy." They told me I didn't understand the assignment, and I told them they didn't understand life.
>
> Attributed to John Lennon but probably apocryphal

For years I have been trying to make my students care, learn, and become absorbed in activities that matter. I want the clock forgotten, and thoughts of parties or what time ice cream will be available to be displaced.

I want them engaged, involved, caring about the material not because it's easy or hard, because it will be tested, because they need the grade, the class, the degree. I want them interested, fascinated, intrigued by the subject so that the work is exciting and gains them some measure of understanding of the world that they did not have prior to the class. I want them to read an article that turns their world upside down and then go back to the dorm and tell their roommate, "You won't believe what I read today!"

Good luck to me.

Joy, Flow, Meaning

I remember when I first heard murmurings—could it be true?—that the small, remote country of Bhutan measured gross national *happiness*—

GNH—instead of gross national product.[1] I wondered how this terribly poor country could possibly consider itself "happy."

But the time was right for this question; measures of happiness are now compared worldwide.

No longer the unique province of theology and philosophy and New Age gurus, in the past few decades the study of "happiness" has gone academic (though almost always gauged individually, reflecting American preoccupations. By contrast, the Bhutanese happiness experts emphasize that "the pursuit of happiness is collective, though it can be experienced deeply personally." They incorporate into their measurement *other-regard,* that is, concern for others, and *responsibility*, which are observed in the nine domains of GNH: psychological well-being, health, time use, education, cultural diversity and resilience, good governance, community vitality, ecological diversity and resilience, and living standards).[2] The "scientific" study of happiness has revealed much that is relevant for my project.

It was Mihaly Csikszentmihalyi's work on *flow* that set in motion the "positive psychology" movement, so named by Martin Seligman of the University of Pennsylvania. (In 2011 Seligman began to use the term *flourishing* instead; some speak of *well-being* and others of *meaning*, though that may sound too grand.)[3] Csikszentmihalyi studied "optimal experience" by having people record how they felt at arbitrary moments throughout the day, a measure that he termed Subjective Well Being (SWB). These optimal experiences were found to occur not when people were relaxing on the beach in Cancún or achieving riches through the lottery. People's most significant moments came after struggle, after hard work that mattered to them in some sense. Such well-being is not easy, effortless, painless, or even fun. Athletes' greatest moments, for example, were accompanied by pain, effort, and struggle. Absorption in the activity is the key.[4]

When people are absorbed in their work, time evaporates. They forget to eat; they are unaware of the clock; they feel sad when they have to stop. Most people have had the feeling of absorption, whether it is reading a book or watching a movie, playing a game, or cleaning out a messy room, and this is something that rewards itself. I especially experience flow (when it works) when I write, read, garden, walk, or talk with the right people at the right moment. This *flow* is "the state in which people are so involved in an activity that nothing else seems to matter; the experience itself is so enjoyable that people will do it even at great cost, for the sheer sake of doing it."[5]

Like all wisdom traditions, from Aristotle and Kongzi ("Confucius") to the writers of the Talmud and Gospels, Sufis and Tibetan Buddhists, the contemporary proponents of happiness or well-being remind us that happiness does not result from wealth or material possessions (though lack of basic needs can cause unhappiness). People are happy when they are content with their lot; when they have a social group with a place for themselves; when they have some kind of activity over which they feel mastery; when they get absorbed at least some of the time in an activity.[6]

Prestige does not provide happiness, and in fact the pursuit of prestige is well established as deleterious to happiness. Consumption—especially the addictive need for constant purchasing that some call the *hedonic treadmill*—is self-defeating.[7] There may be a momentary pleasure in buying something new, but that must be replaced by another new item, just as consumption of sugary foods leads to addiction to sugary foods. Even good health is not required for happiness, and winning the lottery does not produce it.[8]

One of the central questions we must ask as we set up a world for our children and youth is: How can we do our best to create happy and meaningfully engaged—not pleasure-craving—fellow beings? Learning and acting, sometimes alone and sometimes with others, is one way to produce meaning both in the educational process and as a foundation for later.

We also know some surefire ways for young people *not* to be happy: focusing on grades, consumption, appearance, comparison with others. Happiness does not result from students' being kept off-guard, struggling, biding their time until they can leave school. Well-being results from the alignment of desire, ability, and expectation; it results when people know that they are good at what they do. In *Happiness and Education,* Nel Noddings follows many thinkers, from Aristotle on, in distinguishing pleasure from happiness, expressed from inferred needs (as opposed to wants). Adults, of course, have to determine what students *need*, but one of the things they may need is to learn to enjoy learning. Yet a regular school classroom is exactly the opposite of what is desired and desirable. It is not surprising that students tune out, opt out, or "vote with their feet" and drop out.

Defining Well-Being

Psychologists, economists, theologians, health entities all attempt to define *well-being*.[9] Common elements include meaning and mattering; ease

Definition of Well-Being

Figure 10.1 The well-being balance.
Source: Dodge et al. 2012:230. Reprinted with permission.

following effort; solidity; just-enough challenge; usefulness; a sense of virtue, obligation, limitations, security, connections; flourishing; being accountable. Rachel Dodge and her colleagues emphasize a balance between challenges and resources. (See Figure 10.1.)

We can detect absence of well-being easily enough, using information about rates of depression, suicide, and even the need for psychological therapy. Madeleine Levine has worked extensively with materially advantaged youth who are psychologically miserable.[10] Depression afflicts almost half of all college students at some point.[11] Suicide is the tenth-most-common cause of death worldwide, and the second-most-common cause of death in adolescents. Millions of incomplete suicide attempts occur as well—anywhere from ten to forty attempts for every death by suicide.[12] It occurs with some regularity among the college population, often at the most selective schools, and by very high-achieving students.[13] One college president wrote vividly about his experience with parents whose children died at their own hand.[14]

Many have written about the dramatic increase in the diagnosis of unhappiness, mental illness, anxiety, lack of fit, ADD/ADHD, depression, and other psychological problems among all young people, from kindergarten to college. Students have higher rates of depression than nonstudents.[15]

Is school, as it is conventionally set up, in part responsible?

Happiness and Meaning as School Goals

In some vague sense, we would probably find all educators agreed that what they want is "what is best for the students." But this can mean many things. Engineers and designers work toward specified goals. Nel Noddings writes of "aims": What do you really want to get out of the system? Roger Marples writes explicitly of well-being as one of the aims of education.[16] I have a pile of books with titles like *What Is College For?* and *The Aims of College*. The question is far from settled. As parents, teachers, citizens, we have implicit answers to the question of goals, but we often come upon methods that contradict them. What is the nature of the good life? How can we create meaning in our lives? What is the balance between individual and community? Where is the happiness in school? A sense of satisfaction? Friends? Teachers' praise? A high GPA? (Actually, research shows that students with 3.8 GPAs are happier than those with 4.0s.)[17]

There is frequent confusion, too, between ultimate and proximate goals. Why should every child be required to master algebra? The reason given is that it is required because the SAT tests it, and because students need it to go to college. But this is a proximate goal. Noddings suggests that if the *ultimate* quest is for equity, and most disadvantaged students reach an impasse at algebra, we should rethink the requirement that every student has to study it. A colleague reminded me, however, of the dangerous racial and classist implications of determining early who is not college-bound. She points out that "it would require a lot of cultural re-education to imagine not going to college as a positive option."[18]

Understanding (Un)well-Being: Psychological, Economic, Personal

In the years prior to carrying out this project, I suspected my students of slacking off, of not working, of wanting something for nothing. But they come into my office earnest, crying. They have depression. They are in the midst of their parents' divorce. They have undiagnosed stomach problems. They are not sure school is for them. They want to study anthropology and yoga but their parents want them to be doctors or financial analysts. They want an adventure in China but instead opt for safe jobs at home. They have been high-achieving, ahead of all their peers, but now they fear losing their competitive edge; they may be one test away from failing to enter med school.

The pressures of college, especially a residential college, are enormous. Fit in! Have fun! Come party with us! Drink another! Hook up in front of everyone! Show you're independent!

Lots of people use drugs, alcohol, and sex to treat underlying problems, but these treatments can increase the problems. Many such underlying weaknesses are revealed when students leave home for the first time. They are supposed to find these the best years of their lives. But it can be a dangerous and vulnerable stretch. Some don't make it (alcohol poisoning, suicide, accidents, violence), but most, miraculously, do. They get through this period of pushing the limits and get jobs, find partners, have children.

College staff are alarmed about student anxiety and distress. But there is a serious question about the connection between the classroom and students' lives and selves, and whether classroom interaction can make any difference.

In 2014 Wake Forest University began to assess the well-being of its students and alumni, following a Gallup study of "engagement" at work, correlated with engagement years earlier in college.[19] So far there seems to be some connection between engagement in college and a sense of well-being in adult life, though this does not show that college engagement *causes* later well-being.

Permitting Joy and Good Laughter

Korean anthropologist Hyang Jin Jung conducted fieldwork in an American urban junior high school with a good reputation as "the best in town"—turning the tables on the usual direction of research—always contrasting it with her own experience of having been a teacher in a South Korean junior high. I have drawn many lessons from her illuminating book, *Learning to Be an Individual*, but one that keeps jumping into my brain is that in the United States, Jung missed what she calls "good laughter."[20]

From what I understand, "good laughter" can happen only when a group is sharing an experience. She explains it as releasing tension, providing shared moments. In the American school, where students sat alone and did "desk work," where working in groups was anathema, where students were isolated and emphasis was placed on self-control and autonomy, what stood out for her was the lack of joy. (When I was in Seoul, what I noticed was all the kids *touching* one another. It seemed so comforting, despite all the other stresses in their lives.)

And it is worse in disadvantaged schools. But shouldn't even poor children be permitted a scintilla of joy?

Loving Children's Spirits, Not Squeezing and Killing Them

In October 2010 Jonathan Kozol spoke at Saint Mary's College in Indiana about education and inequality. For four decades he has been steadfastly working toward equality and integration, and speaking forcefully against inequality and segregation. His conviction comes from the time he spends directly interacting with children in underresourced nearly-all-minority public schools. His affection and amazement showed clearly as he talked about the bossy kids and the funny little boy who looked like a flying grape. When he spoke of a courageous teacher, Francesca, who insisted on loving the children and hugging them every morning, in contrast to the ones who dutifully posted the incoherent state standards, chapter and verse, on the chalkboard, his appreciation for her warmed us all. This is in contrast to the "drill and kill" regime now foisted upon almost every low-income school in the country, where principals have no choice but to direct all teachers' attention to testing. Teachers spend up to six weeks just teaching about testing. The irony, of course, is that rich, multifaceted teaching is much more likely to improve test scores, but it does so much more than that.

I would disagree slightly with Kozol, though. He contrasts these schools with white suburban schools where things are so much better. And of course that is true. He talks of the importance of having beautiful, not merely functional, school buildings. He speaks longingly of art and music—subjects too frivolous for those needy minority kids who have to be held in line. (He told a moving story about visiting a school in the Bronx with Fred Rogers, where teachers hugged "Mr. Rogers" and cried, and a little kid welcomed him to *his* neighborhood. The point is that there are not two ways of being a kid—the white way and the minority way—but that all kids need an adult friend.) Certainly the seminar discussions in the best suburban schools might be wonderful and stimulating and enriching.

But then again, such schools also teach to the test—in this case the SAT or ACT or AP or college admissions. Students might be intrigued by a subject, or they might be going through the motions to please a teacher who has the power to grade them, which may determine not just their future but even their self-conception, because it sorts them into best/pretty good/not so good. William Deresiewicz has accused top colleges of turning high-achieving students into "zombies."

This kind of teaching kills learning. It kills curiosity. And more tragically, it kills the soul.

It squeezes and tightens until all that is left of an eager, "twinkly" young person is a withered pile of scores and bitterness. Some students end up hating the system and all teachers. Some end up hating themselves for failing. Some end up hating adults for putting them into this position. And some end up—as do many of my students—pegging their sense of worth to the way they are measured in the system, accepting its authority over their every move. *Yes sir, yes ma'am.* This is one product: a pleasing, homework-doing young girl who has no will of her own left. She does everything she is told and is affirmed when she succeeds. She does not squirm or giggle. She consults her calendar hourly and perseveres in reaching a set of concrete goals. She knows how to achieve them, one-two-three-four. She can assess the people around her and use them for her purposes. And she is a winner. She might cheat, or she might develop anxiety disorders. Anything to be successful.

A series of books details these pressures. Alison Quart writes of the pressure on children to be "gifted" and to become ever more impressive. She herself had such an experience and clearly found it oppressive. In *The Overachievers* by Alexandra Robbins, in *The Price of Privilege* by Madeline Levine, we see similar despair at the burdens placed on today's children.[21]

The anti-high-stakes-testing crowd—and I am certainly among their numbers—like to repeat Einstein's adage "Not everything that can be counted counts, and not everything that counts can be counted." So what does count?

Joy? Pleasure? Glee? Discipline? Test scores? Kozol spoke of the best teachers, the ones who can communicate joy, beauty, mystery, and mischief. He recounted stories of kids who raised and waved their hands, looking as if they would absolutely explode in a second if they weren't called on, and when acknowledged had nothing to say. They just wanted to be called on!

And so I have my really well-behaved students who would never challenge authority. They are all good at keeping track of things and apologetic when they fall short. Even mental illness on their part provokes an apology. All I want to do now is tell them it's not that important, to relax and put it all in perspective.

Hunger for the Body

Human beings generally know things kinesthetically as well as cognitively. We—at least most of the human race—cannot live purely in our heads.

In his mesmerizing book *Shop Class as Soulcraft*, Matthew Crawford addresses deeply the problematic, increasing distance we feel from the material realities of our lives. He contrasts our need for tools, for making, fixing, knowing, or at least wondering how things work with the current seamless nature of our electronic lives, the lack of reality in the work lives of "knowledge workers," the lack of depth in our higher education. Sure, we "learn how to learn," but we don't really know anything profoundly. This leaves us all aching, missing something. I know that sometimes all I want to do is laundry or weeding, something that is physical and concrete with a visible result and that engages my body, perhaps leaving me sore and exhausted.

Cooking, farming, sewing—all show that we feel the need to be physically involved in the making and carrying on of our real lives. Once upon a time we scorned farmers and their closeness to animals, to dirt. Someday—I imagined when I was young, if I even thought of it at all—we wouldn't need farmers or even farms. Factories would produce our food miraculously, cleanly. This was the modernist fable. *The Jetsons*, *Soylent Green*: no bodies required.[22]

So to the extent that we expect students to learn in a disembodied fashion, they are unlikely to genuinely master our academic material or to be transformed. They will not experience joy, happiness, a "starts in my toes" kind of tingle, the pleasure of accomplishment and knowing and sharing, the meaning of living. They will wait for all that, wait for someday.

The Chain

If the key to happiness is meaningful work, and the key to work is to learn how to do it, and the key to learning how to do it is attention, and the key to attention is motivation, then there is a line of causality, the *Happiness Chain*, that goes like this:

Motivation → Attention → Learning → Action/Mastery/Flow →
Happiness (well-being)

As a teacher, I can intervene at any of these stages prior to happiness. I can work hard on motivation from need or desire or curiosity, trying to make the subject and the task *matter*. I can try to force, urge, invite attention to the task at hand. I can set things up to maximize learning. I can create exercises in which students employ what they have learned in some kind of activity, in which they ideally experience mastery. If all goes well, this contributes to their sense of happiness.

There is a different chain, though. I call it the *Happiness Deferral Chain*.

Sitting → Learning school topics → Avoiding negative consequences → Gaining positive attention, good grades, approval from parents and teachers → Using learning for the next level of school → Graduation → Credential → Job? → Money/Satisfaction → Happiness

---

Despite its familiarity, this one is much more challenging to make work out right. The good stuff is far away from the moment, and attention is always directed forward.

Humans can thrive only when all facets of their being are cared for. They will seek ways to ensure this, just as trees bend to the light no matter how many obstacles are put in their path. You've seen rounded trunks distorted because the light is obscured.

Many of our students are like those twisted trunks. They seek fulfillment and passion and meaning. Nourishment. If they cannot get it from the thin pabulum of our cognitive curriculum, they will look for it in beer pong and football chants and fast food work and all those places outside our classrooms.

Those who can sit still and memorize effectively may have figured out a way to add a dash of intrinsic motivation, of playfulness, into their otherwise tasteless fare.

But the more educators can create places for *meaning*, the more possible it becomes that our aims will align with those of our young charges. The tragedy is that the education system, in its chaos, is not set up that way.

Part IV

A Revolution in Learning

The essence of any liberated school is that it would be a community—not a
hierarchy of principal, teachers, support staff, and students but a place where
people gather to engage in interesting activities. . . . Not all schools would
attempt to do the same things; each would do what it was best at. Schools
would vary the way individuals vary. I've never seen an ideal school, but
I've visited many schools with enlightened and enthusiastic administrators
encouraging liberated teachers in liberated classrooms.

FRANK SMITH, *The Book of Learning and Forgetting*

We've imbibed complaints focused on a variety of aspects of college. We've
glanced at a sweep of goals. I've told stories. I've provided background information about college, growing up, learning, human nature, the weird
invention of compulsory universal schooling. And I've suggested that the
more in-school learning resembles out-of-school learning—to the logical
end of *being* out of school—the more likely it is to be both successful and
humane.

To be perfectly blunt, it seems clear to me that the whole model—
paradigm, in Thomas Kuhn's formulation—of institutionalizing learning is flawed. Increasingly I see all the tinkering as simply "saving the
phenomena"—just as the Ptolemaic astronomical system was retained for
centuries with adjustments, protestations, and all possible efforts to retain
the old model before it was replaced by the Copernican system.

I believe the institution of school has outlived its usefulness. It rarely
succeeds. There is chaos in discussing its aims, implementation, measures.
As a system of educating, its returns on genuine learning are shameful. As

a signaling game and credential competition, it is incredibly wasteful. As a way of trying to squeeze all individuals into a tight mold, it is abusive and creates suffering. This system began, basically, with the Common School movement. We can't significantly improve a conceptually flawed system; we can only replace it.

Because our industrial mass education system is so recent—only about a hundred years old—it should be possible to change it. But when I said at the beginning of the book that this is a system with intertwined parts and that no genuine improvement can occur unless we address the whole thing, you can see now what I mean. I have tried my own experiments in my classes, but they are limited by existing within a structure filled with profoundly contrary values.

Yet while I advocate revolution, I recognize the flawed record of utopian movements—Transcendentalist farms, kibbutzim, people's communes. I am a China specialist, after all. Almost all of them have seen retreat, and most suffered corruption in their realization.

In education, there are many places where experimentation is occurring: Waldorf schools, Sudbury Valley schools, Montessori schools. Some emphasize play, some the "whole child." We see colleges such as Prescott, where physical challenges and environmental knowledge are integrated. Others like Evergreen State have challenged the modularity of courses and created a rich multidisciplinary structure for learning. These tend to be elite, expensive, available only to those who already have much, while the disadvantaged are given "no excuses" "traditional" schools like the KIPP academies. But the multiplicity of experiments reveals both the shared sense that something is wrong and multiple courageous, creative, and industrious efforts devoted to providing alternatives.

I don't know how the economics of my dream would work out. I know that politically, education is currently a minefield, with right, left, center all jumbled and traditional alliances unraveled. There are enormous corporate and interest-group elements that would challenge any dismantling of the half-trillion-dollar system. There are school lunch providers and textbook publishers, testing companies and test-prep organizations, student life professionals and college architects. There are counselors and advisors and accrediting organizations. All are employers; their employees would have to be absorbed somehow into the workforce as the industrial educational machine shrank.

I don't see a clear, simple, swift path from here to there. In the current system, it is correct to argue that individuals should get as much schooling as possible and do as well as they can. But this is, as I've shown, because of the competitive nature of credential inflation and is tangential to learning. Yes, someone who gets a lot of schooling and does well may in fact learn a lot. But learning happens everywhere, all the time, and some of what passes for learning in schools is an imitation of learning—as is demonstrated time and again when students who have done well in class completely forget the course material within a year of completion.

So I consider some ways a wholesale rethinking of institutional learning might occur, and the more realistic but less thorough changes that people have been employing to try to improve the experience of schooling.

11

Both Sides Now of a
Learning Revolution

We need to kill the poison plant we created. School reform is not enough.
The notion of schooling itself must be challenged.

JOHN TAYLOR GATTO, *The Underground History of American Education*

I genuinely believe a revolution is looming, evidenced in all the challenges and problems and experiments in contemporary education, all the instability of analysis and goal. Yet we are not *quite* on the other side. So in this chapter I talk about both the revolutionary and not-yet-revolutionary ways to address the question "How can we prepare young people for adulthood, perhaps in college?"

I. Who Needs College?

For perfectly well-intentioned reasons, many people advocate "college for all." But going to college, as Bryan Caplan puts it, "is a lot like standing up at a concert to see better. Selfishly speaking, it works, but from a social point of view, we shouldn't encourage it."[1]

College for All?

Promoting "college for all" as a way to increase equality is a complicated, confusing, and ultimately illogical means to a worthy end.[2] As David Labaree points out, with competitive schooling as we have it, "someone has to fail."[3] Even if every individual attended college, not every individual would become "successful," just as not all individuals will be above average. Nor will sending every individual to college eradicate poverty or inequality. The "haves" will still have more. Even if everyone had a four-year degree, there would not be jobs for all graduates, at least not jobs requiring the content of those educations. So if the goal of college is full employment or inequality eradication, this goal will not be met. In John Marsh's book *Class Dismissed: Why We Cannot Teach or Learn Our Way Out of Inequality*, he explains why "college for all" is bound to be unsuccessful—at least at the level of an entire society. (For individuals it may be different.) The reason has mainly to do with getting the argument backward: first we need to address poverty. Education may follow.

In fall 2012 the *New York Times* hosted a debate: Should everyone go to college,[4] or is college a waste of time?[5] (The *Chronicle of Higher Education* had a similar forum in 2009; one commenter noted that if even the Chronicle of *Higher Education* was questioning this, we are far down the road of doubt.)

The question is usually framed as: Is college worth the (economic) investment? Economists give competing answers, though the general belief is that despite the expense and forgone wages, the lifetime earnings of college graduates are much higher than those of high school graduates: the "college premium."[6] An allied inquiry asks *which* schools and *which* majors provide the highest "return on investment."[7]

But, say the old elite, such as the Phi Beta Kappa society (full disclosure: I'm a member), college is not simply about getting a job. The model of a liberal arts education, with a rich, wide-ranging curriculum that establishes a floor for what young students may need to know in the future, hangs on in some colleges and universities: Great Books, Kant, postcolonialism, critical thinking, the basics of relativity theory, and so on. (I believed in this all my adult life, until I began to ask the questions that led to this book.)

In community colleges and in the increasingly popular vocational training for business, engineering, information technology, medical professions, education, and the like, there is no time for Kant when examinations have to be passed and bills have to be paid. (There are those "gen eds," but even here probably not too much Kant.) Getting the credential as quickly and cheaply as possible is the primary goal.

At a farm-to-table dinner in Chautauqua, New York, I met a young woman who worked in recruiting at a nearby community college. Though she herself had a four-year degree, she was passionate about the "value" provided by the community college. "Why would you pay so much more for the basic classes in a four-year school," she asked, "when you could do it comfortably at the local community college, and live at home?"

In summer 2014 Starbucks partnered with Arizona State University to offer some employees compensation for enrolling in ASU's online courses.[8] (There are complicated caveats, but the goal is noble.)

The costs are real. Individuals, right now, don't have time to wait for the revolution.

One of the ideas from the 2011 Occupy movement that caught on easily (and led to an offshoot, Occupy Student Debt) had to do with college debt, now staggering, and filled with treacherous traps for a lifetime.[9] Senator Elizabeth Warren, President Barack Obama, and many others have attempted to get at this problem from the side of banks and the government, limiting the amount students are obligated to repay.

From the economic point of view, with the issue of cost front and center, suggestions have included designing cheap degrees, paying for college for promising students,[10] or skipping college entirely. For an individual, it is statistically advantageous to go to college, and preferably complete it, though the likelihood of (1) enrolling, (2) succeeding, and (3) completing a degree, especially a four-year degree, is low for disadvantaged youth, first-generation college students, and minorities.[11] Not only that, but they often end up financially worse off than they were when they began.

In a system where the college degree signals a certain kind of commitment and the character that accompanies it, anyone without a degree will be seen as falling short—unless she can signal this information in some other form.

Those already solidly in the middle class, with all the cultural and social capital they need, already knowing "how to learn" and reading at a high level, confident about their abilities, able to make calls to top executives, can take PayPal investor Peter Thiel up on his offer of $50,000 for two years to carry out an entrepreneurial objective as long as they do not go to college; or they can get connected with "UnCollege," pay $31,000, and be led on a yearlong self-creation journey after high school.[12] In the increasingly unequal United States, those who already have evidence of their virtue can forgo proving it through the college degree and can concentrate on the substance of what they are learning, whether in or out of school. Those desperate to confirm their abilities have no option other than sitting in classrooms for as long as it takes.

Yes, the substance of college *can* be transformative. It *can* be the pivotal moment in a young life. It *can* be a needed and substantive step to a complex career. It *can* change lives. Or it can be an empty but costly slog through dreaded, meaningless requirements.

But if it is merely for a credential, then let us please stop.

Détente

In the expensive and wasteful credentials race, where increasingly four-year degrees are required to do jobs that were formerly done by high school graduates—*how else can you weed out the huge number of applicants?*—we need to call a halt. Just as the United States and the Soviet Union agreed to dial back on their nuclear weapons in the 1970s, so do we need some version of credentials détente. It may seem obvious that nobody is willing to be the first one to give up on the degree, but in fact people are increasingly asking the question, creating alternatives, and generally reconsidering the necessity of attending college merely for a diploma. I expect more of this soon.

But the other problem with college, as we know so well by now, has to do with how little learning occurs, despite the time and money spent. Reformers have been tweaking the model for a very long time.

II.   Revolutionary Schools: Tinkering with the Model

Progressive, constructivist, democratic, alternative, utopian: as John Dewey once remarked, "The fundamental issue is not of new versus old education or of progressive against traditional education but a question of what anything whatever must be to be worthy of the name *education*."[13]

As compulsory education swept the Euro-American world, challenges arose along with it. There were educational experiments long before this, of course. Looking at the kinds of education advocated by Plato, or the Common Schools of Massachusetts, or the colleges founded in the mid-1800s—from Oberlin and Antioch to the land grant universities—reminds us that notions of education are intimately intertwined with political and cultural movements. Utopian movements have tended to include educational components. Women's movements from the suffragists on have always included a focus on education. *Who goes?* is one of the perennial concerns for all levels and forms of education, as the expansion of education has proceeded along with the expansion of rights. But some reformers have mounted challenges even more radical than these.[14]

In *Émile*, Jean-Jacques Rousseau, perhaps the most prominent educational radical of all, advocated following children's "nature," rejecting school, though not teaching, entirely.[15] A surprising number of prominent figures—Benjamin Franklin, Theodore Roosevelt, Margaret Mead—never attended ordinary schools, or not until beginning college (in eras when "college" was not what it is now).

A movement in the nineteenth century, championed by Transcendentalists such as Ralph Waldo Emerson and Bronson Alcott, favored non-schooling. Early twentieth-century reformers and radicals like John Dewey, Maria Montessori, and Rudolph Steiner retained the structure of schooling while challenging the rigid industrial model, advocating more natural or more humane practices, giving rise to "child-centered" education. In the 1960s and 1970s Paolo Freire, John Holt, and A. S. Neill, founder of Summerhill, connected their critique of schooling with a critique of social values evident in treatment of children. As Neill argued:

> Obviously, a school that makes active children sit at desks studying mostly useless subjects is a bad school. It is a good school only for those who believe in *such* a school, for those uncreative citizens who want docile, uncreative children who will fit into a civilization whose standard of success is money. . . . When my first wife and I began [Summerhill], we had one main idea: *to make the school fit the child*—instead of making the child fit the school.[16]

Since the 1970s, the world of "alternative education" has become vast. It emphasizes in one place physical wellness, in another creativity, in another real connection to the world and work, in another individual shaping of the curriculum, in yet another people's innate curiosity and social cooperation.[17] Some alternative schools are more total in their challenge to convention than others, but all represent ambitions to reject the received model of "real schools." Some look to Finland for examples,[18] others to Italy.[19] Some create models from scratch, like Big Picture Learning.[20] Expeditionary Learning includes schools that embody ten principles: (1) the primacy of self-discovery, (2) the having of wonderful ideas, (3) the responsibility for learning, (4) empathy and caring, (5) success and failure, (6) collaboration and competition, (7) diversity and inclusion, (8) [respect for] the natural world, (9) solitude and reflection, (10) service and compassion.[21]

An organization in the United States, the Alternative Education Resource Organization (AERO), established in 1989, includes the following kinds of schools in its network: "Montessori,[22] Waldorf (Steiner),[23] Public Choice and At-Risk, Democratic, Homeschool, Open, Charter, Free Sudbury,[24] Holistic, Virtual, Magnet, Early Childhood, Reggio Emilia,[25] Indigo, Krishnamurti, Quaker, Libertarian, Independent, Progressive, Community, Cooperative, and Unschooling."[26]

Accepting the universal and compulsory role of schools, alternative schools, including charters, may occupy one pole or the other of the perennially competing goals (buzzwords) of "progressive" versus "traditional" education: an emphasis on "equity" (meaning uniformity?) or "excellence" (sometimes meaning individuation, which can lead to tracking); a focus on academic or vocational training; an orientation toward individual or social goals. Some organizations such as LeapNow and LeapYear, with their emphasis on gap year/"cool school," aim to help with the transitions between home and independence, high school and college, adolescence and adulthood.[27] Open Road Learning and Open Road for Teens are school-less schools.[28]

While in general the focus has been on earlier levels of education,[29] alternative, progressive, experimental, or utopian colleges have also played a role.[30] Constance Cappel visited fifty "utopian" and regular colleges in the 1980s in preparation for her feminist book *Utopian Colleges*. Some are now out of business and some endure; her touchstone school, Sarah Lawrence, is still going strong (though its small endowment has made its tuition among the highest in the country), but probably not quite as strong as in the eighties. As with the challenges at lower levels of education, these colleges have queried varying aspects of higher education including content, method, roles of participants, and location. Some implemented historically radical policies such as admitting women or African Americans. Many required "work" of one sort or another. Most aimed to be democratic and cooperative rather than hierarchical and competitive. Many emphasize creativity and the arts, as well as social justice. In the 1960s the rallying cry was "relevance!" Students were to become empowered. Some colleges included venturing off campus or even offered entirely nonresidential programs; this is commonplace now. Some seek to cultivate innovation and entrepreneurship via "disruption." Online education (including MOOCs), low-residency programs, "blurred" or "mixed" classes in which some of the work is done online and some face-to-face, "flipping the classroom"—all of these are part of the wholesale rethinking of what would transform schools.[31]

Alternatives arise from various perceived shortcomings. Some are radical and others are more incremental. While wholesale transformation may be desirable in the long term, fixes to the status quo are more likely to be possible in the short term.

III. Bricoloage: Bits and Pieces

In some ideal fantasy world children and youth are integrated into the lives of their communities, learning because of need or desire. Specialized tracks for careers can be developed quickly and the pieces can be sped up, as long as everyone has basic literacy and numeracy to build on. But barring such a utopian, Rousseaian, John Lennonesque world, the Marxist world where people farm in the morning and fish in the afternoon, the postrevolutionary cosmos, we have actual worlds to live in. And in just about every world, schooling is problematic.

Students dislike school because classes are boring, time-demanding, impersonal; or they are in big lectures and nobody knows their name; or standards are inconsistent. Some find it irrelevant. Many find it indefensibly expensive. Some of this dissatisfaction is a result of the model they have absorbed of industrial checklists and rubrics. Some has to do with immature attention spans. Some is completely appropriate.

I want to be clear that students' "liking" or "hating" school is not a *consumer* problem. I am not merely trying to please them, the way political pollsters see what plays well in each gerrymandered district, or sports drink companies vary the flavors of their product according to customers' tastes. This is not about pleasure or fun—though I do believe (from my own experience, from theories, and from other people's research) that deep learning provides deep pleasure.

Ruth Paradise published a short article in 1998 laying out all the ways learning in schools differs from learning in the rest of life. Learning in life, or in her words "in family and community settings," has higher immediate stakes; people desire the learning for its own sake and for its usefulness. She notes especially the decontextualized nature of school learning and the production of failure in school; in other contexts learning is a "by-product" of involvement in social life[32] and is motivated by need and desire, bringing with it intensity and involvement, with novices sharing identity with teachers and mentors.[33]

The more learning aligns with the way humans *are* and with the way they learn "in the wild," the more successful, joyous, and humane it will be.

I've argued that humans are immature capable curious emotional social animals. Experts show that in non-school settings people learn in a variety of ways: They learn by doing, or when they have a need or desire to learn; or they learn by teaching others, by being active. People learn when they are physically involved and when there are genuine consequences. They learn by trial and error, observation, play, and in guided participation (sometimes apprenticeship). But we also know when they *don't* learn: People don't learn when they don't care. People don't learn by cramming quickly for tests, or when their goal is to get through the learning to something else. They don't learn when things are unidimensional or when they simply glide on the surface in order to perform.

If we cannot change the entire institution of schooling, or if we cannot create our own school, what should an ordinary teacher/professor do? If "natural" learning does not fit schools' ways of teaching, teachers can try to address what they perceive as the *central* or *most important* failings. For example, if one of the key challenges is lack of intrinsic motivation—recognizing that teachers have influence over only some portion—we might focus on increasing it by giving students something *real* or *tangible* or at least fascinating that connects with their lives. Give them some genuine responsibility, at least to one another if it can't be out in the world. Helpful resources containing concrete examples abound. Five useful books are *How Learning Works, What the Best Teachers Do, How People Learn, Creating Significant Learning Experiences,* and *Teaching What You Don't Know.*[34]

Educational experimentation has proliferated, from yoga in underserved classrooms[35] to team projects, community-based learning, self-designed projects, student-led discussions, "games" and activities, actual games—the "gamification" (in a good way) of including play. Some classes employ "total physical response" or music; some emphasize students' developing relationships with one another or people outside the class; some incorporate actual blogs on the actual Internet (real audiences). There are myriad good examples of fostering students' curiosity: showing a pool filling with a hose and emptying through a hole to foster curiosity about rate and volume. Some teachers experiment with bestowing no grades for trying, or using portfolios or contract grading.[36]

Many extol the benefits of "flipping the classroom," so named when Salman Khan created his Khan Academy, a free online resource with thousands of short videos explaining a range of topics. Schools can partner with Khan Academy and track their students' progress through both their viewing of the videos and their achievement on little quizzes. In class, students work on problems or ask for help on things they were unable to do on their own, at home. In the traditional model, they come to class with their homework done and get graded on it. If they understood it, that comes out fine, but if they didn't, they are penalized. If the goal of school is to get students to learn, then this is more likely to happen if failure is taken as information that tells a teacher what is necessary. This is not a brand-new idea, of course. Seminars involve students' preparing, reading, thinking on their own, and the time spent together in class is for deepening their understanding, raising questions, making connections, suggesting applications, and more. Students take responsibility, which gives them a social and genuine reason to master material. Real consequences are much better than fake consequences.

A radical-sounding approach suggests that all teachers model learning; learn with students; teach what they don't know. Therese Huston's *Teaching What You Don't Know* is chock-full of great ideas and points out the problem with the whole framework of presuming an all-knowing teacher and a fixed and firm "it" (content) that can be known and transmitted once the disparate topics are "covered."

Here are some approaches I've been experimenting with to try to make my classes as un-school-like as possible within the framework of conventional academic disciplines.

Self-Evaluation

If I could make only one change to conventional schooling, it would be to stop giving grades. Yet I teach within a system that requires me to evaluate my students. I have tried to address this contradiction by asking them to evaluate themselves through "self-evaluations," something I've been using for several years to wean my students from teacher-directed assignments, combat their fixation on grades, and help them develop their own standards. Along with their paper, essay, blog post, or whatever, they submit a sheet that looks something like the form in Figure 11.1. They grade themselves, and I usually let their grade stand. This avoids the "I did a crummy job and hope she won't notice" phenomenon. Some classes have tougher standards than others. The last time I used this system, my undergraduates were quite pleased with their own work.

"Jigsaw" Approach: Responsibility

To give students a genuine sense of responsibility, I have for years assigned them reading that is different from their classmates' and made each of them the expert who has to summarize and evaluate the reading for the others. In this way we can "cover" more viewpoints, and students read for a genuine purpose. For example, in my New Media class I had each student read one recent book about the benefits or detriments of new media (*The world is going to hell; Paradise awaits*). In the class of about twenty-four students, I assigned eight books, so we formed three groups. Each group heard from every student about her or his book, and then they had to come up with a synthesis and a decision about what it all added up to. This work is social and real.

Study Partner: *Chavruta*

When our department began a new doctoral program in fall 2014, I taught one of the first courses. Since people tend to learn when they interact, learning by teaching, I put my graduate theory students, who arrived with different backgrounds and different goals, into partner pairs, following the

Anthropology 45865

The Anthropology of Childhood and Education
Fall 2014

Self-Evaluation

(Your name: _____) (Topic: _____)

Your goals for this project:

How you addressed your goals:

Strengths of your paper:

    Content

    Form

Weaknesses of your paper:

    Content

    Form

Why you were able to do the positive things you did:

Why you were unable to do all the positive things you wanted:

Things you would like help with:

Things you might do differently:

Comments:

	Excellent	Good	Fair
Argument			
Knowledge of and incorporation of course material and reading			
Writing style			
Creativity and independent thought			

Your grade: _____

Figure 11.1 Self-Evaluation

Talmudic study method of being in a *chavruta*, a study friendship. Rabbi Yossi bar Hanina is quoted as saying that "scholars who sit alone to study the Torah . . . become stupid."[37] Some found this helpful, as they had a classmate to work with. I have discovered at least one contemporary academic trying to incorporate this method of "collaborative critical text-based learning."[38]

Individual Learning Plans

Sarah Lawrence College incorporates into every class an individual learning plan. Students have to clarify their own goals for the class, in consultation with the professor. In fall 2014 both my classes were small, so I met with every student at the beginning and end of the semester (at least) to discuss their goals and accomplishments beyond "fulfilling requirements" and "getting an A." It was partially successful. I'd give myself a B- on this experiment.

On my website (SusanBlum.com) I have a page called "Good Learning," where I collect other examples of educational experimentation. Please contribute!

IV. Easier Said Than Done

If you want to start a revolution, you can expect a little pushback. Or a lot. As Thomas S. Kuhn writes in *The Structure of Scientific Revolutions:*

> Lifelong resistance, particularly from those whose productive careers have committed them to an older tradition of normal science, is not a violation of scientific standards but an index to the nature of scientific research itself. The source of resistance is the assurance that the older paradigm will ultimately solve all its problems.[39]

I have observed resistance every time I present my ideas for change.

Faculty Resistance

Faculty always have to decide how to handle classes when we are away: Cancel them? Show movies? Ask a colleague to guest teach? Reschedule? I have discussed having to miss class for a legitimate reason with colleagues at various institutions. Two such conversations especially stand out, one with a professor of a foreign language and one with a faculty member in science.

When I said that in the last few years I've had my students meet at class, but without me, they looked shocked. What could students possibly do without a teacher observing, judging, directing?

I gave my spiel: Our students are camp directors. They tutor children. They run their own organizations. Why can't they meet in class for an hour and get something done? I give them a task for which they are accountable.

They raised objections: *What do you have them produce?*

Their objections illustrate resistance even on the part of creative, effective faculty to new approaches to the role of teachers.

But [the language I teach] is so hard! said the language professor.

I have taught Chinese. Surely [language X] isn't harder?

Oh, it is!

Maybe they could read children's books in the foreign language?

No, children's books are the hardest!

Maybe they could have a discussion, I suggested.

Oh, no, they are not at a high enough level in the foreign language.

Maybe they could read a poem?

Too hard.

I explained the practice of Sugata Mitra, who left a computer in the square in a village in India and the students figured it out themselves with the help of Internet resources such as Google Translate.

I forbid Google Translate.

Maybe you could have them compare Google Translate and some other dictionaries? That way they could see for themselves why Google Translate isn't a great tool.

I don't even want to mention Google Translate. But I could have them translate poems in groups and compare their translations.

This seemed promising!

But they might feel that this is even more work than I have already asked of them.

How about [a well-known pop song] or something else from popular culture?

[It] doesn't even use regular words.

Some other kind of popular culture?

Maybe . . . But I'm getting the idea.

The science professor similarly could not imagine his graduate students functioning without him. They hate discussions; in their seminar class-room on their own they rearrange the seats to face the blackboard.

Maybe you could bring in a relevant item and have them figure out what it is?

In a regular classroom? Not possible.

Isn't there anything that they could figure out with the Internet?

No. They need the lab. But every semester I give my students a challenging problem that encourages independent and creative thinking.

I don't mean to single out these professors. Both are devoted to teach-ing and spend a lot of energy thinking about their classes. But the un-conventional idea of having students meet without a professor—this was unthinkable for them. And this is a simple example.

A visiting faculty member in our department did try it, with great success, when she had a series of interviews for a permanent job, which we could not give her. She gave her students a task to accomplish, a structure to follow, and a framework for reporting back. The students commented that they re-ally liked it: they liked being trusted, they liked doing something different, they liked talking frankly with their classmates without being overheard. They were so engaged in their discussions that they all stayed the whole time.

Like parents, faculty have ideas about "real teaching" that are trans-formed only partially, with difficulty, or not at all. In fall 2014 I tried whole-sale radicalism within the context of academic convention—encouraging student experimentation, tailoring assignments to students' goals, confer-ences, self-evaluations. Most days it went really well. One day, though, I could tell that the students hadn't done much reading. And I observed a physical battle within myself as I tried to decide if I should smile compas-sionately or frown with disappointment. It took a lot of self-control not to slip back into my familiar judgmental role. And I'm not even sure if that was the right decision.

Institutional Resistance

Colleges and universities are institutions with expectations, needs, and demands that endure beyond the individuals who occupy roles. Clark Kerr from the University of California coined the term *the multiversity* in

1963—the golden age of U.S. higher education—to point out that research universities have multiple functions. They serve many masters. At around the same time, in 1962 Paul Goodman called higher education "the machine" and rejected it entirely for its production of only an *appearance of learning*.

> The machine has no educative use, but it occupies the time of the students (in a period of youth unemployment), it pays the salaries of scholars, and it manufactures licenses and marketable skills. Yet these are not its purposes. Like the American economy itself, the system of universities is really a machine for its own sake, to run and produce brand goods for selling and buying. Utility is incidental. More revolutionary products like free spirit, individual identity, vocation, community, the advancement of humanity are, rather, disapproved. But frictionless and rapid running is esteemed; and by clever co-ordination of the moving parts, and lots of money as lubrication, it can be maximized.[40]

The "machine" of college is a big business; in 2011 postsecondary institutions in the United States spent $483 billion, or 3.2 percent of GDP.[41] This is no cozy little enterprise.

These "machines," these all-purpose universes for the growth, care, feeding, and entertaining of a very broad segment of the population, are what Erving Goffman called *total institutions*. As microcosms of the larger society, they reflect every virtue and every shortcoming of our, or any, society. Mental illness? They have clinics. Need for entertainment? They have video arcades, movie theaters, rock bands, nationally televised football and basketball games. This has nothing to do with learning chemistry or preparing for accounting exams, nor with understanding the web of history. But as complete human beings, students have a range of needs. Birth control. Cravings for different pizza toppings. Unitarian prayer. Stronger pecs. Support for coming out. Meditation. Hole punches. Kind of mind-boggling, as we think about how to address every possible need of thousands of human beings. Goodman continues:

> The colleges and universities are, as they have always been, self-governing communities. But the personal relations in such communities have come less and less to consist in growing up, in the meeting of veterans and students, in teaching and learning, and more and more in every kind of communication,

policing, regulation, and motivation that is relevant to administration. The community of scholars is replaced by a community of administrators and scholars with administrative mentalities, company men and time-servers among the teachers, grade-seekers and time-servers among the students. And this new community mans a machine that, incidentally, turns out educational products.[42]

The fact that this was written in the 1960s reminds us that my observations are not really new.

Such mammoth institutions usually have, as one of their units, learning and teaching centers, which may advocate profound pedagogical change. At the same time, other components support the status quo. Removing the emphasis on credit hours, for instance, would likely be embraced by learning specialists, while financial aid and the registrar would be thrown into utter turmoil.

Student Resistance

So ... We bring all kinds of new ideas to our classrooms. We try to be radical, progressive, student-centered. Sometimes it works; sometimes it flops.

Students often have an idea of "real schools." They know when a professor is "doing her job": lecturing, giving assignments, grading. A professor who shows up and asks students—in a conventional setting—"What do you want to learn?" may find that they don't know.

A colleague at Notre Dame told me about her experiences in trying to incorporate more flexible, student-centered material. When there were no grades, given the system the students were raised in, she told me with disappointment, they just spent their time on their other classes—where the learning "counted." In my fall 2014 attempt at wholesale experimentation, I found the same thing. Some students tried to slide by. One course alone cannot truly challenge the system within which it functions—especially for the winners whose expertise is in the game of school.

Change *could* be embraced, perhaps, for those with nothing to lose. Rita Smilkstein, a fellow-traveler pedagogical revolutionary, tells an amazing story in *We're Born to Learn*. She was assigned a class of eighteen male working-class "losers" in ninth-grade English who were so disruptive that after two weeks of miserable ("I felt I would not be able to go on") chaos, she offered her students a deal: If they didn't want to learn, fine. They just had to be quiet, because the principal really valued order. Most of them were eighteen; once summer came, they would be able to leave. They had been relegated to, essentially, a holding tank. She offered them a chance to approach her if there was something they wanted to learn.

> But when I turned to them, I saw they had all pushed their chairs up to my desk, as close and as jammed together as possible. We looked at each other, into each other's eyes. Time stopped. Something happened to us. I started crying. After wiping away my tears with my fingers, I asked them what they wanted to learn. They said they wanted to learn how to read and write.[43]

She used this, and other experiences, and research, to understand the "natural human learning process"—almost exactly what I've discovered in my own experience.

Downsizing Higher Ed

One thing colleges tend to succeed at—if only because conventionally students are at this late-adolescent age—is the "human development" part of growing up: developing ethics and morals, becoming independent, having responsibility and relationships. But this is separate from the academic part of college and, as we all know, often conflicts with it. Immature students in traditional college, directionless, have a lot on their minds besides knowing the difference between *structuralism* and *structural functionalism*.

If we are going to keep conventional high school (something that I *strongly* advise against),[44] I advocate regular implementation of a period before college, possibly involving service with civilian work corps and military options. Surely our society needs things done for which we lack labor power. A two-year service term following high school would address maturing. It could be there that young people learn to do their laundry, wake themselves in the morning, refrain from excessive drinking, and become accountable. They would be exposed to people from a variety of backgrounds and could encounter a lot of potential fields of interest. Consequences of their work would be real.

Once this period is finished, those who decide they need or want further education could pursue it. Some people could enter a jobs-preparation program. And some could go to college.

As it is, college is expensive, huge. It does employ a lot of people, so there would have to be a redirection of labor toward other things. (I'm dreaming . . . How about a thirty-five-hour work week? Living wages? Limits on CEO earnings in relation to workers' pay? Universal health coverage?) And for the schools that remain, changes could be undertaken, either wholesale or incrementally.

Solving . . . Which Problem? All Problems? Some Problems?

"For over a century and a half," David Tyack and Larry Cuban observe, "Americans have translated their cultural anxieties and hopes into dramatic demands for educational reform."[45] But school, including college, cannot fix everything that is wrong with society or individuals.

This insight has been discovered over and over, just as the various movements to repair or improve education at all levels have washed over us for centuries. Beginning with the Common School movement begun by Horace Mann in the 1870s, which brought the idea of universal, compulsory public schooling to the United States, through the Morrill Act which introduced land grant universities, through the GI Bill following World War II which paid for returning service members to go to college, through the shifting focus on morality and character, science and math, vocational education, "comprehensive high schools" to prepare all children for college, Pell grants, school-to-work programs, senior thesis and undergraduate research culture, writing across the curriculum, "standards," "outcomes assessment," costs and "return on investment," access, college admissions, retention, completion, character education, cultural literacy, information literacy, STEM education, ideas, practice, skills, concepts, competition of individuals, national and international competition, GDP, infrastructure, an educated workforce, self-control and discipline, leadership, innovation . . . through all these moments of inspiration and hard work, salesmanship and despair, training and retraining, research and dissemination, the hope is that [insert problem here] will improve with education.

And for some, maybe even for many, it does.

Conclusion

Learning versus Schooling: A Professor's Reeducation

When I was young, I admired clever people. Now that
I am old, I admire kind people.

ABRAHAM JOSHUA HESCHEL, *The Wisdom of Heschel*

And so my journey—this one—ends. From that time years ago when a student claimed, "I don't think Professor Blum likes college students," until today, I have been undertaking a journey without a map—an education without a curriculum. First I *needed* to understand; then I developed questions; then I observed; then I researched; always I read; I had new questions; I found a lot of fellow travelers; and slowly I altered not only my teaching but myself.

By 2013, my experience was completely different. At the end of my thirty-nine students' presentations during our exam period, I cried—both because it was clear that they had learned so much and because I was sad at the thought of parting. Then something happened: one after another they asked if they could hug me. This time, it was clear that neither of us hated the other. Even though there was another door that they could have slipped out, almost all the students filed past and hugged me, even the tall stiff guys who had always been the hardest for me to reach. A receiving line; all but maybe ten students gave me hugs. I had never experienced anything like it. It was not like when students clap at the end of a great lecture. It was like partners acknowledging through touching that there had been a connection.

And then the following week, Emmy Dawson, my teaching assistant for two courses, prefaced a suggestion this way: "Daniel [her husband, a Ph.D. student] and his friends read a book about teaching every year. Have you ever thought of writing one?"

Here is the book.

So, it is clear by now that formal schooling, institutions, residential colleges, high-prestige sorting, the focus on predetermined curriculum, age segregation, and the like are "unnatural" and lead, each in its own way, to every manner of problem. In my ideal world, the young are not students. People have curiosity, and the world around them works in concert to give them all the tools to meet their needs.

In that ideal world there is also no poverty, no inequality, no consumerism, no environmental destruction, no suburban sprawl, maybe no automobiles . . .

Meanwhile, back down here on earth, we have schools.

We have a childhood that is focused on school and, for the aspiring, on college. Some lucky students attend liberal arts colleges that are not factories churning out masses of credentialed widgets.

And some faculty at some schools are lucky enough to have the time, the security, the resources, and the freedom to think and experiment with their classes.

And sometimes it all comes together to work.

There is a handful of students who are interested in the course.

The classroom has the right *fengshui*. Or as my spiritual medium friend Dusten says, the spirits are happy.

It is the right time of day. The weather cooperates. Whatever.

When all this happens, students may linger on the last day and the air twinkles with magic.

A Magic Moment

The class was Fundamentals of Linguistic Anthropology. In my department our majors (I don't really believe in majors) are required (and I don't believe in requirements) to select three of four basic anthropology courses. From the time I arrived at Notre Dame until fall 2013, I was the only one teaching this course. Class size has fluctuated from about twenty-two to forty-eight. I like it on the larger side, because this gives us energy and buzz and a lot of experience (cultural, linguistic) that we can draw on. I also taught essentially the same course at my previous university for about eight years, so by 2013 I had approximately twenty years' experience with it.

Some of my most miserable teaching experiences have occurred in this course. And that year, one of my best teaching experiences occurred here.

Over the years I have changed almost all the readings, almost all the exercises and projects, and the formats. I have published two books of readings based on what I use in the course, since I couldn't find anything quite suitable, though I have never been satisfied with my texts either.

I have thought long and hard about my goals for the course, which have become ever simpler: *What do fellow citizens need to know about language? What can I contribute to the curiosity of educated students, and anthropology students, about language? And what misconceptions do students arrive with that really should be replaced?*

For the most part these students are not going to be professional anthropologists, much less linguistic anthropologists. For most students on their way to medical school, law, teaching, business, this is a last requirement, or maybe an intriguing subject at best. I had one student in the decade who went on to graduate school at one of the best programs in linguistic anthropology. After spending three years there, she exited with a master's degree (instead of the Ph.D. as planned) and has become a nurse-midwife. Another has an MA in teaching English to speakers of other languages and a third in speech therapy—but I've taught thousands.

So it doesn't matter if the students get every bit of the field.

It matters that they get *something*. We are all investing a lot of time and energy—and money—in the enterprise.

I have worked hard to refine every dimension of the class. I've gone from writing an outline on the board to putting it on PowerPoint, though in no sense is the class dominated by lectures and slides. My goal is to get everyone talking.

The 2012 class had been a complete dud. Perhaps I had too many detached students. Perhaps I was too distracted by my first year as department chair. Perhaps the classroom was too unwieldy and my daily attempts to rearrange the furniture put everyone off. In any case, I spent a lot of the year thinking about how to improve it.

So here is what I did in spring 2013.

Student Voices

The first day of class is always crucial. Students have to talk and move around. They have to connect with at least some other people, and not only the ones they already know. They have to recognize that they know something, and that they can connect the subject with their lives.

I always have them make introductions and then analyze the introductions, calling attention to the kinds of interactions, scripts, and goals that are evident. They are amused by the obvious conversations. They also have to speak, and learn that their voices are not just welcome but needed. This also usually lets us enjoy some shared humor early on.

In 2013 I introduced something I called "Language Links." Once a semester each student would present, at the beginning of class, something— anything in the world—related to the day's topic. Students could have talked about experiences or brought in articles, but the first ones used videos and then everyone else did too. This was enjoyable and also illustrated the ubiquity of everything we were talking about, demonstrating the applicability of our sometimes abstract learning.

There were four "mini-projects," one big project, and two "Controversies," which were group projects. Initially I gave weekly quizzes until, toward the end of the semester, a student challenged me when I admitted that quizzes didn't align with my pedagogical beliefs. "So," he said, "why don't you get rid of them?" And I did.

The Quizzes and the Reading

About ten years earlier I had been trying to lead a discussion on William Labov's famous study of the way New Yorkers of different social classes pronounce the sound /r/ either at the end of words (*floor*) or before another consonant (*fourth*). As I tried to get a discussion going, it became clear from the evasive way students seemed to be hoping someone else would talk that few of them had done the reading. I sprang a pop quiz, that horrible, punitive, and fear-intending exercise of power, asking about the location of the study described in the reading and one or two major and obvious points that anyone who had glanced at the reading would have grasped.

About two-thirds had clearly not read it. Not even looked at it.

I dismissed class early, with a berating lecture about their education and the need for preparation.

The next time the class met I gave another pop quiz, and half had still not done the reading.

By the third class, more had.

I asked them in a little survey, *What would make you do the reading? Quizzes.*

Thus were born the weekly quizzes in Ling Anth.

I tried to make them very basic, the kinds of things that anyone could get just from quick reading, and recycled questions to emphasize that everything was relevant in every section and to help them review for the final.

But students dreaded them. There was actually a pretty sizable correlation between doing well on the quizzes and grasping the material, but there were always some students who flopped on the quizzes and still seemed to understand the course material. The quizzes counted very little—140 points for all seven quizzes (the lowest score could be dropped) out of 1,000 in this latest incarnation—but students fixated on the points.

As you know by now, I don't believe in grades and I don't really believe in tests. The quizzes lived on. Until now.

In the ill-fated 2012 class where students sat stone-faced or dozing, not even the quizzes could prod them into life. I consulted with Christina Rogers, my undergraduate assistant, who has since headed off to graduate school in cognitive neuroscience. She mentioned that in some of her classes students had to turn in cards at each class. I had done that before in some classes, and introduced it mid-semester. Each student then had to enter class with a card listing (1) something she or he learned, (2) two questions, and (3) a quotation.

It didn't work in 2012, but it did work in 2013. That year I made the effort to comment on every student's card, every time. I did get a little behind sometimes, but the students knew I would read them. As you know, I don't think classes should emphasize the centrality of pleasing the teacher, but these folks were trained. Like little circus dogs: Jump for the teacher!

And if they like the teacher, even though this shouldn't be what it is all about, they care more.

Another thing I did—and I can feel my overworked colleagues at most institutions of higher education completely abandoning any hope of replicating this—was to meet with every student early in the semester.

This idea came to me the previous semester when I had had a small class. One sophomore met me in the bookstore café to talk about her session leading the class, and when we were done she said it was amazing because no professor had ever before asked her how she was. I wanted to replicate this amazement, if possible.

So during the first month of class I met every student, in batches of four, for thirty minutes, at the bookstore café. Emmy did it too (in the library café). Students signed up, and most of them remembered to go. We had no script, no agenda. I heard about their hometowns and their families and their experience abroad, and sometimes the conversation rose above the level of platitudes. I bought them tea or coffee. Altogether it cost about $80 for Emmy's and my generosity. Some students didn't want anything to drink.

And it took me about five hours. I was chair of my department and had ten to twenty meetings each week, but given the size of the class—large for our department—I thought I should do everything I could to break down the barriers.

I'm shy, and I'm busy, but I think these meetings helped. They reduced the physical and social space between faculty and students.

What other preliminaries?

Oh, yes. I invited them to call me *Susan*.

I used to find this absolute pandering. I had a colleague who signed all his notes to students with his first name. I thought this the most absurd attempt to be friendly.

What's In a Name?

I have written, anthropologically, about naming. I have made the point theoretically speaking that names create relationships.

So *Professor Blum* or *Dr. Blum* says something, and does something.

And don't forget that I don't think age or status should be the central focus of education.

My daughters both went to small liberal arts colleges where faculty were always called by their first names. This emphasized students' maturity and equality as adults rather than their status as juniors in the relationship. I listened to the ways my daughters spoke of their teachers and liked it.

So I began in my smaller classes in 2011. "Feel free to call me Susan if you like." Most did, especially once the braver ones began. Something about larger classes made me wish to retain the distance. But then in fall 2012, in a small class, one of my students did her research project on how students address faculty. She observed, interviewed, and read. And her conclusion was that no matter what, students want to be told explicitly how to address their teachers.

So for the first time in a large class, in this magical spring of 2013, I issued this invitation: *Feel free to call me Susan.*

Again, for some of my colleagues reading this, you will not want to do so.

I recognize all the implicit privilege that I am relying on here.

I am a white woman, middle class, and now middle aged. I am a full professor and was at the time department chair. I have every advantage except that I'm female and short. So in terms of "authority," I did not risk losing it by excessive friendliness.

Don't get me wrong. I'm not one of those easy-to-hang-around-and-swear-with faculty. Nobody would ever confuse me with a buddy. I'm serious and academic. I love books. I've had to work very hard to get comfortable with such a range of students, beyond the ones like myself. When I was younger, I worried that students would not take me seriously.

But for those of you who have nothing to lose, or who want to try something different, or who are in a setting where this could make a beneficial difference, you could try it. If you are at a small progressive college, or if your students are older, you may already use first names. If you are in a socially traditional setting, it might even be against the rules. If "discipline" is a problem, you may not be able to risk it. My students are very well behaved and always acknowledge authority, so they may have needed such a prod in a way that differs from institution to institution.

But think about naming. It always matters.

Back to Class

For the first weeks, I gave little exercises almost every day in which students had to define something, or explain something, or generate ideas, so that they worked in pairs or groups of three or four at their tables. Social interactions were regular occurrences. Everyone had to be active. The room was noisy—what the Chinese call *renao*—with involvement: physical, social, intellectual.

Oh, yes, the room. The room was also magic.

Notre Dame has a lot of terrible classrooms. It seems as if, when the buildings were built, someone said, "What is our stereotypical view of college? Someone lecturing from the front of the room." And then when PowerPoint became all the rage, they said, "Let's add technology to the front of the room." This is great for talking *at* students, but we have few classrooms that make discussion natural.

Room B034 Geddes Hall is one of those rooms. The tables are movable. When I taught the class in spring 2011 it was in that room, but sometimes we would arrive and the tables would be in rows facing front. Other times they would be in the "dinner table" configuration of four tables for ten. Sometimes the arrangement was messy and we would try to make a circle.

In spring 2013 it was all dinner tables, all the time.

There were screens both front and back, so even my little PowerPoint items could be visible to everyone.

And despite my initial discomfort (to be honest, it rarely leaves), I made myself circulate physically among all the students so at some point I could be looking directly at each one of them.

So in this magic room I made the students I'd gotten to know, a little, talk to one another. After a few weeks the room vibrated with talking. The students began to get to know their classmates.

Early on they had their first group project, "Controversy 1," a presentation requiring them to take a stand about the issue of linguistic relativity, the so-called Sapir-Whorf hypothesis that language shapes thought. There were six topics. Half the groups presented in class and half posted their material on the class wiki.

They got extra credit points for consulting with a librarian. I'd started this practice several years earlier when one of my students claimed, "Nobody cares about gender pronouns," and used as his sole source an outdated non-scholarly article he'd found through Yahoo. Since then I've made information literacy another quiet goal.

I know that students really dislike group projects. They have to deal with scheduling nightmares. They have to sort out uneven commitment and responsibility and ability on the part of their group mates. I never once did a group project when I was in school. In fact I don't think I ever did a project. We just wrote papers on our own.

But group projects force increased involvement in the activity because people have to talk about it, so I start the semester with one. This means they all have someone's phone number and have to meet outside class.

By mid-February, everything was rolling along pretty nicely. It was all a huge amount of work on everyone's part: mine, Emmy's, the students'. It was magic, but it was not effortless.

More projects: an "ethnography of speaking" and a little online project to gain some information about a language—from Spanish to Yucatec Maya—and get students thinking about what kinds of things we need to know when we think about "a language," and some practice in digital media.

And then in March their conversation analysis: Record a conversation—after getting signed consent—and transcribe and analyze five minutes. It is never what they expect, and they are always transformed afterward. They work hard and write a lot—from about five to nearly thirty pages, depending on the kind of writer each one is—but this always sticks with them. They can always read a transcript after it, too.

And a mini-project on identity, one on the nature of language or writing. "Controversy 2" is about real-world language issues, such as bilingual education and English-only laws. They grapple with "Ebonics" and gender.

And this year, instead of a cumulative final exam, which I used to like because it forced students to review, I gave three options: to write a "language myth" analogous to the myths we'd read about; to revisit one of the earlier projects, using a YouTube video for data; or to make a movie addressing the question "What is language?"

Did I ever tell you *this* story about the class?

A Teacher's Delight: My Students Are Talking about Class Behind My Back—But in a Good Way

I found out by accident. I had a meeting in a building across campus and one of my students had a job there staffing the reception desk. She is one of those students every professor always hopes to get:

insightful, very well trained, a terrific writer, great sense of humor. She also brought personal experience in multilingualism and multiculturalism to a class on linguistic anthropology. I am hesitant to ask any individual to represent a topic or group, so I had not completely mined her for what she could contribute, but she had lived many of the class subjects.

We chatted about this and that. And then I said something about how much there is to talk about in the class and how I feel we always run out of time. I also expressed regret that we had not spoken about her country's complex background as much as I would have liked.

"It's okay. We talk about it on our own."

What? This was something I rarely heard.

"Our table goes out to lunch after every class" (that's three times a week!) "and we talk about the class. You should come with us sometime."

This is the Holy Grail. This is winning the teacher's lottery. This is getting a golden ticket. This is all I've ever wanted in my decades of teaching: for students to care and to want to learn the subject. I don't have any genuine stake in whether they remember the names of Sapir and Whorf and Hockett or if they know what *duality of patterning* is, even though we talk about such things. Whether they can define *language revitalization* or *pidgins* and *creoles* or *adjacency pairs* or *negative politeness* or *index* and *icon* ten years from now . . . that is not the point. All I really want is that they become intrigued by the complexity of language and culture and the mysteries of human social interaction.

So by my own criteria, I passed this particular course with flying colors!

I worked hard to make this magic happen, as I realize that not all students come to class as excited about the subject as I am, but there are also mysterious ingredients—one student with a passion, two students with particular experience—that transform a group of people going through the motions and fulfilling requirements into a tight-knit body of eager discussants. I do not claim credit for this success. The alchemy of any group of humans is beyond the analysis of *this* anthropologist.

But however it happened, I wanted to savor it.

So you can bet I went to lunch with them. I wanted to listen and bask in our joint accomplishment: making something learned in school come alive with possibility and meaning.

Sometimes formal education works. And when it does, when the students are buzzing with interest in the subject, when they don't even tell the teacher about their out-of-class conversations—this is worth every moment.

I went to lunch. Stayed two hours. That's where the student challenged me to drop the quizzes. The class ended. At graduation the students from that class, that table, sought me out. I told them I was going to write about the class and they were thrilled. But this rare exemplary class is tough to replicate.

Not all was ideal in this class. In a survey I did at the end of the semester, students reported working one to three or four to six hours a week, on average, for this demanding class. (I thought the numbers should be higher.) Some of them cut corners. Their final projects were somewhat disappointing. They struggled to integrate class readings into ethnographic discoveries or papers about their viewpoints. Some of their work was superficial. Few of them really understood the nature of the sign. Not every student cared. One student pushed me to my limit by not turning in half the assignments until after finals but appealing cleverly to my interest in her "learning." I had to get the dean's office to help me explain things to her. One student plagiarized from the work of a student in the previous year's class. But that student hugged me too on the last day of class. After our journey through the honor code process, I feel that we are connected for life.

I know I'll keep getting email from the students for a while, as they encounter language-related articles and videos. And then they, and I, will move on, forming new attachments, writing new papers, designing new courses.

But for me this magic memory will endure. I will seek replication. If it works, then I will know I have finally, after twenty-five years, learned something about teaching. My guess is that sometimes I will succeed, and sometimes I won't.

Like being a parent, being a teacher is humbling. We have some power and influence, but the world is vast. Students, like children, come from many places and are subject to many influences. I am glad I am not solely responsible for either category; the trust and opportunity are daunting. Sometimes I feel I've earned them and am worthy. At best, I could dance and sing and celebrate. When I feel the opposite, it is the worst feeling in the world.

Meeting My Younger Self and Knowing She Was Gone

Still floating high after my successful class ended, I met a new colleague, just finished with her first year of teaching. She teaches literature in a foreign language, and is trying simultaneously to teach language and writing and critical thinking skills. I could feel from her first complaining comments that it wasn't going well. "I told them not to say, 'This book is about such-and-such a topic,' which is a simple thing they must have learned in high school. Even though I keep telling them, they keep doing it." We were at a spontaneous lunch with two other faculty members as well. We started giving suggestions: *Begin with something easier than traditional literary works in anthologies. Don't expect them to care about literature; what about email? You can't teach by telling them things.* We—mostly I—talked about the complicated extracurricular lives our students have. She had no idea.

And then she said, "I spend an hour on each paper, correcting everything they do wrong. And they don't improve."

This is tragic in every possible way.

Nobody had guided this well-intentioned academic in how to teach. Students cannot receive a paper full of corrections and make anything meaningful of it. I can imagine her resenting and being frustrated by her students, and vice versa. She is the strict teacher who cannot reach a single student unless it is someone exactly like her. She had grown up in another country, where college was for people with plans to focus on the subjects they studied. They took courses only in their own areas. They did nothing but study. They appreciated correction because it led to improvement.

The baffled woman stuck to her righteous insistence that she could not give good grades for poor performance; it would not be ethical.

We suggested looking for one thing at a time. Using peer editing. Focusing on three commonalities in the paper rather than everything that was wrong.

But what struck me, suddenly, was the realization that I had been a lot like her twenty-five years earlier, complaining at the entitled slackers who did not appreciate the distilled perfection that I was offering. As with all learning, though, I could no longer (mostly) feel that way. It was as foreign as not having known Chinese, or local foods, or marriage. Once upon a time I was young and smug. And then I grew up and understood how at the core of each interaction is not judgment and certainty but goodwill and desire.

One Question: From Judgment to Love

My journey has taken me away from my lifetime of evaluating every student and, for that matter, probably every person, on a single scale: How smart are they? How serious? How hard do they work at school? And I have moved from regarding my students with judgment to regarding them with affection, if not always unconditional love. My teaching, and my life, have become transformed.

I remember being in France when I was in my mid-twenties. My friend Don had moved there with his girlfriend, now his wife, and I was visiting during the summer, after a year or two of exciting but stifling graduate school. (I see its stifling nature only in retrospect.) I was disoriented. How did all these people I was meeting measure up? I couldn't place them. I couldn't figure out what kind of college they'd gone to, or what kind of job they had. They mentioned taking part in various *stages* (in French, 'training workshops') and switching from one job to another. So which kind of person were they? My kind? Or the kind I didn't have too much to do with?

Pathetic.

And in teaching, I of course preferred the students like me, the ones who were prepared, having done the reading, who asked questions, who turned in everything on time, and who went beyond the minimal requirements, indicating that they cared. It is easy and gratifying to affirm the worth of people who have already accepted the system completely, don't you think? But I saw it as simply carrying out some absolute standards. If you do it this way, you're good, and you get both A's and approval. Do it some other way, and you get neither. When students didn't seem to care (notice the repetition of that word?), or cared more about other things, I wanted to show them, teach them a lesson, convert them to the proper path, convince them of the superiority of the dominance of academia. Business? Pshaw! Athletics? Come on! Dorm life? Friends? Jobs? All the interests, distractions, competing domains could not possibly measure up to the sacred realm of the academy, with classes, books, and papers at the center. It is a religion when put that way. The students were novices and I the priest. We had sacred texts, rituals, ancestors, rites of passage, rewards.

I had learned this so long ago.

I remember playing school; I always wanted to be the teacher.

I can't quite recall what school, and being the teacher, meant to six-year-old me, though it is clear that the teacher-centered world of school meant that she was the most important person. She had authority. She got to control the attendance books, the chalk and blackboard erasers. She could even use pen, while we pupils had to use pencils. She judged everybody, could make them laugh or cry. She could confer the mantle of goodness, or devastate with the assessment of failure or evil.

Teachers came to our house for lunch in the spring. We spoke of them in awed tones. We took them Christmas and end-of-the-year gifts. Their favor, like God's, made our faces shine. Their judgment was final. If Mrs. Whatever-Her-Name deemed us "smart," especially if it was affirmed by the Testing-from-Above, then we were.

My parents, too, were smart. They skipped grades in school. They were in special classrooms. Dad graduated from college at nineteen then went to medical school. And I was smart. All five of us kids were smart. That made us good.

Didn't it?

When I was twenty I had a boyfriend who had never gone to college. This was a revelation to me. How could any worthy person not go to college? Was he smart? Who would tell me the right answer to this enduring question?

I began to learn that there was more than one question, and that even with that one question there were many possible ways to answer it.

But the centrality of the One Question remained in my mind for decades. It is supported by everything around us: the old-fashioned psychological focus on *g* (general intelligence) or IQ, SAT scores, GPAs, class rank, and current state-by-state annual testing. It is supported by the general competitive nature of our capitalistic society, by puritanical notions of grace as evidenced by success, by a winner-take-all social structure. I didn't know I possessed this view of the One Question, just as most of us are unaware of the guiding principles of our culture. I believed that I was Right to enforce Standards.

When I taught at Oklahoma State and the University of Colorado Denver, I began to confront the multiplicity of backgrounds of the students, the complexity of their lives. I still believed that academic value had to be measured in a single fashion, but I could certainly sympathize with the family, work, and financial pulls outside school. These students were quite interesting, not merely as case studies but as real human beings. They had come from families with no higher education, or from other countries. They had been in the service. They had had children when they were teenagers. Or they had just lived simple, regular lives for a while and then decided to try something else.

College could make a difference for these students. They could learn something new about the world, or they could discover new talents in themselves. They could create new ways of thinking and acting. They could put on new roles, get new jobs, use new words. It was thrilling for me as a teacher, once I got over my sense that only one form of preparation was adequate.

And then I moved to Notre Dame.

The year I arrived, 2000, the school paper was filled with gloating about how superior these students were over all previous years' students. (Each successive year has the same story.) Better grades, better SAT scores, more community service, more athletes, more team captains and class presidents, more musicians. The admission process was more competitive than ever. A smaller percentage of applicants than ever before had been accepted.

They felt *great*! They had been affirmed and praised every step of the way. They were confident and complacent.

So why, when they entered my classroom, did they seem so entitled yet so disappointing? I took it as my task to show them that they weren't so great after all, at least until they did a better job for me. They didn't read carefully. They did only what was asked and no more. They wrote bland, innocuous papers. But they wanted A's for all that.

Not from me you don't!

I didn't experience this period as the comedy I am presenting it as now. It seemed like a righteous battle at the time: They think they're so great? Fine! I would show them what good really meant.

This went on for a few years. I got the teaching evaluation from the student who thought I disliked college kids. (I didn't dislike them all; just the ones who thought they deserved to be called excellent when they weren't . . . so, not all of them, just most of them!)

But I began to get used to the students, a little. I had a few who were really nice and interesting. Within about three years I had gotten to know some of them a little better. And I proposed my plagiarism project, which resulted in *My Word!* It was, I think, intended in part to demonstrate how misguided the attention to extracurricular stuff was and to deplore the lack of attention to academics, and to show that this was the fault not of individual students but of the system of which they and we—I and my colleagues—are a part.

But in the end, this is only a fraction of what happened.

The really big story, as you know by now, is that I began to reevaluate the whole notion of schooling. I have thrown away the One Question. I can see these lovely people as fully embedded in their lives with a range of families, abilities and disabilities, passions and fears. School happens in the context of all this. Students appear in my class one semester, having experienced twenty years or so of life. They want to be liked and loved and admired. They want to enjoy themselves. They want to be recognized as the people they are. They want to learn cool stuff. They generally want to go out and do something, whether it's earning money, finding a calling, getting married, improving the well-being of their fellow humans, or whatever. So my class has a role to play, but it is probably a different role for each of them. This is not a simple-minded "learning styles" discovery; it means that I have no idea, really, how my class fits with each of my students. All I can do is introduce them to this stuff that I love, try to provide a rich enough set of materials so they can find something to connect to, and invite them to delve in and discover its value themselves.

Now, I have always been a complete apologist for/defender of/partisan of the liberal arts. I regarded this as where the wisdom of humanity was stored, where ideas and values were debated, where the mind was at its purest. For me, honed as I was by the whetstone of education, abstraction reigned supreme. I loved the clarity of ideas and the architecture of theory. Should not all children be exposed to such learning? Who knows how many of them may awaken to the subtlety of history, the beauty of language, the importance of theoretical foundations? Some who thought they wanted to sell newfangled gadgets to people might find out that capitalism oppresses the masses and convert to social critique. Some whose parents expected them to spend their lives perfecting others' teeth might discover a love of art and end up sculptors instead of orthodontists (although I know that we also need orthodontists). This hopeful outlook values certain kinds of work and certain kinds of lives above others: mind over matter, abstraction over concreteness.

But for most people, learning is material and concrete and social. They learn all kinds of things when they hang out and watch their friends; they learn skills when they need them. They have no trouble understanding baseball statistics or sales figures. They just can't get really excited about different theoretical approaches to explaining the outbreak of a world war. Should this consign them to more than fifteen years of feeling inadequate and resentful?

Having a single scale—GPA, IQ, and SAT scores—misleads students, parents, and teachers into a way of assessing that will never again apply in their lives. Yes, in jobs and in life some people are more successful than others; but how would we compare a salesman and a carpenter? There is no single scale. In school, however, there is just one, and most people don't get to be on top.

Putting It All Together

As societies cope with the question of how to take their dependent, helpless young and turn them into the kinds of people respected by their own, each society emphasizes its values—fierceness or gentleness, harmony or proud independence—and its young largely learn how to become individuals who enact those values. In the United States, and increasingly everywhere else, a specific image has emerged, through school, of an ideal human: docile in following regulations, adapted to classroom structures, able to sit still for hours at a time, and economically competitive.

Even more than literacy, which is at most three or four thousand years old, schools are a very recent invention, at least for the majority of human beings. It is only in the last two centuries that something approaching universal, compulsory schooling has become common as a desired individual good. At the same time, schooling is often ineffective, or worse, problematic. Critics regard the hegemony of conventional compulsory education as damaging and misguided.[1] Learning, however, is part of our evolutionary endowment. Evidence from biology, psychology, cognitive science, linguistics, anthropology, psychoanalysis . . . all points to the same conclusion, simply grounded differently. Humans are born to learn.

In our contemporary world we need to learn how to read. We need to learn how to pay bills. We need to learn to cook, at least a little. We need to learn how to tie shoes, pump gas, listen to a friend. All kinds of things in our lives are learned through need. In many societies students learn by apprenticing to masters because what they learn will constitute their livelihood. Most people learn to cook by observing, trying, and so forth, rather than by studying principles and being tested.

In our schools we take kids from their families, and we make it so that they learn to cope, to find others to comfort them, to bond with a social group, and to replace the parent with the teacher. The best little ones are those who accept the separation cheerfully. We reward being outgoing, busy, quick, friendly, both self-contained and compliant. Following instructions . . . keeping on task . . . being aware of time constraints; "time on task," self-control, "locus of control," "executive function." These are now seen to predict success later in life. But it's all circular. We name it, try to produce it, measure it, reward it, and then claim success when we get what we have created.

After those first years of inculcating self-control, transference, and sharing, we get all those things that John Taylor Gatto identified as part of schooling: age segregation, teacher focus, feigned attention that can be curtailed in a flash, superficial appearance of learning.

We have come to accept that all individuals should spend their entire childhood in school, even though little of what occurs there matters in the long run. And it even backfires in terms of inculcating obedience without initiative, performance without meaning, achievement without values, activity without joy. Students learn to cheat, cut corners, lie, evade. They are confined to buildings with peers who might bully or mock or cow them into conformity or entice them into dulling the experience through various substances or random sex.

High school is the worst of the bad. Students with energy and passion are forced to sit docilely. Those who can't contain themselves explode or storm off. Given the iron grip of the system, "they are only hurting themselves," but that is simply because we have evolved a system in which the ability to stand such confinement is certified by documents, degrees, diplomas, and anyone without them has not proven herself or himself to be our kind of person. It is really a mark of endurance.

To the extent that students accept this yoke, out of parental discipline or their own desire to please their parent-substitute, the teacher, we may turn out high-scoring test takers, and occasionally poets, musicians, dreamers. But the whole system seems to produce unhappiness along with the constant competition.

The most privileged of the lot internalize the standards, sneaking energy drinks so they can stay up studying till any hour their families deem acceptable. They wear themselves out emotionally and physically, trying to outdo their friends and end up with the cherished dream of admission to a competitive college.

So they arrive at college, having learned how to please teachers, how to get as much done in as little time and with as little effort as possible. They have learned to ask "What do you want?" and hide their displeasure from authorities.

This is frustrating for those of us who entered college teaching because we wanted to share the joy of learning, but we can't really fault our students for wanting to be different from us. We can force them, just barely, to learn what we insist matters, but we can't force them to care about it.

But all this fails to ask: What is it that makes for a good life? What, in that broadest context, is the role of schooling, and even of learning? Jobs and success and achievement and performance are easily weighed and compared. Some kinds of learning can be assessed with widely administered tests. But living a meaningful life is harder to measure.

Humans are flexible; societies differ enormously in how the young are brought up. But if students are failing in so many ways, maybe it is because we are running up against the absolute limits of what it is to be a person: too much cognition and not enough sociality, too much autonomy and not enough physicality.

In *The Structure of Scientific Revolutions,* Thomas Kuhn has a suggestion that is relevant here.

Like Ptolemaic astronomy, which clung to life by its fingertips, adding one minor fix after another to an erroneous system, attempting to "save the phenomena," our entire child-rearing and educational system is ripe for a Copernican revolution. We have tried one small adjustment after another, only to find more discontent and discouragement. But why? And for what genuine ends?

While I await a more humane world, I carry on in my classes. I've spoken of my reeducation and described some of my own attempts to improve things for my students, while acknowledging that my efforts often fall far short of my ideals.

For the Road—Your Road

My hope for you—my colleagues, my students, my children, my neighbors, the kids struggling down the road—is that you find places in your life that absorb you and give you a sense that you matter, that let you do something you like and in which you can feel pride. That does not have to mean "contributing to society"; it can be as simple as enjoying a walk in the park or knowing how to fix your aunt's squeaky stairs, or discovering that you love reading science fiction. It could be teaching your subject to entranced students. Somewhere in each of our lives, long or short, I hope we can find those moments when we feel the peace of involvement in something. It might be a job, career, or profession. It might be a relationship. It might be nature, or entertainment, or the arts.

You may not get prizes. Reward yourself.

The question remaining is how I, as a university teacher whose students necessarily consumed the messages about competition and deferral, about playing the game and mastering the system, can give them a taste of something else.

That has become my principal challenge, and my obsession.

Appendix

A New Metaphor: Permaculture, or Twelve Principles of Human Cultivation

Metaphors dominate our thinking and thus our action. Are we *one big happy family*? Is it a *dog-eat-dog world*? Are humans *cogs in the machine*, or are we *infused with the light of God*? As George Lakoff and Mark Johnson demonstrated in their 1980 book *Metaphors We Live By*, conceptual metaphors organize our cognition, systematically and deeply, and we cannot think in any sort of nonmetaphoric, "literal" or transparent way.[1] So it is worth looking at the metaphors that have been generated to discuss learning and schools. I propose an old-made-new-again metaphor, the Garden—but with a twist—that might help.

School Is War, Prison, Factory, Machine, Business, Game, Life . . . and Other Metaphors

The ancient Greeks, at least some of them, conceptualized a *symposium* as a dinner party. Other ancient Greeks moved and walked while they discussed matters, in the *peripatetic* model. For millennia every Jewish

Talmud student was matched carefully by his teacher in a friendship pair, *chavruta*. Their task was to struggle together. At the same time, the synagogue was conceived as a school, a *shul*, in eastern Europe—a place not only to worship but also to learn.

Talk with students and teachers today and they will offer that school is *war*, with battles and sides; school is a *prison*, with walls and identification cards and guards and metal detectors; school is a *game*, in which the goal is to accumulate points, to learn the arbitrary rules, and to master tricks that give an advantage. College is regarded as a *commodity*, its *costs* weighed against *returns*. Or school is the entirety of *life*, with all needs met, and including every aspect of a young person's being. The sociologist Erving Goffman considered schools *total institutions*, just like hospitals and prisons.

Critics and workers alike sometimes see schools as *machines*: when all the components are well oiled and every part knows its place, the machine can go smoothly and without crisis. Many administrators operate schools like *businesses*: the goal is the bottom line, and the humans involved are simply one aspect of capital to be managed efficiently and flexibly.

In the early twentieth century, a battle ensued between progressive educators conceiving of schooling as a *garden*, where students need nurturing and cultivation, and traditional educators conceiving it as a *factory*, where inputs and outputs and assessments and uniformity reign.

I propose bringing back the metaphor of the *garden*, but this time with a century of ecological knowledge included.

Bear with me as I explore these two dominant metaphors, a *factory* or *industrial model* and a *permaculture model*. Both may be applied to agriculture, and both may be applied to schooling.

The Factory Model: Big Ag and Big Ed

Factories developed especially in the nineteenth century to increase efficiency. Take uniform raw materials, design a single plan, take energy from elsewhere, make a mold or pattern, apply the energy to churn out predetermined uniform products. Subject them to sorting and assessment to ensure quality. Repeat. This works in a limited way, short-term, for steel, cars, and widgets.

During the twentieth century, farming changed from small-scale, diverse family-run landholdings to huge "factory farms" where single products are produced. This has allowed contemporary farmers, for example, to churn out enormous quantities of soybeans and corn to feed to cattle and pigs.

The transformation of schools from one-room schoolhouses or mixed-age academies to large "factory schools" paralleled the transformation of farms. Conventional schooling, like industrial agriculture and industry itself, assumes that children (plants) are like unformed materials, such as steel, and can be stamped out uniformly.

But the model doesn't work in the long term for children, just as it doesn't actually work sustainably for plants or animals.

The inputs are too costly. The by-products are too dangerous. The wastes are unaffordable. The strain is excessive. There is not enough energy.

In agriculture the food produced this way is not even desirable: it's bland, tasteless, often diseased. In the case of education, we find at the worst unhappiness, mental illness, unhealthy competition, dropping out, and superficial performance.

And it is expensive.

Industrial agriculture, "Big Ag," relies on subsidies for petroleum and price supports for the biggest industrial farms, irrigating with water often, as in California or North China, piped in from elsewhere, fertilizing with the by-products of defense industries, employing pesticides that poison the soil, water, workers, and consumers, shipping long distances, and using antibiotics on animals confined in miserable, unhealthy spaces.

For students, the "factory model" of schooling, "Big Ed," represses natural energy and drive rather than harnessing it. It creates rebels. It deforms the spirit. It aims to—but does not in fact—produce uniform humans. These may have been ideal docile factory workers; but all societies, just like all fields, need a robust, healthy, diverse, and complementary set of people.

In contrast to the factory or industrial model and metaphor, we could regard the cultivation of humans—just like the cultivation of food—as something that might be done sustainably, and in the process provides opportunities for both individual and collective well-being.

The Permaculture Model

I propose another analogy between education and growing food, using concepts from the field of "permaculture," a system of design principles that aims to mimic natural principles to yield permanently sustainable results, not only in terms of the physical and biological and botanical worlds, but also incorporating the human, and our practical ("livelihood") as well as spiritual and communal needs. "Waste" is included, as every system produces "waste," but minimizing and planning for it. Though only a metaphor, it actually works quite well to design a humane, sustainable system—including an education system—that works *with* (human) nature rather than constantly and ineffectively battling *against* it. (See Figure A.1.)

Permaculture, according to one of its founders, David Holmgren, is founded on twelve design principles.[2] We can apply these as well to principles for cultivating humans, integrated in a natural, economic, and social world. (See Table A.1.)

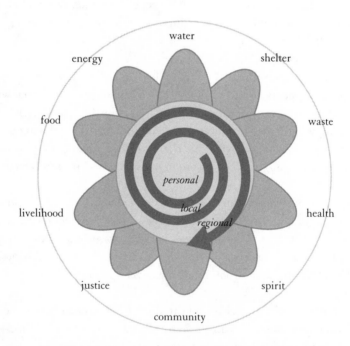

Figure A.1 The Permaculture Flower; modified by Toby Hemenway from David Holmgren. Used by permission of Toby Hemenway.

TABLE A.1   Applying Permaculture Principles to Education

Permaculture principles*	Application to education
1. *Observe and Interact*: "Beauty is in the eye of the beholder."	1. Collect stories and observations of different kinds of educational models and their results.
2. *Catch and Store Energy*: "Make hay while the sun shines."	2. Use children's and young adults' energy.
3. *Obtain a Yield:* "You can't work on an empty stomach."	3. Give students satisfactory harvests all along the way.
4. *Apply Self-Regulation and Accept Feedback:* "The sins of the fathers are visited on the children unto the seventh generation."	4. When it doesn't work—change!
5. *Use and Value Renewable Resources and Services:* "Let nature take its course."	5. Follow natural tendencies.
6. *Produce No Waste:* "A stitch in time saves nine." "Waste not, want not."	6. Be sure you do not waste time on trivia; do not produce negative side effects.
7. *Design from Patterns to Details:* "Can't see the forest for the trees."	7. What are the big goals?
8. *Integrate Rather than Segregate:* "Many hands make light work."	8. Integrate novices and experts, people of different backgrounds, ages, interests. Include non-school participants. Get rid of school walls.
9. *Use Small and Slow Solutions:* "The bigger they are, the harder they fall." "Slow and steady wins the race."	9. Make things livable (e.g., no cramming for tests).
10. *Use and Value Diversity:* "Don't put all your eggs in one basket."	10. Different forms of knowledge and ways of learning are valuable and cannot be prescribed in advance.
11. *Use Edges and Value the Marginal:* "Don't think you are on the right track just because it's a well-beaten path."	11. Those deemed not "normal" or "average" may make valuable contributions.
12. *Creatively Use and Respond to Change:* "Vision is not seeing things as they are but as they will be."	12. Not everything is predictable or changeless.

* http://permacultureprinciples.com/.

I am intrigued by all of this, but I find the concept of "waste" especially relevant for discussions of education. In schooling, some of the "waste" that is produced has been discussed earlier in the book, and includes waste of time, money, human energy, childhood curiosity, and opportunity to do something meaningful. The harmful by-products include mental illness, anxiety, stress. And can we really afford to "discard" the ones self-expelled from the system, the dropouts?

The most tragic form of "waste" is the despair that far too often results from students being told that they are failing, or from their complete disconnection from others and the situation. This lasts years, if not a lifetime.

Beyond Monocropping Children

Education, *permeducation*, is exactly like a garden designed according to concepts of permaculture: we wander in and find everything already there. (The words *culture* and *cultivate* share meanings with agriculture.) Nature must be our ally, not our enemy, but we must firmly grasp natural principles. Diversity and complexity must be the goals so we can withstand whatever arrives in the future.[3] We must design with the entire system and its perpetuation in mind.

For the garden this includes sun and rain and snow and ice; deer and rabbits and snakes; the growth of hidden seeds; the soil; the individual humans who will use it; the community within which it is situated; the economy that sustains it and that it sustains.

For education it is exactly the same. We have to work *with* the tendencies of human beings (tendencies toward movement and sociality); we have to produce diverse results in order to ensure that, whatever comes, some will be prepared to grow; we have to plan as best we can for a variety of users; we have to consider the social and economic contexts.

I take this to refute a number of common institutional practices: a one-size-fits-all curriculum; an assumption that we are beginning with blank slates; an attempt to control every aspect of the process; the need for uniformity of inputs (age, ability), pressures, and outputs, measured by uniform assessments; the hubris to assess everyone in a single fashion; disregard of the human soil—the need to be nurtured and fed.

If all education is cultivation, then it is no surprise that when we *fight* natural forces, we expend energy wastefully, fail to attain our desired results, and produce various pollutants. We cannot produce what we claim to desire. When we work *with* those forces, we produce beauty and bounty.

In that sense, then, the more we can detect these natural forces, the more we experiment with microclimates and persnickety little unique plants, and the more resilience we can build into this system, the better.

So in my little corner of the universe, in a context that I would never have predicted, and if given all the choices in the world might not choose, I try. I make my compost. I give richness back to the soil as best I can. I introduce some joy and color. I hope my young charges can bend in the wind, not break. I embrace the idea that my hundreds and thousands of opportunities to touch young people will yield unexpected harvests.

ACKNOWLEDGMENTS

As you can imagine, since this book draws on my entire personal and professional life, there are countless people to acknowledge, thank, give their due. My memory is pretty good, but I'm sure I've left out really important people. So, please know that if I've forgotten you, I'll remember you as soon as the book goes to production!

My first debt is to the stupendous undergraduate students who helped me directly with this project, including interviewers, transcribers, analysts, interviewees, survey respondents, and partners. Those are Hillary Brass, Jee Seun Choi, Theresa Davey, Christina Gutierrez, Rupa Jose, Lily Jingting Kang, Kate Johnson Kennedy, Barunie Kim, Sarah Kimball, Alexis Palá, Kaitlin Ramsey, Christina Rogers, Michayla Sullivan, Jake Weiler, Aaron (Addy) Wilson, Caitlin Wilson, and the nearly five hundred anonymous interview subjects and survey respondents. Funding all that help were the Institute for Scholarship in the Liberal Arts (ISLA) in the College of Arts and Letters (several grants), the Department of Anthropology, the Office of Research, and the Kellogg Institute for International Studies, all at Notre Dame. The Kellogg Institute and ISLA also supported a conference in 2012 that helped clarify my questions about this topic. Emmy Dawson and Therese Hanlon were invaluable organizers and supporters.

Since I published *My Word!* in 2009, I have been invited to speak at a large number of institutions of all types, always leading to formative and engrossing conversations with faculty, administrators, and students. I thank the following schools for such invitations: Asnuntuck Community College (and Northwestern and Quinebaug Valley Community Colleges), Athens State University, Carleton College, College of Charleston, Culver Military Academy, Delta Kappa Gamma Society, the Haja School (Seoul), Jewish Federation of St. Joseph Valley, John Adams High School (South Bend), Peace House (South Bend), Renmin University (Beijing), Rhode Island College, Seton Hall University School of Nursing, the University of Alabama (Tuscaloosa), the University of Chicago, the University of Michigan, the University of Notre Dame, the University of Virginia, Western Michigan University, Yonsei University (Seoul), and Zayed University (UAE).

Other schools have been formative in my life because I was either a student, parent, or teacher at them. These include Carleton College, Clara Barton Junior High School (Royal Oak, Michigan), Congregation Shaarey Zedek (Southfield, Michigan), Hampshire College, the Inter-University Program (Taipei), Interlochen Arts Camp, the Jewish Community Center of Denver, Jiangsu Institute of Education (Nanjing), John J. Cory Elementary School (Denver), John Marshall Elementary School (South Bend), the Montessori Academy at Edison Lakes, Oklahoma State University, the University of Colorado Denver, the University of Denver, the University of Michigan, the University of Pennsylvania, Sinai Synagogue (South Bend), Southfield-Lathrup Senior High School (Michigan), Stanford University, and Washington Elementary School (Royal Oak, Michigan). Some of the exemplary teachers I've known in my life are Sidney Britton, Shelley Chaiffetz, Kay DeLong, Hung Hsiu-fang, Donna Krasnow, Liang Zhuzhu, Sharon Messinger, Alice Stanley, and Cindy Tachman.

The writing of this book, which took several years (at first I didn't know what I was writing), was assisted by conversations with countless people, some academic and many not. Some of those who were most regularly involved or with whom I had a single formative conversation include Deborah Appleman, Chris Ball, Kevin Barry, Tim Bayer, Jada Benn Torres, Martin Bloomer, Cat Bolten, Mary Jeanne Brenholts, Tamo Chattopadhay, Meredith Chesson, Meghan Chidsey, Cho (Han) Hae-joang, Jee Seun Choi, Chris Clark, Cindy Dell Clark, Emmy Dawson, Peter Demerath, William Deresiewicz, Lise Dobrin, Carolyn Edwards, Lizzie Fagen, Christine Finnan, Vanessa Fong, Agustín Fuentes, Suzanne Gaskins, Lee Gettler, Teresa Ghilarducci, Stuart Greene, John Herzog, Elena (Sassy) Jensen, Hannah Jensen, Lionel Jensen, Rebecca Klenk, David Lancy, Angie Lederach, Katherine Lewandowski, Dennis Littke, Cynthia Mahmood, Jim McKenna, Molly Moon, Leslie Moore, Tami Moore, Hugh Page, Heather Price, Roman Sanchez, Holly Donahue Singh, Elisa (EJ) Sobo, Cara Spinosa, Allison Stoney, Nikita Taniparti, Gabriel Torres, Julie Turner, Bonnie Urciuoli, and Gail Weinstein. Jim McKenna read an early prospectus and has been enthusiastic all along. Agustín Fuentes read a chapter, offering very helpful comments. Cat Bolten and Molly Moon read the entire draft and provided invaluable close reading as well as sensitive and brilliant broader suggestions. I stubbornly retained my own flaws. While I was finishing the draft in the spring and summer of 2014, I talked to friends at Purple Porch Co-op who kept encouraging (and feeding) me. And most magical of all, I spent three days writing at Climbing Vine Cottage in Newfield, New York.

At Cornell University Press, Fran Benson is the ideal editor who can locate the heart of a bold book, and get a writer to help it beat. The editorial team of Emily Powers, Ange Romeo-Hall, and Amanda Heller is a powerhouse of professional and competent people, effective at making manuscripts become books rather than collections of words and pages. And Cathy Small is the manuscript reviewer that I've always hoped for. Sometimes writers' dreams come true.

As always, my unbelievable daughters, Hannah Jensen and Sassy Jensen, were my teachers. They graciously agreed (I checked!) to permit me to write about them and their learning. And Lionel Jensen . . . though I have many words, they fail to convey your foundational support for the entire edifice of my scholarly and personal life. My parents, Joyce and George Blum, taught and modeled love of both learning and school. Long may you learn!

The book is dedicated to my four siblings, Kathi Moss, Bobby Blum, Linda Long, and Barbara Blum-Alexander. They have accompanied me on my lifelong journey to understand this strange human condition, and have provided me with mirrors, sister- and brothers-in-law, nieces and nephews, playmates, pretend pupils, the heartiest laughs, the best cries, and always a place to return. *L'chaim.*

Notes

1. Complaints

1. See Riley 2011 for a complaint against faculty; Bok 2006 about low expectations; Ginsberg 2011 about administrative bloat. Adjuncts. Costs. Debts. Faculty are angry at the ways universities are now regarded as businesses and the students as customers. June 2010 describes the faculty experience of being burned out and tense, all the professional hazards that accompany the tenure track (and, interestingly, affect adjuncts much less). The comments in response to June 2010 are astounding, showing the same kind of resentment at students' entitlement and laziness that I used to feel (Stripling 2010). Tenure is essentially over except at the most prestigious universities and colleges. Seventy percent of all courses are taught by adjuncts—people with no possibility of ever being on the tenure track and who are paid as little as $1,000 per course. Students suffer because their teachers are not really invested in the school and are too busy trying to survive to do justice to the teaching. And it goes without saying that those unable to get secure teaching positions—living in what is now termed *precarity*—fail to thrive.

2. For a professor's experience throughout an entire semester, see Allitt 2005.

3. See, e.g., Vedder 2010. One comment charges that students are not capable of performing "at the real university level" (Eacowan 2010).

4. Arum and Roksa 2011:3.

5. Arum and Roksa 2011:3.

6. Edmundson 2013:26.

7. This quotation appears in Bartleby.com, Chivers 2012; one discussion of its source is in Google Answers 2004. A more thorough discussion of its origin can be found in Quote Investigator 2010.

8. See Lippmann, Bulana, and Wagenaar 2009 for a typical practical and analytical approach to student behavior that is widely recognized as problematic.

9. Affluence and privilege can backfire, though, when accompanied either by parental neglect or by such high expectations that any imperfection leads to serious self-doubt. Madeline Levine, a psychotherapist in Marin County, describes how affluent children, evaluated constantly in terms of their achievement, fold under such constant pressure in her book *The Price of Privilege: How Parental Pressure and Material Advantage are Creating a Generation of Disconnected and Unhappy Kids*. A new form of psychological work has emphasized the need to allow children to learn from their own errors, as in *The Blessing of a Skinned Knee* (Mogel 2001) and its follow-up for older children, *The Blessing of a B-* (Mogel 2010). Wendy Mogel, using Jewish sources, argues that children should be taught values, respect, and responsibility, without any shortcuts that guarantee success. The concept of "resilience," and the idea of being tough, has surfaced in response to this. Author Paul Tough—is naming destiny?—has created a lively conversation with his book *How Children Succeed: Grit, Curiosity, and the Hidden Power of Character*. The backlash against entitlement blames the "self-esteem" flavor of 1990s and 2000s child rearing and the indulgence associated with "attachment parenting" for, as Jean Twenge termed it, "Generation Me."

10. Guinier 2015.

11. Walvoord and Anderson 2010:136.

12. Fairday 2012; emphasis added.

13. See, for example, Hu 2005, Hunt 2008, Johnson 2003, Kohn 2002, Trow 2006, Vedder 2010.

14. Hu 2005.

15. Hunt 2008:202.

16. E.g., Centra 2003.

17. Upper-middle-class students' practices match those of teachers. One of the primary distinctions between successful and unsuccessful students stems from their class capital. See, e.g., Lareau 2011.

18. Systematic challenges do occur occasionally, as with the worldwide attack in the 1960s on inequality in society and in school. That decade saw Paolo Freire's work in Brazil, Mao Zedong's Cultural Revolution (which began in the universities and focused in large part on challenging teachers' authority), France's *soixante-huitards* (revolutionary student/worker protesters of 1968), and the surge of progressive education in the United States as articulated by such writers as Jules Henry, John Holt, Ivan Illich, A. S. Neill (U.K.), John Bruner, and others. This was the period that brought "relevance" and student evaluation of teachers, and a host of sometimes evanescent experiments.

19. http://www.beloit.edu/mindset/.

20. Tapscott 2009.

21. Hoover 2009.

22. http://talk.collegeconfidential.com/parents-forum/1336317-if-youre-stressed-about-college-admissions-pearls-before-swine.html, http://www.gocomics.com/pearlsbeforeswine/2012/05/06#.Uk69YSR4Mso.

23. Reed 2013.

24. Stark 2013a and 2013b is a thoughtful series of blog posts showing what these evaluations do and don't—and can't—mean, while also showing how irrationally they are used on Stark's and other campuses. See also Flaherty 2015, Stark and Freishtat 2014.

25. Smith and Hawkins 2011, Zaino 2015.

26. Stark 2013b; emphasis added.

27. Hobson n.d.

28. Arum and Roksa 2011.

29. Baier et al. 2011.

30. *Chronicle Online* 2011; Volk 2012.

31. National Endowment for the Arts 2007, Neary 2007.

32. National Endowment for the Arts 2013.

33. Pew Internet 2013.

34. Minzesheimer 2013.

35. Brame 2013.

36. See, for example, the research on the neural dimensions of reading in Maryanne Wolf, *Proust and the Squid: The Story and Science of the Reading Brain* (2007); Sven Birkerts, *The Gutenberg Elegies: The Fate of Reading in an Electronic Age* (1994); and John DeFrancis, *Visible Speech: The Diverse Oneness of Writing Systems* (1989), on the nature of writing itself. Some accessible websites showing varieties of media on which writing occur are British Museum n.d. and Spar 2004. For the basic technological deterministic position, see Marshall McLuhan, *Understanding Media: The Extensions of Man* (1964).

37. http://nsse.indiana.edu/html/about.cfm.

38. Boyer Commission 1998: 15.

39. Bonfiglio 2010; Hu, Kuh, and Gayles 2007.

40. Adedokun et al. 2012; Fechheimer, Webber, and Kleiber 2011; Madan and Teitge 2013; Russell, Hancock, and McCullough 2007.

41. Warner 2013.

42. Koc 2013.

43. Greenfeld 2013.

44. Woodhouse 2015.

45. Oehlert and Uggen 2010.

46. White 2013.

47. Taylor 2013.

48. Abbey 2002.

49. In contrast to the prohibitionistic culture of alcohol in the United States, in many societies alcohol and other "drug foods," as we anthropologists term them, are either incorporated in moderation into daily social consumption, as in Mediterranean cultures, or are regarded as sacred. See Chrzan 2013, Douglas 1987. The Amethyst Initiative project points out that when the drinking age was lower, there was less drinking on college campuses. http://www.theamethystinitiative.org/.

50. Knight et al. 2002, Wechsler and Nelson 2008.

51. Chrzan 2013:135.

52. Vincent Felitti and Robert Anda's ACE (Adverse Childhood Experiences) study showed how childhood traumas perfectly predict later suffering and self-destructive behaviors, including obesity, smoking, promiscuity, use of drugs, alcohol, and more; see Felitti, Anda et al. 1998.

53. All names for students, except for my student interviewers, are pseudonyms. Some of these names were selected by interviewees; others were chosen by me.

54. Kadison and DiGeronimo 2004:95.

55. Kadison and DiGeronimo 2004.

56. Center for Collegiate Mental Health 2015:20.

57. Center for Collegiate Mental Health 2015:23.

58. Levine 2013.

2. The Myriad and Muddied Goals of College

1. E.g., Ambrose et al. 2010, Boice 2000, Cronon 1998, Lang 2005.

2. See Friedman 2014 for an account of what Google seeks in employees.

3. Cronon 1998:74.

4. http://www.heri.ucla.edu/cirpoverview.php.

5. Pope 1996, 2000, 2006; see also the website and now organization devoted to "colleges that change lives," http://www.ctcl.org/.

6. Morton 2011.

7. Astin 1993, 1999; Perry 1968.

8. See, e.g., Henry and Beaty 2007, MacIntyre 2009.

9. There is a large body of literature on the "moral" and "patriotic" education that has occupied Chinese educators since the turn of the twentieth century. That includes efforts to "educate" people from minority nationalities—such as Tibetans—to "love the motherland." See, for example, Bass 2005; Fairbrother 2003; Hansen 1999; Kan, Vickers, and Morris 2007; Kipnis 2001; Murphy 2004; Vickers 2009; Wang 2008.

10. Since the 1990s, conservatives have accused universities of having a "liberal bias" and have gone so far as to place observers in classrooms to prevent liberal (communist, socialist) indoctrination. A conservative "Bill of Rights" has been proposed to permit university students to refuse to engage with material they find politically offensive. David Horowitz names professors he regards as "dangerous" because of their liberal attitudes. The 2011–12 legislation in Arizona to prohibit "ethnic studies" is part of this same agenda and the bitter struggle over the purpose of college. History is often where battles for meaning and interpretation are played out, as in China's battle with Japan about how to discuss the Pacific War and Japan's atrocities in China, or about China's claims over the territories of Tibet and Xinjiang. See Cronin 2006, D'Souza 1991, Horowitz 2006, http://www.yaf.org/topconservativecolleges.aspx.

11. See Lee et al. 2011.

12. Tyack 1974.

13. Fallows 2007, Kinsley 2007, Lewin 2007.

14. Arkes 1999, Heywood and Wei 2004, Spence 1973.

15. *Education Week* 2013.

16. OECD 2013.

17. The Wikipedia article on educational attainment in the United States is excellent. See also OECD 2013, United States Census Bureau 2014.

18. Collins 2011:229, 235.

19. "Dean Dad" 2010.

20. According to Pink 2009 and others, choice and autonomy increase intrinsic motivation. See chapter 9, "Motivation Comes in at Least Two Flavors, Intrinsic and Extrinsic."

21. Baum, Ma, and Payea 2013:6.

22. See Baum, Ma, and Payea 2010 for the *Education Pays 2010* report; Armstrong 2010 for a critique of this approach to evaluating the worth of education; Di Meglio 2010 for a contrary view; and Frank and Cook 1995 for a broader social critique.

23. Di Meglio 2010.

24. Leonhardt 2014a, Pew Research 2014.

25. Leonhardt 2014a.

26. Dale and Krueger 2002, 2011.

27. Easterbrook 2004.

28. Kamenetz 2010, Ramsey 2011, Singletary 2011, Vedder 2004.

29. Chetty, Friedman, and Rockoff 2011; Lowrie 2012.

30. Rampell 2013.

31. Schank 2014.

32. Jay and Graff 2012; see also Roche 2010.

33. Inspired by Scott 1985.

34. Christensen and Eyring 2011, Davidson 2011a, Kamenetz 2010, khanacademy.org.

35. Wilson 2010.

36. Phillips 2015.

37. Friedman 2014.

3. Seeing the Air

1. In many countries, such as Germany, cognate terms for *college* and *university* refer to quite distinct entities. I recall a conversation with a German graduate student speaking almost native English who couldn't understand what I was talking about when I explained I was doing research on *college*. A German *Kolleg* is either a research unit of a university or a high school preparatory academy like a *Gymnasium*.

2. Margolis 2001.

3. Tyack and Cuban 1995.

4. Schreiner 2006:10.

5. Crowley 1998:69–73, 75.

6. Graeber 2011.

7. Melton 2003.

8. Labaree 1997:60.

9. Wonderful accounts of one-room schools may be found in the *Anne of Green Gables* (L. M. Montgomery) and *All of a Kind Family* (Sydney Taylor) series of children's books. Scholarly analyses include Rocheleau 2003, Zimmerman 2009.

10. Snyder 1993a:5.

11. Kena et al. 2014:138.

12. See Gatto 2003 for a blistering attack on Fordism.

13. http://www.un.org/en/documents/udhr/.

14. Ashcroft 2010, Brandenburg and Zhu 2007, China Education Center 2012, OECD 2001, Scott 1995.

15. Schofer and Meyer 2005.

16. Trow 2000.

17. Labaree 1997:80.

18. Cobban 1980.

19. Dunbabin 1997:160, 161.

20. Dunbabin 1997:167.

21. Hart 1874:esp. 289.

22. Snyder 1993b:64.

23. Lipka 2013.

24. Kena et al. 2014.

25. Kena et al. 2014:148, 158.

26. Kena et al. 2014:199, 200.

27. OECD 2013:37.

28. Hughes 2013.

29. Malcolm 2013. See also Huelsman 2014, Newman 2014.

30. Kariya 2011b:247.

31. Kariya 2011a:72, 2011b:249.

32. Kariya 2011a:70.

33. Kariya 2011b:258.

34. Kariya 2011a:88.

35. Kariya 2011a:92.

36. Leonhardt 2009, Morrison 1992.

37. College411 2013, Kena et al. 2014:155, Stevens 2007.

38. Leonhardt 2013.

39. Karabel 2005.

40. Collins 1979.

41. Pelissier 1991; but see Gladwin 1970.
42. Freire 2000 [1970].
43. Chick 2010; Gladwin 1970; Lancy 1980; Lancy, Bock, and Gaskins 2010; Lave 1982, 1988.
44. Labaree 2010.
45. Bourdieu and Passeron 1990. Paul Willis's *Learning to Labour* is a classic: working-class "lads" in a working-class town reject school in favor of what are high-paying jobs for teenagers, a veneer of manliness, and a sense of genuine, physical purpose. In the end, of course, they remain stuck in those jobs with little option.
46. Foroohar 2014.
47. http://sitemaker.umich.edu/klein.356/tracking.
48. Andell 2008; Ashwill et al. 1999; Fuhr 1997; Klein 2012; LeTendre, Hofer, and Shimizu 2003; Noack 1999; Schnabel et al. 2002; Schnepf 2002; Werum 2000; Wilson 2000; Wolf 2002.
49. Moltz 2009.
50. Hdr.undp.org/en/statistics/hdi/, Social Science Research Council 2013.
51. Inoue et al. 2008, Lock 1986, Morioka et al. 2014.
52. http://nces.ed.gov/Timss/, http://www.oecd.org/pisa/.

4. Wagging the Dog

1. http://www.hackcollege.com/blog/2013/11/18/how-to-guess-like-a-pro-on-multiple-choice-tests.html, http://www.kaptest.com/college-prep.
2. Elman 2000; but see Kirkpatrick and Xu 2012.
3. Zhao 2009:75.
4. Lee 1999 [1960]:19.
5. Davidson 2011a, 2011b, 2012.
6. Howard 1965:137.
7. Bahner 1966:58.
8. http://www.in.gov/collegegoweek/2540.htm.
9. Bahner 1966, Howard 1965.
10. Ernest Boyer, president of the Carnegie Foundation, declared it obsolete in 1993.
11. Carnegie Foundation 2012, Laitinen 2012.
12. Carnegie Foundation 2012, Laitinen 2012.
13. European University Association 2003.
14. See Heath 1982 for different forms of language socialization, and different types of questions.
15. See http://www.parentsasteachers.org/. My argument is not that children living in poverty should not get the tools for success available to advantaged families; it is that the argument about success via schooling is a circular one, and one that has been challenged for half a century. See, e.g., Avineri et al. 2015, Blum 2014. See Lareau 2011 for the concept of "concerted cultivation."

5. "What Do I Have to Do to Get an A?"

1. Jacobs and Hyman 2009.
2. Ben-David and Bhandari 2013, Princeton University 2014, Windemuth 2014.
3. Fendrich 2012; some emphasis added.
4. Walvoord and Anderson 2010:1, 2.
5. https://www.criticalthinking.org/pages/college-wide-grading-standards/441.
6. http://www.cmu.edu/teaching/designteach/teach/rubrics.html.
7. Demerath 2009, Khan 2011, Levine 2006, Long and Moore 2010, Pope 2001, Robbins 2006, Stevens 2007.
8. To follow the logic to its conclusion, the focus on high-achieving students demonstrates the U.S. higher educational system at its optimal and most successful. On "studying up" see Gusterson 1997, Nader 1974 [1969].

9. On high school, see Varenne, Goldman, and McDermott 1998. An obvious question is how representative the experiences of my student consultants are: Are they representative of all high-achieving students? Or do high-achieving students represent all students? To the first question, the answer is that I don't know, but from the work of others it seems likely that there are similarities. To the second, it seems that the answer is no. See, among many other studies, Willis 1981 [1977] and Eckert 1989. The public college students profiled in Moffatt 1989 and Nathan 2005 may have been less affected by the increasing professionalization of affluent, elite students in the context of neoliberalism than those quoted in this chapter. See also Urciuoli 2008, 2014.

10. These quotations are very lightly edited transcripts of interviews. Some hesitation markers and repetitions are deleted. Sometimes identifying characteristics of people mentioned are modified to maintain anonymity.

11. Nespor 1990.

12. Lepper 1983:300.

13. Milton, Pollio, and Eison 1986:121.

14. Guess 2008.

15. Lynd and Lynd 1956 [1929]:188.

16. Gatto 2005 [1992], Labaree 1997, Smith 1998:45–48.

17. Chudacoff 1989.

18. Levin 1991.

19. Kvale 2007.

20. Elman 2000, Miyazaki 1981 [1963], Suen and Yu 2006.

21. Stray 2001:39.

22. Foucault 1979 [1977], Lucas 2006.

23. Langan 2012.

24. Labi 2009, Nicola and Szabor, personal communication, O'Malley 2015.

25. Davidson 2011a:111.

26. Horowitz 1987:33.

27. Stray 2001:40–41.

28. Davidson 2011a:112. Durm 1993, following Smallwood 1935, gives the fascinating details.

29. Rojstaczer 2012. "Utopian" college such as the University of California, Santa Cruz (UCSC), Evergreen State University, Antioch College, and Hampshire College began experimenting with grade-free higher education in the 1960s and 1970s (Cappel 1999), using narrative evaluations instead. In 2001 UCSC ended an agonizing debate by instituting regular grades (Rogoff 2001). Evergreen State and Hampshire remain grade-free.

30. Gould 1996 [1981].

31. Lemann 1999.

32. Ravitch 2010. In the twenty-first century, serious questions have arisen about the role of higher education in promoting lifelong earnings (C. Kelly 2012, http://www.thielfellowship.org/). A correlation between college and employment, and college and earnings, is robust; the disagreement lies in whether this correlation is caused by college or by social position. But clearly, entrance into selective institutions depends on grades, which may thus influence life outcomes. In 2014 the College Board announced a thorough revision of the SAT, in part to combat obvious advantages to wealthier students. See Balf 2014, Jaschik 2014.

33. Kirschenbaum, Simon, and Napier 1971.

34. Moffatt 1989, Nathan 2005:116–18.

35. Espeland and Sauder 2007.

36. Becker, Geer, and Hughes 1968; Kvale 2007.

37. Demerath 2009:81–82.

38. McNamee and Miller 2004.

39. Young 1958.

40. Merry 2011:S83.

41. Gould 1996 [1981], Lesko 2001.

42. Among the significant changes to the SAT in 2014, the College Board announced that no longer would knowledge of rarely used vocabulary be tested. See Lemann 1999 for a detailed history of testing.

43. The beneficence of the Carnegies and other super-rich (Gates, Walton) in taking their surplus wealth and conferring it on "the poor" (but not on their workers) in the form of schools, libraries, and museums is deconstructed in Marsh 2011.

44. Scott 2011.

45. Foucault 1979 [1977], Rose 1999.

46. Apple 2005, Bosco 2011–12, Foucault 1979 [1977], Greenhouse 2010, Power 1997, Rose 1999, Strathern 2000.

47. Shore and Wright 2001:760.

48. Merry 2011:S90.

49. Simmel 1978 on money; Nespor 1990 on grades.

50. Becker, Geer, and Hughes 1968; Deci 1971; Grigsby 2009; Kohn 1999 [1993], 2011.

51. Weiner 1992.

52. Simmel 1978:357.

53. Merry 2011:S86–87.

54. Merry 2011:S89.

55. Rose 1999.

56. Espeland and Stevens 1998:331.

57. Merry 2011:S84.

58. Espeland and Stevens 2008:412.

59. Merry 2011:S84.

60. Davidson 2010, Jaschik 2010.

61. Bourdieu and Passeron 1990 [1970], Collins 2009.

62. Labaree 2010; Varenne 1974; Varenne, Goldman, and McDermott 1998.

63. Deci 1971; Kohn 1999 [1993], 2011.

64. Lancy 2010, Paradise 1998.

65. E.g., Ravitch 2010, Valenzuela 2007.

66. Genova 2010, Scott 2011.

6. Campus Delights

1. Genova 2010.

2. Valles 2014.

3. Milton, Pollio, and Eison 1986:157.

4. Psychological research on college-age students ranges from a focus on the specific forms of learning and the cognitive to "moral development" to psychosexual independence. Perry (1968) sketches a model of development including a shift from an absolutist to a relativist perspective. Theories of student involvement (Astin 1999) suggest recruiting student involvement of time and energy in order to enhance educational experience. More recent work on learning and engagement (Kuh 2005, Pascarella and Terenzini 2005) emphasizes *affective* and *relational* approaches (Arnett 2004, Walker n.d.). Ecological models, such as Bronfenbrenner 1994, go beyond relationships with individuals to include relationships with the wider society. Sociological perspectives (as in, e.g., Karabel 2005, Martin 2012) illuminate the powerful ways in which socioeconomic factors intersect with success in formal schooling.

5. Trow 2000.

6. Walker n.d.

7. Deresiewicz 2014, Karabel 2005.

8. This discussion largely excludes students on nonresidential or nonselective campuses, many of whom are older, and whose "real lives"—jobs, families, communities—exercise a far greater pull than do their courses.

9. Feldman and Matjasko 2007; Fredricks and Eccles 2006; Kaplan et al. 2003; Luthar, Shoum, and Brown 2006; Marsh 1992; Okamoto, Herda, and Hartzog 2013.

10. See Renn and Arnold 2003, Shiah et al. 2013 on college extracurricular participation, and Fischer 2007, Martin 2012, and Rivera 2011 on correlation with social status.

11. Martin 2012.

12. See Arum and Roksa 2011.

13. Arum and Roksa 2011.

14. Johnson 2003, Rojstaczer 2012, Vedder 2010.

15. Seaman 2005.

16. Bogle 2008.

17. Hacker and Dreifus 2010.

18. Sperber 2000.

19. Lang 2013, McCabe 2005.

20. Becker, Geer, and Hughes 1968; Moffatt 1989; Nathan 2005.

21. Riley 2011.

22. Bloom 1987.

23. Washburn 2005.

24. Blum 2009, Grigsby 2009, Gusfield 1987, Nathan 2005.

25. And then there is the reading. Many students clearly do little reading, no matter how much is assigned. I have been annoyed and puzzled by students complaining that there is so much reading assigned that they have not even begun it. Shouldn't they at least do some of it before complaining there's too much?

26. Lancy, Bock, and Gaskins 2010.

27. Crawford 2009, Rose 2004, Sennett 2008.

28. Noddings 2003. Shirley Brice Heath and others have been studying the contrasting approaches to learning in school and other settings. See her work on softball and coaching in Heath and Langman 1994, and on the arts and theater and "informal learning" in Heath 2012a and 2012b. See also Bekerman, Burbules, and Silberman-Keller 2006 on "informal education."

29. Willingham 2009, Gardner 1995.

30. Lancy 2014, Zelizer 1985.

31. Gaskins 2008, Levison 2000.

32. Herndon 1971, Willis 1981 [1977].

33. Paradise 1998.

34. The nature of compulsion has been seen as violence; see, e.g., Harber 2004.

35. Carini, Kuh, and Klein 2006; Kuh 2005, 2009.

36. Demerath 2009, Pope 2001.

37. Khan 2011.

38. Bourdieu and Passeron 1990 [1970].

39. Gusterson 1997, Nader 1974 [1969].

40. Deci 1971, Kohn 1999 [1993], Ryan and Deci 2000.

41. http://www.thegoodproject.org/, Noddings 2003.

42. Grigsby 2009:134–37.

43. Immordino-Yang and Damasio 2007.

44. Stewart 2013.

45. Ackerman 1999, Chudacoff 2007, Gray 2013, Huizinga 1950 [1938], Yee 2006.

46. Bateson 1972.

7. Beyond Cognition and Abstraction

1. Immordino-Yang and Damasio 2007:4.

2. Henrich, Heine, and Norenzayan 2010.

3. Fuentes and Visala forthcoming.

4. Brown 1991. Claims about universals can be hugely problematic, as people take their own experience and project it backward to the beginnings and nature of humankind. For example, evolutionary psychologists claim to demonstrate that humans prefer hourglass-shaped bodies (Manning, Anderton, and Washington 1996) or that women are less likely to accept one-night stands than men (Clark and Hatfield 1989), or that humans have an aesthetic preference for savanna landscapes (Adevi and Grahn 2012). Others, including me, regard these as "just-so stories." Complicated but not clear-cut research shows a tendency for "basic color terms" to follow certain patterns. See Berlin and Kay 1969, but also Lucy and Shweder 1979.

5. Gibbons 2008, Konner 2010, Lancy 2014.

6. Kline 2014.

7. See, e.g., Chick 2010, Gibbons 2008.

8. Sterelny 2012 presents a powerful account of the importance of learning for human evolution.

9. DeSilva and Lesnik 2008, Portmann 1990, Rosenberg and Trevathan 1995.

10. Bock 2010.

11. Spindler 1997 [1967].

12. Bock 2010:27.

13. See, e.g., Lancy 2014, Scheper-Hughes 1993, Topley 1974.

14. Turner 1969.

15. See, e.g., Ottenberg 1989.

16. Tinto 1987; but see Tierney 1992.

17. Lott 2014. Two communities that do retain significant rites of passage for adolescents are American Jews with the bar and bat mitzvah, and Latinas with the *quinceañera*. The latter seems to acknowledge sexual maturity while emphasizing delay in sexual activity. See Alvarez 2007. Some explain "gangs" as arising from structural conditions of inequality in adolescence. Gangs create their own rites of passage, especially initiation ceremonies, their own challenges, their own symbols of belonging.

18. Kett 1977:6, 13–14.

19. Grinspan 2014.

20. Age is a very recent defining characteristic of humans. See Chudacoff 1989.

21. Kett 1977:18.

22. Kett 1977:20.

23. Arnett 2007, Cohen 2011 [1972], Hall 1904, Lesko 1996, Savage 2007.

24. Tyack 1974.

25. Mead 1961 [1928].

26. It is common now to hear news stories about studies demonstrating that people's brains are still developing in their teens and early twenties, especially the part of the brain that leads to judgment and planning. Using functional magnetic resonance imaging (fMRI), researchers can show which "part" of the brain is active in lab settings, with certain tasks. Usually using North American college students, they find evidence that "the brain" continues to develop until the mid-twenties. Some problems with this conclusion are that the focus on North American college students cannot represent all people (Henrich, Heine, and Norenzayan 2010); development of the brain depends on the demands made of it; functions may be more distributed than localized; people must be motionless and not genuinely interacting while scanned. Because brains respond to the tasks asked of them—referred to as *neuroplasticity*—and we ask our college students to stay active in learning, it is not surprising that their brains keep developing.

27. Arnett 2004:228.

28. Brooks 2007, 2015.

29. Arnett 2011 discusses whether this is just a "process" or a genuine psychological "stage."

30. Arnett 2004:10–11.

31. Arnett 2004. Henig and Henig 2012 ask about the contemporary folks who are "twenty-something": What *is it* about them? They conclude that although there are some new features, mostly such people are the "same as they ever were."

32. Arnett 2004:15.

33. ACLU 2014, Amnesty International 2014, Human Rights Watch 2014.

34. Bronfenbrenner 1979:52–53.

35. For this account, see Ochs and Izquierdo 2009.

36. See Lancy 2014, chapter 7; Gaskins 2008; Lancy 2010; Rogoff 1990, 2003.

37. Crawford 2009, Rose 2004, Sennett 2008.

38. Klein 2012.

39. Foroohar 2014.

40. Castle 2012.

41. Panksepp and Biven 2012:14.

42. Immordino-Yang and Damasio 2007:9. See also Damasio 1999.

43. Immordino-Yang and Damasio 2007:3–4.

44. Immordino-Yang and Damasio 2007:7.

45. Damasio 1999.

46. Panksepp and Biven 2012:103.

47. Sterelny 2012, Whiten and Erdal 2012.

48. Herrmann et al. 2007:1360.

49. Gaskins 2013.

50. Enfield and Levinson 2006:3.

51. Gaskins 2013.

52. Gray 2013.

53. Lancy 2014, chapter 7.

54. Hewlett et al. 2011.

55. The specific figures for women are an average of 5.8 ± 1.7 kilometers daily and for men 11.4 ± 2.1. See Pontzer et al. 2012.

56. Cordain n.d. reports the data as "personal communication from Kim Hill."

57. Comments on one article pointed out that we as human beings need to get much more exercise than any of the studies admit, but they can't say so because it would scare all of us urban office workers away, or into deep despair. See Reynolds 2013.

58. Carr 2008.

59. Wray 2014.

60. Asher 1969.

61. Connor 2011, Schwartz and Cohen 2013.

8. Learning in the Wild, Learning in the Cage

1. A particularly formal version of this arrangement developed in Europe in the Middle Ages, with some unfortunate features such as the master's right to beat the apprentice. But other versions can be humane and effective, as Barbara Rogoff describes in *Developing Destinies*, showing how a Yucatec woman she has known for over thirty years became a midwife. A particular kind of French apprenticeship, *compagnonnage*, developed in the Middle Ages, and endures today. See Herzog 2013.

2. Neill 1960:25.

3. Brown, Roediger, and McDaniel 2014:131–61; Willingham 2009:113–29.

4. Sternberg and Williams 2002:41.

5. Holt 1982 [1964]:231.

6. Willingham 2009:67.

7. Ambrose et al. 2010:108.

8. Lave 1988:18.

9. Lave 1988:14. Goldman 2006 shows basically the same thing: families use all kinds of math but don't think of it as such and don't see what they are doing as connected with what their children are learning in school. Lave's emphasis was on trying to get the families to see the similarities so families could embrace school math; another conclusion might be that the schools' approaches to math must change.

10. Gardner 1995.

11. Herndon 1971:106.

12. Spindler and Spindler 1989.

13. Ochs and Schieffelin 1984 is the formative article, comparing language socialization across three different societies.

14. The scholarly study of language acquisition and socialization is enormous. For one version, see Duff and Hornberger 2010.

15. For an accessible and fascinating account, see Norman Doidge's book *The Brain That Changes Itself: Stories of Personal Triumph from the Frontiers of Brain Science*.

16. Some cognitive scientists suggest that the more expert people are, the less able they are to teach a subject. Ambrose and colleagues state, "Ironically, expertise can be a liability as well as an advantage when it comes to teaching" because of "expert blind spot" (2010:95, 99). Huston 2009 says much the same thing.

17. Brosch 2014:87.

18. Byrne 2005; Pardo et al. 2011; Rizzolatti and Craighero 2004; Stephens, Silbert, and Hasson 2010; Thomason 2001.

19. Iacoboni 2008:270.

20. Gaskins and Paradise 2010.

21. Basso 1996.

22. Nisbett 2003.

23. Gaskins 2013.

24. The term comes from Lave and Wenger 1991.

25. Basso 1996, Gaskins and Paradise 2010, Nisbett 2003.

26. Lancy 2013:3.

27. Lancy 2013:13.

28. Mitra 2003, 2005; Mitra and Rana 2001.

29. Gray 2013, Konner 2010, Rogoff 2003.

30. Hewlett et al. 2011:1169–70.

31. Hewlett et al. 2011:1176.

32. Hewlett et al. 2011:1175.

33. Hewlett et al. 2011:1173.

34. Rogoff 1990:110–34; Greenfield 1984, Greenfield and Lave 1982. For learning right hand from left hand by the age of two, see Freed and Freed 1981:60; for adult !Kung learning trances, see Katz 1982.

35. Hewlett et al. 2011:1169.

36. Hutchins 1995:289.

37. Hutchins 1995:289.

38. Hutchins 1995:370.

39. Duffy 2011.

40. Harvey 2011.

41. Whitehouse 2002.

42. Smith 1984.

43. Marzluff and Angell 2012, especially chapter 6, "Frolic."

44. Chudacoff 2007:xii.

45. Chick 2010:119.
46. Chick 2010:119.
47. Chick 2010:121.
48. Twain 1982 [1876]:33.
49. Hagen and Bryant 2003, Hagen and Hammerstein 2009, Mithen 2007, Sherzer 2002. Dissanayake 1988 also explains the nature of art for our species.
50. Denis Dutton (2009) writes of the "art instinct." I don't know that I would consider it an instinct, but certainly humans take pleasure in this kind of creative and artistic play. Some work suggests that the origins of language lie in music. See Masataka 2009, Mithen 2007.
51. See Chrzan 2013 and Tan 2012 about college drinking; also Wechsler et al. 2002, Wechsler and Nelson 2008.
52. Gusfield 1987.
53. Chang 2013.
54. Brown, Roediger, and McDaniel 2014:23–66; Willingham 2009:41–66, 81–95.
55. Ambrose et al. 2010; Brown, Roediger, and McDaniel 2014; Davis, Sumara, and Luce-Kapler 2008; Gardner 1995; Thomas and Brown 2011; Willingham 2009.
56. Lave 1988:14.
57. Mac Donald 2011.
58. http://www.roadscholar.org/about/history.asp.
59. Bekerman, Burbules, and Silberman-Keller 2006; Heath 2012b.
60. National Geographic 2006.
61. Thomas and Brown 2011:92.

9. Motivation Comes in at Least Two Flavors, Intrinsic and Extrinsic

1. Willingham 2009.
2. Labaree 1997:145; see also Green 2014 on the moment-to-moment training of excellent teachers.
3. Tyack and Cuban 1995.
4. We do not begin life desiring fairness for others, only for ourselves, but by the time we are adults we often—at least sometimes—wish for fairness even when it does not have direct value for ourselves. Evolutionary psychologists call this *altruism*.
5. Of course, manners are one thing, impersonal rules another. And some of the latter have become part of our school system, imperceptibly, over decades and centuries: measurement, assessment, ranking, percentiles. All this puts carts before horses. We have to sit in rows in school because it makes it easier for teachers to observe us. We have to take tests so college admissions officers can judge us against our peers. Bells and buzzers, just like in factories, have been naturalized. But allowing children to use bathrooms only with permission gives an institution an undue amount of control over one's person. On a crowdsourcing site one person aiming to offer an alternative high school posted that one of the "rewards" for a $250 donation would be "We will never make you ask permission to use the bathroom." https://www.incited.org/en/projects/4868-Open-Road-Learning-Community-for-Teens—Self-Directed-Learning-Takes-Off.
6. In the 2000s, children's self-control, "executive function," and "grit" have been emphasized as even more important for success than cognitive accomplishment or ability. See Mogel 2001, 2010; Tough 2012. Earlier research now seen as seminal is found in Rotter 1960.
7. Deci 1971, Kohn 1999 [1993], Pink 2009.
8. Deci 1971.
9. Ryan and Stiller 1991.
10. Lepper 1983, Lepper and Greene 1975.
11. Kruglanski, Stein, and Riter 1977.
12. Ryan and Deci 2000:59.

13. http://www.kzoo.edu/studentlife/?p=fye.

14. This discussion is drawn from Ambrose et al. 2010:71–73.

15. Ambrose et al. 2010:73.

10. On Happiness, Flourishing, Well-Being, and Meaning

1. A. Kelly 2012.

2. Ura et al. 2012:1, 8.

3. Seligman 2011.

4. Davidson 2011, Jackson 2009.

5. Csikszentmihalyi 1990:4.

6. All of philosophy and theology, in some sense, and now psychology, politics, and econom-ics, revolve around the question: What is the good life? To dip a toe into this literature, you could start with Eric Weiner's *Bliss*, Seligman's *Flourish*, Csikszentmihalyi's *Flow*, along with the writ-ings of That Ninh Thich and the Dalai Lama, Robert Bellah's *The Good Society*, Aristotle. For the "capabilities approach" to "flourishing" of Martha Nussbaum and Amartya Sen, in the context of international development, which is a completely different direction that would take me too far from my original query, see Nussbaum 2003, Sen 2009.

7. See Brickman, Coates, and Janoff-Bulman 1978; and Diener and Seligman 2004. But see Diener, Lucas, and Scollon 2006 for a more recent revision.

8. Brickman, Coates, and Janoff-Bulman 1978.

9. Centers for Disease Control 2013, Dodge et al. 2012.

10. Levine 2006.

11. American Psychological Association 2010, National Institute of Mental Health 2012, Neighmond 2011, Tartakovsky 2008.

12. Hawton and van Heeringen 2009.

13. Snyder 2014, Suicide.org n.d., Centers for Disease Control 2012.

14. Chace 2006:294–96.

15. Kadison and DiGeronimo 2004, Levine 2006.

16. Marples 1999.

17. Seligman et al. 2005.

18. Cat Bolten, personal communication.

19. Rivard 2014a, 2014b.

20. Jung 2007:63.

21. Levine 2006; Quart 2006, 2007; Robbins 2006.

22. Amazingly someone is at it again—but for real! Manjoo 2014.

11. Both Sides Now of a Learning Revolution

1. Caplan 2009.

2. Rosenbaum 2001.

3. Labaree 2010.

4. Fishman 2012.

5. C. Kelly 2012.

6. *Huffington Post* 2012.

7. *Wall Street Journal* 2014.

8. Straumsheim 2014.

9. Collins 2012, Hiltonsmith 2013. But see Leonhardt 2014b for a contrary view.

10. Anonymous benefactors in Kalamazoo, Michigan, offer promising young students fully paid college tuition if they complete high school, and this is encouraging at-risk children to stick it out. They may not be there for the sake of what they are learning. But they have to toe the line

and swallow their restlessness in order to board the train that may lead them, if all goes well, to the middle class.

11. DeAngelo et al. 2011, Tough 2014.

12. http://www.uncollege.org/.

13. Dewey 1988 [1938]:115.

14. For an introduction to these ideas, see for example David B. Tyack's *The One Best System: A History of American Urban Education* (1974), Thomas C. Hunt's *The Impossible Dream: Education and the Search for Panaceas* (2001), and Henry J. Perkinson's *The Imperfect Panacea: American Faith in Education, 1865–1965* (1968).

15. *Émile* is not really about education. It uses education as a way to discuss more profound aspects of human nature. Perhaps this book, like so many others, will do so as well.

16. Neill 1960:4.

17. Mitra 2003, 2005; Mitra and Rana 2001.

18. Abrams 2011, Compton 2011.

19. Edwards et al. 2013.

20. Littky 2004.

21. Neill 2005.

22. Seldin and Epstein 2006.

23. Sobo 2013.

24. Gray 2013.

25. http://www.education.com/reference/article/Ref_Reggio_Emilia/.

26. http://www.educationrevolution.org/store/about/. See my website, SusanBlum.com, for more examples.

27. http://www.leapnow.org/leapyear/.

28. https://www.incited.org/en/projects/4868-Open-Road-Learning-Community-for-Teens—Self-Directed-Learning-Takes-Off, http://openroadteens.org/7-guiding-principles/.

29. David Tyack and Larry Cuban talk about some of these efforts in *Tinkering toward Utopia: A Century of Public School Reform* (Tyack and Cuban 1995). It is supremely humbling to see how many of my discoveries have been made over and over again by many committed reformers.

30. Cappel 1999.

31. Some examples are Berea College (emphasizing responsibility, work, no tuition); Evergreen State (self-directed, integrated curriculum, no grades); Sarah Lawrence (self-directed, narrative evaluations, seminars, and reflections); Goddard (low-residency); Antioch (low-residency, work); Bennington (self-directed); Prescott (physical, sustainability, expeditionary); Costa Rica's Earth University (which aims to teach about sustainability and to use principles of sustainability in its teaching); polytechnics of various forms (http://studywesterneurope.eu/study/polytechnics); apprenticeships; Chautauquas and other adult learning; Elderhostels; HASTAC: Humanities, Arts, Science, and Technology Alliance and Collaboratory; "free universities" (UK, Germany, Europe, South America); service learning; entrepreneurship; UnCollege (structured self-designed gap year); University of the People: Tuition-Free Online University (http://uopeople.edu/). The Union for Research and Experimentation in Higher Education was formed in 1964 by ten presidents of small experimental colleges, mostly in the northeast United States, to share experience and outlook. (These included Sarah Lawrence, Bard, and Antioch.) After several name and mission changes, it is now the Union Institute and University and offers degrees, though it does so without residential programs.

32. This idea comes from Meyer Fortes's work from 1938. See Fortes 1970 [1938]:15.

33. Paradise 1998.

34. Ambrose et al. 2010; Bain 2004; Bransford, Brown, and Cocking 2000; Fink 2003; Huston 2009.

35. Finnan and Rose 2013.

36. Davidson 2011b.
37. American Jewish World Service n.d., Holzer 2015, Schultz n.d., Sinclair 2008.
38. Holzer 2015:64.
39. Kuhn 1962:150.
40. Goodman 1962, 1964:227.
41. National Center for Education Statistics 2012. The 2014 edition gives the figure of "more than $488 billion" spent in 2011-12. National Center for Education Statistics 2014:182.
42. Goodman 1962, 1964:238.
43. Smilkstein 2011:13–14.
44. See http://openroadteens.org/7-guiding-principles/ for an approach that embraces teenagers.
45. Tyack and Cuban 1995:1.

Conclusion

1. For some of the main critics, see Gatto 2005 [1992]; Goodman 1964; Henry 1963; Holt 1982 [1964], 2004 [1976]; Illich 1970; Neill 1960.

Appendix

1. See Derrida 1974 [1971] on the impossibility of finding "degree zero" of thought.
2. Hemenway 2009, Holmgren 2002.
3. Taleb 2012.

Works Cited

Abbey, Antonia. 2002. Alcohol-Related Sexual Assault: A Common Problem among College Students. *Journal of Studies on Alcohol* Supplement 14: 118–28.

Abrams, Samuel E. 2011. The Children Must Play: What the United States Could Learn from Finland about Education Reform. *New Republic*, January 28. http://www.tnr.com/article/politics/82329/education-reform-Finland-US?page=0,0.

Ackerman, Diane. 1999. *Deep Play*. New York: Random House.

ACLU. 2014. End Juvenile Life without Parole. https://www.aclu.org/human-rights_racial-justice/end-juvenile-life-without-parole.

Adedokun, Omolola A., Dake Zhang, Loran Carleton Parker, Ann Bessenbacher, Amy Childress, and Wilella Daniels Burgess. 2012. Understanding How Undergraduate Experiences Influence Student Aspirations for Research Careers and Graduate Education. *Journal of College Science Teaching* 42 (1) (September/October): 82–90.

Adevi, Anna A., and Patrik Grahn. 2012. Preferences for Landscapes: A Matter of Cultural Determinants or Innate Reflexes That Point to Our Evolutionary Background? *Landscape Research* 37 (1): 27–49.

Allitt, Patrick. 2005. *I'm the Teacher, You're the Student: A Semester in the University Classroom*. Philadelphia: University of Pennsylvania Press.

Alvarez, Julia. 2007. *Once Upon a Quinceañera: Coming of Age in the USA*. New York: Viking.

Ambrose, Susan A., Michael W. Bridges, Michele DiPietro, Marsha C. Lovett, and Marie K. Norman. 2010. *How Learning Works: 7 Research-Based Principles for Smart Teaching*. San Francisco: Jossey-Bass.

American Jewish World Service. N.d. Babylonian Talmud, Brachot 63B. On1Foot. http://www.on1foot.org/text/babylonian-talmud-brachot-63b.

American Psychological Association. 2010. College Students Exhibiting More Severe Mental Illness, Study Finds. August 12. http://www.apa.org/news/press/releases/2010/08/students-mental-illness.aspx.

Amnesty International. 2014. Demand Juvenile Justice. http://www.amnestyusa.org/our-work/issues/children-s-rights/juvenile-life-without-parole.

Andell, Katelyn. 2008. A Country Divided: A Study of the German Education System. Student Research. College of William and Mary. http://web.wm.edu/so/monitor/issues/14–1/2-andell.pdf.

Anderson, Benedict. 2006 [1983]. *Imagined Communities: Reflections on the Origin and Spread of Nationalism*. Rev. ed. London: Verso.

Apple, Michael W. 2005. Education, Markets, and an Audit Culture. *Critical Quarterly* 47 (1–2): 11–29.

Arkes, Jeremy. 1999. What Do Educational Credentials Signal and Why Do Employers Value Credentials? *Economics of Education Review* 18 (1) (February): 133–41.

Armstrong, Lloyd. 2010. College Real Return on Investment Continues to Fall. *Changing Higher Education*. October 6. http://www.changinghighereducation.com/2010/10/the-college-board-has-recently-published-an-interesting-report-entitled-education-pays-2010-the-benefits-of-higher-education.html.

Arnett, Jeffrey Jensen. 2004. *Emerging Adulthood: The Winding Road from the Late Teens through the Twenties*. New York: Oxford University Press.

———. 2007. *Adolescence and Emerging Adulthood: A Cultural Approach*. 3rd ed. Upper Saddle River, NJ: Pearson.

———. 2011. *Debating Emerging Adulthood: Stage or Process*. New York: Oxford University Press.

Arum, Richard, and Josipa Roksa. 2011. *Academically Adrift: Limited Learning on College Campuses*. Chicago: University of Chicago Press.

Ashcroft, Kate. 2010. Ethiopia: Dilemmas of Higher Education Massification. *University World News*, September 5. http://www.universityworldnews.com/article.php?story=20100903174508343.

Asher, James J. 1969. The Total Physical Response Approach to Second Language Learning. *The Modern Language Journal* 53 (1): 3–17. DOI: 10.1111/j.1540–4781.1969.tb04552.x.

Ashwill, M. A., W. Foraker, R. Nerison-Low, M. Milotich, and U. Milotich. 1999. *The Educational System in Germany: Case Study Findings*. http://www.ed.gov/pubs/GermanCaseStudy/notes.html.

Astin, Alexander. 1993. *What Matters in College? Four Critical Years Revisited*. San Francisco: Jossey-Bass.

———. 1999. Student Involvement: A Developmental Theory for Higher Education. *Journal of College Student Development* 40 (5): 518–29.

Avineri, Netta, et al. 2015. Invited Forum: Bridging the "Language Gap." *Journal of Linguistic Anthropology* 25 (1): 66–86. DOI: 10.1111/jola.12071.

Ayers, William. 2003. *On the Side of the Child:* Summerhill *Revisited.* New York: Teachers College Press.

Bahner, John M. 1966. The Demise of the Carnegie Unit. *The Clearing House* 41 (1): 58.

Baier, Kylie, Cindy Hendricks, Kiesha Warren Gorden, James E. Hendricks, and Lessie Cochran. 2011. College Students' Textbook Reading, or Not! *American Reading Forum Annual Yearbook* 31. http://www.americanreadingforum.org/year book/11_yearbook/volume11.htm.

Bain, Ken. 2004. *What the Best College Teachers Do.* Cambridge: Harvard University Press.

Balf, Todd. 2014. The Story Behind the SAT Overhaul. *New York Times,* March 6. http://www.nytimes.com/2014/03/09/magazine/the-story-behind-the-sat-overhaul. html.

Bartleby.com. 2015. Socrates' quotation. http://www.bartleby.com/73/195.html.

Bass, Catriona. 2005. Learning to Love the Motherland: Educating Tibetans in China. *Journal of Moral Education* 34 (4): 433–49.

Basso, Keith. 1996. *Wisdom Sits in Places: Landscape and Language among the Western Apache.* Albuquerque: University of New Mexico Press.

Bateson, Gregory. 1972. A Theory of Play and Fantasy. In *Steps to an Ecology of Mind,* 177–93. New York: Ballantine Books.

Bauerlein, Mark. 2008. *The Dumbest Generation: How the Digital Age Stupefies Young Americans and Jeopardizes Our Future (Or, Don't Trust Anyone under 30).* New York: Jeremy P. Tarcher/Penguin.

Baum, Sandy, Jennifer Ma, and Kathleen Payea. 2010. *Education Pays 2010: The Benefits of Higher Education for Individuals and Society.* New York: College Board Advocacy and Policy Center. Trends in Higher Education Series.

——. 2013. *Education Pays 2013: The Benefits of Higher Education for Individuals and Society.* N.p.: College Board. Trends in Higher Education Series.

Becker, Howard S., Blanche Geer, and Everett C. Hughes. 1968. *Making the Grade: The Academic Side of College Life.* New York: Wiley.

Bekerman, Zvi, Nicholas C. Burbules, and Diana Silberman-Keller, eds. 2006. *Learning in Places: The Informal Education Reader.* New York: Peter Lang.

Bellah, Robert N. 1991. *The Good Society.* New York: Knopf.

Ben-David, Yuval, and Rishabh Bhandari. 2013. As Yale Talks Grade Deflation, Princeton Pulls Back. *Yale News,* November 22. http://yaledailynews.com/blog/2013/11/22/ as-yale-talks-grade-deflation-princeton-pulls-back/.

Benei, Véronique. 2008. *Schooling Passions: Nation, History, and Language in Contemporary Western India.* Stanford: Stanford University Press.

Berlin, Brent, and Paul Kay. 1969. *Basic Color Terms: Their Universality and Evolution.* Berkeley: University of California Press.

Birkerts, Sven. 1994. *The Gutenberg Elegies: The Fate of Reading in an Electronic Age.* Winchester, MA: Faber and Faber.

Bloom, Allan. 1987. *The Closing of the American Mind: How Higher Education Has Failed Democracy and Impoverished the Souls of Today's Students.* New York: Simon and Schuster.

Blum, Susan D. 2009. *My Word! Plagiarism and College Culture.* Ithaca: Cornell University Press.

———. 2014. "The Language Gap": Liberal Guilt Creates Another Not-So-Magic Bullet. *Huffington Post Education*, April 30. http://www.huffingtonpost.com/susan-d-blum/language-gap-liberal-guilt-creates-ano_b_5233638.html.

Bock, John. 2010. An Evolutionary Perspective on Learning in Social, Cultural, and Ecological Context. In *The Anthropology of Learning in Childhood*, edited by David F. Lancy, John Bock, and Suzanne Gaskins, 11–34. Walnut Creek, CA: AltaMira.

Bogle, Kathleen A. 2008. *Hooking Up: Sex, Dating, and Relationships on Campus*. New York: New York University Press.

Boice, Robert. 2000. *Advice for New Faculty Members: Nihil Nimus*. Boston: Allyn and Bacon.

Bok, Derek. 2006. *Our Underachieving Colleges: A Candid Look at How Much Students Learn and Why They Should Be Learning More*. Princeton: Princeton University Press.

———. 2013. *Higher Education in America*. Princeton: Princeton University Press.

Bonfiglio, Jeremy D. 2010. Gladly Would They Learn. *Notre Dame Magazine*, Summer. http://magazine.nd.edu/news/15955/.

Bosco, Joseph. 2011–12. The Formula as a Managerial Tool: Audit Culture in Hong Kong. *Journal of Workplace Rights* 16 (3–4): 383–403.

Bourdieu, Pierre, and Jean-Claude Passeron. 1990 [1970]. *Reproduction in Education, Society, and Culture*. Translated by Richard Nice. Newbury Park, CA: Sage.

Boyer Commission on Educating Undergraduates in the Research University. 1998. *Reinventing Undergraduate Education: A Blueprint for America's Research Universities*. Stony Brook: State University of New York at Stony Brook for the Carnegie Foundation for the Advancement of Teaching.

Brandenburg, Uwe, and Jiani Zhu. 2007. *Higher Education in China in the Light of Massification and Demographic Change: Lessons to be Learned for Germany*. Gütersloh: Centrum für Hochschulentwicklung.

Bransford, John D., Ann L. Brown, and Rodney Cocking, eds. 2000. *How People Learn: Brain, Mind, Experience, and School*. Expanded ed. National Research Council, Committee on Developments in the Science of Learning, and Committee on Learning Research and Educational Practice. Washington, DC: National Academy Press.

Brickman, P., D. Coates, and R. Janoff-Bulman. 1978. Lottery Winners and Accident Victims: Is Happiness Relative? *Journal of Personality and Social Psychology* 36 (8): 917–27.

British Museum. N.d. A Brief History of Writing. http://www.britishmuseum.org/explore/young_explorers/discover/videos/a_brief_history_of_writing.aspx.

Bronfenbrenner, Urie. 1979. *The Ecology of Human Development: Experiments by Nature and Design*. Cambridge: Harvard University Press.

———. 1994. Ecological Models of Human Development. In *International Encyclopedia of Education*, vol. 3, 2nd ed., 1643–47. Oxford: Elsevier.

Brooks, David. 2007. The Odyssey Years. *New York Times*, October 9. http://www.nytimes.com/2007/10/09/opinion/09brooks.html.

———. 2015. How Adulthood Happens. *New York Times*, June 12. http://www.nytimes.com/2015/06/12/opinion/david-brooks-how-adulthood-happens.html?rref=collection%2Fcolumn%2Fdavid-brooks&_r=0.

Brosch, Tobias. 2014. Neurocognitive Mechanisms of Attentional Prioritization in Social Mechanisms. In *Collective Emotions: Perspectives from Psychology, Philosophy, and Sociology*, edited by Christian von Scheve and Mikko Salmela, 78–93. Oxford: Oxford University Press.

Brown, Donald E. 1991. *Human Universals*. New York: McGraw-Hill.

Brown, Peter C., Henry L. Roediger III, and Mark A. McDaniel. 2014. *Make It Stick: The Science of Successful Learning*. Cambridge: Belknap Press of Harvard University Press.

Byrne, Richard W. 2005. Social Cognition: Imitation, Imitation, Imitation. *Current Biology* 15 (13): R498–500.

Cahill, Thomas. 2008 [2006]. *Mysteries of the Middle Ages: And the Beginning of the Modern World*. New York: Anchor.

Caplan, Bryan. 2009. Are Too Many Students Going to College? *Chronicle of Higher Education*, November 8. http://chronicle.com/article/Are-Too-Many-Students-Going-to/49039/.

Cappel, Constance. 1999. *Utopian Colleges*. New York: Peter Lang.

Carey, Kevin. 2015. *The End of College: Creating the Future of Learning and the University of Everywhere*. New York: Penguin (Riverhead).

Carini, Robert M., George D. Kuh, and Stephen P. Klein. 2006. Student Engagement and Student Learning: Testing the Linkages. *Research in Higher Education* 47 (1): 1–32.

Carnegie Foundation. 2012. Carnegie Foundation for the Advancement of Teaching Receives Funding to Rethink the Carnegie Unit. Carnegie Foundation for the Advancement of Teaching, December. http://www.carnegiefoundation.org/newsroom/press-releases/carnegie-foundation-receives-funding-rethink-the-carnegie-unit.

Carr, Nicholas. 2008. Is Google Making Us Stupid? What the Internet Is Doing to Our Brains. *Atlantic*, July–August. http://www.theatlantic.com/magazine/archive/2008/07/is-}google-making-us-stupid/306868/.

Castle, Terry. 2012. Don't Pick Up: Why Kids Need to Separate from their Parents. *Chronicle Review*, May 6. http://chronicle.com/article/The-Case-for-Breaking-Up-With/131760/.

Center for Collegiate Mental Health. 2015. *2014 Annual Report*. Publication No. STA 15-30 (January).

Centers for Disease Control. 2012. Suicide. Facts at a Glance. http://www.cdc.gov/violenceprevention/pdf/Suicide_DataSheet-a.pdf.

———. 2013. Well-Being Concepts. http://www.cdc.gov/hrqol/wellbeing.htm.

Centra, John A. 2003. Will Teachers Receive Higher Student Evaluations by Giving Higher Grades and Less Course Work? *Research in Higher Education* 44 (5): 495–518.

Chace, William M. 2006. *100 Semesters: My Adventures as Student, Professor, and University President, and What I Learned Along the Way*. Princeton: Princeton University Press.

Chang, Deborah. 2013. Harriet Ball Teaching Multiplication Facts. https://www.youtube.com/watch?v=U55i6LFN2-s.

Chetty, Raj, John N. Friedman, and Jonah E. Rockoff. 2011. The Long-Term Impacts of Teachers: Teacher Value-Added and Student Outcomes in Adulthood. *National Bureau of Economic Research Working Paper Series*, no. 17699. http://www.nber.org/papers/w17699.

Chick, Garry. 2010. Work, Play, and Learning. In *The Anthropology of Learning in Childhood*, edited by David F. Lancy, John Bock, and Suzanne Gaskins, 119–43. Walnut Creek, CA: AltaMira.

China Education Center. 2012. Higher Education Law of China. http://www.chinaed ucationcenter.com/en/cedu/hel.php.

Chivers, Tom. 2012. Kids, Disrespecting their Elders since 500 BC. *The Telegraph*, July 27. http://blogs.telegraph.co.uk/news/tomchiversscience/100172911/kids-disrespecting-their-elders-since-4000bc/.

Christensen, Clayton M., and Henry J. Eyring. 2011. *The Innovative University: Changing the DNA of Higher Education from the Inside Out*. San Francisco: Jossey-Bass.

Chronicle Online (Lorain County). 2011. Oberlin's Steve Volk Named Professor of Year. November 18. http://chronicle.northcoastnow.com/2011/11/18/oberlin%E2%80% 99s-steve-volk-named-professor-of-year/.

Chrzan, Janet. 2013. *Alcohol: Social Drinking in Cultural Context*. Routledge Series for Creative Teaching and Learning in Anthropology. New York: Routledge.

Chua, Amy. 2011. *Battle Hymn of the Tiger Mother*. New York: Penguin.

Chudacoff, Howard P. 1989. *How Old Are You? Age Consciousness in American Culture*. Princeton: Princeton University Press.

———. 2007. *Children at Play: An American History*. New York: New York University Press.

Clark, Russell D., and Elaine Hatfield. 1989. Gender Differences in Receptivity to Sexual Offers. *Journal of Psychology & Human Sexuality* 2 (1): 39–55.

Cobban, Alan B. 1980. Student Power in the Middle Ages. *History Today* 30 (2). http://www.historytoday.com/alan-b-cobban/student-power-middle-ages.

Cohen, Stanley. 2011 [1972]. *Folk Devils and Moral Panics: The Creation of the Mods and Rockers*. 3rd ed. Abingdon: Routledge.

College Board. 2004, 2007, 2010, 2013. *Education Pays: The Benefits of Higher Education for Individuals and Society*. http://trends.collegeboard.org/education-pays.

College411. 2013. Understanding College Selectivity. http://www.collegedata.com/cs/content/content_choosearticle_tmpl.jhtml?articleId=10004.

Collins, Gail. 2012. The Lows of Higher Ed. *New York Times*, September 14. http://www.nytimes.com/2012/09/15/opinion/collins-the-lows-of-higher-ed.html.

Collins, James. 2009. Social Reproduction in Classrooms and Schools. *Annual Review of Anthropology* 38: 33–48.

Collins, Randall. 1979. *The Credential Society: An Historical Sociology of Education and Stratification*. New York: Academic Press.

———. 2011. Credential Inflation and the Future of Universities. *Italian Journal of Sociology of Education* 2: 228–51. Originally published in *The Future of the City of Intellect*, edited by Steven Brint, 23–46. Stanford: Stanford University Press, 2002.

Compton, Robert. 2011. *The Finland Phenomenon: Inside the World's Most Surprising School System*. Washington, DC: Broken Pencil Productions.

Connor, Daniel F. 2011. Problems of Overdiagnosis and Overprescribing in ADHD. *Psychiatric Times*, August 11. http://www.psychiatrictimes.com/adhd/problems-overdiagnosis-and-overprescribing-adhd/page/0/1.

Cordain, Loren. N.d. Run with the Hunt: How Do Your Workouts Compare? The Paleo Diet. http://thepaleodiet.com/run-hunt-workouts-compare/.

Crawford, Matthew B. 2009. *Shop Class as Soulcraft: An Inquiry into the Value of Work*. New York: Penguin.

Cronin, Mike. 2006. Conservatives Push to Counter Liberal Professors. *Arizona Republic*, August 12. http://www.azcentral.com/arizonarepublic/news/articles/0812 professors.html.

Cronon, William. 1998. Only Connect . . . : The Goals of a Liberal Education. *American Scholar* (Autumn): 73–80.

Crowley, Sharon. 1998. The Invention of Freshman English. In *Composition in the University: Historical and Polemical Essays*, 46–78. Pittsburgh: University of Pittsburgh Press.

Csikszentmihalyi, Mihaly. 1990. *Flow: The Psychology of Optimal Experience*. New York: Harper and Row.

Dale, Stacy Berg, and Alan B. Krueger. 2002. Estimating the Payoff to Attending a More Selective College: An Application of Selection on Observables and Unobservables. *Quarterly Journal of Economics* 117 (4) (November): 1491–1528.

——. 2011. Estimating the Return to College Selectivity over the Career Using Administrative Earnings Data. NBER Working Paper no. 17159, June. http://www.nber.org/papers/w17159.

Damasio, Antonio R. 1999. *The Feeling of What Happens: Body and Emotion in the Making of Consciousness*. New York: Harcourt Brace.

Davidson, Cathy. 2010. No Grading, More Learning. HĀSTAC. May 3. http://www.hastac.org/blogs/cathy-davidson/no-grading-more-learning.

——. 2011a. *Now You See It: How the Brain Science of Attention Will Transform the Way We Live, Work, and Learn*. New York: Viking.

——. 2011b. Strangers on a Train. *Academe*, September–October. http://www.aaup.org/article/strangers-train#.U4d1t5QYbzc.

——. 2012. Should We Really ABOLISH the Term Paper? A Response to the NY Times. HĀSTAC. January 21. http://www.hastac.org/blogs/cathy-davidson/2012/01/21/should-we-really-abolish-term-paper-response-ny-times.

Davis, Brent, Dennis J. Sumara, and Rebecca Luce-Kapler. 2008. *Engaging Minds: Learning and Teaching in a Complex World*. New York: Routledge.

"Dean Dad." 2010. Get Your Gen Eds Out of the Way. *Inside Higher Ed*, June 7. http://www.insidehighered.com/blogs/confessions_of_a_community_college_dean/get_your_gen_eds_out_of_the_way.

DeAngelo, Linda, Ray Franke, Sylvia Hurtado, John H. Pryor, and Serge Tran. 2011. *Completing College: Assessing Graduation Rates at Four-Year Institutions*. Los Angeles: Higher Education Research Institute at UCLA. http://heri.ucla.edu/DARCU/CompletingCollege2011.pdf.

De Botton, Alain. 2009. *The Pleasures and Sorrows of Work*. New York: Pantheon.

Deci, Edward L. 1971. Effects of Externally Mediated Rewards on Intrinsic Motivation. *Journal of Personality and Social Psychology* 18: 105–15.

DeFrancis, John. 1989. *Visible Speech: The Diverse Oneness of Writing Systems*. Honolulu: University of Hawai'i Press.

Delbanco, Andrew. 2012. *College: What It Was, Is, and Should Be.* Princeton: Princeton University Press.

Demerath, Peter. 2009. *Producing Success: The Culture of Personal Advancement in an American High School.* Chicago: University of Chicago Press.

Deresiewicz, William. 2014. *Excellent Sheep: The Miseducation of the American Elite and the Way to a Meaningful Life.* New York: Simon and Schuster.

Derrida, Jacques. 1974 [1971]. White Mythology: Metaphor in the Text of Philosophy. *New Literary History* 6 (1): 5–74.

DeSilva, Jeremy M., and Julie J. Lesnik. 2008. Brain Size at Birth throughout Human Evolution: A New Method for Estimating Neonatal Brain Size in Hominins. *Journal of Human Evolution* 55: 1064–74.

Dewey, John. 1988 [1938]. *Experience and Education: The 60th Anniversary Edition.* West Lafayette, IN: Kappa Delta Pi.

Diener, Ed, Richard E. Lucas, and Christie Napa Scollon. 2006. Beyond the Hedonic Treadmill: Revising the Adaptation Theory of Well-Being. *American Psychologist* 61 (4): 305–14.

Diener, Ed, and M. E. P. Seligman. 2004. Beyond Money: Toward an Economy of Well-Being. *Psychological Sciences in the Public Interest* 5 (1) (July): 1–31.

DiMartino, Joseph, and John H. Clarke. 2008. *Personalizing the High School Experience for Each Student.* Alexandria, VA: Association for Supervision and Curriculum Development.

Di Meglio, Francesca. 2010. College: Big Investment, Paltry Return. *Bloomberg Businessweek,* June 28. http://www.businessweek.com/bschools/content/jun2010/bs20100618_385280.htm.

Dissanayake, Ellen. 1988. *What Is Art For?* Seattle: University of Washington Press.

Dodge, Rachel, Annette P. Daly, Jan Huyton, and Lalage D. Sanders. 2012. The Challenge of Defining Wellbeing. *International Journal of Wellbeing* 2 (3): 222–35. DOI: 10.5502/ijw.v2i3.4.http://www.internationaljournalofwellbeing.org/index.php/ijow/article/viewFile/89/238.

Doidge, Norman. 2007. *The Brain That Changes Itself: Stories of Personal Triumph from the Frontiers of Brain Science.* New York: Viking.

Douglas, Mary, ed. 1987. *Constructive Drinking: Perspectives on Drink from Anthropology.* Cambridge: Cambridge University Press.

Douthat, Ross. 2005. *Privilege: Harvard and the Education of the Ruling Class.* New York: Hyperion.

D'Souza, Dinesh. 1991. *Illiberal Education: The Politics of Race and Sex on Campus.* New York: Free Press.

Duff, Patricia A., and Nancy H. Hornberger, eds. 2010. *Language Socialization.* Encyclopedia of Language and Education. Vol. 8. New York: Springer.

Duffy, Thomas P., M.D. 2011. The Flexner Report—100 Years Later. *Yale Journal of Biology and Medicine* 84 (3): 269–76.

Dunbabin, Jean. 1997. Jacques Le Goff and the Intellectuals. In *The Work of Jacques Le Goff and the Challenges of Medieval History,* edited by Miri Rubin, 157–67. Woodbridge: Boydell Press.

Durm, Mark W. 1993. An A Is Not An A Is Not An A: A History of Grading. *Educational Forum* 57 (Spring): 1–4.

Dutton, Denis. 2009. *The Art Instinct: Beauty, Pleasure, and Human Evolution*. Oxford: Oxford University Press.

Eacowan. 2010. Comments on Vedder 2010. June 21. http://chronicle.com/blogPost/Student-Evaluations-Grade/24926/.

Easterbrook, Gregg. 2004. Who Needs Harvard? *Atlantic*, October. http://www.theatlantic.com/magazine/archive/2004/10/who-needs-harvard/303521/.

Eckert, Penelope. 1989. *Jocks and Burnouts: Social Categories and Identity in the High School*. New York: Teachers College Press.

Edmundson, Mark. 2013. *Why Teach? In Defense of a Real Education*. New York: Bloomsbury.

Education Week. 2013. Diplomas Count 2013, June 6. http://www.edweek.org/ew/toc/2013/06/06/index.html?intc=EW-DPCT13-AP.

Edwards, Carolyn Pope, Keely Cline, Lella Gandini, Alga Giacomelli, Donatella Giovannini, and Annalia Galardini. 2013. Books, Stories, and the Imagination at "The Nursery Rhyme": A Qualitative Case Study of the Learning Environment at an Italian Preschool. In *Learning In and Out of School: Education across the Globe*, edited by Susan D. Blum. Conference proceedings. http://kellogg.nd.edu/learning/Edwards.pdf.

Elman, Benjamin A. 2000. *A Cultural History of Civil Examinations in Late Imperial China*. Berkeley: University of California Press.

Enfield, N. J., and Stephen C. Levinson. 2006. Introduction: Human Sociality as a New Interdisciplinary Field. In *Roots of Human Sociality*, edited by N. J. Enfield and Stephen C. Levinson, 1–35. Oxford: Berg.

Erikson, E. H. 1963. [1950] *Childhood and Society*. New York: Norton.

Espeland, Wendy Nelson, and Michael Sauder. 2007. Rankings and Reactivity: How Public Measures Recreate Social Worlds. *American Journal of Sociology* 113 (1): 1–40.

Espeland, Wendy Nelson, and Mitchell L. Stevens. 1998. Commensuration as a Social Process. *Annual Review of Sociology* 24: 313–43.

——. 2008. A Sociology of Quantification. *European Journal of Sociology* 49 (3) (December): 401–36. DOI: 10.1017/S0003975609000150.

European Commission. 2011. Education and Training: The Bologna Process; Toward the European Higher Education Area. http://ec.europa.eu/education/higher-education/doc1290_en.htm.

European Higher Education Area. 2010. The Official Bologna Process Website 2010–2012. http://www.ehea.info/.

European University Association. 2003. European Credit Transfer and Accumulation System (ECTS). http://www.eua.be/eua/jsp/en/upload/ECTS%20Key%20Features.1068807879166.pdf.

Fain, Paul. 2012. College Credit Without College. *Inside Higher Ed*, May 7. http://www.insidehighered.com/news/2012/05/07/prior-learning-assessment-catches-quietly.

Fairbrother, Gregory P. 2003. The Effects of Political Education and Critical Thinking on Hong Kong and Mainland Chinese University Students' National Attitudes. *British Journal of Sociology of Education* 24 (5): 605–20.

fairday. 2012. Blog comment on Fendrich 2012.

Fallows, James. 2007. About Credentialism and the Marilee Jones/MIT Case. *Atlantic*, April 30. http://www.theatlantic.com/technology/archive/2007/04/about-credentialism-and-the-marilee-jones-mit-case/7592/.

Fechheimer, Marcus, Karen Webber, and Pamela B. Kleiber. 2011. How Well Do Undergraduate Research Programs Promote Engagement and Success of Students? *CBE–Life Sciences Education* 10 (Summer): 156–63. DOI: 10.1187/cbe.10-10-0130.

Feldman, A. F., and J. L. Matjasko. 2007. Profiles and Portfolios of Adolescent School-Based Extracurricular Activity Participation. *Journal of Adolescence* 30: 313–32.

Felitti, Vincent J., Robert F. Anda, et al. 1998. Relationship of Childhood Abuse and Household Dysfunction to Many of the Leading Causes of Death in Adults. *American Journal of Preventive Medicine* 14 (4): 245–58.

Fendrich, Laurie. 2012. Making the Grade. *Chronicle of Higher Education*, May 22. http://chronicle.com/blogs/brainstoa.rm/making-the-grade/47185?sid=cr.

Fink, L. Dee. 2003. *Creating Significant Learning Experiences: An Integrated Approach to Designing College Courses*. San Francisco: Jossey-Bass.

Finnan, Christine, and Lauren Rose. 2013. Learning, Sense of Self, and Yoga in a High-Poverty Urban Elementary School. In *Learning In and Out of School*, edited by Susan D. Blum. Conference proceedings. http://kellogg.nd.edu/learning/Finnan.pdf.

Fischer, Mary J. 2007. Settling into Campus Life: Differences by Race/Ethnicity in College Involvement and Outcomes. *Journal of Higher Education* 78 (2): 125–61.

Fish, Stanley. 2008. *Save the World on Your Own Time*. New York: Oxford University Press.

Fishman, Ted C. 2012. Why These Kids Get a Free Ride to College. *New York Times*, September 13. http://www.nytimes.com/2012/09/16/magazine/kalamazoo-mich-the-city-that-pays-for-college.html?_r=1&.

Flaherty, Colleen. 2015. Flawed Evaluations. *Inside Higher Ed*, June 10. https://www.insidehighered.com/news/2015/06/10/aaup-committee-survey-data-raise-questions-effectiveness-student-teaching.

Foroohar, Rana. 2014. The School That Will Get You a Job. *Time*, February 13. http://time.com/7066/the-school-that-will-get-you-a-job/.

Fortes, Meyer. 1970 [1938]. Social and Psychological Aspects of Education in Taleland. In *From Child to Adult: Studies in the Anthropology of Education*, edited by John Middleton, 14–74. Garden City, NY: The Natural History Press.

Foucault, Michel. 1979 [1977]. *Discipline and Punish: The Birth of the Prison*. Translated by Alan Sheridan. New York: Vintage.

Frank, Robert H., and Philip J. Cook. 1995. *The Winner-Take-All Society: How More and More Americans Compete for Ever Fewer and Bigger Prizes, Encouraging Economic Waste, Income Inequality, and an Impoverished Cultural Life*. New York: Free Press.

Fredricks, Jennifer A., and Jacquelynne S. Eccles. 2006. Is Extracurricular Participation Associated with Beneficial Outcomes? Concurrent and Longitudinal Relations. *Developmental Psychology* 42 (4): 698–713.

Freed, R. S., and S. A. Freed. 1981. Enculturation and Education in Shanti Nagar. New York: American Museum of Natural History.

Freire, Paolo. 2000 [1970]. *Pedagogy of the Oppressed*. Translated by M. B. Ramos. New York: Continuum.

Friedman, Thomas. 2014. How to Get a Job at Google. *New York Times*, February 22. http://www.nytimes.com/2014/02/23/opinion/sunday/friedman-how-to-get-a-job-at-google.html?_r=0.

Fuentes, Agustín, and Aku Visala, eds. Forthcoming. *Verbs, Bones, and Brains: Interdisciplinary Perspectives on Human Nature*. Notre Dame: University of Notre Dame Press.

Fuhr, C. 1997. *The German Education System since 1945: Outlines and Problems*. Bonn: Inter Nationes.

Gardner, Howard. 1995. *The Unschooled Mind: How Children Think and How Schools Should Teach*. New York: Basic Books.

Gaskins, Suzanne. 2008. Children's Daily Lives among the Yucatec Maya. In *Anthropology and Child Development: A Cross-Cultural Reader*, edited by Robert A. LeVine and Rebecca S. New, 280–88. Malden, MA: Blackwell.

——. 2013. Open Attention as a Cultural Tool for Observational Learning. In *Learning In and Out of School: Education across the Globe*, edited by Susan D. Blum. Conference proceedings. http://kellogg.nd.edu/learning/Gaskins.pdf.

Gaskins, Suzanne, and Ruth Paradise. 2010. Learning through Observation in Daily Life. In *The Anthropology of Learning in Childhood*, edited by David F. Lancy, John Bock, and Suzanne Gaskins, 85–118. Lanham, MD: AltaMira.

Gatto, John Taylor. 2003. *The Underground History of American Education: A Schoolteacher's Intimate Investigation into the Prison of Modern Schooling*. Oxford, NY: The Oxford Village Press.

——. 2005 [1992]. *Dumbing Us Down: The Hidden Curriculum of Compulsory Schooling*. Gabriola Island, BC: New Society Publishers.

Geertz, Clifford. 1973. Deep Play: Notes on the Balinese Cockfight. In *The Interpretation of Cultures*, 412–53. New York: Basic Books.

Genova, Jane. 2010. "C" Students More Successful Than "A" Students. *AOL Jobs*, November 16. http://jobs.aol.com/articles/2010/11/16/c-students-more-successful-than-a-students/.

Gibbons, Ann. 2008. The Birth of Childhood. *Science* 322 (November 14): 1040–43.

Ginsberg, Benjamin. 2011. *The Fall of the Faculty: The Rise of the All-Administrative University and Why It Matters*. New York: Oxford University Press.

Gladwin, Thomas. 1970. *East Is a Big Bird: Navigation and Logic on Puluwat Atoll*. Cambridge: Harvard University Press.

Goldman, Shelley. 2006. A New Angle on Families: Connecting the Mathematics of Life with School Mathematics. In *Learning in Places: The Informal Education Reader*, edited by Zvi Bekerman, Nicholas C. Burbules, and Diana Silberman-Keller, 55–76. New York: Peter Lang.

Goodman, Paul. 1962, 1964. *Compulsory Mis-education and The Community of Scholars*. New York: Vintage.

Google Answers. 2004. Quote About Ill-Behaved Kids—Aristotle? Socrates? Plato? http://answers.google.com/answers/threadview?id=398104.

Gould, Stephen Jay. 1996 [1981]. *The Mismeasure of Man*. Rev. ed. New York: Norton.

Graeber, David. 2011. *Debt: The First 5,000 Years*. Brooklyn, NY: Melville House.

Gray, Peter. 2013. *Free to Learn: Why Unleashing the Instinct to Play Will Make Our Children Happier, More Self-Reliant, and Better Students for Life*. New York: Basic Books.

Green, Elizabeth. 2014. *Building a Better Teacher: How Teaching Works (and How to Teach It to Everyone)*. New York: W.W. Norton.

Greenfeld, Karl Taro. 2013. My Daughter's Homework Is Killing Me. *Atlantic*, September 18. http://www.theatlantic.com/magazine/archive/2013/10/my-daughters-homework-is-killing-me/309514/.

Greenfield, Patricia Marks. 1984. A Theory of the Teacher in the Learning Activities of Everyday Life. In *Everyday Cognition: Its Development in Social Context*, edited by Barbara Rogoff and Jean Lave, 117–38. Cambridge: Harvard University Press.

———. 2004. *Weaving Generations Together: Evolving Creativity in the Maya of Chiapas*. Santa Fe, NM: SAR Press.

Greenfield, Patricia Marks, and Jean Lave. 1982. Cognitive Aspects of Informal Education. In *Cultural Perspectives on Child Development*, edited by Daniel Wagner and Harold Stevenson, 181–207. San Francisco: Freeman.

Greenhouse, Carol J., ed. 2010. *Ethnographies of Neoliberalism*. Philadelphia: University of Pennsylvania Press.

Grigsby, Mary. 2009. *College Life through the Eyes of Students*. Albany: State University of New York Press.

Grinspan, Jon. 2014. The Wild Children of Yesteryear. *New York Times*, May 31. http://www.nytimes.com/2014/06/01/opinion/sunday/the-wild-children-of-yesteryear.html?src=me&ref=general&_r=0.

Guess, Andy. 2008. Stanford Law Drops Letter Grades. *Inside Higher Ed*, June 2. http://www.insidehighered.com/news/2008/06/02/stanford.

Guinier, Lani. 2015. *The Tyranny of the Meritocracy: Democratizing Higher Education in America*. Boston: Beacon Press.

Gusfield, Joseph. 1987. Passage to Play: Rituals of Drinking Time in American Society. In *Constructive Drinking*, edited by Mary Douglas, 73–90. Cambridge: Cambridge University Press.

Gusterson, Hugh. 1997. Studying Up Revisited. *PoLAR: Political and Legal Anthropology Review* 20 (1): 114–19.

Hacker, Andrew, and Claudia Dreifus. 2010. *Higher Education? How Colleges Are Wasting Our Money and Failing Our Kids—and What We Can Do About It*. New York: Henry Holt.

Hagen, Edward H., and G. A. Bryant. 2003. Music and Dance as a Coalition Signaling System. *Human Nature* 14: 21–51.

Hagen, Edward H., and P. Hammerstein. 2009. Did Neanderthals and Other Early Humans Sing? Seeking the Biological Roots of Music in the Loud Calls of Primates, Lions, Hyenas, and Wolves. *Musicae Scientiae*: 291–320.

Hall, G. Stanley. 1904. *Adolescence: Its Psychology and Its Relations to Physiology, Anthropology, Sociology, Sex, Crime, Religion, and Education*. Vol. 2. New York: D. Appleton.

Hansen, Mette Halskov. 1999. *Lessons in Being Chinese: Minority Education and Ethnic Identity in Southwest China*. Seattle: University of Washington Press.

Harber, Clive. 2004. *Schooling as Violence: How Schools Harm Pupils and Societies*. London: RoutledgeFalmer.

Hart, James Morgan. 1874. *German Universities: A Narrative of Personal Experience. Together with Recent Statistical Information, Practical Suggestions, and a Comparison of the German, English and American Systems of Higher Education*. New York: G. P. Putnam's Sons.

Harvey, Nelson. 2011. Why Are Young, Educated Americans Going Back to the Farm? *Huffington Post*, August 2. http://www.huffingtonpost.com/turnstyle/why-are-young-educated-am_b_916263.html.

Hawton, Keith, and Kees van Heeringen. 2009. Suicide. *The Lancet* 373 (9672): 1372–81. http://www.thelancet.com/journals/lancet/article/PIIS0140–6736(09)60372-X/fulltext.

Heath, Shirley Brice. 1982. What No Bedtime Story Means: Narrative Skills at Home and School. *Language in Society* 11: 49–76.

———. 2012a. Informal Learning. In *Encyclopedia of Diversity in Education*, edited by James A. Banks, 1194–1202. New York: Sage.

———. 2012b. Seeing Our Way into Learning Science in Informal Environments. In *Research on Schools, Neighborhoods, and Communities: Toward Civic Responsibility*, edited by W. F. Tate, 249–67. New York: Rowman & Littlefield.

Heath, Shirley Brice, and Juliet Langman. 1994. Shared Thinking and the Register of Coaching. In *Sociolinguistic Perspectives on Register*, edited by Douglas Biber and Edward Finegan, 82–105. New York: Oxford University Press.

Hemenway, Toby. 2009. *Gaia's Garden: A Guide to Home-Scale Permaculture*. White River Junction, VT: Chelsea Green.

Henig, Robin Marantz, and Samantha Henig. 2012. *Twentysomething: Why Do Young Adults Seem Stuck?* New York: Penguin.

Henrich, Joseph, Steven J. Heine, and Ara Norenzayan. 2010. The Weirdest People in the World? *Behavioral and Brain Sciences* 33 (2–3): 61–83. DOI: 10.1017/S0140525X0999152X.

Henry, Douglas V., and Michael R. Beaty, eds. 2007. *The Schooled Heart: Moral Formation in American Higher Education*. Waco, TX: Baylor University Press.

Henry, Jules. 1963. *Culture Against Man*. New York: Random House.

Herndon, James. 1971. *How to Survive in Your Native Land*. New York: Simon and Schuster.

Herrmann, Esther, Josep Call, Maria Victoria Hernández-Lloreda, Brian Hare, and Michael Tomasello. 2007. Humans Have Evolved Specialized Skills of Social Cognition: The Cultural Intelligence Hypothesis. *Science* 317 (5843): 1360–66. DOI: 10.1126/science.1146282.

Hersh, Richard H., and John Merrow, eds. 2005. *Declining by Degrees: Higher Education at Risk*. New York: Palgrave Macmillan.

Herzog, John D. 2013. Reflecting on Compagnonnage: Or Real World vs. Schoolroom Learning. In *Learning In and Out of School: Education across the Globe*, edited by Susan D. Blum. Conference proceedings. http://kellogg.nd.edu/learning/Herzog.pdf.

Hewlett, Barry S., Hillary N. Fouts, Adam H. Boyette, and Bonnie L. Hewlett. 2011. Social Learning among Congo Basin Hunter-Gatherers. *Philosophical Transactions of the Royal Society B* 366: 1168–78. DOI: 10.1098/rstb.2010.0373.

Heywood, John S., and Xiangdong Wei. 2004. Education and Signaling: Evidence from a Highly Competitive Labor Market. *Education Economics* 12 (1) (April): 1–16.

Hiltonsmith, Robert. 2013. At What Cost? How Student Debt Reduces Lifetime Wealth. Dēmos, August 1. http://www.demos.org/what-cost-how-student-debt-reduces-lifetime-wealth.

Hobson, Eric H. N.d. Getting Students to Read: Fourteen Tips. The IDEA Center. Paper 40. http://www.theideacenter.org/research-and-papers/idea-papers/idea-paper-no-40.

Holland, Dorothy C., and Margaret A. Eisenhart. 1990. *Educated in Romance: Women, Achievement, and College Culture*. Chicago: University of Chicago Press.

Holmgren, David. 2002. *Permaculture: Principles and Pathways Beyond Sustainability*. Hepburn, Victoria (Australia): Holmgren Design Services.

Holt, John. 1982 [1964]. *How Children Fail*. Rev. ed. Cambridge, MA: Da Capo.

———. 2004 [1976]. *Instead of Education*. Boulder: Sentient Publications.

Holzer, Elie. 2015. Welcoming Opposition: *Havruta* Learning and Montaigne's *The Art of Discussion*. *Journal of Moral Education* 44 (1): 64–80. http://dx.doi.org/10.1080/03057240.2014.1002462.

Hoover, Eric. 2009. The Millennial Muddle: How Stereotyping Students Became a Thriving Industry and a Bundle of Contradictions. *Chronicle of Higher Education*, October 11. http://chronicle.com/article/The-Millennial-Muddle-How/48772/.

Horowitz, David. 2006. *The Professors: The 101 Most Dangerous Academics in America*. Washington, DC: Regnery.

Horowitz, Helen Lefkowitz. 1987. *Campus Life: Undergraduate Cultures from the End of the Eighteenth Century to the Present*. Chicago: University of Chicago Press.

Howard, Alvin W. 1965. The Carnegie Unit: Is This Bugaboo Still with Us? *The Clearing House* 40 (3): 135–39.

Howe, Neil, and William Strauss. 2000. *Millennials Rising: The Next Great Generation*. New York: Vintage.

———. 2007. *Millennials Go to College: Strategies for a New Generation on Campus. Recruiting and Admissions, Campus Life, and the Classroom*. 2nd ed. Great Falls, VA: LifeCourse Associates.

Hu, Shouping. 2005. *Beyond Grade Inflation: Grading Problems in Higher Education*. ADSHE Higher Education Report. Vol. 30, no. 6. Hoboken, NJ: Wiley Periodicals.

Hu, Shouping, George D. Kuh, and Joy Gaston Gayles. 2007. Engaging Undergraduate Students in Research Activities: Are Research Universities Doing a Better Job? *Innovative Higher Education* 32 (3): 167–77.

Huelsman, Mark. 2014. Yes, Large Student Debt Burdens Are Overblown. But We Still Have a Huge Student Debt Problem. Dēmos, June 24. http://www.demos.org/blog/6/24/14/yes-large-student-debt-burdens-are-overblown-we-still-have-huge-student-debt-problem.

Huffington Post. 2012. Which Colleges Have the Best Return on Investment? April 19. http://www.huffingtonpost.com/2012/04/19/college-roi-rankings-best-worst_n_1438699.html.

Hughes, Katherine. 2013. The College Completion Agenda: 2012 Progress Report. College Board. Completionagenda.collegeboard.org.

Huizinga, Johan. 1950 [1938]. *Homo Ludens: A Study of the Play-Element in Culture*. Boston: Beacon Press.

Human Rights Watch. 2014. US/OAS: End Juvenile Life-without-Parole Sentences. March 25. http://www.hrw.org/news/2014/03/25/usoas-end-juvenile-life-without-parole-sentences.

Hunt, Lester H., ed. 2008. *Grade Inflation: Academic Standards in Higher Education*. Albany: State University of New York Press.

Hunt, Thomas C. 2001. *The Impossible Dream: Education and the Search for Panaceas*. New York: Peter Lang.

Huston, Therese. 2009. *Teaching What You Don't Know*. Cambridge: Harvard University Press.

Hutchins, Edwin. 1995. *Cognition in the Wild*. Cambridge: MIT Press.

Iacoboni, Marco. 2008. *Mirroring People: The New Science of How We Connect with Others*. New York: Picador.

Illich, Ivan. 1970. *Deschooling Society*. London: Marion Boyars.

Immordino-Yang, Mary Helen, and Antonio Damasio. 2007. We Feel, Therefore We Learn: The Relevance of Affective and Social Neuroscience to Education. *Mind, Brain, and Education* 1 (1): 3–10.

Inoue, Ken, et al. 2008. Current State of Refusal to Attend School in Japan. Letter to the Editor. *Psychiatry and Clinical Neurosciences* 62: 622. DOI: 10.1111/j.1440–1819. 2008.01857.x.

Jackson, Maggie. 2009. *Distracted: The Erosion of Attention and the Coming Dark Age*. Amherst, NY: Prometheus Books.

Jacobs, Lynn F., and Jeremy S. Hyman. 2009. 15 Secrets of Getting Good Grades in College. *US News Education*, August 19. http://www.usnews.com/education/blogs/professors-guide/2009/08/19/15-secrets-of-getting-good-grades-in-college.

——. 2010. *The Secrets of College Success*. San Francisco: Wiley.

James, William. 1903. The Ph.D. Octopus. *Harvard Monthly* 36 (March): 1–9.

Jaschik, Scott. 2010. No Grading, More Learning. *Inside Higher Ed*, May 3. http://www.insidehighered.com/news/2010/05/03/grading.

——. 2014. A New SAT. *Inside Higher Ed*, March 5. http://www.insidehighered.com/news/2014/03/05/college-board-unveils-new-sat-major-overhaul-writing-exam#sthash.aPsyjxDU.dpbs.

Jay, Paul, and Gerald Graff. 2012. Fear of Being Useful. *Inside Higher Ed*, January 5. http://www.insidehighered.com/views/2012/01/05/essay-new-approach-defend-value-humanities.

Johnson, Valen E. 2003. *Grade Inflation: A Crisis in College Education*. New York: Springer.

June, Audrey Williams. 2010. Faculty Burnout Has Both External and Internal Sources, Scholar Says. *Chronicle of Higher Education*, June 9. http://chronicle.com/article/Faculty-Burnout-Has-Both/65843/.

Jung, Hyang Jin. 2007. *Learning to Be an Individual: Emotion and Person in an American Junior High*. New York: Peter Lang.

Kadison, Richard, and Theresa Foy DiGeronimo. 2004. *College of the Overwhelmed: The Campus Mental Health Crisis and What to Do about It*. San Francisco: Jossey-Bass.

Kamenetz, Anya. 2010. *DIY U: Edupunks, Edupreneurs, and the Coming Transformation of Higher Education*. White River Junction, VT: Chelsea Green.

Kan, Flora, Edward Vickers, and Paul Morris. 2007. Keepers of the Sacred Flame: Patriotism, Politics, and the Chinese History Subject Community in Hong Kong. *Cambridge Journal of Education* 37 (2): 229–47.

Kaplan, Celia Patricia, et al. 2003. Health-Compromising Behaviors among Vietnamese Adolescents: The Role of Education and Extracurricular Activities. *Journal of Adolescent Health* 32: 374–83.

Karabel, Jerome. 2005. *The Chosen: The Hidden History of Admission and Exclusion at Harvard, Yale, and Princeton*. Boston: Houghton Mifflin.

Kariya, Takehiko. 2011a. Credential Inflation and Employment in "Universal" Higher Education: Enrollment, Expansion and (In)equality via Privatization in Japan. *Journal of Education and Work* 24 (1–2): 69–94.

——. 2011b. Japanese Solutions to the Equity and Efficiency Dilemma? Secondary Schools, Inequity and the Arrival of "Universal" Higher Education. *Oxford Review of Education* 37 (2): 241–66.

Katz, Richard. 1982. *Boiling Energy: Community Healing among the Kalahari Kung*. Cambridge: Harvard University Press.

Kelly, Annie. 2012. Gross National Happiness in Bhutan: The Big Idea from a Tiny State That Could Change the World. *The Guardian*, December 1. http://www.theguardian.com/world/2012/dec/01/bhutan-wealth-happiness-counts.

Kelly, Caitlin. 2012. Forgoing College to Pursue Dreams. *New York Times*, September 15. http://www.nytimes.com/2012/09/16/business/the-thiel-fellows-forgoing-college-to-pursue-dreams.html.

Kena, Grace, Susan Aud, Frank Johnson, Xiaolei Wang, Jijun Zhang, Amy Rathbun, Sidney Wilkinson-Flicker, and Paul Kristapovich. 2014. *The Condition of Education 2014* (NCES 2014-083). U.S. Department of Education. Washington, DC: National Center for Education Statistics. http://nces.ed.gov/pubsearch.

Kerr, Clark. 2001. *The Uses of the University*. 5th ed. Cambridge: Harvard University Press.

Kett, Joseph F. 1977. *Rites of Passage: Adolescence in America, 1790 to the Present*. New York: Basic Books.

Khan, Shamus Rahman. 2011. *Privilege: The Making of an Adolescent Elite at St. Paul's School*. Princeton: Princeton University Press.

Kinsley, Michael. 2007. MIT Dean Marilee Jones Flunks Out. *Time*, May 3. http://www.time.com/time/magazine/article/0,9171,1617508,00.html.

Kipnis, Andrew. 2001. The Disturbing Educational Discipline of "Peasants." *The China Journal* 46: 1–24.

Kirkpatrick, Andy, and Zhichang Xu. 2012. The Ba Gu Wen. In *Chinese Rhetoric and Writing: An Introduction for Language Teachers*, 75–91. Fort Collins, CO: WAC Clearinghouse and Parlor Press.

Kirn, Walter. 2009. *Lost in the Meritocracy: The Undereducation of an Overachiever*. New York: Doubleday.

Kirschenbaum, Howard, Sidney B. Simon, and Rodney W. Napier. 1971. *Wad-ja-get? The Grading Game in American Education*. New York: Hart Publishing.

Klein, Joe. 2012. Learning That Works. *Time*, May 14. http://content.time.com/time/magazine/article/0,9171,2113794,00.html.

Kline, Michelle Ann. 2015. How to Learn about Teaching: An Evolutionary Framework for the Study of Teaching Behavior in Humans and Other Animals. *Behavioral and Brain Sciences* 38 (January): e31. DOI: 10.1017/S0140525X14000090.

Knight, John R., Henry Wechsler, Meichun Kuo, Mark Seibring, Elissa R. Weitzman, and Marc A. Schuckit. 2002. Alcohol Abuse and Dependence among U.S. College Students. *Journal of Studies on Alcohol and Drugs* 63 (3): 263–70.

Koc, Elif. 2013. My Insane Homework Load Taught Me How to Game the System. *Atlantic*, September 24. http://www.theatlantic.com/education/archive/2013/09/my-insane-homework-load-taught-me-how-to-game-the-system/279876/.

Kohn, Alfie. 1999 [1993]. *Punished by Rewards: The Trouble with Gold Stars, Incentive Plans, A's, Praise, and Other Bribes*. Boston: Houghton Mifflin.

———. 2002. The Dangerous Myth of Grade Inflation. *Chronicle of Higher Education* 49 (11) (November 8): B7.

———. 2011. The Case against Grades. *Educational Leadership*, November. http://www.alfiekohn.org/teaching/teaching/tcag.htm.

Konner, Melvin. 2010. *The Evolution of Childhood: Relationships, Emotion, Mind*. Cambridge: Belknap Press of Harvard University Press.

Kozol, Jonathan. 1991. *Savage Inequalities: Children in America's Schools*. New York: Crown.

———. 2005. *The Shame of the Nation: The Restoration of Apartheid Schooling in America*. New York: Crown.

Kruglanski, Arie W., Chana Stein, and Aviah Riter. 1977. Contingencies of Exogenous Rewards and Task Performance: On the "Minimax" Strategy in Instrumental Behavior 1. *Journal of Applied Social Psychology* 7 (2): 141–48.

Kuh, George D. 2005. *Student Success in College: Creating Conditions That Matter*. San Francisco: Jossey-Bass.

———. 2009. What Student Affairs Professionals Need to Know about Student Engagement. *Journal of College Student Development* 50 (6): 683–706.

Kuhn, Thomas S. 1962. *The Structure of Scientific Revolutions*. Chicago: University of Chicago Press.

Kvale, Steinar. 2007. Contradictions of Assessment for Learning in Institutions of Higher Learning. In *Rethinking Assessment in Higher Education: Learning for the Longer Term*, edited by David Boud and Nancy Falchikov, 57–62. London: Routledge.

Labaree, David F. 1997. *How to Succeed in School without Really Learning: The Credentials Race in American Education*. New Haven: Yale University Press.

———. 2010. *Someone Has to Fail: The Zero-Sum Game of Public Schooling*. Cambridge: Harvard University Press.

Labi, Aisha. 2009. In Europe, Skeptics of New 3-Year Degrees Abound. *Chronicle of Higher Education*, June 11. http://chronicle.com/article/In-Europe-Skeptics-of-New-/44467/.

Laing, R. D. 1969. *The Divided Self*. New York: Pantheon.

Laitinen, Amy. 2012. Cracking the Credit Hour. New America Foundation and Education Sector. September 5. http://newamerica.net/publications/policy/cracking_the_credit_hour.

Lakoff, George, and Mark Johnson. 1980. *Metaphors We Live By*. Chicago: University of Chicago Press.

Lancy, David F. 1980. Becoming a Blacksmith in Gbarngasuakwelle. *Anthropology and Education Quarterly* 11 (4): 266–74.

——. 2010. Learning "From Nobody": The Limited Role of Teaching in Folk Models of Children's Development. *Childhood in the Past* 3: 79–106.

——. 2013. The Lost Skills: What Happens When "Culture" Is Learned from Teachers and Books. Paper presented at the American Anthropological Association meeting, Chicago, November 23.

——. 2014. *The Anthropology of Childhood*. 2nd ed. Cambridge: Cambridge University Press.

Lancy, David F., John Bock, and Suzanne Gaskins, eds. 2010. *The Anthropology of Learning in Childhood*. Walnut Creek, CA: AltaMira.

Lang, James M. 2005. *Life on the Tenure Track: Lessons from the First Year*. Baltimore: Johns Hopkins University Press.

——. 2013. *Cheating Lessons: Learning from Academic Dishonesty*. Cambridge: Harvard University Press.

Langan, Elise. 2012. The Normative Effects of Higher Education Policy in France. *International Journal of Educational Research* 53: 32–43.

Lareau, Annette. 2011. *Unequal Childhoods: Class, Race, and Family Life*. 2nd ed. Berkeley: University of California Press.

Lave, Jean. 1982. A Comparative Approach to Educational Forms and Learning Processes. *Anthropology and Education Quarterly* 13 (2): 181–87.

——. 1988. *Cognition in Practice: Mind, Mathematics and Culture in Everyday Life*. Cambridge: Cambridge University Press.

Lave, Jean, and Etienne Wenger. 1991. *Situated Learning: Legitimate Peripheral Participation*. Cambridge: Cambridge University Press.

Lee, Harper. 1999 [1960]. *To Kill a Mockingbird*. New York: HarperCollins.

Lee, John Michael, Jr., Kelcey Edwards, Roxanna Menson, and Anita Rawls. 2011. *The College Completion Agenda 2011 Progress Report*. The College Board. http://completionagenda.collegeboard.org/reports.

Lemann, Nicholas. 1999. *The Big Test: The Secret History of the American Meritocracy*. New York: Farrar, Straus and Giroux.

Leonhardt, David. 2009. Q. & A.: The Real Cost of College. *New York Times*, November 19. http://economix.blogs.nytimes.com/2009/11/19/q-a-the-real-cost-of-college/?_r=0.

——. 2013. What Makes a College "Selective"—And Why It Matters. *New York Times*, April 4. http://economix.blogs.nytimes.com/2013/04/04/what-makes-a-college-selective-and-why-it-matters/.

——. 2014a. Is College Worth It? Clearly, New Data Say. *New York Times*, May 27. http://www.nytimes.com/2014/05/27/upshot/is-college-worth-it-clearly-new-data-say.html?ref=economy&_r=0.

——. 2014b. The Reality of Student Debt Is Different from the Clichés. *New York Times*, June 24. http://www.nytimes.com/2014/06/24/upshot/the-reality-of-student-debt-is-different-from-the-cliches.html?_r=0.

Lepper, Mark R. 1983. Extrinsic Reward and Intrinsic Motivation. In *Teacher and Student Perceptions: Implications for Learning*, edited by John M. Levine and Margaret C. Wang, 281–317. Hillsdale, NJ: Erlbaum.

Lepper, Mark R., and David Greene. 1975. Turning Play into Work: Effects of Adult Surveillance and Extrinsic Rewards on Children's Intrinsic Motivation. *Journal of Personality and Social Psychology* 3 (3): 479–86.

LeShan, Eda J. 1967. *The Conspiracy against Childhood*. New York: Atheneum.

Lesko, Nancy. 1996. Denaturalizing Adolescence: The Politics of Contemporary Representations. *Youth & Society* 28 (2): 139–61.

———. 2001. *Act Your Age! A Cultural Construction of Adolescence*. New York: Routledge Falmer.

LeTendre, G. K., B. K. Hofer, and H. Shimizu. 2003. What Is Tracking? Cultural Expectations in the United States, Germany, and Japan. *American Educational Research Journal* 40 (1): 43–89.

Levin, Robert A. 1991. The Debate over Schooling: Influences of Dewey and Thorndike. *Childhood Education* 68 (2) (Winter): 71–75.

Levine, Bruce E. 2013. How Our Society Breeds Anxiety, Depression and Dysfunction. Alternet.org. August 21. http://www.alternet.org/personal-health/how-our-society-breeds-anxiety-depression-and-dysfunction.

Levine, Madeline. 2006. *The Price of Privilege: How Parental Pressure and Material Advantage Are Creating a Generation of Disconnected and Unhappy Kids*. New York: HarperCollins.

Levison, Deborah. 2000. Children as Economic Agents. *Feminist Economics* 6 (1): 125–34.

Lewin, Tamar. 2007. Dean of Admissions at M.I.T. Resigns. *New York Times*, April 26. http://www.nytimes.com/2007/04/26/education/26cnd-mit.html.

Lipka, Sara. 2013. As Typical Student Changes, So Do Worries about Costs. Almanac of Higher Education 2012. *Chronicle of Higher Education*. http://chronicle.com/article/As-Typical-Student-Changes/133930/.

Lippmann, Stephen, Ronald E. Bulana, and Theodore C. Wagenaar. 2009. Student Entitlement: Issues and Strategies for Confronting Entitlement in the Classroom and Beyond. *College Teaching* 57 (4): 197–204.

Littky, Dennis, with Samantha Grabelle. 2004. *The Big Picture: Education Is Everyone's Business*. Alexandria, VA: Association for Supervision and Curriculum Development.

Lock, Margaret. 1986. Plea for Acceptance: School Refusal Syndrome in Japan. *Social Science and Medicine* 23 (2): 99–112.

Long, Nick, and Henrietta Moore. 2010. The Social Life of Achievement. Conference website. http://www.socanth.cam.ac.uk/2010/09/the-social-life-of-achievement/.

Lott, Tim. 2014. Adolescents Need a Rite of Passage to Ease Them into Adulthood. *The Guardian*, January 3. http://www.theguardian.com/lifeandstyle/2014/jan/03/adolescents-need-rites-passage-into-adulthood.

Lowrie, Annie. 2012. Big Study Links Good Teachers to Lasting Gain. *New York Times*, January 5. http://www.nytimes.com/2012/01/06/education/big-study-links-good-teachers-to-lasting-gain.html?_r=1.

Lucas, Christopher J. 2006. *American Higher Education: A History*. 2nd ed. New York: Palgrave Macmillan.

Lucy, John A., and Richard A. Shweder. 1979. Whorf and His Critics: Linguistic and Nonlinguistic Influences on Color Memory. *American Anthropologist*, n.s. 81 (3): 581–615.

Luthar, Suniya S., Karen A. Shoum, and Pamela J. Brown. 2006. Extracurricular Involvement among Affluent Youth: A Scapegoat for "Ubiquitous Achievement Pressures"? *Developmental Psychology* 42 (3): 583–97.

Lynd, Robert S., and Helen Merrell Lynd. 1956 [1929]. *Middletown: A Study in Modern American Culture*. New York: Harcourt Brace.

Mac Donald, Heather. 2011. Great Courses, Great Profits. *City Journal* (Summer). http://www.city-journal.org/2011/21_3_the-great-courses.html.

MacIntyre, Alasdair. 2009. *God, Philosophy, Universities: A Selective History of the Catholic Philosophical Tradition*. Lanham, MD: Rowman & Littlefield.

Madan, Christopher R., and Braden D. Teitge. 2013. The Benefits of Undergraduate Research: The Student's Perspective. *The Mentor: An Academic Advising Journal*, May 1. https://dus.psu.edu/mentor/2013/05/undergraduate-research-students-perspective/.

Malcolm, Hadley. 2013. Millennials' Ball-and-Chain: Student Loan Debt. *USA Today*, July 1. http://www.usatoday.com/story/money/personalfinance/2013/06/30/student-loan-debt-economic-effects/2388189/.

Manjoo, Farhad. 2014. The Soylent Revolution Will Not Be Pleasurable. *New York Times*, May 28. http://www.nytimes.com/2014/05/29/technology/personaltech/the-soylent-revolution-will-not-be-pleasurable.html?hpw&rref=technology&_r=0.

Manning, J. T., R. Anderton, and S. M. Washington. 1996. Women's Waists and the Sex Ratio of Their Progeny: Evolutionary Aspects of the Ideal Female Body Shape. *Journal of Human Evolution* 31 (1): 41–47.

Margolis, Eric, ed. 2001. *The Hidden Curriculum in Higher Education*. New York: Routledge.

Marples, Roger. 1999. Well-Being as an Aim of Education. In *The Aims of Education*, edited by Roger Marples, 133–44. London: Routledge.

Marsh, Herbert W. 1992. Extracurricular Activities: Beneficial Extension of the Traditional Curriculum or Subversion of Academic Goals? *Journal of Educational Psychology* 84 (4): 553–62.

Marsh, John. 2011. *Class Dismissed: Why We Cannot Teach or Learn Our Way Out of Inequality*. New York: Monthly Review Press.

Martin, Nathan D. 2012. The Privilege of Ease: Social Class and Campus Life at Highly Selective, Private Universities. *Research in Higher Education* 53: 426–52.

Marzluff, John M., and Tony Angell. 2012. *Gifts of the Crow: How Perception, Emotion, and Thought Allow Smart Birds to Behave Like Humans*. New York: Free Press.

Masataka, Nobuo. 2009. The Origins of Language and the Evolution of Music: A Comparative Perspective. *Physics of Life Reviews* 6 (1): 11–22.

McCabe, Donald L. 2005. Cheating among College and University Students: A North American Perspective. *International Journal for Educational Integrity* 1 (1). http://ojs.ml.unisa.edu.au/index.php/IJEI/article/view/14/9.

McLuhan, Marshall. 1964. *Understanding Media: The Extensions of Man*. Berkeley, CA: Gingko Press.

McNamee, Stephen J., and Robert K. Miller. 2004. The Meritocracy Myth. *Sociation Today* 2 (1) (Spring). http://www.ncsociology.org/sociationtoday/v21/merit.htm.

Mead, Margaret. 1961 [1928]. *Coming of Age in Samoa: A Psychological Study of Primitive Youth for Western Civilisation*. New York: Morrow.

Melton, James Van Horn. 2003. *Absolutism and the Eighteenth-Century Origins of Compulsory Schooling in Prussia and Austria*. Cambridge: Cambridge University Press.

Merry, Sally Engle. 2011. Measuring the World: Indicators, Human Rights, and Global Governance. *Current Anthropology* 52 (S3): S83–95.

Milton, Ohmer, Howard R. Pollio, and James A. Eison. 1986. *Making Sense of College Grades*. San Francisco: Jossey-Bass.

Minzesheimer, Bob. 2013. E-Books Are Changing Reading Habits. *USA Today*, October 7. http://www.usatoday.com/story/life/books/2013/10/06/e-books-reading/2877471/.

Mithen, Steven. 2007. *The Singing Neanderthals: The Origins of Music, Language, Mind, and Body*. Cambridge: Harvard University Press.

Mitra, Sugata. 2003. Minimally Invasive Education: A Progress Report on the "Hole-in-the-Wall" Experiments. *British Journal of Educational Technology* 34 (3): 367–71.

———. 2005. Self-Organizing Systems for Mass Computer Literacy: Findings from the "Hole in the Wall" Experiments. *International Journal of Development Issues* 4 (1): 71–81.

Mitra, Sugata, and V. Rana. 2001. Children and the Internet: Experiments with Minimally Invasive Education in India. *British Journal of Educational Technology* 32 (2): 221–32.

Miyazaki, Ichisada. 1981 [1963]. *China's Examination Hell: The Civil Service Examinations of Imperial China*. Translated by Conrad Schirokauer. New Haven: Yale University Press.

Moffatt, Michael. 1989. *Coming of Age in New Jersey: College and American Culture*. New Brunswick, NJ: Rutgers University Press.

Mogel, Wendy. 2001. *The Blessing of a Skinned Knee: Using Jewish Teachings to Raise Self-Reliant Children*. New York: Penguin.

———. 2010. *The Blessing of a B-: Using Jewish Teachings to Raise Resilient Teenagers*. New York: Scribner.

Moltz, David. 2009. Skills Training à la Carte. *Inside Higher Ed*, August 12. http://www.insidehighered.com/news/2009/08/12/kellogg#sthash.5mg2Wn95.dpbs.

Morioka, Hisayoshi, Osamu Itani, Yoshitaka Kaneita, Hajime Iwasa, Maki Ikeda, Ryuichiro Yamamoto, Yoneatsu Osaki, Hideyuki Kanda, Sachi Nakagome, and Takashi Ohida. 2014. Factors Affecting Unhappiness at School among Japanese Adolescents: An Epidemiological Study. *PLoS One* 9(11): e111844. DOI: 10.1371/journal.pone.0111844.

Morrison, Richard. 1992. Price Fixing among Elite Colleges and Universities. *University of Chicago Law Review* 59 (2): 807–35.

Morton, Brian. 2011. Falser Words Were Never Spoken. *New York Times*, August 29. http://www.nytimes.com/2011/08/30/opinion/falser-words-were-never-spoken.html?_r=0.

Murphy, Rachel. 2004. Turning Peasants into Modern Chinese Citizens: "Population Quality" Discourse, Demographic Transition and Primary Education. *China Quarterly* 177: 1–20.

Nader, Laura. 1974 [1969]. Up the Anthropologist: Perspectives Gained from Studying Up. In *Reinventing Anthropology*, edited by Dell Hymes, 284–311. New York: Vintage.

Nathan, Rebekah [Cathy Small]. 2005. *My Freshman Year: What a Professor Learned by Becoming a Student*. Ithaca: Cornell University Press.

National Center for Education Statistics. 2012. Expenditures of Educational Institutions Related to the Gross Domestic Product, by Level of Institution. Digest of Education Statistics, 2012, table 28. http://nces.ed.gov/programs/digest/d12/tables/dt12_028.asp?referrer=report.

———. 2014. Expenses of Postsecondary Institutions. In *The Condition of Education 2014*. Institute of Education Sciences, U.S. Department of Education. http://nces.ed.gov/pubs2014/2014083.pdf.

National Endowment for the Arts. 2007. To Read or Not To Read: A Question of National Consequence. Research Report no. 47. Washington, DC.

———. 2013. National Endowment for the Arts Presents Highlights from the 2012 Survey of Public Participation in the Arts. September 26. http://arts.gov/news/2013/national-endowment-arts-presents-highlights-2012-survey-public-participation-arts.

National Geographic. 2006. Survey of Geographic Literacy. http://www.nationalgeographic.com/roper2006/index.html.

National Institute of Mental Health. 2012. Depression and College Students. http://www.nimh.nih.gov/health/publications/depression-and-college-students/index.shtml.

———. 2014. Attention Deficit Hyperactivity Disorder (ADHD). http://www.nimh.nih.gov/health/topics/attention-deficit-hyperactivity-disorder-adhd/index.shtml.

Neary, Lynn. 2007. Reading Study Shows Remarkable Decline in U.S. NPR. November 17. http://www.npr.org/templates/story/story.php?storyId=16435529.

Neighmond, Patti. 2011. Depression on the Rise in College Students. NPR. January 17. http://www.npr.org/2011/01/17/132934543/depression-on-the-rise-in-college-students.

Neill, A. S. 1960. *Summerhill: A Radical Approach to Child Rearing*. New York: Hart Publishing Company.

Neill, James. 2005. Ten Expeditionary Learning Principles (Based on the Ideas of Kurt Hahn and Other Educational Leaders). March 9. http://wilderdom.com/experiential/tenELOBprinciples.html.

Nespor, Jan. 1990. Grades and Knowledge in Undergraduate Education. *Journal of Curriculum Studies* 22 (6): 545–56.

Newman, Jonah. 2014. Student-Debt Debate Is Stoked by Caveats about Data. *Chronicle of Higher Education*, June 25. http://chronicle.com/blogs/data/2014/06/25/student-debt-debate-is-stoked-by-caveats-about-data/.

Nisbett, Richard. 2003. *The Geography of Thought: How Asians and Westerners Think Differently . . . and Why*. New York: Free Press.

Noack, Ernest G. 1999. Comparing U.S. and German Education: Like Apples and Sauerkraut. *Phi Delta Kappan* 80 (10): 773–76.

Noddings, Nel. 2003. *Happiness and Education*. Cambridge: Cambridge University Press.

Nussbaum, Martha. 2003. Capabilities as Fundamental Entitlements: Sen and Social Justice. *Feminist Economics* 9 (2–3): 33–59.

Ochs, Elinor, and Carolina Izquierdo. 2009. Responsibility in Childhood: Three Developmental Trajectories. *Ethos* 37 (4): 391–413.

Ochs, Elinor, and Bambi B. Schieffelin. 1984. Language Acquisition and Socialization: Three Developmental Stories. In *Culture Theory: Essays on Mind, Self, and Emotion*, edited by Richard A. Shweder and Robert A. LeVine, 276–320. Cambridge: Cambridge University Press.

OECD (Organisation for Economic Co-operation and Development). 2001. How Many Students Will Enter Tertiary Education? *Education at a Glance.* Indicator C2: 308–17.

——. 2013. Education at a Glance 2013: OECD Indicators. OECD Publishing. http://dx.doi.org/10.1787/eag-2013-en.

Oehlert, Gary, and Chris Uggen. 2010. CLA 2015 Committee Final Report to Dean James A. Parente Jr. University of Minnesota College of Liberal Arts. http://images.cla.umn.edu/cla2015/CLA2015_Complete_FINAL.pdf.

Okamoto, Dina G., Daniel Herda, and Cassie Hartzog. 2013. Beyond Good Grades: School Composition and Immigrant Youth Participation in Extracurricular Activities. *Social Science Research* 42: 155–68.

O'Malley, Brendan. 2015. Universities Demand New System of Grading of Degrees. *University World News* 369, May 29. http://www.universityworldnews.com/article.php?story=20150530063736450.

Ottenberg, Simon. 1989. *Boyhood Rituals in an African Society: An Interpretation.* Seattle: University of Washington Press.

Panksepp, Jaak, and Lucy Biven. 2012. *The Archaeology of Mind: Neuroevolutionary Origins of Human Emotions.* New York: W. W. Norton.

Paradise, Ruth. 1998. What's Different about Learning in Schools as Compared to Family and Community Settings? *Human Development* 41: 270–78. DOI: 10.1159/000022587.

Pardo, Jennifer S., Rachel Gibbons, Alexandra Suppes, and Robert M. Krauss. 2011. Phonetic Convergence in College Roommates. *Journal of Phonetics* 40: 190–97. DOI: 10.1016/j.wocn.2011.10.001.

Parents as Teachers. 2007. The Parents as Teachers Program: Its Impact on School Readiness and Later School Achievement. http://www.parentsasteachers.org/images/stories/documents/Executive20Summary_of_K_Readiness.pdf.

Pascarella, Ernest T., and Patrick T. Terenzini. 2005. *How College Affects Students.* Vol. 2. A Third Decade of Research. San Francisco: Jossey-Bass.

Pelissier, Catherine. 1991. The Anthropology of Teaching and Learning. *Annual Review of Anthropology* 20: 75–95.

Perkinson, Henry J. 1968. *The Imperfect Panacea: American Faith in Education, 1865-1965.* New York: Random House.

Perry, William. 1968. *Forms of Intellectual and Ethical Development in the College Years: A Scheme.* New York: Holt, Rinehart and Winston.

Pew Internet. 2013. New Reading Data from the NEA's Survey of Public Participation in the Arts. Pew Internet & American Life Project. October 2. http://libraries.pewinternet.org/2013/10/02/new-reading-data-from-the-neas-survey-of-public-participation-in-the-arts/.

Pew Research. 2014. The Rising Cost of Not Going to College. Social & Demographic Trends. February 11. http://www.pewsocialtrends.org/2014/02/11/the-rising-cost-of-not-going-to-college/.

Phillips, Matt. 2015. Face It: America's Experiment with For-Profit Colleges has Failed. *Quartz,* June 9. http://qz.com/423501/face-it-americas-experiment-with-for-profit-colleges-has-failed/.

Pink, Daniel H. 2009. *Drive: The Surprising Truth about What Motivates Us*. New York: Riverhead Books.

Pontzer, Herman, David A. Raichlen, Brian M. Wood, Audax Z. P. Mabulla, Susan B. Racette, and Frank W. Marlowe. 2012. Hunter-Gatherer Energetics and Human Obesity. *PLOS One* 7 (7): e40503. July 25. http://www.plosone.org/article/info:doi/10.1371/journal.pone.0040503.

Pope, Denise Clark. 2001. *"Doing School": How We Are Creating a Generation of Stressed Out, Materialistic, and Miseducated Students*. New Haven: Yale University Press.

Pope, Loren. 1996, 2000, 2006. *Colleges That Change Lives: 40 Schools That Will Change the Way You Think about Colleges*. New York: Penguin.

Portmann, Adolf. 1990. *Essays in Philosophical Zoology by Adolf Portmann: The Living Form and Seeing Eye*. Lewiston, NY: E. Mellen Press.

Postman, Neil. 1994 [1982]. *The Disappearance of Childhood*. New York: Vintage.

Power, Michael. 1997. *The Audit Society: Rituals of Verification*. Oxford: Oxford University Press.

Princeton University. 2014. Grading at Princeton. Office of the Dean of the College. http://odoc.princeton.edu/faculty-staff/grading-princeton.

"Professor X." 2011. *In the Basement of the Ivory Tower: Confessions of an Accidental Academic*. New York: Viking.

Quart, Alissa. 2006. *Hothouse Kids: The Dilemma of the Gifted Child*. New York: Penguin.

———. 2007. *Hothouse Kids: How the Pressure to Succeed Threatens Childhood*. New York: Penguin.

Quote Investigator. 2010. Misbehaving Children in Ancient Times? Plato or Socrates? http://quoteinvestigator.com/2010/05/01/misbehaving-children-in-ancient-times/.

Rampell, Catherine. 2013. It Takes a B.A. to Find a Job as a File Clerk. *New York Times*, February 19. http://www.nytimes.com/2013/02/20/business/college-degree-required-by-increasing-number-of-companies.html?pagewanted=all.

Ramsey, Dave. 2011. What's Wrong with Buying a Mobile Home? Fox Business. November 29. http://www.foxbusiness.com/personal-finance/2011/11/28/whats-wrong-with-mobile-home/#ixzz1kOIyyJH0.

Ravitch, Diane. 2010. *The Death and Life of the Great American School System: How Testing and Choice Are Undermining Education*. New York: Basic Books.

Reed, Matt. 2013. What If Student Learning Counted in Performance Funding? *Inside Higher Ed*, December 4. http://www.insidehighered.com/blogs/confessions-community-college-dean/what-if-student-learning-counted-performance-funding#sthash.lYG7b5J1.dpbs.

Renn, Kristen A., and Karen D. Arnold. 2003. Reconceptualizing Research on College Student Peer Culture. *Journal of Higher Education* 74 (3): 261–91.

Reynolds, Gretchen. 2013. The Rise of the Minimalist Workout. *New York Times*, June 24. http://well.blogs.nytimes.com/2013/06/24/the-rise-of-the-minimalist-workout/?_php=true&_type=blogs&_r=0.

Riley, Naomi Schaefer. 2011. *The Faculty Lounges and Other Reasons Why You Won't Get the College Education You Paid For*. Lanham, MD: Ivan R. Dee.

Rivard, Ry. 2014a. Gauging Graduates' Well-Being. *Inside Higher Ed*, May 6. http://www.insidehighered.com/news/2014/05/06/gallup-surveys-graduates-gauge-whether-and-why-college-good-well-being#sthash.DeP7hI65.dpbs.

——. 2014b. Well-Being and Time. *Inside Higher Ed*, April 29. http://www.inside-highered.com/news/2014/04/29/wake-forest-u-tries-measure-well-being#sthash. Cz0efHTL.dpbs.

Rivera, Lauren A. 2011. Ivies, Extracurriculars, and Exclusion: Elite Employers' Use of Educational Credentials. *Research in Social Stratification and Mobility* 29: 71–90.

Rizzolatti G., and L. Craighero. 2004. The Mirror-Neuron System. *Annual Review of Neuroscience* 27: 169–92.

Robbins, Alexandra. 2006. *The Overachievers: The Secret Lives of Driven Kids*. New York: Hyperion.

Roche, Mark William. 2010. *Why Choose the Liberal Arts?* Notre Dame, IN: University of Notre Dame Press.

Rocheleau, Paul. 2003. *The One-Room Schoolhouse*. New York: Universe.

Rogoff, Barbara. 1990. *Apprenticeship in Thinking: Cognitive Development in Social Context*. New York: Oxford University Press.

——. 2001. Why a Nonconventional College Decided to Add Grades. *Chronicle of Higher Education*, September 14.

——. 2003. *The Cultural Nature of Human Development*. New York: Oxford University Press.

——. 2011. *Developing Destinies: A Mayan Midwife and Town*. New York: Oxford University Press.

Rojstaczer, Stuart. 2012. Where A Is Ordinary: The Evolution of American College and University Grading, 1940–2009. *Teachers College Record* 114 (7): 1–23.

Rose, Mike. 2004. *The Mind at Work: Valuing the Intelligence of the American Worker*. New York: Penguin.

Rose, Nikolas. 1999. *Governing the Soul: The Shaping of the Private Self*. London: Free Association.

Rosenbaum, James E. 2001. *Beyond College for All: Career Paths for the Forgotten Half*. New York: Russell Sage Foundation.

Rosenberg, Karen, and Wenda Trevathan. 1995. Bipedalism and Human Birth: The Obstetrical Dilemma Revisited. *Evolutionary Anthropology* 4 (5): 161–68.

Rotter, Julian B. 1960. Generalized Expectancies of Internal versus External Control of Reinforcements. *Psychological Monographs* 80 (1): 1–28.

Rousseau, Jean-Jacques. 1979 [1762]. *Émile or On Education*. Translated by Allan Bloom. New York: Basic Books.

Russell, Susan H., Mary P. Hancock, and James McCullough. 2007. Benefits of Undergraduate Research Experiences. *Science* 316 (5824) (April 27): 548–49. http://www.sciencemag.org/content/316/5824/548.full. DOI: 10.1126/science.1140384.

Ryan, Richard M., and Edward L. Deci. 2000. Intrinsic and Extrinsic Motivations: Classic Definitions and New Directions. *Contemporary Educational Psychology* 25: 54–67. DOI: 10.1006/ceps.1999.1020.

Ryan, Richard M., and Jerome Stiller. 1991. The Social Contexts of Internalization: Parent and Teacher Influences on Autonomy, Motivation, and Learning. *Advances in Motivation and Achievement* 7: 115–49.

Sacks, Peter M. 1997. *Generation X Goes to College: An Eye-Opening Account of Teaching in Postmodern America*. Chicago: Open Court.

Savage, Jon. 2007. *Teenage: The Creation of Youth Culture*. New York: Viking.

Schank, Roger. 2014. The Old University System Is Dead—Time for a Professional University. January 31. http://educationoutrage.blogspot.com/2014/01/the-old-university-system-is-dead-time.html.

Scheper-Hughes, Nancy. 1993. *Death without Weeping: The Violence of Everyday Life in Brazil*. Berkeley: University of California Press.

Schlegel, Alice, and Herbert Barry III. 1991. *Adolescence: An Anthropological Inquiry*. New York: Free Press.

Schnabel, K. U., C. Alfeld, J. S. Eccles, O. Koller, and J. Baumert. 2002. Parental Influence on Students' Educational Choices in the United States and Germany: Different Ramifications—Same Effect? *Journal of Vocational Behavior* 60 (2): 178–98.

Schnepf, Sylke Viola. 2002. A Sorting Hat That Fails? The Transition from Primary to Secondary School in Germany. Innocenti Research Centre. Florence: United Nations Children's Fund, International Child Development Centre. http://www.unicef-irc.org/publications/341.

Schofer, Evan, and John W. Meyer. 2005. The Worldwide Expansion of Higher Education in the Twentieth Century. *American Sociological Review* 70: 898–920.

Schreiner, Samuel A., Jr. 2006. *The Concord Quartet: Alcott, Emerson, Hawthorne, Thoreau, and the Friendship That Freed the American Mind*. New York: John Wiley & Sons.

Schultz, Rachel Gelfman. N.d. Havruta: Learning in Pairs. My Jewish Learning. http://www.myjewishlearning.com/practices/Ritual/Torah_Study/How_to_Study_Torah/Havruta_Learning_in_Pairs_.shtml.

Schwartz, Alan, and Sarah Cohen. 2013. A.D.H.D. Seen in 11% of U.S. Children as Diagnoses Rise. *New York Times*, March 31. http://www.nytimes.com/2013/04/01/health/more-diagnoses-of-hyperactivity-causing-concern.html?pagewanted=all&_r=0.

Scott, James C. 1985. *Weapons of the Weak: Everyday Forms of Peasant Resistance*. New Haven: Yale University Press.

Scott, Peter. 1995. *The Meanings of Mass Higher Education*. Buckingham: SRHE Open University Press.

Scott, Sarah. 2011. Revenge of the C Plus Student. *Huffington Post*, June 22. http://www.huffingtonpost.ca/sarah-scott/failing-students-success_b_881163.html.

Seaman, Barrett. 2005. *Binge: Campus Life in an Age of Disconnection and Excess*. Hoboken, NJ: John Wiley.

Seldin, Tim, and Paul Epstein. 2006. Dr. Montessori's Legacy. The Montessori Foundation. September 19. http://www.montessori.org/index.php?option=com_content&view=article&id=262:dr-montessoris-legacy&catid=7:faqs&Itemid=25.

Seligman, Martin E. P. 2011. *Flourish: A Visionary New Understanding of Happiness and Well-Being*. New York: Free Press.

Seligman, Martin E. P., Tracy A. Steen, Nansook Park, and Christopher Peterson. 2005. Positive Psychology Progress: Empirical Validation of Interventions. *American Psychologist* 60 (5): 410–21.

Sen, Amartya. 2009. *The Idea of Justice*. London: Allen Lane.

Sennett, Richard. 2008. *The Craftsman*. New Haven: Yale University Press.

Shernoff, David J., and Mihaly Csikszentmihalyi. 2009. Flow in Schools: Cultivating Engaged Learners and Optimal Learning Environments. *Handbook of Positive*

Psychology in Schools, edited by Rich Gilman, Eugene Scott Huebner, and Michael J. Furlong, 131–45. New York: Routledge.

Sherzer, Joel. 2002. *Speech Play and Verbal Art*. Austin: University of Texas Press.

Shiah, Yung-Jong, et al. 2013. School-Based Extracurricular Activities, Personality, Self-Concept, and College Career Development Skill in Chinese Society. *Educational Psychology* 33 (2): 135–54.

Shore, Cris, and Sue Wright. 2001. Comment: Audit Culture and Anthropology. *Journal of the Royal Anthropological Institute* 7 (4): 759–63.

Simmel, Georg. 1978. *The Philosophy of Money*. Translated by Tom Bottomore and David Frisby. London: Routledge & Kegan Paul.

Sinclair, Rabbi Julian. 2008. Chavruta. *The Jewish Chronicle*, November 5. http://www.thejc.com/judaism/jewish-words/chavruta.

Singletary, Michelle. 2011. A Bachelor's Degree for $10,000? Imagine the Impact. *Washington Post*, September 10. http://www.washingtonpost.com/a-bachelors-degree-for-10000-imagine-the-impact/2011/09/07/gIQA4B5FIK_story.html.

Smallwood, M. L. 1935. *Examinations and Grading Systems in Early American Universities*. Cambridge: Harvard University Press.

Smilkstein, Rita. 2011. *We're Born to Learn: Using the Brain's Natural Learning Process to Create Today's Curriculum*. 2nd ed. Thousand Oaks, CA: SAGE (Corwin).

Smith, Bettye P., and Billy Hawkins. 2011. Examining Student Evaluations of Black College Faculty: Does Race Matter? *The Journal of Negro Education* 80 (2) (Spring): 149–62.

Smith, Frank. 1998. *The Book of Learning and Forgetting*. New York: Teachers College Press.

Smith, Peter K. 1982. Does Play Matter? Functional and Evolutionary Aspects of Animal and Human Play. *Behavioral and Brain Sciences* 5 (1): 139–55.

———, ed. 1984. *Play in Animals and Humans*. Oxford: Blackwell.

Snyder, Susan. 2014. Addressing Suicide among Seemingly Successful College Students. *The Inquirer,* February 10. Philly.com. http://articles.philly.com/2014–02–10/news/47171516_1_college-campuses-college-students-parking-garage.

Snyder, Thomas D. 1993a. Education Characteristics of the Population. In *120 Years of American Education: A Statistical Portrait*, edited by Thomas D. Snyder, 5–23. Washington, DC: National Center for Education Statistics. U.S. Department of Education.

———. 1993b. Higher Education. In *120 Years of American Education: A Statistical Portrait*, edited by Thomas D. Snyder, 63–94. Washington, DC: National Center for Education Statistics. U.S. Department of Education.

Sobo, Elisa. 2013. "This Is Not Head-to-Head Education": Whole Child Development in a Waldorf School. In *Learning In and Out of School: Education across the Globe*, edited by Susan D. Blum. Conference proceedings. https://kellogg.nd.edu/learning/Sobo.pdf.

Social Science Research Council (SSRC). 2013. Measure of America. About Human Development. www.measureofamerica.org/human-development/.

Spar, Ira. 2004. The Origins of Writing. In Heilbrunn Timeline of Art History. New York: Metropolitan Museum of Art, 2000–. http://www.metmuseum.org/toah/hd/wrtg/hd_wrtg.htm.

Spence, Michael. 1973. Job Market Signaling. *Quarterly Journal of Economics* 87 (3): 355–74. DOI: 10.2307/1882010.

Sperber, Murray. 2000. *Beer and Circus: How Big-Time College Sports Is Crippling Undergraduate Education*. New York: Henry Holt.

Spindler, George D. 1997 [1967]. The Transmission of Culture. In *Education and Cultural Process: Anthropological Approaches*, edited by George D. Spindler, 275–309. 3rd ed. Long Grove, Ill.: Waveland.

Spindler, George, and Louise Spindler. 1989. There Are No Dropouts among the Arunta and the Hutterites. In *What Do Anthropologists Have to Say about Dropouts?*, edited by Henry T. Trueba, George Spindler, and Louise S. Spindler, 7–15. New York: Falmer Press.

Stark, Philip. 2013a. Do Student Evaluations Measure Teaching Effectiveness? The Berkeley Blog. October 14. http://blogs.berkeley.edu/2013/10/14/do-student-evaluations-measure-teaching-effectiveness/.

——. 2013b. What Exactly Do Student Evaluations Measure? The Berkeley Blog. October 21. http://blogs.berkeley.edu/2013/10/21/what-exactly-do-student-evaluations-measure/.

Stark, Philip B., and Richard Freishtat. 2014. An Evaluation of Course Evaluations. *ScienceOpen*, September 26. https://www.scienceopen.com/document/vid/42e6aae5-246b-4900-8015-dc99b467b6e4?0. DOI: 10.14293/S2199-1006.1.SOR-EDU.AOFRQA.v1.

Stephens, Greg J., Lauren J. Silbert, and Uri Hasson. 2010. Speaker-Listener Neural Coupling Underlies Successful Communication. *PNAS Neuroscience Early Edition*, July 26. DOI: 10.1073/pnas.1008662107.

Sterelny, Kim. 2012. *The Evolved Apprentice: How Evolution Made Humans Unique*. Cambridge: MIT Press.

Sternberg, Robert J., and Wendy M. Williams. 2002. *Educational Psychology*. Boston: Allyn and Bacon.

Stevens, Mitchell L. 2007. *Creating a Class: College Admissions and the Education of Elites*. Cambridge: Harvard University Press.

Stewart, James B. 2013. Looking for a Lesson in Google's Perks. *New York Times*, March 15. http://www.nytimes.com/2013/03/16/business/at-google-a-place-to-work-and-play.html.

Strathern, Marilyn, ed. 2000. *Audit Cultures: Anthropological Studies in Accountability, Ethics and the Academy*. London: Routledge.

Straumsheim, Carl. 2014. The Starbucks-ASU Contract. *Inside Higher Ed*, June 23. http://www.insidehighered.com/news/2014/06/23/contract-reveals-arizona-state-u-starbucks-partnership-details#sthash.YLfLkQVG.dpbs.

Stray, Christopher. 2001. The Shift from Oral to Written Examination: Cambridge and Oxford 1700–1900. *Assessment in Education: Principles, Policy & Practice* 8 (1): 33–50.

Stripling, Jack. 2010. Burned Out, and Fading Away. *Inside Higher Ed*, June 10. http://www.insidehighered.com/news/2010/06/10/aaup.

Suen, H. K., and L. Yu. 2006. Chronic Consequences of High-Stakes Testing? Lessons from the Chinese Civil Service Exam. *Comparative Education Review* 50 (1): 46–65.

Suicide.org. N.d. College Student Suicide. http://www.suicide.org/college-student-suicide.html.

Taleb, Nassim Nicholas. 2012. *Antifragile: Things That Gain from Disorder*. New York: Random House.

Tan, Andy Soon Leong. 2012. Through the Drinking Glass: An Analysis of the Cultural Meanings of College Drinking. *Journal of Youth Studies* 15 (1): 119–42.

Tapscott, Don. 2009. *Grown Up Digital: How the Net Generation Is Changing Your World*. New York: McGraw-Hill.

Tartakovsky, Margarita. 2008. Depression and Anxiety among College Students. Psych-Central. http://psychcentral.com/lib/depression-and-anxiety-among-college-students/0001425.

Taylor, Kate. 2013. Sex on Campus: She Can Play That Game, Too. *New York Times*, July 12. http://www.nytimes.com/2013/07/14/fashion/sex-on-campus-she-can-play-that-game-too.html?pagewanted=all&_r=0.

Thomas, Douglas, and John Seely Brown. 2011. *A New Culture of Learning: Cultivating the Imagination for a World of Constant Change*. Lexington, KY.

Thomason, Sarah Grey. 2001. *Language Contact: An Introduction*. Edinburgh: Edinburgh University Press.

Tierney, William G. 1992. An Anthropological Analysis of Student Participation in College. *Journal of Higher Education* 63 (6): 603–18.

Tinto, Vincent. 1987. *Leaving College: Rethinking the Causes and Cures of Student Attrition*. Chicago: University of Chicago Press.

Tomar, Dave. 2012. *The Shadow Scholar: How I Made a Living Helping College Kids Cheat*. New York: Bloomsbury.

Topley, Marjorie. 1974. Cosmic Antagonisms: A Mother-Child Syndrome. In *Religion and Ritual in Chinese Society*, edited by Emily Martin and Arthur P. Wolf, 233–49. Stanford: Stanford University Press.

Tough, Paul. 2012. *How Children Succeed: Grit, Curiosity, and the Hidden Power of Character*. New York: Houghton Mifflin Harcourt.

———. 2014. Who Gets to Graduate? *New York Times Magazine*, May 15. http://www.nytimes.com/2014/05/18/magazine/who-gets-to-graduate.html?_r=0.

Trow, Martin A. 2000. From Mass Higher Education to Universal Access: The American Advantage. *Center for Studies in Higher Education, UC Berkeley*. March 1. http://escholarship.org/uc/item/9f02k0d1.

———. 2006. Reflections on the Transition from Elite to Mass to Universal Access: Forms and Phases of Higher Education in Modern Societies since WWI. In *International Handbook of Higher Education*, edited by J. J. F. Forest and P. G. Altbach, 243–80. Dordrecht: Springer.

Turner, Victor. 1969. *The Ritual Process: Structure and Anti-Structure*. Ithaca: Cornell University Press.

Twain, Mark [Samuel Langhorne Clemens]. 1982 [1876]. *The Adventures of Tom Sawyer*. Berkeley: University of California Press.

Twenge, Jean. 2006. *Generation Me: Why Today's Young Americans Are More Confident, Assertive, Entitled—And More Miserable Than Ever Before*. New York: Free Press.

Tyack, David B. 1974. *The One Best System: A History of American Urban Education*. Cambridge: Harvard University Press.

Tyack, David B., and Larry Cuban. 1995. *Tinkering toward Utopia: A Century of Public School Reform*. Cambridge: Harvard University Press.

Tyack, David B., and William Tobin. 1994. The 'Grammar' of Schooling: Why Has It Been So Hard to Change? *American Educational Research Journal* 31 (3): 453–79.

United States Census Bureau. 2012. College Enrollment. Table 283. *The 2012 Statistical Abstract*. http://www.census.gov/compendia/statab/cats/education/higher_education_institutions_and_enrollment.html.

———. 2014. Educational Attainment. https://www.census.gov/hhes/socdemo/education/.

Ura, Karma, Sabina Alkire, Tshoki Zangmo, and Karma Wangdi. 2012. A Short Guide to Gross National Happiness Index. Thimphu, Bhutan: The Center for Bhutan Studies. http://www.grossnationalhappiness.com/wp-content/uploads/2012/04/Short-GNH-Index-edited.pdf.

Urciuoli, Bonnie. 2008. Skills and Selves in the New Workplace. *American Ethnologist* 35(2): 211–28.

———. 2014. The Semiotic Production of the Good Student: A Peircean Look at the Commodification of Liberal Arts Education. *Signs and Society* 2(1): 56–83.

Valenzuela, Angela, ed. 2007. NCLB Special Issue. *Anthropology & Education Quarterly* 38 (1).

Valles, Sean A. 2014. Don't Call Them 'Kids.' *Inside Higher Ed*, June 17. http://www.insidehighered.com/views/2014/06/17/essay-criticizes-way-professors-call-their-students-kids#sthash.OaoFe328.dpbs.

van Gennep, Arnold. 1960 [1909]. *The Rites of Passage*. Translated by Monika B. Vizedom and Gabrielle L. Caffee. Chicago: University of Chicago Press.

Varenne, Hervé. 1974. From Grading and Freedom of Choice to Ranking and Segregation in an American High School. *Anthropology & Education Quarterly* 5 (2): 9–15.

Varenne, Hervé, Shelley Goldman, and Ray McDermott. 1998. Racing in Place. In *Successful Failure: The School America Builds*, by Hervé Varenne and Ray McDermott, with Shelley Goldman, Merry Naddeo, and Rosemarie Rizzo-Tolk, 106–28. Boulder: Westview.

Vedder, Richard K. 2004. *Going Broke by Degree: Why College Costs Too Much*. Washington, DC: AEI Press.

———. 2010. Student Evaluations, Grade Inflation, and Declining Student Effort. *Chronicle of Higher Education,* June 19. http://chronicle.com/blogPost/Student-Evaluations-Grade/24926/.

Vickers, Edward. 2009. Selling "Socialism with Chinese Characteristics," "Thought and Politics," and the Legitimisation of China's Developmental Strategy. *International Journal of Educational Development* 29: 523–31.

Volk, Steve. 2012. Size Matters: How Much Reading to Assign (and Other Imponderables). Center for Teaching Innovation and Excellence at Oberlin College. September 24. http://languages.oberlin.edu/ctie/blog/2012/09/23/size-matters-how-much-reading-to-assign-and-other-imponderables/.

Walker, Mike. N.d. Working with College Students & Student Development Theory Primer. Studentdevelopmenttheorybymwalker.pdf.

Wall Street Journal. 2014. From College Major to Career. June 13. http://graphicsweb. wsj.com/documents/NILF1111/#term=.

Walvoord, Barbara E., and Virginia Johnson Anderson. 2010. *Effective Grading: A Tool for Learning and Assessment in College*. 2nd ed. San Francisco: Jossey-Bass.

Wang, Zheng. 2008. National Humiliation, History Education, and the Politics of Historical Memory: Patriotic Education Campaign in China. *International Studies Quarterly* 52: 783–806.

Warner, John. 2013. A's for Everyone! *Inside Higher Ed*, September 3. http://www.insidehighered.com/blogs/just-visiting/everyone.

Washburn, Jennifer. 2005. *University, Inc.: The Corporate Corruption of Higher Education*. New York: Basic Books.

Wechsler, Howard, et al. 2002. Trends in College Binge Drinking during a Period of Increased Prevention Efforts. Findings from 4 Harvard School of Public Health College Alcohol Study Surveys: 1993–2001. *Journal of American College Health* 50 (5): 203–17.

Wechsler, Howard, and T. F. Nelson. 2008. What We Have Learned from the Harvard School of Public Health College Alcohol Study: Focusing Attention on College Student Alcohol Consumption and the Environmental Conditions That Promote It. *Journal of Studies on Alcohol and Drugs* 69 (4): 481–90.

Weiner, Annette B. 1992. *Inalienable Possessions: The Paradox of Keeping-While-Giving*. Berkeley: University of California Press.

Weiner, Eric. 2008. *The Geography of Bliss: One Grump's Search for the Happiest Places in the World*. New York: Twelve.

Werum, Regina E. 2000. The Ethnic Dimensions of Social Capital: How Parental Networks Shape Track Placement in Germany. Paper presented at the American Educational Research Association, New Orleans, April.

White, Byron P. 2013. Take It from an Ex-Journalist: Adapt or Die. *Chronicle of Higher Education*, September 23. http://chronicle.com/article/Take-It-From-an-Ex-Journalist-/141779/.

Whitehouse, Harvey. 2002. Modes of Religiosity: Towards a Cognitive Explanation of the Sociopolitical Dynamics of Religion. *Method & Theory in the Study of Religion* 14: 293–315.

Whiten, Andrew, and David Erdal. 2012. The Human Socio-Cognitive Niche and Its Evolutionary Origins. *Philosophical Transactions of the Royal Society B* 367: 2119–29. DOI: 10.1098/rstb.2012.0114.

Willingham, Daniel T. 2009. *Why Don't Students Like School? A Cognitive Scientist Answers Questions about How the Mind Works and What It Means for the Classroom*. San Francisco: Jossey-Bass.

Willis, Paul E. 1981 [1977]. *Learning to Labour: How Working Class Kids Get Working Class Jobs*. New York: Columbia University Press.

Wilson, David N. 2000. The German "Dual System" of Occupational Training: A Much-Replicated but Oft-Failed Transfer. Paper presented at the annual meeting of the Comparative and International Education Society, San Antonio, March 8–12. http://files.eric.ed.gov/fulltext/ED450264.pdf.

Wilson, Robin. 2010. For-Profit Colleges Change Higher Education's Landscape. *Chronicle of Higher Education*, February 7. http://chronicle.com/article/For-Profit-Colleges-Change/64012/.

Windemuth, Anna. 2014. After Faculty Vote, Grade Deflation Policy Officially Dead. *Daily Princetonian*, October 6. http://dailyprincetonian.com/news/2014/10/breaking-after-faculty-vote-grade-deflation-policy-officially-dead/.

Wolf, Alison. 2002. *Does Education Matter? Myths about Education and Economic Growth*. London: Penguin.

Wolf, Maryanne. 2007. *Proust and the Squid: The Story and Science of the Reading Brain*. New York: Harper Perennial.

Wolfe, Tom. 2004. *I Am Charlotte Simmons*. New York: Farrar, Straus, Giroux.

Woodhouse, Kellie. 2015. Arts and Sciences Deficits. *Inside Higher Ed*, June 4. https://www.insidehighered.com/news/2015/06/04/colleges-arts-and-sciences-struggle-deficits-enrollment-declines.

Wray, Herbert. 2014. Ink on Paper: Some Notes on Note-taking. *Huffington Post,* January 28. http://www.huffingtonpost.com/wray-herbert/ink-on-paper-some-notes-o_b_4681440.html.

Yee, Nick. 2006. Motivations for Play in Online Games. *CyberPsychology & Behavior* December 9 (6): 772–75.

Young, Jeffrey R. 2012. "Badges" Earned Online Post Challenge to Traditional College Diplomas. *Chronicle of Higher Education*, January 8. http://chronicle.com/article/Badges-Earned-Online-Pose/130241/?sid=wb&utm_source=wb&utm_medium=en.

Young, Michael. 1958. *The Rise of the Meritocracy 1870–2033: An Essay on Education and Society*. London: Thames and Hudson.

Zaiger, Alan Scher. 2010. College for All? Experts Say Not Necessarily. *Huffington Post,* May 14. http://www.huffingtonpost.com/2010/05/13/college-for-all-experts-s_n_575396.html.

Zaino, Jeanne. 2015. Gender Bias in Student Evaluations. *Inside Higher Ed*, February 23. https://www.insidehighered.com/blogs/university-venus/gender-bias-student-evaluations.

Zelizer, Viviana A. 1985. *Pricing the Priceless Child: The Changing Social Value of Children*. New York: Basic Books.

Zencey, Eric. 2009. G.D.P. R.I.P. *New York Times*, August 10. http://www.nytimes.com/2009/08/10/opinion/10zencey.html?pagewanted=all&_r=0.

Zhao, Yong. 2009. *Catching Up or Leading the Way: American Education in the Age of Globalization*. Alexandria, VA: ASCD.

Zimmerman, Jonathan. 2009. *Small Wonder: The Little Red Schoolhouse in History and Memory*. New Haven: Yale University Press.

INDEX

Page numbers followed by letters *f* and *t* refer to figures and tables, respectively.

ABOUT THE AUTHOR

Susan D. Blum loves complicated questions. This led her to anthropology, the study of humans in our full diversity embedded in all manner of contexts. She has been teaching for more than twenty-five years and is currently Professor of Anthropology at the University of Notre Dame. Recipient of a National Endowment for the Humanities fellowship, among other forms of recognition, she is the author of *Portraits of "Primitives": Ordering Human Kinds in the Chinese Nation*, *Lies That Bind: Chinese Truth, Other Truths*, *My Word! Plagiarism and College Culture*, and *Language and Social Justice* (forthcoming); editor of four books; and author of many articles and book chapters. Please visit her website, SusanBlum.com, for her latest thoughts on education, schooling, and learning.